This book contributes substantively to the current state of art of macroeconomic modeling by providing a method for modeling large collections of possibly heterogeneous agents subject to nonpairwise externality called field effects, that is, feedback of aggregate effects on individual agents or agents using state-dependent strategies. By adopting a level of microeconomic description that keeps track of compositions of fractions of agents by types or strategies, time evolution of the microeconomic states is described by (backward) Chapman–Kolmogorov equations. Macroeconomic dynamics naturally arise from these equations by expansion of the solutions in some power series of the number of participants. Specification of the microeconomic transition rates thus leads to macroeconomic dynamic models. This approach provides a consistent way for dealing with multiple equilibria of macroeconomic dynamics by ergodic decomposition and associated calculations of mean first passage times, and stationary probabilities of equilibria provide further useful information on macroeconomic behavior.

This book ends with a set of elaborations, sketches of further topics of research, and a collection of supporting materials in the Appendix.

New Approaches to Macroeconomic Modeling

New Approaches to Macroeconomic Modeling

Evolutionary Stochastic Dynamics, Multiple Equilibria, and Externalities as Field Effects

MASANAO AOKI
University of California, Los Angeles

CAMBRIDGE
UNIVERSITY PRESS

PUBLISHED BY THE PRESS SYNDICATE OF THE UNIVERSITY OF CAMBRIDGE
The Pitt Building, Trumpington Street, Cambridge CB2 1RP

CAMBRIDGE UNIVERSITY PRESS
The Edinburgh Building, Cambridge CB2 2RU, United Kingdom
40 West 20th Street, New York, NY 10011-4211, USA
10 Stamford Road, Oakleigh, Melbourne 3166, Australia

First published 1996
First paperback edition 1998

Library of Congress Cataloging-in-Publication Data is available.

A catalog record for this book is available from the British Library.

ISBN   0-521-48207-0 hardback
ISBN   0-521-63769-4 paperback

Transferred to digital printing 2004

To My Mother

CONTENTS

Part II   Modeling Interactions

Part III Hierarchical Dynamics and Critical Phenomena

PREFACE

This book is an attempt to reformulate macroeconomic modeling as currently practiced by the macroeconomic profession.

The need to improve macroeconomic models certainly is felt widely by the economic profession. A short list of the defects that we recognize in macroeconomic modeling includes extensive and almost exclusive use of the assumption of representative agents, of largely deterministic dynamic models, and inadequate attention paid to off-equilibrium dynamic phenomena. More specifically, we do not have a satisfactory model for explaining sluggish responses of macroeconomic phenomena and the distributional effects of policy actions. We lack adequate treatments of the dynamic adjustment behavior of microeconomic units in the presence of externalities of the kind designated "field effects" in this book, and are known variously in the economic literature as social influence, social consumption, or group sentiments or pressure.

This book collects my recent investigations to provide an alternative manner for building and analyzing models in macroeconomics; it is addressed to macroeconomists and advanced graduate students in macroeconomics. The book is arranged in three parts. Part I consists of three chapters. After a short introductory discussion of motivation for developing a new way to construct and analyze macroeconomic models in Chapter 1, Chapter 2 provides some simple, motivating examples of the proposed approaches. An explicitly stochastic or statistical approach is taken in Chapter 3. It collects some material that I use in the remainder of the book, since this material is not usually in the toolkit of practicing macroeconomists and is not taught in traditional economics graduate courses.

Part II, consisting of Chapters 4 through 6, presents models of interacting microeconomic units via jump Markov processes and the derivation of macroeconomic dynamics by backward Chapman–Kolmogorov equations. Time evolution of a large collection of microeconomic units is described in terms of probability densities, and is governed by the master equation. Under certain conditions, the equilibrium probability distributions are Gibbs distributions. Chapter 4 addresses situations in which each of the microeconomic units has a finite number of choices, and thus extends the literature on discrete choice to include interacting agents.

Chapter 5 is a further elaboration of the ideas presented in Chapter 4. It focuses on the type of externalities that I call field effects. Field effects are such that each agent is influcenced by the aggregate effects, and hence are usually weak and diffuse. These effects are in contrast with the pairwise interactions between two, possibly anonymous, agents. In Chapter 5 as well as in Chapter 4, a new way of aggregating microeconomic units to produce macroeconomic equations is illustrated. The issue associated with the existence of multiple macroeconomic equilibria naturally arises. In the explicitly stochastic framework of this book, dynamic models with well-behaved basins of attractions for locally stable equilibria behave in such a way that each basin will be visited with a positive probability, and the expected time of transition from one locally stable equilibrium to another is shown to depend on the height of a potential barrier separating the two basins. Finally, pairwise interactions are taken up in Chapter 6.

Part III, composed of Chapters 7 and 8, examines properties of dynamics with a large state space, which are organized hierarchically. The characteristic feature of such dynamics is sluggishiness in the dynamic responses. Once disturbed off an equilibrium dynamic path, a hierarchical state-space model returns to it at rates slower than the usual exponential ones exhibited by dynamics with state spaces that are not similarly organized. Chapter 8 treats gathering of agents into the same state (or beliefs), as in bubbles and other critical phenomena. The book ends with a collection of supporting materials in the Appendix.

Some of the topics have been presented in my graduate course on economic modeling at the University of California, Los Angeles, as well as in special courses or sequences of seminars that I was invited to present in the past three years at the University of Tokyo, the Åbo Academy University, the European University Institute, the University of Siena, and elsewhere. I thank my former students as well as seminar participants for their reactions and comments. I thank H. Yoshikawa, K. G. Nishimura, L. Punzo, R. Fiorito, M. Salmon, and R. Östermark for arranging such special seminars or courses.

Professor Weidlich was very helpful in an early stage of the book writing as well. I have benefited from my colleagues, Axel Leijonhufvud and John McCall in particular, through their insights, suggestions, and wide knowledge of the economic and stochastic-processes literature. William McKelvey, Michael Orszag and Arthur Havenner read parts of the early drafts and made many useful comments. Max Rhee corrected my English by his careful reading of a draft. I thank them all for their help.

I also acknowledge support from the Shin Nittetsu Endowed Chair to Tokyo Institute of Technology, grants-in-aid from Toshiba Corporation, and the academic senate research grants from University of California, Los Angeles.

Masanao Aoki
Los Angeles, California
July 14, 1995

CHAPTER 1

Introduction

The macroeconomic profession is well aware of the shortcomings of the current state of macroeconomic modeling, and is generally dissatisfied with the models it uses, as documented, for example, in Kirman (1992b) or Leijonhufvud (1993, 1995). The need to improve macroeconomic models is certainly felt widely. To cite a few examples, we do not have a satisfactory explanation of why some macroeconomic variables move sluggishly, or how policy actions affect segments of the economy differently, and we lack adequate tools for treating dynamic adjustment behavior of microeconomic units in the presence of externalities of the kind termed "social influence" by Becker (1990) and others, or in models with multiple equilibria.

Leijohnhufvud (1995) argues that the Rationality Postulate has such a strong hold on economists that, although they are aware of the notion of the Invisible Hand, a self-regulating order emerging in a complex system from the interactions of many microeconomic agents without this being part of their intentions, they are generally blind to hierarchical complexity and some of its consequences and averse to learning from other fields in which emergent properties and distributive information processing are also studied.

This book is concerned with modeling a large collection of not necessarily homogeneous microeconomic agents or units in a stochastic and dynamic framework. Major ingredients that distinguish this book from other books on macroeconomics are the following: (a) use of jump Markov processes to model interacting microeconomic agents; (b) focus on the multiplicity of microeconomic states that are consistent with given sets of macroeconomic observables, and introduction of exchangeable agents in addition to the usual distinguishable agents, since they affect the multiplicity counts; (c) a new type of analysis of multiple equilibria and calculation of mean first-passage times between equilibria, and introduction of the notion of ergodic components to describe state spaces with several basins of attraction; and (d) introduction of hierarchical structures to explain complex and sluggish dynamic responses of some macroeconomic variables in large dimensional state space. We take up some of these points next.

1.1   Multiplicity

This book discusses models composed of a large number of microeconomic agents. That a large number of microeconomic agents interact in our model has several important consequences. The most important one is undoubtedly the fact that a large number of microeconomic states are compatible with a given macroeconomic state. We call this the multiplicity of microeconomic states or the degeneracy of macroeconomic state. Although this fact is completely ignored in the existing macroeconomic literature, it has profound effects on the behavior of the macroeconomic models that we construct by aggregating models of microeconomic agents, because the multiplicity determines how uncertainty in the model affects macroeconomic behavior. In addition to the usual distributional effects of changes in macroeconomic states affecting segments of the economy differently, degeneracy affects equilibirum probability distribution of macroeconomic states. The probability distributions of microeconomic states consistent with a set of macroeconomic variables or observables are obtained by applying the Gibbs conditioning principle in Chapter 3.[1]

This is the reason why we discuss entropy and Gibbs distributions in Chapters 2 and 3. As we make clear there, entropy is a measure of the degree of multiplicity of microeconomic states, that is, degeneracy of a macroeconomic state. This point becomes more transparent when we discuss the exponents of the equilibrium probability distribution of the exponential type later in Chapter 5, where we observe that a given performance or cost index must be modified by a measure of the degeneracy of the optimal solution, which is measured by entropy.

Put differently, degeneracy is relevant to us because we take the view that the state space of an economy possesses basins of attraction that are associated with macroeconomic equilibria and, around them, states of the economy randomly move about, occasionally jumping from one basin to another. An economy may stay in this new basin for a while until it jumps out again. A basin is composed of microeconomic configurations that are compatible with or converge to the given macroeconomic state. We also can calculate the average time for the system to travel between two local equilibria, and show that the mean travel time will depend on the difference in the potentials[2] of the local equilibria.

---

[1] Fragments of this procedure are found in random utility models or random coefficient choice models, but these models are static rather than dynamic.

[2] For now, think of potentials as the exponents in exponential distributions.

1.2   Multiple equilibria

Multiple equilibria are likely to be present in dynamic models that have a large number of microeconomic agents. Multiple equilibria bring out the essential difference between deterministic and stochastic formulations of dynamic models. Suppose that a deterministic dynamic macroeconomic model has multiple equilibria with well-defined basins of attraction for each locally stable equilibrium. One important and natural question to pose for such a model is how the model can settle on an economically desirable equilibrium. With deterministic models, the only way to reach the desired equilibrium is to be initially in the basin of attraction associated with that equilibrium. Otherwise, the models must jump to the right basin. This is the issue of history versus perfect-foresight expectations addressed by Krugman (1991).

Unlike deterministic models, multiple equilibria present no conceptual difficulty to stochastic models. In the stochastic formulation in this book, we show that there are positive steady-state or stationary probabilities that the model state is in each basin, and the state moves from one equilibrium to another with positive probabilities, and mean first-passage times between these equilibria can, in principle, be calculated. The essence of this situation is captured by the example in Chapter 2, where the expected first-passage time from one equilibrium to another has been shown to depend exponentially on the height of the barrier separating the two basins, even though the equilibrium probabilities are independent of the height. Use of probabilistic or stochastic concepts and models allows us to regard macroeconomic regularities as statistical laws, and we employ empirical distributions and large deviation techniques to state statistical findings. Instead of a single ergodic system, we have ergodic decompositions in general. Each locally stable equilibrium has associated with it an ergodic component. There are positive probabilities associated with each ergodic component, and there are positive probabilities of transitions from one basin of attraction to another. Some of the mean first-passage times could be very long, indicating sluggishness of responses of macroeconomic phenomena.

The importance of and need to (re)cast choice or optimization problems of microeconomic units in a stochastic framework have been hinted at. Briefly, such reformulations involve three ingredients: spaces of states or strategies (decisions), which are called state spaces; transition rates that specify rates of changes of probabilities of transitions from one microeconomic state to another; and the deterministic equation for time evolution of the probabilities of states.

Long ago, Bellman (1961), pointed out that the state of a dynamic system (composed of microeconomic agents) is the probability distribution of (their microeconomic) states, because knowledge of the distribution determines uniquely probabilistically how the system evolves with time in the future. In this extended sense, state equations are deterministic. Unlike the evolutionary game literature, however, it is not the strategy mixes themselves that evolve deterministically. It is the probability distribution of the strategy mixes that evolves deterministically.[3] Because we choose microeconomic states to be discrete, we deal directly with sets of probabilities of the states, which we also call distributions. The so-called replicator dynamics in the literature of evolutionary games or Malthusian dynamics of Friedman are replaced with the backward Chapman–Kolmogorov equation. The fitness function of Friedman is replaced with transition rates that contain some functions, like the fitness function, that affect the rates. When transition rates satisfy the detailed balance conditions, the equilibrium distributions in the form of the Gibbs distribution exist, as discussed by Kelly (1979). These matters are discussed in Chapters 3 and 4.

1.3   Jump Markov processes

Next, we explain why we use jump Markov processes to model the behavior of microeconomic agents. Economic literature introduces many examples that show that (optimal) adjustment behavior by microeconomic units is not always continuous or small. Rather, adjustments are made at some discrete points in time by some finite magnitudes. Similar adjustment behavior is known to be optimal or used as convenient suboptimal rules in several classes of problems in finance, operations research, and control. Many of these reported results show that adjustment or decision (control) rules are of the threshold type: A specific action or decision is chosen or triggered when some gap variable, which measures gap or discrepancy between a desired or ideal value and the actual one, reaches or exceeds (becomes larger or smaller than) some preset threshold or trigger level. Adjustments could be in one direction only or they could be bidirectional, that is, adjustments could be upward or downward. More generally, when state variables of a microeconomic unit are in a certain subset of states, and when the unit receives a specific shock or signals from other units, then the decision of the unit is to choose a particular adjustment from a discrete-choice set. Microeconomic agents following these decision rules then act or adjust intermittently. Although the variable that represents the gap lies between the thresholds, no action or adjustment is undertaken. Adjustments of labor forces by firms and decisions of entry and exit by firms are also of this type.

In the economics literature, we find many examples of aggregate variables affecting microeconomic decisions, although they are not called field effects. Becker (1974, 1990), for example, examines an individual consumer's demand for some goods that depends on the demands by other customers, such as de-

---

[3] See the survey of Friedman (1991) on evolutionary games.

mands for popular restaurant seats, theater tickets, and best sellers. What Becker calls the effects of social consumption is an example of what we call field effects, and is further discussed in Section 5.6. In the phenomena examined by Becker, there is no reason to think of interactions among agents as pairwise interactions, anonymous or otherwise. Caballero and Lyons (1990, 1992) also discuss the effects of aggregate output on sectoral or other country outputs. Becker (1974), Schelling (1978), Akerlof (1980), Friedman (1993), Friedman and Fung (1994), and Aoki (1995a) are also examples of field effects.[4] It is important to recognize that our method deals with interactions over time without the curse of dimensionality of the dynamic programming approach commonly used in the discrete-choice literature. The reader should note that none of the examples mentioned above, which are drawn from economic and related literature, analyzes interaction among microeconomic units.[5] At any given point in time, microeconomic agents have chosen some decisions, typically from finite-choice sets. Joint effects of their choices affect the economic environments in which they perform and make further choices in the future, that is, there is feedback from aggregate decisions to individual choices. Therefore, the agents operate in endogenous stochastic and dynamic environments, or they are subject to stochastic and dynamic externality. Effectiveness, desirability, or utility of their decisions is affected by the joint effects of other agents' actions, which determine the state variables of the models. We discuss interactions among microeconomic agents in Chapters 4 through 7.

Jump Markov processes provide an appropriate framework for modeling a class of models known as market participation models [see Stoker (1993)] or another class of models in which agents choose types interactively. There can be several types of microeconomic agents that interact in a model: optimizers and imitators, informed and uninformed, purchasers and nonpurchasers of information, investers and noninvestors, or holders of one kind of assets or another. Possibilities are many. Furthermore, random encounters of microeconomic agents of several types also can be modeled this way advantageously. Clearly, agents can choose their roles or types in addition to adjusting gap variables as part of their strategy or decision processes, and the problem can be described as a large collection of interacting jump Markov processes, or a birth-and-death process with state-dependent and possibly nonlinear transition rates.

---

[4] It is interesting to read in Friedman (1991) that biologists use the expression "playing the field" to indicate interactions with a whole population. According to him, background environments and prevalence of alternative behavior traits or patterns in a population affects fitness of a particular biological trait or behavioral pattern in biological models.

[5] For example, as we discuss later, Caballero (1992), and Caballero and Engel (1992) use the Glivenko–Cantelli lemma to deal with the cross-sectional distribution of firms by discrete choices that they make. This theorem requires that firms' states are independent random variables.

We propose to model all these and other related problems that involve discrete choices made at intermittent time points as interacting jump Markov processes. Population compositions or mixes of agents with alternative decisions will evolve over time according to jump Markov processes. Specifications of decision processes for microeconomic agents determine probabilistic or stochastic mechanisms for the agents to change their decisions over time. These specifications are then translated into those of transition rates between microeconomic states. Transition rates between microeconomic states are generally easier to construct than direct specifications of macroeconomic models.

Our approach is easier to apply, and generally more powerful in circumstances in which specifying transition rates is easier than directly specifying macroeconomic behavior for the whole collection of microeconomic agents. In the applications of Chapter 5, the state space is discrete, or agents' choice sets are discrete, and the degree of knowledge of the system is such that the microeconomic states of the system are the vectors of the fractions of agents with the same decisions or microeconomic states, as the case may be. At whatever level of detail we wish to describe stochastic dynamics, the master equation, which is a version of the backward Chapman–Kolmogorov equation, governs time evolution of the probabilities of the states in the form of probability flows into and out of them.

How do we construct macroeconomic models? Microeconomic specifications of agent interactions imply macroeconomic models via the process of aggregations that is implemented in this book. There is some superficial similarity between our specification of transition rates for jump Markov processes and fitness functions in the evolutionary game literature to express the idea that better choices win over converts, but there are some essential differences. For example, we do not impose deterministic rules for strategy mixed as in the game literature, but rather examine stochastic processes for this conversion process by backward Chapman–Kolmogorov equations which govern the time evolution of the probability distribution of the mixes of agents or strategies.

We develop two novel aggregation procedures in Chapters 5 and 7 in order to obtain macroeconomic dynamics of a large collection of interacting microeconomic units. One is via the master equation (Chapman–Kolmogorov equation) to describe probability flows of agents moving among states. Specifying behavior of microeconomic units in terms of transition probabilities or rates is a useful way of constructing macroeconomic models when certain technical conditions, called the detailed (or partial) balance conditions, are met, because the equilibrium probability distributions, called Gibbs distributions, then exist. The first term of an approximate expansion solution method of the equation yields the dynamic equation for the aggregate or macroeconomic variables. This is one way, first introduced in Chapter 4 and further developed in Chapter 5.

The aggregate or macroeconomic equations keep track of the time evolution of the expected fractions or something like conditional means of the population, whereas fluctuations about the means are described in some cases by Fokker–Planck equations.

The second way to derive aggregate models is via renormalization group theory associated with hierarchy, which is discussed in Chapter 7. By adopting a more disaggregate and explicitly stochastic dynamic framework than is traditional in economic modeling, we demonstrate in Chapters 4, 5, and 7 that we have new ways of aggregating microeconomic units, and can explain sluggishness of responses of some macroeconomic phenomena. We discuss interactions among microeconomic agents in Chapters 4 through 7. These two novel aggregation procedures allow us to examine macroeconomic dynamics of a large collection of interacting microeconomic units.

To summarize, we model agents as interacting jump Markov processes, and the dynamic version of market participation models and other discrete-choice models are put in this framework. Our reformulation of the macroeconomic modeling procedure involves recasting the deterministic models into a stochastic framework of jump Markov processes in some of the examples cited above. In other cases where the original formulations are already in stochastic terms, there is a need to recognize or reformulate the problems as those involving jump Markov processes. Specifics of how these reformulations are carried out, of course, vary from problem to problem. All involve specifying interactions of microeconomic units probabilistically in terms of transition probabilities (discrete time) or transition rates (continuous time) of Markov chains, and use a version of Chapman–Kolmogorov equations to derive time evolutions of probability distributions of state variables, suitably defined. See Sections 4.7 and 5.1 for further discussions of the basic ingredients of such reformulations.

This book illustrates that our framework goes some way in improving the state of economic modeling. Concepts and techniques that are not in the toolkit of traditional macroeconomists also are developed in this book to support this framework. New model construction methods for interacting microeconomic units that we advocate in this book give us results that have not been possible in the traditional framework of deterministic and representative agents.

Having decided to use jump Markov processes to model microeconomic agents, let us next mention the types of interaction among agents considered in this book.

In Chapter 4, we introduce jump Markov processes to pave our way for modeling a large collection of interacting agents. We defer to Chapter 6 our discussion of pairwise interaction or interaction with randomly matched (drawn) anonymous microeconomic units. In Chapter 5, we concentrate on the type of interaction or externality that does not lend itself to modeling with pairwise interaction. We call these externalities **mean-field effects** or simply **field effects**. This terminology is chosen to convey the notion that interaction with a whole population or class of microeconomic units is involved, that is, aggregate (macroeconomic) effects due to contributions from a whole population of microeconomic units or composition of the whole in the sense that fractions of units in various states or categories are involved.

A good case in which to examine the field effects is a study of the dynamic behavior of a group of agents who interact through the choices they make in circumstances in which each agent has a set of finite decisions from which to choose, and in which they may change their minds as time progresses, possibly at some cost. In such situations, an agent's choice is influenced by the vector of the fractions of agents who have selected the same decisions, because the agent's perceived profit or benefit from a decision change will be a function of this vector, that is, the composition of agents with the same decisions in the whole population of agents.

1.4   Hierarchical state spaces

We have mentioned the multiplicity of microeconomic states and multiple equilibria. The third consequence of large models is the complexity of dynamic behavior in a large dimensional state space, or complex behavior of performance indexes or cost structures of dynamic models in such large dimensional state spaces. The problems are similar to those of complex landscapes of performance indexes in difficult optimization problems or energy landscapes of large neural networks, the kind that requires sophisticated numerical optimization algorithms, such as simulated annealing, in seeking optimal solutions. One way to think of hierarchical or tree-structured state space is to recognize that some subsets of state spaces with high dimensions are rarely occupied by models, and trees are introduced to approximate such state spaces.[6]

Large state spaces without any structure are difficult to deal with. The state spaces of our models, however, have some structures which we exploit in modeling. These state spaces are organized into tree or hierarchical structure, and we introduce the notion of ultrametrics or tree distance to discuss similarity of states in nodes of trees. This is the way we deal with complex landscapes of performance indexes or cost structures of large models. These are introduced in Chapter 2, and discussed in detail in Chapter 7.

---

[6] Doyle and Snell (1984) have an interesting discussion of approximating random walk in the three-dimensional space by a tree space. Another way to introduce trees is to map local minima and maxima of functions with complex behavior into a tree as in Aldous and Vazirani (1993).

1.5   Scope of modeling

The proposed modeling procedure can be applied whenever and wherever speci-fications of optimization problems or behavior rules for microeconomic agents can be transformed into those of transition rates between configurations of microeconomic states of a collection of such agents. Some indications of how such transformations can be accomplished are given in Chapters 4 through 6. Chapter 5, in particular, shows by examples how the knowledge or specifications of transition rates allows us to specify the dynamics as the master equations for a composition of the population of microeconomic agents. In general, the master equations do not admit closed-form solutions. In Chapter 5 we give some of the approximate-solution methods of van Kampen (1965, 1992) and Kubo (1975). We also show the reader the importance of the multiplicity of microeconomic agents in interpreting the equilibrium probability distributions of the master equations. Whenever the vectors of fractions of agents are appro-priate microeconomic states for interacting agents, we can employ the master equations to describe time evolution of the population. The proposed approach, therefore, is limited only to the extent that the equations prove to be analytically or computationally intractable.

One of the major aims of this book is to examine consequences of changing patterns of agent interaction over time. We view these patterns as distributions of agents over possible types or categories over time, and we endevour to discover stable distributions of patterns of interactions among agents.

Equilibrium distributions of patterns of classification describe stable emer-gent properties of the model. Some simple and suggestive examples are dis-cussed in Chapters 4 and 5.

In models with a small number of types, choices or classes, the methods developed in Chapter 5 are quite effective. When the number of classes becomes large, (numerical) solutions of the master equations may become cumbersome. An attractive alternative is to examine equilibrium distributions directly. We outline this method in the concluding section of this book by drawing on the literatures of population genetics and statistics.

CHAPTER 2

Simple illustrative and motivating examples

This chapter introduces concepts and techniques that are further developed in the main body of this book, mostly via simple examples. The objective is to introduce to the reader our approaches, viewpoints, and techniques of modeling that are possibly unfamiliar to the economics profession, and to illustrate them in simple context so that basic ideas can be easily grasped. For simplification, some examples are artificial, but suggestive enough to demonstrate relevance of the notions or methods in more realistic macroeconomic models.

The examples focus on the statistical, dynamic, and state-space properties of economic variables and models. They help to introduce to the reader the notions of distinguishable and exchangeable microeconomic agents, multiplicity of microeconomic states and entropy as a measure of multiplicity, empirical distributions and related topics such as Sanov's theorem and the Gibbs conditional principle, and dynamics on trees, among others.

All of these examples are intended to suggest why certain concepts or modeling techniques, possibly not in the mainstream of the current macroeconomic literature, are useful in, or provide a new way of examining, aggregate behavior of a large number of interacting microeconomic agents.

2.1 Stochastic descriptions of economic variables

We treat all micro- and macroeconomic variables as random variables or stochastic processes, although macroeconomic variables become deterministic in the limit of the number of microeconomic units approaching infinity. Relationships among economic variables are statistical in an essential way, and are not made so by having additive disturbances or measurement errors superimposed on deterministic relationships.

In this book we consistently model economic systems as stochastic, not as deterministic. As mentioned in Chapter 1, if time evolution of an economy is modeled as the outcome of a deterministic process, then different locally stable equilibria are separated by basins of attractions, and once in a basin of a particular equilibrium the economy is trapped in it forever. This is why the distinction between history, that is, initial conditions of dynamic systems, and perfect foresight (expectations) is crucial and various selection criteria of multiple equilibria occupy a large part of the literature on deterministic dynamic models. In stochastic systems, this distinction disappears. There is a small but positive probability that an economy in a basin may escape or jump into another basin. Indeed, there are equilibrium probability distributions on the set of local equilibria, and the system wanders among them with finite first-passage times. A simple example of this notion is found in Section 2.4.2.

2.1.1   Distinguishable and exchangeable agents

There are two complementary ways to proceed with economic modeling. One is to deduce from economic considerations the probability of joint microeconomic variables, and to calculate the statistical properties of interesting macroeconomic variables by integrating (averaging) over some set of microeconomic variables. Another is to proceed from the opposite direction. Given a set of selected macroeconomic signals that are observed, what is the most probable distribution of microeconomic variables? This is how Sanov's theorem, which is described in Section 2.3.3 and in Chapter 3, is applied to obtain the conditional-limit theorems for unobserved microvariables. The maximum-entropy principle of Jaynes (1985) is a special case of this theorem under the uniform prior probabilities. Chapter 3 delves into greater detail on these concepts.

A simple example of the first approach is illustrated as follows. We let $\mathbf{x} = (x_1, x_2, \ldots, x_N)$ be a complete description of the economic states of N distinguishable agents, where x_i is a set of microeconomic-state variable(s) of agent i. We assume that x_i can take values on a discrete set with K elements, $x_i = a_j$, for some j, $j = 1, 2, \ldots, K$. Consequently, the vector $\mathbf{x}$ takes values on a set with K^N elements. These elements are called microeconomic configurations (or simply configurations).

If we assume that all these configurations are equally likely, then a macroeconomic variable, X, for example, is a function of x_i with expected value calculated (in principle) as

$$E(X) = \frac{1}{K^N} \sum_{x_1=a_1}^{a_K} \cdots \sum_{x_N=a_1}^{a_K} X(x_1, \ldots, x_N).$$

A less detailed description would be to keep track of the number N_j of agents in state j, $j = 1, \ldots, K$, without specifying the identity of individual agents in the same state. This describes the composition of the total population of microeconomic agents, that is, the fractions of population in each state, which is related to the notion of empirical distributions of agents introduced later in Chapters 2–5.

At this level of description, the state of the collection of N agents is described by specifying the number of agents in each of K microeconomic states. This is the classic occupancy problem in probability theory. The probability of a particular vector of occupancy numbers $\{N_j\}$ is given by the multinomial distribution

$$Pr(N_1, N_2, \ldots, N_K) = \frac{N!}{\prod_j N_j!} K^{-N},$$

where $N_j \geq 0$. Notice that each of the K^N configurations is regarded as equally probable. We call this the distinguishable (Maxwell–Boltzmann) form of the classic occupancy problem.

More generally, we can classify microeconomic agents into distinct and non-overlapping categories, that is, we partition the set of agents into classes or types (urns), just as we put distinguishable or indistinguishable balls into urns in the classic occupancy problems as in Feller (1957). Categories or classes correspond to urns, and balls to microeconomic agents. Suppose there are M non-empty categories. Let L_i be the number of agents in class i, and N be the total number of agents. First we put one agent in each of M categories to ensure that they are non-empty. Assuming that each agent is distinguishable, each has a probability of M^{-1} of being placed in a category. Thus $\{L_i - 1\}$ has the binomial distribution based on $N - M$ trials with probability of success M^{-1}.

Suppose there are g_j microeconomic states in category j, $j = 1, \ldots, M$. We can let $q_i = g_i / G$, where $G = \sum g_j$, be the a priori probability of configurations in category i. Then, the factor K^{-N}, above, is replaced by $\prod_i q_i^{N_i}$. The total number of possible microeconomic states, each of which is regarded as equally probable, is important in our consideration of the model's properties. We denote it by $W(N)$, where we explicitly indicate the total number of agents, N, in the argument

$$W(N) = \sum_j \frac{N!}{\prod_j N_j!} \prod_j g_j^{N_j} = \left(\sum_j g_j \right)^N.$$

This function is called the state-sum, or partition, function. If $g_j = 1$ for all j, and if $M = K$, then we recover $W(N) = K^N$.

In the above, agents in different categories are assumed to be distinguishable, even though those in the same category are not. The alternative is an exchangeable (Bose–Einstein) form of the classic occupancy problem. If we assume that agents are not distinguishable even in different categories, that is, exchangeable in the technical terminology of the probability literature, (see Chow and Teicher 1978 and Kingman 1978a for examples) then the total number of possible configurations is given by

$$W(N) = \prod_j \frac{(N_j + g_j - 1)!}{N_j!(g_j - 1)!},\tag{2.1}$$

where g_j is the number of possible microeconomic states that an agent can assume. Recall that the number of ways n identical balls can be placed in g boxes is given by $(n + g - 1)!/n!(g - 1)!$.

If none of the M categories is assumed to be zero, then the total number of configurations is $_NC_{M-1} = (N - 1)!/[(M - 1)!(N - M)!]$, since M agents are allocated to each of M categories to ensure that they are non-empty, and the remaining $N - M$ agents can be distributed to M categories without constraint, and $(N - M) + M - 1 = N - 1$.

In short, this first modeling approach proceeds by specifying microunits and their interactions, and then examines the implied macrospecifications. In Chapters 4 and 5, we follow this approach. Interactions among microeconomic agents are specified as transition probabilities or transition rates among the configurations. Specification of the stochastic behavior of microeconomic agents uniquely determines macroeconomic laws, under the technical conditions discussed in these chapters. This is how macrodynamics emerge out of Chapman–Kolmogorov equations or their equivalent – the master equations – and, when certain moments are assumed to exist, fluctuations about macroeconomic equilibria emerge as the Fokker–Planck equations.

To summarize, with distinguishable agents, the joint probability of $\{L_i\}$ numbers of agents in M categories is

$$P(L_1, L_2, \ldots, L_M \mid N, M) = \frac{(N - M)!}{\prod_{i=1}^M (L_i - 1)!} M^{-(N-M)},$$

and in the exchangeable case

$$P(L_1, L_2, \ldots, L_M \mid N, M) = {}_{N-1}C_{M-1}^{-1}.$$

Chen (1978) introduced a distribution that is a mixture of multinomial distribution where the mixture is a symmetric (exchangeable) Dirichlet distribution, and has shown that his Dirichlet–multinomial distribution reduces to the Bose–Einstein and Maxwell–Boltzmann distributions. The multinomial distribution is

$$P(L_1, L_2, \ldots, L_M \mid N, M, \alpha, \mathbf{p}) = \frac{(N - M)!}{\prod_{i=1}^M (L_i - 1)!} \prod_i p_i^{L_i-1},$$

where $\mathbf{p} = (p_1, p_2, \ldots, p_M)$ itself is distributed with a density function

$$f(\mathbf{p}) = \frac{\Gamma(M\alpha)}{\Gamma(\alpha)^M} \prod_i p_i^{\alpha-1},$$

which is an exchangeable version of the Dirichlet distribution

$$\frac{\Gamma(\alpha_1 + \alpha_2 + \cdots + \alpha_M)}{\prod_{i=1}^{M} \Gamma(\alpha_i)} p_1^{\alpha_1 - 1} \cdots p_M^{\alpha_M - 1} dp_1 dp_2 \cdots dp_{M-1}.$$

Integrating out the dependence on **p**, we arrive at

$$P(L_1, \ldots, L_M \mid N, M, \alpha) = \frac{(N - M)!}{\Gamma(N - M + M\alpha)} \frac{\Gamma(M\alpha)}{\Gamma(\alpha)^M} \prod_i \frac{\Gamma(L_i + \alpha - 1)}{\Gamma(L_i)}.$$

See the Appendix for further detail. With the parameter value $\alpha = 1$, this distribution reduces to the Bose–Einstein distribution, and the limit of α going to infinity is the Maxwell–Boltzmann distribution.

We remark that $E(L_i/N) = M^{-1}$ in both cases. The variance of L_i/N goes to zero as N goes to infinity in the Maxwell–Boltzmann case, but the variance remains finite in the Bose–Einstein case. In other words, in the case where N is much larger than M, the Maxwell–Boltzmann distribution implies sharper knowledge of L_i/N than does the Bose–Einstein one.

2.2 Entropy: A measure of economic activity

We consider an industry composed of N exchangeable firms, each of which can produce outputs at the rate y_s, $s = 1, 2, \ldots$. Firms producing outputs at a rate y_s can be in one of g_s internal states.[1] Thus, each firm occupies one of these g_s states, for some s. We denote by n_s the number of firms in state s. We know that

$$N = \sum_s n_s, \tag{2.2}$$

and we are given the aggregate output rate Y, that is,

$$Y = \sum_s n_s y_s. \tag{2.3}$$

The number of possible ways for firms to occupy states, or the number of configurations or microeconomic states of the industry is given by

$$W(N, Y) = \sum_{n_s} \prod_s \frac{(n_s + g_s - 1)!}{n_s!(g_s - 1)!}, \tag{2.4}$$

where the sum over n_s is taken subject to Eqs. (2.2) and (2.3), since we assume here that the random variables n_s are exchangeable.

---

[1] We assume that the number of firms not in production, $y_0 = 0$, is negligible. See Chapter 8, on the other hand, for situations in which this state becomes heavily occupied.

2.2.1   *Maximizing entropy*

Later in Chapter 3, we discuss entropy that is defined to be proportional to the logarithm of $W(N, Y)$. With the constant of proportionality set to 1 for convenience, we define

$$S(N, Y) = \ln W(N, Y) \tag{2.5}$$

as the entropy of the industry consistent with the two macroeconomic variables of Eqs. (2.2) and (2.3), which has $W(N, Y)$ configurations given in Eq. (2.4). Since this summation is difficult to carry out, we look for the maximum term in the sum subject to the macroeconomic constraints on N and Y by maximizing the Lagrangian

$$L = \ln\left\{ \frac{(n_s + g_s - 1)!}{n_s!(g_s - 1)!} \right\} + \alpha\left(N - \sum n_s \right) + \beta\left(Y - \sum n_s y_s \right),$$

where α and β are Lagrange multipliers associated with the constraints Eqs. (2.2) and (2.3). We approximate $(n_s + g_s - 1)!$ by $(n_s + g_s)!$ because n_s is expected to be large.

The maximum is realized by

$$n_s^* = \frac{g_s}{e^{y_s} - 1},$$

where, for convenience, we set $y_s = \alpha + \beta y_s$.

On substitution of this expression into the definition of the entropy Eq. (2.5), the entropy is approximated by the logarithm of the maximized term in W, which becomes

$$S(N, Y) \approx \alpha N + \beta Y - \sum_s (g_s - 1) \ln\{1 - e^{-y_s}\}.$$

This expression is important because it indicates that the parameters α and β, which were introduced as Lagrange multipliers that incorporate the constraints imposed by the observed macroeconomic signals, can actually be interpreted as the semielasticity of the partition function with respect to the macroeconomic signals.[2] The partial derivative of the entropy with respect to N is equal to

$$\alpha = \frac{\partial S}{\partial N},$$

and the partial derivative with respect to the other macroeconomic signal Y gives

$$\beta = \frac{\partial S}{\partial Y}.$$

---

[2] See our discussion of Sanov's theorems.

In carrying out the partial derivatives, dependence of these parameters on N and Y, such as $\partial \alpha / \partial Y$, cancel out. We later see that the parameter β is often interpretable as a measure of uncertainty in the economy, or as a measure of the level of economic activity in the model.

2.2.2   Laplace transform and moment-generating functions

We usually take Laplace transforms of functions of time to solve (sets of) ordinary differential equations by converting them to algebraic relationship of Laplace transforms. Given a function of time $f(t)$, $t \geq 0$, we define $\hat{f}(s) = \int_0^\infty e^{-st} f(t) dt$ as its Laplace transform for some s with positive real part to make the integral well defined.

Breiman (1968, sec. 8.13) shows that the exponentials $(e^{-\lambda x})$, with real and nonnegative λ, separate the distribution functions for nonnegative random variables in the sense that the equality of the transforms

$$\int e^{-\lambda x} F(dx) = \int e^{-\lambda x} G(dx)$$

implies equality of the two distribution functions F and G. This relationship is also a Laplace transform. The equality of Laplace transforms implies the equality of the distribution functions.[3]

We use the Laplace transform in this generalized way because it is convenient. Below is an example of how we will use it in Chapter 3. Instead of using the sum in Eq. (2.4), we can take its Laplace transform, or its discrete-version probability-generating function. Accordingly, we define

$$\Xi = \sum_{N=0}^{\infty} W(N, Y) e^{-\alpha N - \beta Y} = \prod_{s} \sum_{n_s=0}^{\infty} \frac{(n_s + g_s - 1)!}{n_s!(g_s - 1)!} e^{-n_s(\alpha + \beta y_s)},$$

since the sum over n_s can now be carried out independently. Noting that

$$\sum_{n} \frac{(n + g - 1)!}{n!(g - 1)!} a^n = (1 - a)^{-g},$$

where $|a| \leq 1$, we can write Ξ as

$$\Xi = \prod_{s} \left[1 - e^{-(\alpha + \beta y_s)} \right]^{-g_s}.$$

---

[3] For a discrete random variable taking values of $0, 1, \ldots$, the probability-generating function is defined as

$$P(t) = \sum_{0}^{\infty} p_n t^n; \quad -1 \leq t \leq 1.$$

We can set $t^n = e^{-\alpha n}$ for some nonnegative α if we wish.

We recover the macroeconomic variables by

$$-\frac{\partial \ln(\Xi)}{\partial \alpha} = N,$$

and

$$-\frac{\partial \ln(\Xi)}{\partial \beta} = Y.$$

We use this type of transformation in Chapter 8, and other places as well.

2.2.3 Replacing the sum with the maximum term

In the preceeding, we replaced the sum with its maximum term in evaluating the partition function. To illustrate that this method is surprisingly accurate, we evaluate the known sum

$$\sum_s \frac{N!}{\prod_s N_s!} \prod_s q_s^{N_s} = \left(\sum_s q_s \right)^N.$$

We use Stirling's formula to evaluate the factorials

$$\ln N! \approx \ln[(N/e)^N] + O(\ln N/N)$$

where we ignore the second term. Maximizing the Lagrangian of a single term in the summation

$$L = \ln N! - N_s[\ln(N_s - 1)] + N_s \ln q_s + \alpha \left(N - \sum_s N_s \right)$$

yields

$$N_s^* = q_s e^{-\alpha},$$

where α is determined by the constraint equation to be

$$e^\alpha = \sum_s q_s/N.$$

Now, we evaluate this maximal term to see that

$$\frac{N!}{\prod_s N_s^*!} \prod_s q_s^{N_s^*} = \left\{ \frac{N}{e} \right\}^N \prod_s \left(\frac{eq_s}{N_s^*} \right)^{N_s^*} = N^N e^{N\alpha} = \left(\sum_s q_s \right)^N,$$

where α is substituted out by $e^\alpha = \sum_s q_s/N$.

We observe that the method of maximum term reproduces the correct result up to $O(\ln N/N)$.

In another example, we let X_i be independent and identically distributed Poisson random variables with rate λ. Then, the sum $S_N = X_1 + \cdots + X_N$ is a Poisson random variable with rate $N\lambda$. Take a to be larger than λ, and consider the probability

$$P(S_N \geq na) = \sum_{j=Na}^{\infty} \frac{(N\lambda)^j}{j!} e^{-N\lambda}.$$

We evaluate this probability by replacing the sum with the largest term, which is the one with $j = na$, since a is larger than λ:

$$\frac{(N\lambda)^{Na}}{(Na)!} e^{-N\lambda} \approx (2\pi Na)^{-1/2} \exp\{-N[\lambda - a + a \ln(a/\lambda)]\}.$$

Since the ratio of the term with $j = Na+k$ over that with $j = Na$ is less than $(\lambda/a)^k$, for $k = 1, 2, \ldots$, the error in making this approximation is of $O(N)$, and actually, it is independent of N.

2.3   Empirical distributions

How can we model seemingly random movements of macroeconomic conditions, for instance, those of suitably detrended real GNP? One possibility is to partition an interval of the real line into a finite number of subsets in which such deviational movements from the trend take place, and provide some probabilistic description or mechanism for movements from one subset to another.

Indeed, Hamilton (1989) attempts something like this by using available past records of booms and depressions to construct a two-state Markov chain to describe business-cycle movements of real Gross National Product (GNP). Two states of such a Markov chain can correspond to unobserved shifts between two regimes or turning points in time series. Neftci (1984) classifies the state of the economy into one of two categories, depending on whether unemployment is rising or falling.

Such a description of the macroeconomy may be empirically satisfactory, and may even forecast future states of the economy well, but it is hardly satisfactory as a theoretical explanation of why business cycles arise.

If, however, such macroeconomic movements are linked to shifting economic conditions of an underlying set of microeconomic agents, then it may be the beginning of a useful model of movements of GNP, unemployment, and so on. To such an end, we can quantize the possible values of microeconomic states of an agent into a finite or denumerable set of values, so that we can deal with a large but finite dimensional collection of agents. For example, if each microeconomic variable is binary and there are N agents, then the set of configurations of the collection of N agents has 2^N elements. Extensions are immediate to more than binary quantization as well as to microeconomic-state vectors, each component of which is quantized to a finite level.

However, our knowledge of microeconomic states is limited. We do not know the microeconomic variables of each and every agent in the model. At most, we can construct empirical distributions, that is, we know the number of times a particular microeconomic-state variable has occurred in a given sample of agent configurations, and, of course, we know the value of macroeconomic variables that are presumably functions of these microeconomic variables, such as arithmetic averages.

2.3.1 Examples

Suppose that a random variable x_i can take on three values $-1, 0$, and -1. There are five agents, $i = 1, 2, \ldots, 5$, and we observe a sample $X = (1, -1, 0, 1, 0)$. Then, the empirical distribution assigns probability 2/5 to 1, 2/5 to 0, and 1/5 to -1, that is, the probability distribution of this realization is $P_X = (2/5, 2/5, 1/5)$.

Next, suppose that each agent's microeconomic state, x, is either $+1$ or -1, and there are N agents. We assume, the x's are independent and identically distributed. Then, all possible ways that we observe ± 1 are $(0, N), (1, N - 1)$, $\ldots, (N, 0)$, where $(k, N - k)$ means that k of N agents are in state 1, and the remainder of $N - k$ agents are in state -1. Therefore, the empirical distributions are

$$\left\{ [P(1), P(-1)] : \left(\frac{0}{N}, \frac{N}{N} \right), \left(\frac{1}{N}, \frac{N-1}{N} \right), \ldots \left(\frac{N}{N}, \frac{0}{N} \right) \right\}.$$

What is important in this example is that there are 2^N number of configurations, but there are only $(N + 1)$ choices for the vector of empirical distributions.

More generally, if microeconomic variables can take on K distinct values, $a_j, j = 1, \ldots, K$, then the empirical distribution is defined by $P(a_j) = N_j/N$, $j = 1, \ldots, K$, where $\sum_j N_j = N$. There are K^N number of configurations, whereas there are, at most, $(N + 1)^{K-1}$ choices for empirical distributions, since each component can take on $N + 1$ values. Since there are an exponential number of configurations among the polynomial number of empirical distributions, at least one empirical distribution has exponentially many configurations corresponding to it.

2.3.2 Multiplicity of microstates

We illustrate that a given macroeconomic state is compatible with many microeconomic states or configurations. In addition to the obvious observation that this fact is important in discussing the distributional effects of any policy action, there is the far less obvious but very important fact that this multiplicity determines how macroeconomic equilibria are affected by uncertainty in the model. The notion of entropy naturally arises as a measure of degree of degeneracy or multiplicity of microstates, which must be included in evaluating particular model performances or costs. The exponent of a Gibbs distribution includes the effects of multiplicity or degeneracy in this sense. We encounter this notion, which corresponds to the idea of free energy in physics, in Chapters 3 and 5.

Let x_i, $i = 1, \ldots, N$, be independent and identically distributed binary random variables with prior probabilities

$$q = Pr(x_i = 1),$$

and

$$1 - q = Pr(x_i = -1),$$

for $i = 1, \ldots, N$.

In this simple example, the macroeconomic or aggregate signal is the arithmetic average of individual microeconomic agents' state variables:

$$m = \frac{1}{N} \sum_{i=1}^{N} x_i.$$

We note that a permutation of the agent indexes does not change the average. This is one indication that these are exchangeable random variables. In many economic models, microeconomic agents are not representative agents, but rather exchangeable agents. We have more to say on this in Chapter 3. A realization (a sample) is an N-dimensional vector, $\mathbf{x} = (x_1, \ldots, x_N)$, called a state vector, which records a realized value of the random variables. It is also called a configuration (of N random variables or microeconomic variables).

When k of the N variables take on the value of 1, the arithmetic average is given by

$$m = \frac{k - (N - k)}{N} = \frac{2k - N}{N}.$$

We solve this for k:

$$k = (1 + m)/2,$$

which is the value k that is compatible with the observed average. Since there are $_N C_k$ ways of choosing k agents out of N, the same average value is compatible with $_N C_k$ microeconomic configurations or samples. By a simple combinatorial argument,

$$Pr[m = (2k - N)/N] = {_N C_k}\, q^k (1 - q)^{N-k}. \tag{2.6}$$

To get a feel for the magnitude of this expression when N is large, we note first that

$$_NC_k \approx \exp[NH(k/N)],$$

that is, $(1/N)\ln(_NC_k)$ is approximately equal to $H(k/N)$, which is the base e Shannon entropy, that is,

$$H(k/N) = -(k/N)\ln(k/N) - (1 - k/N)\ln(1 - k/N).$$

This is a measure of the multiplicity of the average m, that is, the multiplicity of microstates that generate the same average.

Another way to see this is to use Stirling's formula for large factorials:[4]

$$M! \approx \sqrt{2\pi M}(M/e)^M.$$

Using this approximation, we can rewrite Eq. (2.6) as

$$Pr[m = (2k - N)/N]$$
$$\approx \exp\{N[H(k/N) + (k/N)\ln(q) + (1 - k/N)\ln(1 - q)]\}.$$

We can rewrite this expression by utilizing the Kullback–Leibler distance measure as follows. First, define the empirical distribution P_X of a sample $X = (X_1, \ldots, X_N)$ as the fraction of the times 1 and -1 are observed in the sample. When k of the components of X are ones in sample X, then P_X has two components $P_+ = k/N$, and $P_- = 1 - k/N$.

Therefore, we can write the exponent above as

$$P_+ \ln(q) + P_- \ln(1 - q) = -H(k/N) + D(P_X; Q),$$

where $D(P_X; Q)$ is called the Kullback–Leibler divergence between two distributions P_X and Q, where they have two components $p, 1 - p$, and $q, 1 - q$, respectively,

$$D(P; Q) = p\ln(p/q) + (1 - p)\ln[(1 - p)/(1 - q)],$$

in the case for distributions of binary variables. The Kullback–Leibler distance is also called the relative entropy.

Combining the two above, we have derived the probability distribution of the macrovariable m as

$$Pr\left(m = \frac{2k - N}{N}\right) \approx e^{ND(P_X; Q)}.$$

[4] See the method of Laplace in the Appendix for a derivation of this formula.

Suppose next that X_i are independent and identically distributed Poisson random variables with rate λ. Then, the sum $S_n = X_1 + \cdots + X_n$ is also a Poisson random variable with rate $n\lambda$. By direct calculation,

$$
\begin{aligned}
P(S_n/n \geq a) &= \sum_{j=na}^{\infty} \frac{(n\lambda)^j}{j!} e^{-n\lambda} \\
&\approx \frac{(n\lambda)^{na}}{(na)!} \\
&\approx (2\pi na)^{-1/2} (a/\lambda)^{-na} e^{-n(\lambda-a)}
\end{aligned}
$$

for $a \geq \lambda$. The right-hand side is of the form $e^{-nc(a)+o(n)}$ where $c(a) = (\lambda - a) + a \ln(a/\lambda)$. This is a simple illustration of the type of results yielded by the large-deviation techniques discussed in Chapter 3. There, we also discuss how this bound is related to the Kullback–Leibler divergence measure. An example in Section 5.9 shows how the multiplicity as measured by Shannon entropy jointly determines the equilibrium probability distribution together with expressions of cost or profits in a large collection of interacting agents.

2.3.3   Sanov's theorem

Sanov's theorem is a statement about the probabilities of a collection of empirical distributions that are compatible with observed macroeconomic conditions. Here is a numerical example to give a flavor of how Sanov's theorem and the conditional-limit theorem discussed in Section 2.3.4 can be used.

Suppose that a random variable X_i, $i = 1, \ldots, N$, represents a microeconomic condition for N agents. This variable is independent and identically distributed by assumption, and takes on the values $+1$ and -1 with probabilities q and $1 - q$. The a priori probability distribution is thus $Q = (q, 1 - q)$.

Suppose that their average m is observed to be 0.6. This means that the empirical distribution $P = (p, 1 - p)$ must be such that $2p - 1 \geq 0.6$.

Sanov's theorem, discussed in Chapter 3, estimates this probability by

$$
Pr(m \geq 0.6) \approx e^{-ND(P^*;Q)},
$$

where the empirical distribution P^* minimizes the Kullback–Leibler divergence measure $D(P; Q)$ subject to the constraint on the observed average.

After a simple calculation, this minimization yields the optimal estimate

$$
p^* = \frac{qe^{-2\lambda}}{1 - q + qe^{-2\lambda}},
$$

where the value of λ is chosen to yield the average of 0.6. When this is done, p^* is given by 0.8, that is, the solution of $2p^* - 1 = 0.8$. If $q = 0.8$, then

$Pr(m \geq 0.6) = 1$. If $q = 0.7$, then $P(m \geq 0.6) \approx e^{-0.026N}$, and when $q = 0.5$, this probability becomes approximately equal to $e^{-0.19N}$. For example, with $N = 100$, this last probability is practically zero, since it is 0.6×10^8. With $N = 20$, it is about 0.022.

2.3.4   Conditional-limit theorem

Related to this is the conditional-limit theorem, which gives the probability of $x_1 = 1$, given that the average is 0.6, by

$$Pr(x_1 = 1 \mid m \geq 0.6) \to p^*,$$

as N becomes very large, that is, about 0.8.

We let the arithmetic average of N binary variables be given by

$$\bar{l} = (1/N) \sum l_i,$$

where $Pr(l_i = 1) = q$, and $Pr(l_i = -1) = 1 - q$, for all $i = 1, \ldots, N$.

The conditional-limit theorem states that

$$Pr(l_1 = 1 \mid \bar{l}) = p^*(l_1 = 1),$$

where the distribution $P^* = (p^*, 1 - p^*)$ minimizes the Kullback–Leibler measure $D(P^*; Q)$, subject to the macroeconomic constraint that the average is equal to $\bar{l}$.

On carrying out this constrained minimization, we derive

$$p^* = \frac{q e^\lambda}{q e^\lambda + (1 - q)e^{-\lambda}},$$

where the parameter λ is adjusted to yield $\bar{l}$ as the average, that is,

$$e^{2\lambda} = \frac{(1 + \bar{l})(1 - q)}{(1 - \bar{l})q}.$$

From this, we see that $p^* = (1 + \bar{l})/2$, or, more directly, from the expression for the average $\bar{l} = p^* - (1 - p^*)$.

2.4   Stochastic dynamics and processes

2.4.1   Mean first-passage times

We use a simple discrete-time Markov chain with two states to illustrate a method to calculate the average first-passage time from one state to the other.

We have occasion to carry out such calculations on a more realistic model in Chapter 5.

Suppose that the transition probability is given by

$$P = \begin{bmatrix} 1-a & a \\ b & 1-b \end{bmatrix},$$

where a and b are the transition probability from state 1 to state 2, and from state 2 to state 1, respectively.

Denoting the probability that the system is in state i at time n by $p_i(n)$, $i = 1, 2$, we define $\rho(n) = [p_1(n)\, p_2(n)]$. Then we multiply $P^{n+1} = P^n P$ from the left by this row vector of probabilities to see that it evolves with time according to

$$\rho(n + 1) = \rho(n)P.$$

Since $p_2(n) = 1 - p_1(n)$, we focus on the time evolutions of the probability that the system occupies state 1. This probability is governed by

$$p_1(n + 1) = (1 - a)p_1(n) + bp_2(n) = b + (1 - a - b)p_1(n).$$

This is an example of a class of the Chapman–Kolmogorov equations we later call the master equations. This Markov chain has a stationary, or equilibrium probability, distribution:

$$p_1(\infty) = \frac{b}{a + b}.$$

The equilibrium probability depends on the transition probabilities only through their ratio.

The probability of the first passage from state 1 to state 2, which happens at step k, denoted by $f_{12}(k)$, is given by

$$f_{12}(k) = a(1 - a)^{k-1}, \quad k = 1, 2, \ldots.$$

The expected first-passage time from state 1 to state 2, denoted by m_{12}, is then given by

$$m_{12} = \sum_{k=1}^{\infty} k f_{12}(k) = \frac{1}{a},$$

where we use the fact that $\sum k\gamma^{k-1} = d/d\gamma(\sum \gamma^k)$ for $\gamma < 1$ in magnitude.

Unlike the equilibrium probabilities, the mean first-passage time depends on the transition probability, and not on the ratio. To see a dramatic implication of this difference, suppose that

$$a = e^{-(V+v)},$$

and

$$b = e^{-V},$$

where $V \gg v \geq 0$. Then,

$$b/(a + b) = 1/(1 + e^{-v}),$$

but

$$m_{12} = e^{(V+v)} \gg 1.$$

With the value of v nearly zero, the system has a nearly equal probability of being in state 1 or state 2, but the transition from state 1 to state 2, and similarly that from state 2 to state 1 will take a long time. The standard deviation is of the same order of magnitude, since the variance is $e^{(V+v)}[e^{(V+v)} - 1]$.

2.4.2 Dynamics with multiple equilibria

In a simple model of stochastic dynamics with two locally stable equilibria, we let $X(t)$ be a scalar-valued state variable of this model, which is either a or c. In other words, there are two states in the state space, $S = \{a, c\}$. Unlike the more complex models of Chapters 5 and 7, we can solve this example simply. This model is an extremely simplified version of stochastic dynamics with many local equilibria. Figure 2.1 is a sketch of a function (the exponent of a Gibbs distribution, called the potential), with two local equilibria and its relation to our model. We write $Pr[X(t) = a]$ as $P_a(t)$ for shorter notation, and similarly, $P_c(t)$.

Since $P_c(t) + P_a(t) = 1$ for all $t \geq 0$, we examine only probability $P_c(t)$ as an example. The equation for it can be written as

$$dP_c(t)/dt = w_{a,c} P_a(t) - w_{c,a} P_c(t),$$

where $w_{a,c}$ is the transition rate from state a to state c. It is the derivative of $Pr[X(t) = c \mid X(0) = a]$ with respect to time t, that is, the probability of moving from state a to state c in a small positive time interval, Δt, is equal to $w_{a,c}\Delta t + o(\Delta t)$. Chapter 4 delves into more detail on this important concept. Similar statements can be made for $w_{c,a}$. This equation is an example of a class of Chapman–Kolmogorov equations called the master equations, and is discussed extensively in Chapters 4 and 5.

In this example, we assume that the transition rate from state a to state c is $w_{a,c} = e^{-\beta(V+v)}$, and that from state c to state a, it is given by $w_{c,a} = e^{-\beta V}$,

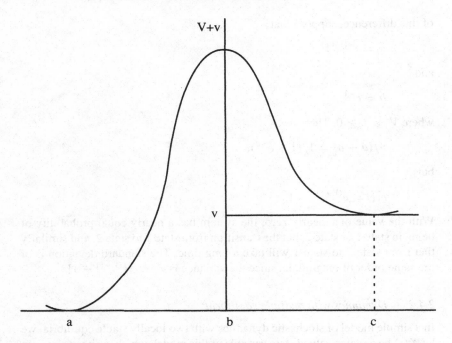

Fig. 2.1. Two basins of attractions separated by a barrier in a two-state Markov process.

where the parameter β is taken to be nonnegative.[5] These transition rates reflect the fact that to go from state a to state c, there is a barrier of height $V + v$, and from state c to state a, the height of the barrier is V. We assume that v is (much) smaller than V.

The equilibrium probability for the state variable $X(t)$ to lie in state a, or in state c, is obtained simply by setting the derivative to zero in the above differential equation. These are equilibrium probabilities, denoted by π_a and π_c, respectively. They satisfy the relation

$$\pi_a w_{a,c} = \pi_c w_{c,a},$$

which states that the probability of jumping from state a to state c, and the reverse probability, balance out in equilibrium. This equation is an especially simple example of the detailed balance condition that we discuss in Section 3.3.2

---

[5] Even though we treat it simply as a parameter, we use β in this book as something that reflects the level of economic activity in models, or the level of uncertainty that is present in the economy. We may think roughly that the level of economic activity and that of uncertainty are inversely related.

in detail. The detailed balance condition implies that the equilibrium distribution is a Gibbs distribution. See Chapter 3 or Kelly (1979), for example. The equilibrium probability is given by

$$\pi_c = (1 + e^{\beta v})^{-1}.$$

The assumed form of the transition rates implies that we measure the potential in the exponent of the Gibbs distribution from that of state a, and assume that the value of the potential function at state c differs only slightly from the first by the amount v, but that these two stable equilibria are separated by a barrier of height V, as shown in Fig. 2.1. Note that these equilibrium probabilities are independent of the height of the barrier.

Dropping the subscript c, we rewrite the differential equation as

$$dP/dt = e^{-\beta(V+v)} - \gamma P = -\gamma(P - \pi_c), \tag{2.7}$$

where $\gamma = e^{-\beta V} + e^{-\beta(V+v)}$. This probability monotonically approaches its equilibrium value. Although these equilibrium probabilities are independent of the height of the barrier, the time constant $1/\gamma$ does depend on V. Lowering the value of β increases the probability of moving from one state to the other. This can be interpreted as a reflection of a higher level of economic activity or a lower degree of uncertainty in the model. In equilibrium the model is more likely to be in state a than in state c, as β becomes large.

We next consider varying the β parameter over time in such a way that the path to equilibrium is the quickest possible. Put differently, we ask: If we can manipulate the value of β, how do we adjust β to hasten convergence to an equilibrium state? Such a β can be obtained by maximizing the rate of change of P, that is, the right-hand side of Eq. (2.7) with respect to β:

$$\frac{\partial}{\partial \beta}\left[e^{-\beta(V+v)} - \gamma P\right] = 0. \tag{2.8}$$

For a simpler explanation, we set the initial condition to zero, $P(0) = 0$. Then,

$$P(t) = \pi_c(1 - e^{-\gamma t}),$$

and the right-hand side of Eq. (2.7) becomes $\exp[-\beta(V + v) - \gamma t]$. By minimizing the exponent of this expression, we obtain

$$V + v = -(\partial \gamma / \partial \beta)t,$$

as a necessary and sufficient condition for maximizing the right-hand side of Eq. (2.7), that is, Eq. (2.8). This expression becomes

$$t = \frac{e^{\beta V}}{e^{-\beta v} + V/(V + v)},$$

or

$$\beta V \approx \ln t,$$

by noting that β becomes large as t increases.[6] Comparing this result with those obtained for our hierarchical models in Chapter 7 we notice a similar sluggish response pattern.

One interpretation we make of this example is that under the best of circumstances, the approach to equilibrium is sluggish, that is, at most at a rate $\ln t$, and not exponential for stochastic dynamics with multiple equilibria.

2.4.3   Random partition of agents by types

2.4.3.1   Pólya's urn
An urn contains b black balls and g green balls initially. Each time a ball is drawn it is returned to the urn with one more ball of the color drawn. Let X_n be the fraction of green balls after the nth draw, i.e., after the ball drawn is returned and a new ball added.[7]

After n draws, the probability of getting green balls on the first m draws and black balls on the next $l = n - m$ draw is

$$\frac{g}{g+b}\frac{g+1}{g+b+1}\cdots\frac{g+m-1}{g+b+m-1}\frac{b}{b+g+b+m}\cdots\frac{b+l-1}{g+b+n-1}.$$

Note that any other outcomes of the first n draws with m green balls drawn have the same denominator, and the numerators are merely permuted, i.e., the probability is the same.

It is easy to verify that X_n is a martingale and $X_n \to X_\infty$ as n goes to infinity. See Durrett (1991, p. 208). The random variable X_∞ is distributed as

$$\frac{\Gamma(g+b)}{\Gamma(g)\Gamma(b)}(1-x)^{g-1}x^{b-1}.$$

More generally, we could assume that initially there are K colors.

2.4.3.2   Generalized Pólya urn model
Next, we describe a generalized Pólya urn model. At time zero an urn contains only θ black balls. At time $1, 2, \ldots,$ a ball is drawn at random from the urn, and

---

[6] This result is interesting because of the similarity with the optimal annealing schedule in the simulated annealing literature (see Kirkpatrick, Gelatt, and Vecchi 1983; Geman and Geman 1984; and Kabashima and Shinomoto 1991).

[7] We think of the balls of different color as economic agents with different characteristics, i.e., of different type. This point of view is not too relevant in this example but becomes more so in the next example.

returned after noting its color. When a black ball is drawn, then a ball is added of a color which has not been seen before. When a non-black ball is drawn, a ball of the same color is returned. In other words, drawing a black ball introduces a ball of new color (type) into the urn.[8] Label new colors as color 1, color 2, etc, in the order of appearance. The device of black balls is used to introduce new types, new algorithms or choices to a set of interacting agents. It may also be useful in introducing innovations in consumption goods at random instants.

Initially, there are only black balls. The first ball drawn is always black, and a new color, color 1, is introduced after the first draw. At the $(n + 1)$ the draw there are $\theta + n$ balls in the urn. Hence the probability of drawing a black ball next is $\theta/(\theta + n)$. Denote by n_j the number of balls of color (type) j after n draws. The probability of drawing color j next is given by $n_j/(\theta + n)$.

Then

$$Pr(n_1 = i) = E_x\{_{n-1}C_{i-1}x^{i-1}(1 - x)^{n-i}\},$$

where x is the fraction of color 1 balls.

If the density for x is given by

$$p(x) = \theta(1 - x)^{\theta-1},$$

$0 \leq x \leq 1$, then this probability becomes

$$Pr(n_1 = i) = \left(\frac{\theta}{n}\right)\frac{_nC_i}{_{\theta+n-1}C_i}.$$

See Hoppe (1987), and Kelly (1979).

If we let i and n go to infinity while keeping $x = i/n$, we recover

$$f(x)\Delta x = \frac{1}{n}f(x) = \frac{\theta}{n}(1 - x)^{\theta-1}.$$

Interpreting colors as types of agents, distributions of agents over possible types or choices can thus be examined statistically. See Chapter 4 of this book, Aoki (1995c), and Ewens (1990) for further comments.

2.5   Hierarchical state spaces

In this book, dynamic systems are Markovian processes, usually with denumerable state spaces. By suitable selections of variables to serve as a state vector, that is, by describing models in enough detail, we can render the dynamics Markovian. A microscopic state is thus a complete dynamic description of the model. Dynamics can be continuous, or discrete, in time. The former is called

---

[8] In the above, θ need not be an integer. If you like, think of a black ball of weight θ, all non-black balls weighing a unit. Think of the selection probability being determined by relative weights.

a continous-time Markov chain, and the latter a discrete-time Markov chain when the states are denumerable at most.

Dynamics of a model composed of a large number of agents have a high-dimensional state space. We often find, however, that all states are not equally occupied. Some subset of the state space is occupied with much higher probabilities than other subsets. In such cases, we find it advantageous and useful to impose some structure into state spaces and to work with subsets of states by partitioning the original state space into hierarchically organized subsets, where a subset on a level is further partitioned into a set of smaller subsets on the next level. For example, we can partition states in such a way that states in a given leaf all have the same pairwise correlations. We present examples in this chapter and in Chapter 7 where we associate martingales with tree nodes. Alternatively, we can regard trees as an approximation to (Euclidean) high-dimensional state space.

This hierarchical organization of subsets can be visualized as an upside-down tree with the root at the top.[9] The root is the original state space containing all of the states. At level 1, counting the root as level 0, a binary tree has two nodes, each of which is a partitioned subset of the state space that is divided into two distinct non-overlapping subsets.[10] At the bottom, each subset is called a leaf. The leaves contain one or more configurations, that is, one or more states of the original state space.

Economic models with many agents have a huge number of internal configurations, that is, their state spaces contain a large number of states even when states of microeconomic agents are very simple. For example, with each of N agents, numbered from 1 to N, in one of two possible states, the state space is a collection of $x = (x_1, x_2, \ldots, x_N)$, where $x_i = \pm 1$ for all i from 1 to N. There are 2^N states. To have some idea of the magnitudes, observe that $2^{10} = 1024$, $2^{20} = 1.05 \times 10^6$, and 2^{50} is about 1.13×10^{15}. Increasing N to 100, we have $2^{100} = 1.27 \times 10^{30}$. This is the total number of configurations when each of 100 agents is in one of two alternative microeconomic or microstates. This is indeed a very large number.[11] Clearly, some of these configurations can be lumped together in our modeling of the system to form coarser-grained configurations or states.

Put differently, dynamics in the state space can be approximated with advantage by dynamics on trees in the sense that we describe subsequently.[12]

Instead of partitioning microeconomic states into subsets to construct trees, we can alternatively partition the set of microeconomic agents into tree nodes. A

---

[9] Numerical taxonomy and other fields such as biology also use tree classification schemes.

[10] A tree need not be binary. It can have any finite number of nodes at a given level.

[11] Recall that the Avogadro number (the number of particles in 1 mole of gas) is approximately 6×10^{23}.

[12] See Doyle and Snell (1984, p. 113) for an example of random walks on trees that approximate random walks in three-dimensional Euclidean space.

subset of agents can be further partitioned into subgroups of more homogeneous agents in some sense, for example. Or, the range of some macroeconomic variable can be partitioned into a tree structure.

Dynamics of Markov chains are characterized by transition probabilities or transition rates – depending on discrete-time or continuous-time formulation – to indicate how a state in one leaf can move to a state in another leaf. We often consider the transition rates as functions of the tree distance between leaves, which is defined as the number of levels of trees retraced toward the root until a common node shared by the leaves is found for the first time. This is an example of the ultrametric distance.

In investigating the macroscopic properties of material known as spin glasses, the physicists Mezard and Virasoro (1985) proposed a hierarchical structure for energy levels of spin glasses and used an ultrametric distance to organize them into trees. They also conjectured that ultrametrics and the associated hierarchical organization of space may exist not only in spin glasses but in other complex optimizing systems.[13] We follow up on their conjecture in our search for alternative macroeconomic modeling approaches in this chapter. See the examples in Chapter 2 and in Section 7.1 for motivation and illustrations.

Before we proceed with this plan, a word about ultrametric spaces is in order. This notion is explained in an introductory book by Schikhof (1984) and the notion of p-adic numbers behind it is explained in Mahler (1973). According to Rammal and Toulouse (1986), the theory of p-adic numbers was developed by K. Hensel in 1897. The p-adic numbers have a natural ordering not along a line as the ordinary real numbers have, but on hierarchical generating trees.[14] Rammal and Toulouse (1986) credit M. Krasner as the person who coined the word ultrametric in 1944.

Hierarchical structures are self-similar in that their subsets have the same form as the original structure. Schikhof (1984) has an interesting illustration of figures within figures in the inside cover of his book. Hierarchies also are used in the literature on numerical taxonomy. See Jardine and Sibson (1971). Biological species are classified into families and then genera which are trees. Genealogical trees are another example.[15]

---

[13] There is some work that draws attention to similarities between the energy structures of spin glasses and the cost structures of some difficult (combinatorial) optimization problems, such as the traveling-salesman problem, graph-partitioning problems, and the like. See Vannimenus and Mezard (1984), Kirkpatrick and Toulouse (1985), or Mezard, Parisi, and Virasoro (1987, Chap. VII), Aldous and Vazirani (1993), for example.

[14] The p-adic representations have many interesting applications, such as Gray code used in analog-to-digital converters. See Clarke (1992).

[15] The literature of numerical taxonomy discusses algorithms for constructing hierarchies, such as the single-linkage clustering method, minimal spanning trees, and the subdominant ultrametrics. See Sokal and Sneath (1963), Jardine and Sibson (1971), or Murtagh (1983).

2.5.1   *Examples of hierarchically structured state spaces*

Here we focus on structures of state spaces, namely, how these microeconomic states are organized. Fortunately, not all of these numerous configurations are equally likely in equilibrium. In dynamic context, the transition from a current state to one of these states is not equally likely either. Certain states are more likely to follow than others. Situations are analogous with deterministic linear dynamics. Not all states are equally accessible from initial states in a given amount of time, for example.

How do we build such structural information or constraints into the model state spaces? There are several ways, as discussed in Chapter 7. For example, we can classify states into clusters or subsets corresponding to some measure of similarity or distance. As the measure of distance is changed, a cluster can be further subdivided into a set of subclusters, so that clusters and subclusters, and so forth, become partially nested, that is, form nodes of trees. In other words, we partition state spaces into smaller and smaller subsets of states. By construction, states in a given node are closer or more similar to each other than those in different clusters. Clearly, we need a measure of similarity or dissimilarity of states by which to partition sets of states. We describe an example later in this section to point out that an intuitively reasonable idea of using correlations does not always work, and that we need a stronger notion of ultrametrics.

2.5.1.1   *Coin-tossing spaces.*

The first example is not an economic example, but is mentioned here because it is a very well-known example in probability. It is a space of sequences of ones and zeroes (heads and tails of fair coin tosses). Such sequences are called paths. The space, Ω, is a space of paths, with the usual Borel σ-field, and P is the fair-coin-tossing probability.

The root of this tree stands for the unit interval. At level 1, we have a node labeled 0 and a node labeled 1 corresponding to the binary intervals $[0, 2^{-1}]$ and $[2^{-1}, 1]$. At level j, each node is labeled by a sequence $\delta_1, \delta_2, \ldots, \delta_j$ where δ_k is 1 or 0, $k = 1, 2, \ldots, j$. At this level, binary intervals $[i2^{-j}, (i+1)2^{-j}]$, $i = 0, 1, \ldots 2^j - 1$, are associated with each node. See Fig. 2.2. For each $\omega \in \Omega$, we define random variables X_n by $X_1(\omega), X_2(\omega), \ldots, X_n(\omega)$, where $X_k(\omega)$ is the value of the node hit by ω at level k. We note that

$$P[\omega \mid X_1(\omega) = \delta_1, \ldots, X_n(\omega) = \delta_n] = 2^{-n}.$$

Next, we denote by $(X_j = 1)$ the set of paths with $X_j(\omega) = 1$. Likewise, we define $(X_j = 0)$. For any j not greater than n, we note that the set $(X_j = \delta_j)$ is equal to $\bigcup_{i \neq j}(X_i = \delta_i, i = 1, \ldots, n)$, where the union is over all $i \neq j$. We note that

$$P[(X_j = \delta_j)] = 2^{-n}2^{n-1} = 2^{-1},$$

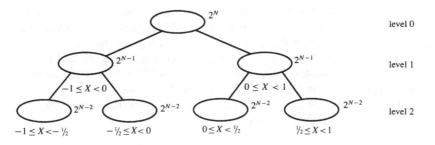

Fig. 2.2. Coin tossing space as a tree.

and

$$P\{[X_j(\omega) = \delta_j, 1 \le j \le n]\} = \prod_1^n P[(X_j = \delta_j)].$$

Another probabilistic or stochastic example is a construction method of a standard Brownian motion from a sequence of normal random variables associated with nodes of the binary tree constructed above. See Freedman (1983). Independent normal random variables with mean 0 and variance 2^{-k} are associated with nodes at level k. The root has a mean zero-normal random variable with variance 1. A random variable, Z_b, where b is the binary rational interval associated with nodes, is defined by

$$Z_{b0} = \frac{1}{2}Z_b - \frac{1}{2}X_b,$$

and

$$Z_{b1} = \frac{1}{2}Z_b + \frac{1}{2}X_b,$$

where the notation $b0$ and $b1$ mean concentration of zeros and ones. By construction, $Z_b = Z_{b0} + Z_{b1}$.

2.5.1.2 K-level classification.
We refer to a vector $\mathbf{x} = (x_1, \cdots, x_N)$ as a sample, a realization, or a configuration (of microvariables, x_i's). With binary random variables $x_i = \pm 1$, there are 2^N configurations in all.

A K-level tree displays how we partition the total of 2^N configurations, each of which is a microeconomic description of the states of N agents, into 2^K subsets of the macroeconomic variables, for some positive integer $K < N$. Changes in K result in macroeconomic descriptions with different detail. We arrange these subsets as the leaves (bottom-level partitions) of a K-level binary (inverted) tree. Reducing the number K corresponds to pruning a tree to have a smaller number of levels. We further discuss the idea of pruning or aggregation in Section 7.3 and explain the use of renormalization group theory.

To get some idea of magnitudes involved, suppose that $N = 30$, and $K = 5$, that is, we have a five-level tree. The root contains $2^{30} = 1.07 \times 10^9$ configurations. The average m is quantized into $2^5 = 32$ intervals of length $2 \times 2^{-5} = 0.06$ each. Each leaf thus contains $2^{30-5} = 3.36 \times 10^7$ numbers of the configurations. More examples can be found in Chapter 7.

2.5.1.3 Pattern classification.
This little example shows that an intuitive notion of using correlation to classify or partition a set of patterns (of economic activity) does not always work.

Suppose we encode information on, or pattern of macroeconomic state with, an N-bit string, $x = (x_1, \ldots, x_N)$, where $x_i = \pm 1$. Such a string may describe the conditions of N microeconomic units or agents, where $+1$ may be interpreted as better than normal, and -1 as worse than normal, for example.

One common way to measure similarity between two such strings is by correlation. If x_i and y_i are ± 1 with equal probabilities, then their correlation is calculated by

$$\rho = (1/N) \sum_{i=1}^{N} x_i y_i.$$

We want to partition a set of all possible strings in such a way that we put into the same cluster or subset all strings that have pairwise correlations higher than, say, some cutoff value, ρ_c.

Feigelman and Ioffe (1991, p. 173) showed that this scheme does not work. Consider the three strings: $\xi^1 = (1, 1, 1, 1)$, $\xi^2 = (1, 1, -1, 1)$, and $\xi^3 = (1, 1, 1, -1)$. We denote the correlation between ξ^i and ξ^j by q_{ij}. We have $q_{12} = q_{13} = 1/2$, but $q_{23} = 0$. If we set ρ_c at $1/2$, then this classification scheme based on correlation breaks down, since we cannot decide whether to put ξ^2 or ξ^3 with ξ^1.

This sort of difficulty has been known in the literature of numerical taxonomy; see Jardine and Sibson (1971), for example. To avoid this intransitivity of correlations as a measure of similarity, we need to impose a condition on measures of similarity s_{ij} so that if $s_{12} \le s_c$ and if $s_{13} \le s_c$, then $s_{23} \le s_c$. Alternatively, we can define a notion of distance between patterns, d_{ij}, to satisfy the condition that if $d_{12} \ge d_c$, and $d_{13} \ge d_c$, then $d_{23} \ge d_c$, where d_{ij} is the distance between patterns or strings i and j.

More generally, we require that

$$s_{ij} \le \min(s_{ik}, s_{kj}),$$

or

$$d_{ij} \geq \max(d_{ik}, d_{kj}),$$

for any triplet of strings or patterns.

This condition is known as the ultrametricity condition, and any distance measure that satisfied the condition is called ultrametric. Note that the usual Euclidean distance satisfies the triangle inequality. The above ultrametric condition is stronger.

When patterns are arranged as leaves of a tree, that is, when patterns are organized into hierarchy, the ultrametric distance is the same as, or some monotone function of, the tree distance, which is the number of levels one needs to trace toward the root to find for the first time a common node from which the leaves separate. We can construct a two-level tree for the example of Feigelman and Ioffe (1991) in which the set (root) containing the three patterns is partitioned into two nodes, where the first contains ξ_1 and ξ_3, and the second ξ_2, and the first node is further subdivided into two nodes, each containing a single pattern, ξ_1 and ξ_3. This tree is constructed by regarding components of the patterns as binary valued, and associating martingales with nodes as we describe them in Section 2.5.2. The notion of ultrametrics is further discussed later in this chapter.

2.5.2 Tree metric and martingales

Martingales can be associated with the nodes of a tree, or, rather, each path from the root to a leaf at the bottom can be interpreted as a sequence of finite-valued random variables which are martingales. A special case is the coin-tossing space introduced earlier, which is a binary tree with the left and right branches associated with heads and tails, for example. Each path is a sequence of heads and tails, which are the outcomes of independent sequences of tosses of a coin.[16]

We introduce a sequence of real numbers, $0 \leq r_1 \leq \cdots \leq r_k \leq \cdots \leq r_K \leq 1$. A superscript denotes a path from the root to a particular node, and to label a random variable associated with that node. We let a random variable at level k, ξ^k, take on values $\pm r_k$ with probability

$$Pr(\xi^k \mid \xi^{k-1}) = (1/2)[1 + \operatorname{sgn}(\xi^k \xi^{k-1}) r_{k-1}/r_k],$$

where we use k to label a random variable at a node at the level k with a slight abuse of notation.

We note that ξ is a martingale, since

$$E(\xi^k \mid \xi^{k-1}) = \xi^{k-1}.$$

---

[16] See Parga and Virasoro (1986) and Bös, Kühn, and van Hemmen (1988).

The variances are equal to $E[(\xi^k)^2] = r_k^2$, $k = 1, 2, \ldots, K$. In this assignment of probabilities, we note that $Pr(+ \mid +) = Pr(- \mid -) \geq 1/2$, and $Pr(+ \mid -) = Pr(- \mid +) \leq 1/2$.

Another possibility is to let ξ^k take on values ± 1 or 0, and assume that $\xi^k = \pm 1$ if $\xi^{k-1} = \pm 1$, and when $\xi^{k-1} = 0$, assign ± 1 to ξ^k with probability $r_k/2$ each and assign 0 to ξ^k with probability $1 - r_k$. In both cases, the random variable $(\xi^k - \xi^{k-1})/\sqrt{r_k^2 - r_{k-1}^2}$ has mean 0 and variance 1.

We can modify this basic scheme and define

$$Pr(\xi^k \mid \xi^{k-1}) = (1/2)[1 + a_k \, \mathrm{sgn}(\xi^k \xi^{k-1}) r_{k-1}/r_k],$$

where a_k is a constant exogenously assigned. Then, $E(\xi^k \mid \xi^{k-1}) = a_k \xi^{k-1}$, and $E[(\xi^k)^2] = r_k^2$. This scheme thus can generate both supermartingales and submartingales depending on whether $|a_k| \leq 1$ or not.

We can consider two random variables, ξ^μ and ξ^ν, and let these variables share a node on level k as the most recent, or closest, node from which the two nodes with these two random variables emanate. In other words, we have two paths $\mu = (\mu' \; \mu'')$, and $\nu = (\mu' \; \nu'')$ from the root, that is, the first k of the labels in μ and ν is common to both if a node on level k is the most recent common ancestor of these two nodes, speaking of the tree as a genealogical tree. Conditional on the random variable associated with this commonly shared node, the random variables are assumed to be independent.

Then, by the martingale property, we see that

$$E(\xi^\mu \xi^\nu) = E[E(\xi^\mu \xi^\nu \mid \xi^{\mu'})] = E[(\xi^{\mu'})^2] = r_k^2.$$

Any two random variables in a cluster share a node from which all branches emanate. Hence, any two random variables in a cluster have the same correlation. Therefore, using correlations to classify martingales, we can construct trees in which each node is a cluster of martingales with the same correlations among themselves, with martingales belonging to different clusters having smaller correlations.

This property characterizes what is called the ultrametric tree or ultrametric distance, which can be thought of as the tree distance between two nodes i and j, $d_{i,j}$. Necessarily, it satisfies the inequality

$$d_{i,j} \leq \max(d_{i,k}, d_{k,j})$$

2.5.3   *Markov chains on binary trees*

A simple way of introducing dynamics is to consider a two-level binary tree, that is, an economy could be in one of four possible macroeconomic states, as shown in Fig. 2.3. We think of these four states as worst, poor, fair, and best

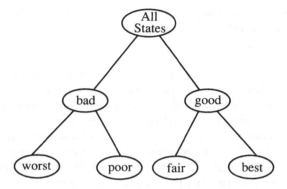

Fig. 2.3. A two-level tree of economic states.

states of the model economy, for example. At one level up, the worst and the poor states share the same node, and the fair and the best states share another node. The four states can represent a refined description of the two states of the economy, bad and good.

We can construct a four-state Markov chain of these states by assigning transition probabilities between states. It seems reasonable to set these probabilities so that the probability of going from worst to fair or best state is smaller than that of going from worst to poor or going from fair to best. To simplify the assignment, suppose that the probabilities are monotone functions of the tree distance, which is defined as the number of levels one must trace the inverted tree toward the root before one finds a common node. By construction then, we have $d(1, 2) = d(3, 4) = 1$, and $d(1, 3) = d(2, 3) = d(2, 3) = d(2, 4)$, where $d(i, j)$ is the tree distance between states i and j, and we assign values 1 through 4 to the states ranging from worst to best. Let ϵ_1 be the transition rate between two states with distance 1, and ϵ_2 the transition rate between two states with distance 2.

Denoting by P_i the probability of being in state i, the continous-time Markov chain is described by the next set of four equations

$$dP_1/dt = \epsilon_1(P_2 - P_1) + \epsilon_2(P_3 - P_1) + \epsilon_2(P_4 - P_1),$$
$$dP_2/dt = \epsilon_1(P_1 - P_2) + \epsilon_2(P_3 - P_2) + \epsilon_2(P_4 - P_2),$$
$$dP_3/dt = \epsilon_1(P_4 - P_3) + \epsilon_2(P_2 - P_3) + \epsilon_2(P_1 - P_3),$$
$$dP_4/dt = \epsilon_1(P_3 - P_4) + \epsilon_2(P_1 - P_4) + \epsilon_2(P_2 - P_4).$$

These equations are special cases of the master equations or Chapman–Kolmogorov equations which keep track of the probability flows into and out of a given state.

Written jointly by defining a four-dimensional vector $\mathbf{P} = (P_1, P_2, P_3, P_4)$, the system evolves with time according to

$$dP/dt = WP,$$

where W is a (4×4) matrix that is symmetric and each column sums to zero. This matrix has four eigenvalues: $\lambda_0 = 0$, $\lambda_1 = -4\epsilon_2$, and $\lambda_2 = -2(\epsilon_2 + \epsilon_1)$, which has multiplicity two. Because of the assumed inequality $\epsilon_1 \leq \epsilon_2$, these eigenvalues are all nonpositive, and ϵ_2 is the largest in magnitude.

The eigenvectors are $(1\ 1\ 1\ 1)'$, and $(1\ 1\ -1\ -1)'$ for λ_0 and λ_1, and $(1\ -1\ 0\ 0)'$ and $(0\ 0\ 1\ -1)'$ for the repeated eigenvalues λ_2, as one can easily verify.

Suppose that the initial condition is $P_1(0) = 1$, and that all other P are zero initially. We can solve the differential equation to see that

$$P_1(t) = 0.25 + 0.25e^{\lambda_1 t} + 0.5e^{\lambda_2 t},$$
$$P_2(t) = 0.25 + 0.25e^{\lambda_1 t} - 0.5e^{\lambda_2 t},$$
$$P_3(t) = 0.25 - 0.25e^{\lambda_1 t},$$
$$P_4(t) = 0.25 - 0.25e^{\lambda_1 t}.$$

2.5.4   Aggregation of dynamics on trees

After an elapse of time of the order, $t \geq 4/|\lambda_2|$, the terms depending on $e^{\lambda_2 t}$ become negligible. Then, the expressions $P_1(t)$ and $P_2(t)$ are identical, and so are those of $P_3(t)$ and $P_4(t)$. This means, of course, that the probabilities of being in states 1 and 2 are (nearly) equal, or that these two states need not be distinguished for t sufficiently large, that is, they can be combined into a single state. Similarly, states 3 and 4 can be combined as a single state. In other words, we can aggregate four states into two states, and the tree with two levels can be aggregated into a tree with one level and two states. We call these states α and β, and define the combined probabilities by

$$q_\alpha = P_1 + P_2,$$

and

$$q_\beta = P_3 + P_4.$$

We derive the dynamics for these vectors from those for the underlying probabilities P_i

$$\frac{dq_\alpha}{dt} = 2\epsilon_2(q_\beta - q_\alpha),$$

and

$$\frac{dq_\beta}{dt} = 2\epsilon_2(q_\alpha - q_\beta).$$

If we rescale time by $\tau = (2\epsilon_2/\epsilon_1)t$, then the differential equations for q become

$$\frac{dq_\alpha}{d\tau} = \epsilon_1(q_\beta - q_\alpha),$$

and

$$\frac{dq_\beta}{d\tau} = -dq_\alpha/d\tau.$$

This last set of equations is identical with a single-level tree model. Hence we have shown that, by rescaling time and redefining state variables, we can aggregate a four-state tree into a two-state tree. This is a simple example of the method of renormalization group which is discussed more fully in Chapter 7.

CHAPTER 3

Empirical distributions: Statistical laws in macroeconomics

This chapter follows up the motivating examples in Sections 2.2 and 2.3, and introduces the reader to some concepts and techniques that are useful in discussing behavior of macroeconomic variables statistically, but are not currently being employed by the majority of the economics profession.

Elementary discussions of entropy, Gibbs distributions and some introductory material from large deviation theory are provided. Entropy is not only important in describing states of macroeconomic systems made up of a large collection of interacting microeconomic agents but also is crucial in providing bounds for probabilities of large deviations from normal states. Gibbs distributions are important because equilibrium distributions of macroeconomic states are of this type. Large deviation theory has obvious distributional implications in macroeconomic policy studies by means of more disaggregate models than currently practiced.

3.1 Model descriptions

3.1.1 Micro and macro descriptions of models

Depending on the level of detail used in explaining economic phenomena, we can have either a micro description, which is a complete description (at least theoretically) of all units or agents in the model, or a macro description, which keeps track only of some of the observables which are some functions of the microscopic or microeconomic variables in the model. Microvariables needed to achieve a complete description, in the sense that models become Markovian, usually are not observed directly (see the examples in Chapter 2).

We let a microscopic or microeconomic state of an agent belong to a finite or denumerable set S. The state vector of N agents in a model is a vector $\mathbf{x} = (x_1, \ldots, x_N)$, $x_i \in S$, for $i = 1, \ldots, N$. This vector is also called a configuration of the system.

Given a set of macroscopic or macroeconomic variables $Y_k, k = 1, \ldots, K$, we denote by $W(N, Y_1, \ldots Y_k; dY_1, \ldots, dY_K)$ the total number of configurations compatible with the number of agents N that can take on values of the macroeconomic variables between Y_k and $Y_k + dY_k$, for all k. We refer to it as the state-sum, or partition, function. If we write this as $\Omega(N, Y_1, \ldots Y_K)dY_1 \cdots dY_K$, then we call Ω a state density. Often we assume that microeconomic states are specified in sufficient detail that microeconomic states are equally probable in equilibrium.

We can clarify this distinction between micro- and macrostates and illustrate some of the implications by using a box with two compartments between which N particles move randomly.[1] Equivalently, we can think of N agents, each of whom is in one of two possible microeconomic states. Agents change their microeconomic states randomly. Other interpretations are also possible. For example, we can think of agents choosing from one of two alternative decisions. They reevaluate their actions at random intervals that are exponentially distributed, and rechoose their actions. These possibilities are discussed further in Chapters 4 and 5. This kind of simple model is useful and important since it indicates the way foward, as Whittle (1992, p. 49) states. We discuss birth-and-death processes, which generalize this model, in Chapters 4 and 5.

If the agents are regarded as identifiable, then a complete description of this model lists the states of all N agents, up to the category in which an agent belongs. This is a micro description. Then, the stochastic process for the state variables $\mathbf{x}(t)$ is a Markov process with 2^N states. If each configuration is equally likely, then all 2^N states have equilibrium probability 2^{-N}. This is unique because the process is irreducible with a finite state space. The transition probability rates are assumed to be

$$w(\mathbf{x}, \mathbf{x}') = w(\mathbf{x}', \mathbf{x}) = \lambda,$$

for some positive parameter λ, and for all $\mathbf{x} \to \mathbf{x}'$ and $\mathbf{x}' \to \mathbf{x}$, where the arrow indicates transitions between the two indicated states.[2]

A less complete description keeps track only of the number of agents in category 1, for example, $n(t)$. This process is also Markovian with $N + 1$ states. This is a macro description. In this description assuming that agents act independently the transitions take place at the rates

$$w(n, n + 1) = \lambda(N - n)$$

---

[1] This is known as the Ehrenfest model. An equivalent description is in terms of an urn containing N balls of one of two types, say the colors red and black. A ball is extracted at random from the urn and replaced with a ball of the opposite color. For this reason, it is called the urn model. See Feller (1957, p. 111) or Whittle (1992, p. 192).

[2] The transition rate is the time derivative of the transition probabilities with respect to the time interval of transition. See our discussion of birth-and-death processes in Section 4.3.1.

and

$$w(n, n - 1) = \lambda n,$$

since, by assumption, the agents act independently of each other.

The important thing to note here is that several, indeed many, microstates correspond to a single macrostate, when N is large. This is the notion of degeneracy of a macrostate, so important in our discussion, and yet neglected in the economics literature. See Aoki (1995b). In other words, it is the number of microstates to which a macrostate corresponds (see our discussion of entropies in Chapter 2). We further elaborate on entropy in Section 3.2, and discuss large deviations in Section 3.6. In this model, a macrostate n has degeneracy given by the binomial coefficient $_NC_n$, since there are that many ways of selecting n agents out of N, and the equilibrium probability of this macrostate is given by

$$\pi(n) = {_NC_n} 2^{-N}.$$

3.1.2 *Multiplicity of microstates*

We continue with the simple example of the previous section. States of a system composed of N agents are described by a vector that specifies microeconomic states for each of N agents, $\mathbf{x} = (x_1, \ldots, x_N)$, where x_i is a variable (vector) that represents the microeconomic condition of agent i.

To consider one of the simplest cases, we suppose that each x_i is a binary variable. Then, there are 2^N configurations of the system, corresponding to each of the N variables taking on one of two possible values independently. If this N-dimensional vector is taken to be the macroeconomic vector of the system composed of N agents, then there is a one-to-one correspondence between the macroeconomic vector and a configuration of microeconomic agents in this simple case.

In general, however, a macroeconomic value is a statistical average or some other function of the microeconomic variables. Consequently, a macroeconomic state is consistent with a (large) number of microeconomic states, so that a constant value of a macroeconomic variable does not imply that microeconomic variables of all agents are likewise constant. There is a distribution of microeconomic states consistent with any value of the macroeconomic-state variable. We stress this point when we discuss empirical distributions of microeconomic states consistent with observed macroeconomic values in Sections 3.3.3 and 3.7.

Suppose that the average of N microeconomic variables is one of the macroeconomic variables observed about this system:

$$Y = (1/N) \sum_i x_i,$$

where x_i is ± 1 with equal probability $1/2$.

Then, with any k of N variables being equal to 1 and the rest equal to -1, the value of Y is equal to $2(k/N) - 1$. There are $_NC_k$ distinct microeconomic states that produce this same average value, where $_NC_k$ is the binomial coefficient. Again we emphasize that a single macroeconomic value is compatible with any one of these microeconomic configurations. Using the notation introduced at the beginning of this chapter, the number of microeconomic states consistent with the average value is

$$W(N, Y) = {}_NC_k,$$

where $k = N(1 + Y)/2$. However, note that there is exactly one k that yields Y in this example. So, we do not write $W(N, Y; dY)$.

The multiplicity of this event is $_NC_k$ where we approximate the binomial coefficient by

$$\frac{1}{N+1} e^{NH(k/N)} \le {}_NC_k \le e^{NH(k/N)},$$

and where

$$H(y) = -y \ln(y) - (1 - y) \ln(1 - y),$$

for $|y| \le 1$. This is the base e Shannon entropy, $H(k/N)$, when y is equated with the average. The upper bound on the binomial coefficient is obtained by noting that

$$1 \ge {}_NC_k(k/N)^k(1 - k/N)^{N-k} = {}_NC_k e^{-NH(k/N)}.$$

The lower bound is obtained by replacing each term of the right-hand side in

$$1 = \sum_k {}_NC_k p^k(1 - p)^{N-k}$$

by the maximum of the $(N + 1)$ terms

$$1 \le (N + 1) \max_k [{}_NC_k p^k(1 - p)^{N-k}],$$

and by noting that the maximum is achieved by setting k to be the integer part of pN, denoted by k^*, that is,

$$1 \le (N + 1){}_NC_{k^*}(k^*/N)^{k^*}(1 - k^*/N)^{N-k^*}.$$

See Cover and Thomas (1991, p. 285). Alternatively, we can use Stirling's formula $\ln(N!) \approx N[\ln(N) - 1] + O[\ln(N)/N]$. One way of deriving this formula is shown in Section A.1.1.

We can consider this simple case in more detail. In our notation, we have $_NC_k = W(N, k)$, and $\sum_k W(N, k) = 2^N$. However, let us pretend that we cannot carry out the summation, and instead look for the maximum term of the sum subject to the constraint that the average is given by Y. In other words, we consider maximizing

$$L = \ln(_NC_k) + \beta[Y - (2k - N)/N],$$

where the constraint is incorporated in the Lagrange multiplier β.

Assuming that N is large, we treat k/N as continuous and denote it by η. We differentiate the above with respect to η, after approximating the binomial coefficient by $e^{NH(\eta)}$. The maximum is achieved by

$$\eta^* = \frac{1}{1 + e^{2\beta/N}}.$$

Of course, $\eta^* = (1 + Y)/2$, and $k^* = N\eta^*$ maximizes $W(N, k)$, subject to the average value constraint. Then, up to $O(1/N)$, the entropy is given by

$$S(N, Y) = \ln[W(N, k^*)] = \ln e^{NH(\eta^*)} = NH(\eta^*).$$

When we differentiate the entropy with respect to Y, we obtain

$$\frac{\partial S}{\partial Y} = \frac{1}{2}\frac{\partial S}{\partial \eta} = \beta,$$

which states that the partial derivative of a suitably defined entropy with respect to the macroeconomic variable is the value of the Lagrange multiplier. This result also supports our use of the maximum term in the summation to approximate the sum.

As in the example in Chapter 2, we can use the Laplace transform to carry out the summation. We define

$$Z(N, \beta) = \sum_k {}_NC_k e^{-\beta Y} = e^{\beta}\sum_k {}_NC_k e^{-2\beta k/N} = e^{\beta}(1 + e^{-2\beta/N})^N,$$

namely

$$\ln[Z(N, \beta)] = \beta + N\ln(1 + e^{-2\beta/N}),$$

and we differentiate this with respect to β to see that

$$\frac{\partial \ln(Z)}{\partial \beta} = 1 - 2\eta^* = -Y. \tag{3.1}$$

The semielasticity of Z with respect to the Lagrange multiplier is the negative of the constraining macroeconomic variable.

As we have hinted by this simple exercise, an important question is how many configurations of microeconomic states are compatible or consistent with a given value of the aggregate, that is, the macroeconomic variable. This is true not only from the view of the distributional effects of macroeconomic states on individual microeconomic agents, but also because degeneracy affects the equilibrium probability of macroeconomic states. This point becomes more transparent when we discuss the exponents of the equilibrium probability distribution later in this chapter, when we observe that a given performance or cost index must be modified by a measure of the degeneracy of the optimal solution, that is, the entropy. This also can be seen in the example in Chapter 5.

To put this point differently, degeneracy is relevant to us because we take the view that the state space of an economy possesses basins of attraction that are associated with macroeconomic equilibria, and, states of the economy randomly move around them, occasionally jumping from one basin to another. An economy may stay in this new basin for a while until it jumps out again. A basin is composed of microeconomic configurations that are compatible with or converge to the given macroeconomic state. The equilibrium probability distributions are affected by the degree of degeneracy as measured by their entropy. See Chapter 5 for details. Later in Chapter 5, we show how to calculate the average time for the system to travel between two local equilibria, and show that it depends on the difference in the potentials[3] of the local equilibria.

3.2 Entropy and relative entropy

We have seen that entropy appears in evaluating the binomial coefficients. More essentially, we have seen that the partial derivative of entropy with respect to the constraining macrosignal is the value of the Lagrange multiplier, and that the negative semielasticity of the Laplace transform of the number of the microeconomic states compatible with a macrosignal with respect to the Lagrange multiplier yields back the macrosignal. Here, we continue our discussion of the notion of entropy and a related notion of relative entropy, or the Kullback–Leibler information measure, also called divergence, between probability distributions. The Kullback–Leibler divergence measures similarities between two probability distributions, and is used to bound probabilities of certain macroeconomic events via large-deviation theory.

Several notions of entropy have been proposed in the past. Historically, it was Ludwig Boltzmann, an Austrian physicist (1844–1906), who introduced a notion of entropy to physical systems composed of many particles. Boltzmann's proposal was to define entropy as being proportional to the logarithm of the partition function, that is, the state sum, $W (\cdots)$ in our notation, which is the sum of the number of microeconomic states consistent with a given macroeconomic signal.

We give a brief account of the case in which agents are treated as distinguishable. The case of exchangeable agents was presented as an example in Chapter 2.

---

[3] For now, we can think of potentials as the exponents in exponential distributions.

Suppose that there are N agents who can be in one of K possible categories (subclasses, subsystems, or substates), C_i, $i = 1, \ldots, K$. Alternatively, there are N independent and identically distributed random variables, each taking on one of K possible values. We let N_i be the number of agents in category C_i, and g_i be the number of microstates (configurations) in category C_i, $|C_i| = g_i$. We assume that agents are independent. The total number of configurations of this system is specified by the state vector $(N_1, \ldots, N_K)$, called occupancy numbers by Feller (1957, p. 36) and Whittle (1992, p. 50), which represents how many agents occupy a particular category. Assuming that the system is closed, that is, N is constant, the total number of configurations consistent with this vector is

$$W(N_1, \ldots, N_K) = \frac{N!}{\prod_i N_i!} \prod_i g_i^{N_i},$$

where the occupation numbers satisfy

$$\sum_i N_i = N.$$

We write $W(N_1, \ldots, N_K)$ as $W[\{N_i\}]$ for convenience. The sum $\sum W[\{N_i\}]$ is equal to G^N, where $G = \sum_i g_i$ is assumed to be finite.

In Section 3.1.2, we saw a measure of multiplicity $(1/N)\ln(C_{N,k}) \sim H(k/N)$. Applying the estimate or, alternatively, using Stirling's formula, $N! \sim (N/e)^N \sqrt{2\pi N}$, we see that

$$\frac{1}{N}\ln(W[\{N_i\}]/G^N) \sim -\sum_i \frac{N_i}{N}\ln\left(\frac{N_i/N}{q_i}\right) + O[\ln(N)/N],$$

where $q_i = g_i/G$. The first term introduces the Kullback–Leibler divergence between two distributions on a finite set, that is, between two probability mass functions, also called distributions:

$$D(p; q) = \sum_i p_i \ln(p_i/q_i),$$

where $p = (p_1, p_2, \ldots, p_K)$, with $p_i = N_i/N$, and where we define $q = (q_1, \ldots, q_K)$.

Clearly then, we have $W[\{N_i\}] \approx G^N e^{-ND(p;q)}$.

3.2.1   Kullback–Leibler divergence measure

For a set of finite events with probabilities p_i, $i = 1, \ldots, K$, the Shannon entropy is defined as $-\sum_{i=1}^{K} p_i \ln p_i$.

In the case of finite events with probabilities p_i and q_i, $i = 1, \ldots, K$, the entroy of p relative to q is defined by the Kullback–Leibler divergence introduced above

$$D(p; q) = \sum_{i=1}^{K} p_i \ln(p_i/q_i).$$

This quantity is nonnegative and clearly is equal to zero if and only if $p_i = q_i$ for all i. It reduces to the (negative) Shannon entropy up to a constant when q_i is constant, $1/n$. In this case, maximizing entropy is equivalent to minimizing the Kullback–Leibler divergence. In essence, this measures the discrepancy or distance between two probability distributions, even though it is not a metric.[4] In the finance literature, Stutzer (1994, 1995) calls it financial entropy where q is an a priori probability distribution of the state of nature, and p is the risk-neutral probability distribution.

For the case of two continuous probability measures μ and ν, where the former is absolutely continuous with respect to the latter, the entropy of measure μ relative to ν, that is, the Kullback–Leibler divergence, is defined as

$$D(\mu; \nu) = \int d\mu \ln(d\mu/d\nu).$$

3.2.2 *Boltzmann and Shannon entropies*

Boltzmann's entropy S of a system of N agents with a macroeconomic signal Y is defined by

$$S(N, Y) = k \ln\left\{ \sum W[\{N_i\}] \right\},$$

where the summation is with respect to all occupation numbers subject to $\sum_i N_i = N$, and the constraint imposed by the macroeconomic variable $Y = \sum_i N_i Y_i$, with k a constant.[5]

Here, we have tacitly assumed that agents belong to different categories, that those belonging to category i have the same output Y_i per agent, and that $|C_i| = g_i$ as before. Suppose that we maximize the logarithm of the maximum term in the summation, $\ln\{W[\{N_i\}]\}$, since the summation is not easy to carry out because of the constraints. We have already seen several examples where this approximation scheme works correctly, in which a sum is approximately evaluated by its maximum term.

---

[4] For example, $D(p; q) \neq D(q; p)$. The symmetrized version $[D(p; q) + D(q; p)]/2$ is not a metric either. Moreover, it does not satisfy the triangle inequality.

[5] This is known as the Boltzmann constant, an important constant in physics. Here, we merely treat it as a constant of proportionality.

In our economic interpretation, the macro variable Y could be total output, total cost, or some other (extensive) variable. The usual Lagrange multiplier method yields the answer to this constrained maximization problem, and we have[6]

$$N_i = Gq_i e^{-\alpha - \beta Y_i}, \tag{3.2}$$

where α and β are some constants (Lagrange multipliers). We define

$$\Xi = \sum q_i e^{-\beta Y_i},$$

which is called the partition function in the physics literature, and express α as $Ge^{-\alpha} = N/\Xi$, that is,

$$p_i = q_i e^{-\beta Y_i}/\Xi, \quad i = 1, \ldots, K,$$

where $p_i = N_i/N$, as was introduced above. We also have the relation

$$Y/N = \sum_i q_i Y_i e^{-\beta Y_i}/\Xi.$$

The maximized expression of $\ln W[(N_i)]$ is given by[7]

$$\ln\{W[\{N_i\}]/G^N\} = N\ln(\Xi) + \beta Y = \ln(N!) + \alpha N + \beta Y.$$

If instead we use $W[\{N_i\}]/(G^N N!)$, the first term of the second equality disappears.[8]

This so-called principle of entropy maximization argues that given observation on macrovariables, such as the total number N and the total output Y, the actual system should be in the configuration that maximizes the entropy subject to macrovariable constraints. See Jaynes (1957, 1979).[9]

We can use any number of macroeconomic variables or signals to carry out the constrained optimization. Suppose that we maximize $\ln(W)$ subject to the total number of agents in the model, and a macrosignal that may be the average

---

[6] Whittle (1992, p. 110) objects to this proof on two accounts: one is the question of whether the most probable values locate limit values in any sense as N is made to approach infinity as in the thermodynamic limit. More seriously, he questions the treatment of integers as continuous variables. Tikochinsky, Tishby, and Levine (1984) proposes an alternative approach to maximum-entropy inference. As Whittle himself points out, these difficulties disappear either by treating the macrovalues as it they are in a narrow band, or by treating the macrovalues as integer multiples of (sufficiently small) units. Khinchin (1949) uses the same device.

[7] Noting that $d\Xi/d\beta = -(\Xi/N)Y$ from Eq. (3.1), we then have $(d/d\beta)(k\ln W) = \beta(dY/d\beta)$, or $d(k\ln W) = \beta dY$. This entropy was named the Boltzmann entropy by W. Pauli.

[8] We divide the partition function by a suitable expression so that its logarithm defines an expression that is extensive with N and define it as the entropy.

[9] In Section 3.7, we view this maximization of entropy as an application of Sanov's theorem.

of some quantity, such as utility, cost, or level of output. For example, we define the following macrovariable when there are N_k agents in class C_k, each of whom has value f_k:

$$\langle f(N) \rangle = \sum_{k=1}^{m} N_k f_k / N,$$

where the notation $\langle \ \rangle$ is defined by the right-hand side. It is an average operation and we use it interchangeably with the expectation notation E. Actually, f_k can be any intensive variable that is characteristic of the state k, such as the wage rate, income per agent, output rate, and so forth. The constrained entropy maximization yields the following maximum likelihood estimate of N_i:

$$N_i^* / N = q_i e^{-\beta f_i} / \Xi$$

with the partition function defined by

$$\Xi = \sum_k q_k e^{-\beta f_k}.$$

At this stage of our discussion, the parameter β is merely a constant (Lagrange multiplier) associated with the constraint that f_k, which is not observed for individual agents, has the macroscopic average, which is observable. Later, we interpret it as an indicator of degree of uncertainty in the model or level of economic activity. As β decreases, $\ln W[\{N_i\}]$ or, more generally, $\ln Z(N, \beta)$ increases. See Eq. (3.1).[10]

By normalizing g_i by dividing it by the sum $\sum g_i$, we can think of the normalized q_i as the probability of finding an agent in category i. The probability q_i is the a priori probability, and $q_i e^{-\beta f_i} / \Xi$ is its maximum-likelihood estimate. The value of the entropy (omitting the constant k) is evaluated as:

$$\ln\{W[(N_i)]\} = N \ln(\Xi) + \beta \langle f(N) \rangle N + o(N).$$

The derivative of the above expression with respect to β is

$$\frac{d(\ln W_N)}{d\beta} = \beta N \frac{d\langle f(N) \rangle}{d\beta},$$

since

$$N \frac{d(\ln \Xi)}{d\beta} = -N \langle f(N) \rangle.$$

---

[10] The parameter β corresponds to the inverse of temperature in physical context. Hence we can speak loosely of increasing or decreasing economic temperature, when we mean to decrease or increase β.

We see that the derivative of this macrovariable with respect β gives information on its variance:

$$\frac{d\langle f(N)\rangle}{d\beta} = -(\langle f^2\rangle - \langle f\rangle^2).$$

A probability measure on a configuration space provides a microscopic or microeconomic definition for states of the economy. We have already given an example of a macroeconomic variable Y that is compatible with a large number of microeconomic configurations. The maximum-entropy approach or maximum-likelihood approach outlined above adopts the view that those values of the macroeconomic variables compatible with the largest number of microeconomic configurations, that is, those with the largest entropy, are the ones actually observed in reality. See Sanov's theorem in Section 3.7 for further discussion.

Using the uniform probability distribution $q_i = N_i/N$, $i = 1, \ldots, K$, the difference between the Boltzmann entropy and the Shannon entropy is

$$|\ln W_N/N - H(N)| = O(\ln N/N).$$

3.3   Gibbs distributions

3.3.1   Discrete-choice models

We have seen how Gibbs distributions arise in maximizing entropy subject to a set of constraints involving macrosignals. This formulation can be thought of as the dual problem of minimizing (nonlinear) functions subject to a set of constraints in nonlinear programming, as shown by Fukao (1990), for example. We also know that Markov processes, which satisfy detailed balance conditions, have stationary Gibbs distributions. See Chapters 4 and 5. For the Gibbs distribution $e^{-\beta f(x)}/\sum_x e^{-\beta f(x)}$, the function $f(x)$ is called the potential. Strauss (1993) shows how Gibbs distributions arise in logistic regressions.

In economics, Gibbs distributions arise in discrete-choice models. See Anderson, de Palma, and Thisse (1993) and Amemiya (1985, Sec. 9.2.8). As a very simple example, we consider the logarithm of odds ratio

$$\ln(p^+/p^-) = a^+ - a^-$$

in a binary-choice situation. Since $p^- = 1 - p^+$, the probability p^+ is obtained in the form of a Gibbs distribution:

$$p^+ = \frac{e^{a^+}}{e^{a^+} + e^{a^-}}.$$

To see a connection with discriminant analysis, suppose that a random variable x_i is governed by a probability density function g_0 or g_1, depending on another random variable y_i being 0 or 1. Suppose that $P(y_i = 1) = q_1$ and $P(y_i = 0) = q_0$. Then, by the Bayes theorem, we obtain the conditional distribution of y_i being 1, given x_i as

$$P(y_i = 1 \mid x_i) = g_1(x_i)q_1/[g_1(x_i)q_1 + g_0(x_i)q_0],$$

which is of the Gibbs distribution form.

Anderson et al. (1993) also offer an interpretation of the parameter in the exponent of a Gibbs distribution in terms of the elasticity of substitution in a constant elasticiy of substitution function. Suppose that there are n goods (choices) and the utility or return of choosing good (choice) i is given by

$$U_i = V(x_i) + \epsilon_i,$$

where $V(x_i)$ is the deterministic part of the return, and ϵ_i is a random disturbance on the return, where x_i indicates that the return depends on the state associated with choice i, for example. The disturbance is standardized to have mean zero, and the same variance. The variance is assumed to be proportional to a positive parameter μ.

They assume that good (choice) i is chosen with probability

$$P_i = \mathrm{Prob}\left(U_i = \max_j U_j\right).$$

In the case of binary choice or two alternatives, the resulting model is called the binomial logit model, whereas the general case is called the multinomial logit model.

In discrete-choice models, the probability distribution of the difference $\epsilon = \epsilon_2 - \epsilon_1$ is specified by the logistic function

$$Pr(\epsilon \leq x) = 1/(1 + e^{-x/\mu}).$$

Then, we have

$$P_1 = Pr(U_1 \geq U_2) = \frac{e^{V(x_1)/\mu}}{e^{V(x_1)/\mu} + e^{V(x_2)/\mu}}.$$

From this expression, we see that a larger μ implies a smaller difference $|P_1 - P_2|$ or, put differently, the smaller that μ is, the closer the probability approaches one, that is, one of the alternatives tends to become dominant.

With more than two alternatives, Anderson et al. (1993) show how choice i is chosen with probability, which is in the form of Gibbs distribution:

$$P_i = \frac{e^{V(x_i)/\mu}}{\sum_j e^{V(x_j)/\mu}},$$

when the disturbance is independent and identically distributed with the double exponential distribution. See Johnson and Kotz (1977) on the specifics of this distribution. It is such that[11]

$$Pr(\epsilon_i \le x) = \exp(-e^{\eta_i/\mu} e^{-x/\mu}).$$

The multinomial logit distribution yields a Gibbs distribution

$$P_i = \exp[V(x_i)/\mu]/Z,$$

where Z is the normalizing constant.

In a discrete model, when there are changes in the deterministic portion of U, then the modified choice probabilities are given by

$$\bar{P}_i = \frac{P_i e^{\delta V(x_i)/\mu}}{\sum_j P_j e^{\delta V(x_j)/\mu}},$$

which shows that P can be treated as prior probabilities. We note that the same expression arises in connection with Sanov's theorem where $V(x_i)$ is some macroeconomic signal. Caplin and Nalebuff (1991) show how similar distributions arise in the context of the so-called voter model.

3.3.2   Detailed balance and Gibbs distributions

We let S be a state space of an irreducible Markov chain or discrete state-space Markov process. We use the indices i, j, k, and so forth to denote states as well as the indexes x, y, z, and so forth. Kelly (1979, p. 5) has shown that a stationary Markov chain or process is reversible if and only if detailed balance conditions are satisfied, that is, there exists the equilibrium distribution $\{\pi_j\}$ such that $\pi_j p_{j,k} = \pi_k p_{k,j}$, $j, k \in S$, in the case of the Markov chain, and $\pi_j w_{j,k} = \pi_k w_{k,j}$ for the Markov process, where $p_{i,j}$ is the transition probability and $w_{i,j}$ is the transition rate from state i to state j, respectively.

Kolmogorov's criteria for reversibility show that the equilibrium probabilities are defined such that they are path-independent. Pick an arbitrary reference state j_0. Because the state space is irreducible, there is a path with positive probability of going from j_0 to j, $j_0 \to j_1 \to j_2 \cdots \to j_n \to j$, for instance. Then the equilibrium probability of state j is

$$\pi_j = C \frac{w(j_0, j_1)w(j_1, j_2) \cdots w(j_{n-1}, j_n)w(j_n, j)}{w(j, j_n)w(j_n, j_{n-1}) \cdots w(j, j_0)},$$

---

[11] One might question the validity of this distribution as being too specialized. We do not need this special assumption.

where C is a normalization constant, and where we write $w(j, k)$ for $w_{j,k}$. A similar expression obtains for the case of a Markov chain. We note from the Kolmogorov criteria that this probability is equal to

$$\pi_j = C \frac{w(j_0, j)}{w(j, j_0)},$$

and is independent of paths from j_0 to j, since another path of positive probability, $j_0 \to j_1' \to \cdots j_m' \to j$, also will define the same probability. In other words,

$$\pi_i = \frac{e^{-V(j)}}{\sum_{k \in S} e^{-V(k)}},$$

where $V(j) - V(j_0) = \ln[w(j, j_0)/w(j_0, j)]$ is the potential of this distribution.

The Kolmogorov criteria are also useful for guessing the expressions for the equilibrium distributions, which are then verified by the detailed balance condition.

3.3.3   *Conditional-limit theorems: Gibbs conditioning principle*

In macroeconomics, we know the averages of some functions of underlying microeconomic variables, and we would like to infer the distribution of these microeconomic variables. We let X_i be basic microeconomic random vectors that are independent and identically distributed with the distribution function, Q. Given the value of the average $m_N = (1/N) \sum_i h(X_i)$, we want to calculate the distribution of X_1 conditional on m_N.[12] By direct calculation we see that as N goes to infinity, the conditional probabilities converge to

$$P_\beta(s_j) = Q(s_j)e^{\langle \beta, h(s_j) \rangle}/M(\beta),$$

where $M(\beta) = \sum_i Q(s_i)e^{\beta h(s_i)}$.

Here, we follow van Campenhout and Cover (1981) to derive a limit theorem for pointwise and interval conditioning for sequences of independent and identically distributed continuous-valued random variables with densities.

We let $q(x)$ be the density for random variables X_i, and $p(y)$ be the density for the random variables $Y_i = h(X_i)$.

The tilted densities are defined by

$$q^*(x) = e^{\beta x}q(x)/M_x(\beta),$$

where the normalizing constant, $M_x(\beta) = \int e^{\beta x}q(x)\,dx$, is assumed to be finite,

---

[12] As it turns out, we can replace the independence assumption with that of exchangeability. See Dembo and Zeitouni (1993, p. 74).

that is, β is such that the integral is finite, and we define

$$p^*(x) = e^{\beta h(x)} p(x)/M_y(\beta);$$

M_y is analogously defined. The densities denoted with an asterisk are the tilted or twisted densities of Section 2.2. For example, α can be given by

$$\frac{dM_x(\beta)/d\beta}{M_x(\beta)} = \int xq^*(x)\,dx = \alpha.$$

Thus, the tilted density has a mean of α that is generally different from the mean of x under the density q.

The tilted density of the sum of $\sum_{i=1}^n h(x_i)$ is denoted by $p_n^*(x)$, and the sum by S_n. Then, using P^* to denote the measure induced by p^* to write the expression for the conditional distributions,

$$P^*\{x_1 \in A, S_n \in B\} = \int_B \left[\int_A P^*\{dx \mid S_n = t\} \right] p_n^*(t)\,dt,$$

we derive

$$P^*\{x_1 \in dx \mid S_n = t\} = q^*(x)p_{n-1}^*[t - h(x)]\,dx/p_n^*(t).$$

Verification that convolution and tilting operations commute is straight forward, and we obtain

$$p_n^*(t) = M_y(\beta)^{-n} e^{\beta t} p_n(t).$$

The conditional distributions are therefore invariant to tilting such that

$$P^*\{x_i \in dx \mid S_N = N\alpha\} = P\{x_1 \in dx \mid S_N = N\alpha\}.$$

In this way, we establish that

$$P\left\{ x_1 \leq x \;\middle|\; \sum_{i=1}^N h(x_i) = N\alpha \right\} \rightarrow \int_{-\infty}^x e^{\beta h(x)} p(x)\,dx/M_y(\beta).$$

In the case of interval conditioning, the distribution

$$F_\beta(x) = \int_{-\infty}^x e^{\beta h(t)} P(x_1 \in dx)/M(\beta)$$

miminizes the Kullback–Leibler distance over all distributions that are absolutely continuous with respect to F induced by p, subject to the constraint

$$\int h(x)\,dF_\beta(x) \in [a, b].$$

See van Campenhout and Cover (1981, Theorem 3).

3.3.3.1 Example of asymptotic independence

We let X_j, $j = 1, 2, \ldots$, be independent and identically distributed discrete random variables taking values on the set $\{1, 2, \ldots, K\}$,[13] with $Pr(X_1 = i) = 1/K, i = 1, 2, \ldots, K$. Then,

$$P\left[X_1 = j \mid (1/n) \sum_{i=1}^{n} X_i = a\right] = P^*(X_1 = j),$$

where

$$P^*(x) = \frac{e^{\beta x}}{\sum_{j=1}^{K} e^{\beta j}},$$

and the value of β is determined by the equality of the mean $\sum_{j=1}^{j} P^*(j) = a$.

If the constant a is the mean of x_1, that is, $(1 + K)/2$, then the parameter β is equal to zero, and $P^*(x_1 = j) = 1/K$. When the constant a is not equal to the mean, we use the tilted probability distributions to make the mean equal to the constant. Since the conditional distributions are independent of tilting, asymptotically as n goes to infinity such that na is an integer, we obtain the asymptotic independence.

3.4   Maximizing equilibrium probabilities or minimizing potential

In complex optimization problems with many parameters, the average cost of configurations is calculated by assuming that configurations are weighted according to Gibbs distributions.

This average cost roughly corresponds to the notion of internal energy in the statistical physics literature. In these problems, we need to balance the average cost with the degrees of freedom, that is, the multiplicity at a given cost. The notion of free energy in physics provides this balance by taking into account these combined effects. In other words, it is roughly equal to the average cost minus a suitably weighted notion of entropy.

At a very large value of β (low level of economic activity, or near-zero temperature in a physical context), the entropy component does not play any role. At a lower value of β (higher level of economic activity, or high temperature), the entropy component becomes more heavily weighted. This is an intuitive reason for the formal definition given below.

As a simple illustration that degeneracies or degrees of freedom of microstates matter, we examine a model with N agents, each of whom can be in one of two possible microstates. We denote the cost or performance index of the

---

[13] This example is in van Campenhout and Cover (1981).

system by $Nu(n)$, when n of N agents is in a positive state, indicating that it is an extensive quantity.

The equililbrium probability distribution of the system is known to be

$$P_e(n) = \Xi^{-1}{}_N C_n e^{-\beta N u(n)},$$

where Ξ is a normalizing constant.[14]

The combinatorial factor is stated as

$$\ln({}_N C_n) = N\left[-\frac{1+x}{2}\ln\left(\frac{1+x}{2}\right) - \frac{1-x}{2}\ln\left(\frac{1-x}{2}\right)\right],$$

up to $O(\ln N/N)$, where $x = (2n - N)/N$. It is equal to N times the entropy $S(p)$, with $p = (1 + x)/2 = n/N$, which we also write as $S(n)$.

The equilibrium probability is then equal to

$$P_e(n) = \frac{1}{\Xi_N}\exp\{N[-\beta f(n)]\},$$

with

$$f(n) = u(n) - s/\beta,$$

where $s(n) = S(n)/N$ is the per-agent entropy, $f(n)$ is the potential (free energy) per agent, and β is a parameter inversely proportional to the level of (economic) activity.[15] When β is small, the right-hand side of f is approximately proportional to the negative of the entropy term. Then, the maximum-likelihood estimate of n is the value of n that minimizes the potential (free energy).

An alternative scheme for calculating free energy is

$$-\beta f(\beta) = \lim_{N\to\infty}\frac{1}{N}\ln(Z_N),$$

where the entropy is given by the Boltzmann expression, that is, the logarithm of the partition function:

$$Z_N = \sum_s e^{-\beta f(s)}.$$

In this expression the summation is over all possible state-space configurations, that is, over the entire state vector s. This alternative expression is only valid when the entropy component dominates the other u component.

---

[14] This formula is derived later in Chapter 5 when we discuss the master equations.
[15] See Footnote 17.

3.4.1   Optimization and Gibbs distributions

Optimization of a cost function $f(x)$ over a feasible set X can be a difficult problem when the terrain of the function, that is, the set of equi-cost function $\{x \in X; f(x) = \text{constant}\}$, has a complicated structure. Here, we assume that x is of high dimension, and we refer to it as a microscopic-state vector. We may not observe the values of the components, but $f(x)$ is something we can observe directly and is of a macroscopic nature.

Often, we replace this original formulation by introducing probability distributions over the feasible set to reflect the fact that we may not know x exactly, or that the value of the cost function may not be known exactly or calculated. Recent uses of simulated annealing in optimization can also be interpreted this way, since the method chooses probabilistically the next point at which to evaluate the cost function. In this reformulation, we minimize over possible distribution functions

$$\min_{p(x)} \sum_x p(x) f(x),$$

subject to a constant value of entropy as a measure of randomness or uncertainty over the set X,

$$\sum_x -p(x) \ln p(x),$$

and the fact that $p(x)$ sums to one.[16] In this formulation, we minimize the average or expected cost subject to a measure of ambiguity or disorder of the set X. Shannon's entropy is used as the measure of uncertainty here.

The optimal distribution is obtained by incorporating the constraints by the Lagrange multiplier,

$$p(x) = e^{-\beta f(x)} / \Xi,$$

with

$$\Xi = \sum_x e^{-\beta f(x)},$$

where the summation is over all possible x. This is a particular example of a probability distribution, called the Gibbs distribution. The function f that is in the exponent is called its potential.

Equivalently, we can work with the dual formulation of this last minimization problem, so that we now have the maximization problem

$$\max_{p(x)} \sum_x p(x) \ln p(x),$$

---

[16] If x is taken to be continuous, then we replace the summation with integration.

subject to

$$\sum_x p(x)f(x) = \langle f(x) \rangle,$$

and $p(x)$ sums to one.

This reformulation states that subject to a known or observed macroscopic signal, distributions over microstates are made as uniform as possible by maximizing the Shannon entropy.[17]

3.5   Finite-state Markov chains

Later in Chapters 4 and 5, we use finite-state Markov chains to model discrete or lumpy adjustment behavior of economic agents. We measure the similarity of two Markov chains or the degree of approximation of stationary stochastic processes by some finite-state Markov chains by the relative-entropy or Kullback–Leibler measure. Suppose there are two Markov chains with transition probabilities $p(j \mid i)$ and $q(j \mid i)$ where i and j range over the set $S = \{1, 2, \ldots, K\}$. We rename the states $s_1, s_2, \ldots, s_K$ as states $1, 2, \ldots, K$ without loss of generality.

When state i is fixed, then $p(j \mid i)$, $j = 1, 2, \ldots, K$, is the usual probability vector, and we can use the Kullback–Leibler divergence

$$D[p(\cdot \mid i); q(\cdot \mid i)] = \sum_{j=1}^{K} p(j \mid i) \ln\left[\frac{p(j \mid i)}{q(j \mid i)}\right]$$

as a measure of discrepancy or dissimilarity between the two probability vectors.

Then, averaging this divergence with respect to the probability of the occurrence of state i, we define the divergence between q and p by

$$D(p; q) = \sum_i p_1(i) D[p(\cdot \mid i); q(\cdot \mid i)],$$

where $p_1(i) = \sum_j p(i, j)$ is the marginal probability.

More generally, we can start with a two-dimensional array of probabilities on $S \times S$, $p(i, j)$, and define the transition probability by

$$p(j \mid i) = p(i, j) \bigg/ \sum_j p(i, j),$$

whenever the sum in the denominator is positive, and use it in the expression for the divergence. Generally, the sum of the array $p(i, j)$ with respect to the first

---

[17] What is missing in the analysis of this section is the element of time. To deduce dynamics of macroeconomic variables, from those of microeconomic variables, we use the notion of the master equations or the backward Chapman–Kolmogorov equations later in Chapter 5.

argument is not the same as the sum with respect to the second argument. When they are the same, that is, when the two marginals are the same, the probability measure q is shift invariant, and there is no ambiguity in defining the transition probabilities from a given array of two-dimensional probabilities.

3.5.1 Entropy maximization

With a two-dimensional array of probabilities $p(i, j)$ for $i, j \in S$ with the same two marginals as above, where S is a finite set, we can construct a Markov chain with the state space S having the transition probabilities $p(j \mid i) = p(i, j)/p(i)$, in which $p(i) = \sum_j p(i, j) = \sum_j p(j, i)$. This set of transition probabilities defines the transition matrix with a unique equilibrium distribution when it is restricted to be irreducible.

We next find a two-dimensional array that maximizes the entropy associated with this Markov chain. The entropy, conditional on the chain being in state i, is $- \sum_j p(j \mid i) \ln[p(j \mid i)]$. The entropy of the Markov chain is defined by averaging this entropy over state i using $p(i)$,

$$H = - \sum_{i,j} p(i)p(j \mid i) \ln[p(j \mid i)]$$

$$= - \sum_{i,j} p(i, j) \ln \left[p(i, j) \bigg/ \sum_j p(i, j) \right].$$

Next we maximize this expression subject to three constraints that $p(i, j)$ defines the same marginals, that it is nonnegative, and that

$$\sum_{i,j} p(i, j)w(i, j) \le c,$$

where $w(i, j)$ is the weight for $p(i, j)$, and c is some constant. By suitably reinterpreting the weights, we shortly show the connection of this entropy maximization problem with the performance-index or cost-minimization problem discussed in Section 3.5.2.

By incorporating these constraints with Lagrange multipliers, we construct the Lagrangian

$$L = H - \beta \sum_{i,j} p(i, j)w(i, j)$$

$$+ \sum_k \xi_k \left[\sum_j p(k, j) - \sum_i p(i, k) \right] + \eta \sum_{i,j} p(i, j),$$

and by differentiating it with respect to $p(i, j)$, we derive the relation

$$p(j \mid i) = \frac{e^{-\beta w(i,j)} r(j)}{\lambda r(i)},$$

where $r(i) = e^{\xi_i}$, $\lambda = e^{-\eta}$, and β is the Lagrange multiplier for the weight constraint. We can easily verify that $r(i)$ is the ith component of the right eigenvector of the matrix $V = \{e^{-\beta w(i,j)}\}$ with the eigenvalue λ. The left eigenvector has the component $l(i) = p(i)/r(i)$. These eigenvectors are normalized by the condition that $\sum_i l(i) r(i) = 1$.

When these expressions are substituted into the expression for H, it becomes

$$H = \ln \lambda + \beta c.$$

Since entropy is maximized subject to the weight constraint, we conclude that the eigenvalue λ must be the largest eigenvalue of the matrix V, that is, the Perron–Frobenius eigenvalue, because the elements of V are all positive. Csiszár (1984) and Justesen and Høhold (1984) obtained similar results.

Earlier, Spitzer (1972) demonstrated the identical idea, namely, that Markov chains have the largest entropy subject to the same cost, by interpreting $w(i, j)$ not as weights but as the cost of going from state i to state j.[18]

We can rename $w(i, j)$ as $U(i, j)$, which is now the cost of going from state i to state j. Then, we introduce a Markov chain with the transition probability matrix W:

$$W(i, j) = \frac{e^{-\beta U(i,j)} r(j)}{\lambda_{max} r(i)},$$

where $r(i)$ is the ith component of the right eigenvector of the matrix W with the maximum eigenvalue λ_{max}. This matrix satisfies Kolmogorov's criterion for reversibility. See Kelly (1979, p. 24). Indeed, for any three distinct states, i, j, and k, we see that $W(i, j)W(j, k)W(k, i) = W(i, k)W(k, j)W(j, i)$, if and only if $U(i, j) + U(j, k) + U(k, i) = U(i, k) + U(k, j) + U(j, i)$. The latter condition is assumed to be satisfied.

For a sequence of N states, $i^N = (i_1, i_2, \ldots, i_N)$, $i_k \in S$, for $k = 1, 2, \ldots, N$, the average cost (of this N-stage process) is defined by averaging the transition costs:

$$G(\mu) = \sum \mu(i^N) \sum_{k=1}^{N-1} U(i_k, i_{k+1}),$$

---

[18] Spitzer (1972) called this the constraint free energy rather than the cost following the usage in the physics literature. Free energy F is defined as $G - \beta^{-1} H$, where G is energy or average potential in physics, and cost or performance index in our usage. We discuss this point briefly in Section 3.5.2.

where the first sum is over all possible i^N and μ is a probability measure introduced over such sequences. This measure is discussed in Section 3.5.2.

3.5.2 Cost minimization with Markov-chain dynamics

We introduce a strictly stationary, that is, shift- or translation-invariant probability distribution μ. In addition, we have its truncation, μ_N, over the sample space Ω, which is constructed as the direct product of S^Z, where Z is the set of positive integers:

$$\mu_N(s) = \mu(\omega: \omega_1 = s_1, \omega_2 = s_2, \ldots, \omega_N = s_N),$$

where $s = (s_1, s_2, \ldots, s_N)$ and where s_k ranges over the set S, for $k = 1, \ldots, K$. When this distribution is a Markov chain with a strictly positive transition matrix, we can write it as the product of the probability of the initial state and the probabilities of the appropriate transition matrices. We encounter this expression shortly.

The average cost or performance index with respect to μ is

$$G_N(\mu) = \sum_{i=1}^{K} \mu_N(i) \sum_{k=1}^{N-1} U(s_k, s_{k+1}).$$

We associate the probability distribution ν_N with this index, which is defined by

$$\nu_N(s) = \phi(s_1) \prod_{k=1}^{N-1} W(s_k, s_{k+1}),$$

where $\phi(k)$ is the kth component of the left eigenvector corresponding to the eigenvalue 1 of the matrix W, that is, $\phi W = \phi$, which is unique with the normalization that the components sum to one. Clearly, we have

$$\phi(k) = l(k)r(k).$$

The relationship between matrix W and the potential U (dropping the subscript max from λ) is given by

$$\beta U(i, j) = -\ln \lambda - \ln W(i, j) + \ln r(j) - \ln r(i),$$

which, when summed over $s = (s_1, s_2, \ldots, s_N)$, becomes

$$\beta \sum_{k} U(s_k, s_{k+1}) = -(N-1)\ln[\lambda(U)] - \sum_{k} \ln W(s_k, s_{k+1})$$
$$- \ln r(s_1) + \ln r(s_N).$$

Substituting out $\sum \ln W(s_k, s_{k+1})$ with $\ln \nu_N(s) - \ln \phi(s_1)$, and averaging over s with respect to the distribution μ_N, we obtain

$$\beta G_N(s) = -N \ln[\lambda(U)] - \sum_s \mu(s) \ln[\nu_N(s)] + c,$$

where c is a constant independent of N. The entropy of the distribution μ is

$$H_N(\mu) = -\sum_s \mu_N(s) \ln \mu_N(s).$$

The definition of potential (free energy) is

$$F_N(\mu) = G_N(\mu) - \beta^{-1} H_N(\mu).$$

Dividing both sides by N, we obtain

$$N^{-1} F_N(\mu) = -\ln[\lambda(U)] + N^{-1}\beta^{-1} \sum_s \mu_N(s) \ln\left[\frac{\mu_N(s)}{\nu_N(s)}\right] + \frac{c}{N}.$$

For the left-hand side of this expression, we define $f(\mu)$ as the limit as N goes to infinity. Since the second term on the right is a positive constant times the Kullback–Leibler divergence, we obtain the inequality

$$N^{-1} F_N(\mu) \geq -\ln[\lambda(U)] + c/N,$$

where the equality holds when μ is identical to ν. By letting N become large, we have the limiting statement

$$f(\mu) \geq -\ln \lambda(U),$$

for any strictly stationary μ. Equality holds when μ is equal to the Markov distribution constructed from U as above. Moreover, Spitzer (1972) shows that if μ is ergodic, then the strict inequality holds.

3.6   Large deviations

In macroeconomics, we want to know the frequencies with which the economy performs poorer than average by more than a certain specified amount. For example, how long is the average duration of a higher-than-normal level of unemployment, or how atypical are some observations on large economies composed of many agents? A body of techniques known loosely as large-deviation theory addresses just such questions and bounds the probabilities of exceptional or rare events. More specifically, consider the example of an average of a number of independent and identically distributed random variables. A question can be stated thus: How large is the probability that the average deviates from its expected value by more than a small positive number ϵ? First, we give a preliminary analysis of upper bounds on some rare events; we return to the subject later when we discuss Sanov's theorem in Section 3.7. Interestingly, large-deviation theory turns out to be closely related to the notion of entropy introduced in Chapter 2 and in Sections 3.2 and 3.3.3 of this chapter.

3.6.1 Example of asset returns

This section discusses the application of large-deviation theory to a specific economic problem. This theory is important for at least two reasons: (1) It is useful in bounding the probabilities of occurrences of rare events such as severe depressions in macroeconomic models; and (2) it is useful for devising methods for simulating these rare events. Ordinary methods cannot deal with rare events because they occur too infrequently in simulations.

This first point is illustrated by the following example concerning the returns to an asset over n periods for large n, $\prod_{i=1}^{n} R_i$, where R_i is the random return to some asset during period i, which is assumed to be independent and identically distributed with mean μ. We let $\alpha = E(\ln R_1)$. To avoid technical complications, we assume that R_i are greater than 1 but less than 2 for all i.[19]

First, by assuming independence and identical distribution, we find that the expected return is

$$E\left(\prod_i R_i\right) = \mu^n,$$

but by the strong law of large numbers, we know that the sum of the logarithms of returns is such that

$$P\left[\frac{1}{n}\sum_{i=1}^{n} \ln(R_i) \to \alpha\right] = 1,$$

and by Jensen's inequality, $\mu = e^{\ln[E(R_i)]} \geq e^{\alpha}$.

These equations mean that the return over n periods, $\prod_i R_i$, is expected to grow at the rate $e^{n\alpha}$, and not at the greater rate of $e^{n\ln(\mu)}$. The reason for this is that even though the mean return is $\mu^n = e^{n\ln(\mu)}$, likely growths are at the exponential rate α, and rare events of a much larger return than that boost the mean return to μ^n, that is, most samples have values of $O(e^{n\alpha})$, but occasionally, samples of the order $O[e^{n\ln(\mu)}]$ are realized. How frequently do we observe such

---

[19] This example is adapted from Shwartz and Weiss (1995). The boundedness assumption allows the use of the Varadhan's integral expression. See the Appendix on the method of Laplace. The return can be interpreted more generally as some growth rate of biological or economic phenomena.

exceptional returns? Suppose that we have

$$P\left(a \le \frac{\sum \ln R_i}{n} \le a + da\right) \approx e^{-nc(a)}da,$$

for some nonnegative function c such that $c(a)/|a| \to \infty$, as $|a| \to \infty$.

We evaluate $E[\exp(n\sum \ln(R_i)/n)]$ by the method of Laplace. The expectation is written as

$$e^{nm}\int \exp\{n[a - c(a) - m]\}da,$$

where $m = \sup_a[a - c(a)]$.[20] By the assumption on c,

$$e^{n(m-\epsilon)} \le E\left(\prod R_i\right) \le e^{n(m+\epsilon)},$$

that is, the expected return to the asset grows exponentially at the rate m. Later in this chapter, we see that $c(a)$ is such that $\sup_a[a - c(a)] = \ln \mu$.

To see this heuristically, we note first that if the supremum is achieved where $c(a)$ is differentiable, then $c'(a) = 1$. We show in Section 3.6.2 that the function $c(a)$ is defined by $\sup_\theta[a\theta - \ln M(\theta)]$ where $M(\theta) = E[e^{\theta \ln(R_1)}]$, and hence $c'(a)$ is equal to the value of θ at which this supremum is achieved, that is, $a = M'(\theta)/M(\theta)$ which shows that this θ is equal to 1. This implies in turn that $m = a - a + \ln M(1) = \ln E[e^{1 \cdot \ln(R_1)}] = \ln E(R_1) = \ln \mu$.

3.6.2   Chernoff bounds

A special case of upper bounds for probabilities of large deviations is very easy to derive (Whittle 1992, p. 233). See also Durrett (1991, Sec. 1.9) for an easy introduction to large deviations.

Let $\chi(X \ge a)$ be the indicator function of some nonnegative random variable. It satisfies the inequality

$$\chi(X \ge a) \le X/a,$$

since X is nonnegative. Taking expectations of both sides, we obtain the Markov inequality

$$P(X \ge a) \le E(X)/a.$$

Now, we let S_N be a sum of N nonnegative independent and identically distributed random variables X_j. Its moment-generating function is denoted by

---

[20] Loosely put, for large $|a|$ the exponent is strictly negative and the integrand goes to zero exponentially fast, except at the point where the maximum of the exponent is achieved.

$M(\theta) = E(e^{\theta X_1})$. Then, by the Markov inequality,

$$P(S_N \geq Na) = P(e^{\theta S_N} \geq e^{\theta Na}) \leq \inf_{\theta \geq 0}[M(\theta)^N e^{-N\theta a}].$$

Carrying out the optimization in the above, we can rewrite it as

$$P(S_N \geq Na) \leq e^{-Nc(a)},$$

where

$$c(a) = \sup_{\theta \geq 0}[\theta a - \ln M(\theta)].$$

is the Legendre transform of the logarithm of the moment-generating function, that is, the cumulant-generating function. This is known as the Chernoff bound. This bound asymptotically becomes sharp as N becomes very large.

For independent and identically distributed Poisson random variables with parameter λ, we have $\ln M(\theta) = \lambda(e^{\theta} - 1)$ and $c(a) = a \ln(\lambda/a) + \lambda - a$ by simple calculations. Hence, we obtain

$$Pr\left(\sum_{i=1}^{N} X_i \geq Na\right) = \left(\frac{a}{\lambda}\right)^{-Na} \exp[-N(\lambda - a) + o(N)],$$

for all $a \geq \lambda$. This upper bound can be written as $e^{-ND(\mu;\nu)}$ where μ and ν are Poisson distributions with rates a and λ, respectively.

For independent and identically distributed Bernoulli random variables with parameter p, that is, $Pr(X_1 = 1) = p$, and $Pr(X_1 = 0) = 1 - p$, we obtain for all $a \geq p$

$$Pr\left(\sum_{i=1}^{N} X_i \geq Na\right) \leq \left(\frac{a}{p}\right)^{-Na} \left(\frac{1-a}{1-p}\right)^{-N(1-a)},$$

in which we also note that the upper bound is expressible as $e^{-ND(\mu;\nu)}$ where μ and ν are distributions $(a, 1 - a)$ and $(p, 1 - p)$, respectively.

We can actually calculate the upper bounds explicitly for these simple examples. For example, for the Bernoulli random variables, we write

$$Pr\left(\sum_{i=1}^{N} X_i \geq Na\right) = \sum_{j=Na}^{N} C_{N,j} p^j (1 - p)^{N-j},$$

and use Stirling's formula to approximate the binomial coefficients. Here again, we can use the largest term, which for j is Na, to approximate the sum, since the rest of the terms contribute only the terms of $O[e^{o(N)}]$.[21]

---

[21] To see this, calculate the ratio of the term for $j = Na+k$ with $k = 1, 2, \ldots$ over that for $j = Na$ and bound the effects of including the omitted terms.

In another example of Bernoulli random variables, we specialize $X_i, i = 1,$ $\ldots, N$, to a sequence of independent and identically distributed random variables taking values 1 and -1 with probability $1/2$. Then, the logarithm of its moment-generating function is

$$c^*(\theta) = \ln M(\theta) = \ln \cosh \theta,$$

and its Legendre transform is defined as

$$c(m) = \sup_{\theta}[\theta m - c^*(\theta)],$$

where, thinking of m as the deviation of the sample mean from the average value of zero, we define m by

$$N_+/N = (1 + m)/2,$$

where N_+ is the total number of random variables taking on the value of 1.

For $|m| \leq 1$, we can differentiate the expression inside the square brackets and ascertain that the supremum is realized by

$$\theta^o = (1/2) \ln[(1 + m)/(1 - m)].$$

When this θ^o is subsituted in the definition, we note that

$$c(m) = \frac{1}{2}[(1 + m) \ln(1 + m) + (1 - m) \ln(1 - m)],$$

which is equal to $D(\mu; \nu)$ for $\mu = [(1 + m)/2, (1 - m)/2]$ and $\nu = (0.5, 0.5)$. We recognize this as the negative of the entropy, $-H(p)$ for $p = (1 + m)/2$.

The function $c(m)$ measures the discrepancy between m and its mean, which is zero, in the sense that $c(m)$ is nonnegative for all m with $c(0) = 0$. The theory of large deviations bounds the probability that m is not zero by

$$Pr(m \geq \epsilon) \leq e^{-Nc(\epsilon)}.$$

We say more on this in Section 3.6.3. See Ellis (1985, Theorem II.3.3). Given ϵ, a large probability of m of falling in an interval $(m - \epsilon, m + \epsilon)$ (i.e., a high multiplicity of microstates corresponding to a macroscopic value m that is close to zero), corresponds to a small value of $c(m)$, (i.e., m near zero). This is in the same sense that we discussed earlier, in that $c(m)$ is a measure of the multiplicity of microscopic states compatible with m. In other words, if m_1 and m_2 are such that $c(m_1) \leq c(m_2)$, then m_1 is more random than m_2. The value of zero is the most random value of the macroeconomic variable m.

With probability densities, large deviations are analyzed using integrals rather than sums. We let μ be a measure on the real line and μ^n be the n-fold tensor product on the n-dimensional Euclidean space. We let μ_n denote the distribution of the arithmetic average of X_i, $i = 1, \ldots, n$, under μ^n. We assume that the integral $\int |x|\mu(dx)$ is bounded, and denote the moment-generating function by

$$\Lambda(\theta) = \int e^{\theta x}\mu(dx).$$

This map from the real line to $[0, \infty)$ is a lower semicontinuous convex function. Next, we take its Legendre transform

$$\Lambda^*(x) = \sup_{\theta}[\theta x - \ln \Lambda(\theta)].$$

This is also a nonnegative and lower semicontinuous function.

We let X_i be independent and identically distributed real-valued random variables. Then, the empirical measure of the sample mean is μ_n. If we consider the set of probability measure v given by

$$C_a = \left\{ v : \int y\, dv(y) \geq a \right\},$$

then we can write

$$P(S_n \geq na) = P(\mu_n \in C_a),$$

where $S_n = X_1 + \cdots + X_n$.

As noted before, the Kullback–Leibler divergence between two probability measures μ and v is given by

$$D(\mu; v) = \int \ln\left(\frac{d\mu}{dv}\right)d\mu.$$

The large-deviations principle states that

$$P(\mu_n \in S_a) \approx \exp\left[-n \inf_{v \in S_a} \int \ln\left(\frac{dv}{d\mu}\right)dv\right],$$

where μ is the distribution of X_i.

We use Lagrange multipliers to incorporate the constraints that

$$\int v(x)d\mu(x) = 1,$$

where $v(x)$ is defined as $dv/d\mu$, and that

$$\int xv(x)d\mu(x) \geq a.$$

The minimization yields a function

$$v(x) = ce^{\theta^* x},$$

where the constants c and θ^* are determined from

$$1 = cE(e^{\theta^* x}) = c\Lambda(\theta^*),$$

and

$$a = cE(xe^{\theta^* x}) = c\Lambda'(\theta*).$$

Then, the Kullback–Leibler divergence measure becomes

$$\int \ln\left(\frac{d\mu}{d\nu}\right) d\mu = \int v(x) \ln[v(x)] \, d\mu(x) = a\theta^* - \ln \Lambda(\theta^*).$$

Noting that we have the relationship

$$a = \frac{\Lambda'(\theta^*)}{\Lambda(\theta^*)},$$

we recognize this to be equal to $\sup_\theta [a\theta - \ln \Lambda(\theta)] = \Lambda^*(a)$.

Collecting these, we establish the relationship

$$P(\mu_n \in S_a) \approx \exp\left[-n \inf_{\nu \in S_a} \int \ln\left(\frac{d\mu}{d\nu}\right) d\mu(x)\right] = \exp[-n\Lambda^*(a)].$$

3.6.3   Tilted distribution and lower Chernoff bound

We let X_i be independent and identically distributed random variables with a common distribution $F(x)$, and choose a constant a greater than the mean $E(X)$. As before, $M(\theta)$ is the moment-generating function $E(e^{\theta X_1})$, and we let θ^* be argmax$[\theta a - \ln M(\theta)]$, which we assume to be an interior maximum, that is,

$$a = M'(\theta^*)/M(\theta^*).$$

We next define another distribution related to F, called twisted or tilted, by

$$dG(y) = \frac{e^{\theta^* y}}{M(\theta^*)} dF(y).$$

A random variable $\tilde{X}$ with this distribution has the mean at a, such that

$$E(\tilde{X}) = \int y \, dG(y) = \frac{1}{M(\theta^*)} \int e^{\theta^* y} y \, dF(y)$$

where the right-hand side is $M'(\theta^*)/M(\theta^*)$, which is a. In other words, the mean of this random variable is shifted to a, hence the name.[22]

A lower bound for $Pr(\sum_{i=1}^{n} X_i \geq na)$ can be obtained by using the tilted distribution as follows. First we note that

$$Pr(X_1 \geq a) = \int \chi_{(X_1 \geq a)} dF(x) \geq \int \chi_{[a \leq X_1 \leq (a+\epsilon)]} dF(x),$$

for any positive ϵ. In terms of the tilted distribution, this last expression is

$$M(\theta^*) \int \chi_{[a \leq X \leq (a+\epsilon)]} e^{-\theta^* x} dG(x).$$

With n independent and identically distributed random variables, we have

$$Pr\left(\sum_i X_i \geq na\right) \geq \int \chi_{[na \leq \sum X_i \leq n(a+\epsilon)]} dF(x_1) \cdots dF(x_n),$$

which is equal to

$$M(\theta^*)^n \int \chi_{[na \leq \sum X_i \leq n(a+\epsilon)]} \exp^{(-\theta^* \sum x_i)} dG(x_1) \cdots dG(x_n).$$

Recalling that the tilted random variables have means located at a, we can state that the integral above is not less than

$$e^{-\theta^* n(a+\epsilon)} Pr\left[0 \leq \frac{\sum_i (\tilde{X}_i - a)}{\sqrt{n}} \geq \sqrt{n}(a+\epsilon)\right],$$

which converges to $1/2$ as n goes to infinity by the central-limit theorem.

Combining these two together, we can establish that

$$Pr\left(\sum_i X_i \geq na\right) \geq e^{-nc(a)+o(n)},$$

and combining this lower bound with the upper bound obtained in the previous section, we have

$$Pr\left(\sum_i X_i \geq na\right) = e^{-nc(a)+o(n)}.$$

---

[22] The same idea is used in proving a lower bound of the Gärtner–Ellis theorem which is described in Section 3.6.5.

3.6.4   *Example of large-deviation analysis*

In the previous example, we have shown that entropy or relative entropy enters in bounding probabilities of certain rare events.

Before we venture further on this, here is a slightly more complicated version of one of the previous examples. Suppose we wish to calculate the correlation

$$q = N^{-1} \sum_i \xi_i s_i,$$

of an N-dimensional random state vector $s = (s_1, s_2, \ldots, s_N)$, with a fixed N-dimensional vector $\xi = (\xi_1, \xi_2, \ldots, \xi_N)$, where the components of these vectors take values of ± 1 with equal probability.

Since the ξ_i are fixed, we can change variables and rename $\xi_i s_i$ as s_i. Since the original state-vector components are distributed equally between 1 and -1 with probability $1/2$ each, so are the s_i redefined above.

Suppose that k of the N components is 1, and the remaining $(N - k)$ components take on the value -1. We denote the sample average by $x = (2k - N)/N$, and express k in terms of x as $k = N(1 + x)/2$. The variable x measures the deviation from the value of the a priori average (which is 0) of the ratio of the components with $+1$ values, where we use p_+ to denote the $+1$ proportion in the N components, $p_+ = k/N = (1 + x)/2$ and, similarly, $p_- = 1 - p_+ = (N - k)/N = (1 - x)/2$. Since the components are independent, the value of q has the binomial distribution

$$Pr(q = x) = {}_N C_k (1/2)^k (1/2)^{N-k},$$

which, after substituting k out by the relation noted above, and using Stirling's formula, becomes

$$Pr(q = x) \approx \exp[NH(p_+)],$$

to the $O[\ln(N)/N]$, and where $H(p_+)$ is the base e Shannon entropy, $H(p) = -p \ln(p) - (1 - p) \ln(1 - p)$ evaluated at p_+. This example is exactly the same as the first one we used to illustrate large-deviation theory, in Section 3.6.1. Using t rather than θ the cumulant-generating function is

$$c^*(t) = \lim N^{-1} \ln E(e^{tNq}) = \ln \cosh(t),$$

since $e^{tNq} = \prod_i e^{ts_i}$, and $E(e^{ts_i}) = (e^t + e^{-t})/2 = \cosh t$ for all i.

Alternatively, using the continuous variable approximation,

$$Pr(x \le q \le x + dx) \approx \exp[NH(x)] dx,$$

we write the logarithm of the moment-generating function as

$$N^{-1} \ln E(e^{tNq}) = N^{-1}\ln\left(\int \exp\{N[xt + H(x)]\} \, dx \right).$$

We evaluate this expression in the limit of $N \to \infty$ by the method of Laplace, on the assumption that the expression in square brackets on the right-hand side has a unique maximum, to see that

$$c^*(t) = \sup_x \{xt - [-H(x)]\}.$$

The supremum is actually achieved at $2t = \ln[(1 + x)/(1 - x)]$, and we obtain $c(t) = \ln\cosh(t)$, which we earlier identified as the cumulant-generating function.

We recover $-H$ by

$$-H(x) = \sup_t [xt - c^*(t)],$$

where the supremum is achieved at $x = dc^*(t)/dt = \tanh(t)$, that is,

$$-H(x) = x \tanh^{-1} x - \ln\{\cosh[\tanh^{-1}(x)]\}.$$

3.6.4.1 Sample mean greater than the expected value

We let X_i be independent and identically distributed random variables taking on values 0 and 1 with equal probability, and we let a be a constant between $1/2$ and 1. Then, we have

$$Pr\left(\sum_{i=1}^{n} X_i \geq na \right) = \sum_{j=na}^{n} {}_nC_j 2^{-n}.$$

The probability that this sum is equal to na is ${}_nC_{na}2^{-n}$ which is equal to $\exp[-D(a; 1/2) + O(n)]$, where by $D(a; 1/2)$, we mean the Kullback–Leibler divergence between the two probability mass functions, $(a, 1 - a)$ and $(1/2, 1/2)$.

We can calculate the rest of the sum

$$\sum_{j=na+1}^{n} {}_nC_j 2^{-n},$$

by noting that

$${}_nC_{na+k} = \gamma^k {}_nC_{na} + o(n),$$

for $k = 1, 2, \ldots$, where $\gamma = (1 - a)/a$.

Therefore, if $\sum_i X_i \geq na$, then the sum is approximately equal to na. Finally, we can actually calculate $E(\sum_i X_i \mid \sum X_i \geq na)$ and show that it differs from na by a number that asymptotically approaches a constant independent of n.

3.6.5   Gärtner–Ellis theorem

In economic applications of large-deviation theory, we use mostly intervals to bound values of macroeconomic variables. For these simple sets, we can generalize large-deviation results to random variables that are not independent and identically distributed. See Dembo and Zeitouni (1993, p. 139) for more abstract sets.

To illustrate this fact, which is known as the Gärtner–Ellis theorem, we let S_n be a sequence of real-valued random variables and define

$$\phi_n(\theta) = \frac{1}{n} \ln E\left(e^{\theta S_n}\right).$$

This expression reduces to the logarithm of the moment-generating function when S_n is the sum of n independent and identically distributed random variables, $S_n = X_1 + \cdots + X_n$ for some X_i.

We assume that the pointwise limit exists such that

$$\phi(\theta) = \lim_{n \to \infty} \phi_n(\theta),$$

for all real θ, and that it is differentiable when it is finite. The value of the limits as well as the values of the function ϕ_n may be ∞.

The rate function is defined as

$$I(x) = \sup_\theta [\theta x - \phi(\theta)].$$

If an interval $[a, b]$ has nonzero intersection with the set on which the rate function is finite, then

$$\limsup_n \left[\frac{1}{n} \ln P\left[\frac{S_n}{n} \in (a, b)\right]\right] \leq - \inf_{x \in [a,b]} [I(x)],$$

and

$$\liminf_n \left[\frac{1}{n} \ln P\left[\frac{S_n}{n} \in (a, b)\right]\right] \geq - \inf_{x \in (a,b)} [I(x)],$$

where we assume that, for any $x \in (a, b)$, there is a θ_x such that

$$x = \phi'(\theta_x).$$

Then, we see that $I(x) = \theta_x x - \phi(\theta_x)$.

3.6.5.1 Examples of dependent asset returns

We let the asset returns in Section 3.6.1 be dependent by assuming that the independent and identically distributed random variables $\ln(R_i)$ are corrupted by additive noises that are bounded random variables, independent of R_i. Then, we let $S_n = \sum_{i=1}^{n}(\ln R_i + \xi_i)$, where R_i are independent and identically distributed and $|\xi|$ is bounded from above by ϵ_i. Whenever $\sum_{i=1}^{n}(\epsilon_i/n)$ goes to zero as n goes to infinity, ϕ_n converges pointwise to ϕ which is the logarithm of the moment-generating function of $\ln(R_i)$.

A more interesting example is when $\ln(R_i)$ is generated by an autoregressive process of order one:

$$Z_{k+1} = aZ_k + \xi_{k+1},$$

where $Z_k = \ln(R_k)$, where a is a constant of magnitude less than one, and where ξ_k are independent and identically distributed bounded random variables. To be specific, suppose that $P(\xi_k = 1) = p$, and $P(\xi_k = 0) = 1 - p$ for all $k = 1, 2, \ldots$. We can take the initial condition to be zero ($Z_0 = 0$) without loss of generality.

To find the upper and lower bounds of the probability that the average S_n/n falls in interval (a, b), we begin by calculating

$$\phi_n(\theta) = (1/n)\ln E\left(e^{\theta S_n}\right).$$

This function has the limit

$$\lim_n \phi_n(\theta) = \ln M(\hat{\theta}),$$

where $M(\theta) = 1 - p + p^\theta$ is the moment-generating function of ξ_1, and where $\hat{\theta} = \theta/(1-\alpha)$. Let $\hat{x} = (1-\alpha)x$.

The supremum of the rate function is achieved at

$$\hat{\theta} = \ln\frac{(1-p)\hat{x}}{p(1-\hat{x})},$$

and the value of the rate function is

$$I(x) = D(\hat{x}; p),$$

where the Kullback–Leibler divergence measures the discrepancy between the distribution $(\hat{x}, 1 - \hat{x})$ and $(p, 1 - p)$.

3.7 Sanov's theorem

How many microeconomic states (configurations) are compatible with observed values of some macroeconomic variables? We have earlier given a preliminary answer. We now proceed to consider possible distributions of microstates that are compatible with a set of observed macrostates, that is, posterior distributions of the microeconomic states, conditional on a set of observed macroeconomic signals. We first describe Sanov's theorem, which has to do with empirical distributions of samples, and then discuss Cramér's theorem, which bounds sample means.[23] In Section 3.7.1, we discuss the Gibbs posterior distributions.

Suppose that agent i's state is represented by a random variable X_i which takes on a value from a finite set of states, $S = \{s_1, s_2, \ldots, s_K\}$. We describe microstates at the level of detail that keeps track of the compositions of states, that is, the fractions of microeconomic agents that take on particular values of states, $s_i, i = 1, 2, \ldots, K$. These fractions lead to the notion of empirical distributions, which are introduced next. For simplicity, we assume that $X_1, \ldots, X_N$ are independent and identically distributed with a distribution $Q(x)$. Then, the joint probability of a sample of size N – $\mathbf{x}$ – is $Q(\mathbf{x}) = \prod_{i=1}^{N} Q(x_i)$, where x_i is a realized (sample) value of X_i.

We define $P_{\mathbf{x}}(s_k)$ as the number of times s_k occurs in the sample $\mathbf{x}$ divided by the sample size, N, that is, $NP_x(s_k)$ is the number of times s_k occurs in the sample, $x_1, \ldots, x_N$.

The empirical distribution is defined by

$$P_{\mathbf{x}} = [P_{\mathbf{x}}(s_1), \ldots, P_{\mathbf{x}}(s_K)].$$

Component i of this K-dimensional vector is the fraction of instances that state s_i occurs in the sample $\mathbf{x}$.[24]

Using the empirical distribution, we can rewrite $Q(\mathbf{x})$ as follows:

$$Q(\mathbf{x}) = \prod_i Q(x_i) = \prod_s Q(s)^{NP_{\mathbf{x}}(s)} = e^{-N[H(P_{\mathbf{x}})+D(P_{\mathbf{x}};Q)]},$$

where $\prod_s$ means that the product is taken over all $s_i, i = 1, \ldots, K$.[25]

We let P_N be an empirical distribution of sample size N (think of a system composed of N agents). For shorter notation, we drop N from it from now on. We define $T(P)$ as the set of samples that produces the same empirical distribution as P,

$$T(P) = \{\mathbf{x} \in S^N : P_{\mathbf{x}} = P\}.$$

---

[23] For multinomial distributions, Sanov's theorem is equivalent to the Chernoff theorem discussed in Sections 3.6.2 and 3.6.3.

[24] For d-dimensional vectors, we let $Y_j = \sum_j \chi(X_i = j)u_j$, where χ is the indicator function, and where u_j is the d-dimensional vector with one in the jth component and zero everywhere else, that is, the jth component of the vector Y_j is one when $X_i = j$. Then, $(Y_1+Y_2+\cdots+Y_N)/N$ is a representation of the empirical measure of $X_1, X_2, \ldots$.

[25] We can see this as follows: We let $q_i = Q(s_i)$ and $p_i = P_{\mathbf{x}}(s_i)$ for shorter notation. Then $q_i^{Np_i} = \exp(Np_i \ln q_i) = \exp\{N[p_i(q_i/p_i) + p_i \ln p_i]\}$. This last expression is rearranged to obtain the expression shown.

This set consists of all permutations of the original sample $\mathbf{x}$, since only the fractions matter in empirical distributions. Therefore, the number of elements in this set is given by the multinomial coefficient of allocating N numbers into N_j, $j = 1, 2, \ldots, K$, where $N_j = NP(s_j)$.

The probability of this set measured by the probability measure Q is

$$Q[T(P)] = \sum_{\mathbf{x} \in T(P)} Q(\mathbf{x}),$$

where $Q(\mathbf{x})$ is as derived above. Since it does not depend on the particular samples, but only on empirical distributions, we have

$$Q[T(P)] = |T(P)| \exp\{-N[H(P) + D(P; Q)]\}.$$

The number of empirical distributions with the same distribution as P can be bounded from above as

$$|T(P)| \leq e^{NH(P)},$$

and hence the probability is bounded from above by

$$Q[T(P)] \leq e^{-ND(P; Q)}. \tag{3.3}$$

This bound can be computed directly by approximating the multinomial coefficient by Stirling's formula, or alternatively as follows. As stated above, all of the empirical distributions in $T(P)$ have the same number, N_j, of realizations (observations) of the value s_j, $j = 1, \ldots, K$, and hence the number of samples is equal to the number of multinomial combinations of dividing the total sample size N into N_j, $j = 1, \ldots, K$. We then note that, writing p_j for $P_{\mathbf{x}}(s_j)$,

$$P_{\mathbf{x}} = \prod_j p_j^{N_j} = e^{-NH(P)},$$

and that

$$1 \geq P[T(P)] = \sum_{\mathbf{x} \in T(P)} P_{\mathbf{x}} = \sum_{\mathbf{x} \in T(P)} e^{-NH(P)} = |T(P)| e^{-NH(P)},$$

which establishes the inequality.

We are then lead to a particular form of Sanov's theorem (Cover and Thomas 1991, p. 292), which bounds the probabilities of empirical distributions, conditional on the sample average, $(1/N) \sum_i h(x_i) \geq$ constant,

$$A = \left[P : \sum_s h(s) P(s) \geq \text{constant} \right],$$

where the sum is over all possible states in the set S.[26]

This is the correct inequality since the sample average is expressible as

$$\frac{1}{N} \sum_i h(x_i) = \sum_j P_\mathbf{x}(s_j) h(s_j).$$

The right-hand side can be written compactly as an inner product $\langle h, P_\mathbf{x} \rangle$ by introducing a K-dimensional vector $\mathbf{h}$ with components $h(s_i)$.

By incorporating the constraint with the Lagrange multiplier β, we derive the result of the constrained minimization as

$$P^*(s_i) = \frac{Q(s_i) e^{\beta h(s_i)}}{\sum_{j=1}^{K} Q(s_j) e^{\beta Q(s_j)}}.$$

For large N, the development of this section shows that if a rare event occurs, then it happens in only one way, according to the tilted distribution shown above. Summing $Q[T(P)]$ over all elements of P in the set $\mathbf{A}$, we have an upper bound

$$Q(\mathbf{A}) = \sum_{P \in \mathbf{A}} Q[T(P)],$$

where by replacing $D(P; Q)$ in the exponent of the upper bound in Eq. (3.3) by the infimum of it over the set $\mathbf{A}$, and noting that there are at most $(N + 1)^K$ number of elements in the set, we can bound it from above by

$$Q(\mathbf{A}) \le (N + 1)^K e^{-ND(P^*; Q)},$$

where P^* is the distribution corresponding to the infimum of $D(P; Q)$ over the set $\mathbf{A}$.

3.7.1   From Sanov's theorem to Cramér's theorem

We derive one of the simplest and most basic large-deviation theorems for sample means of Cramér by the method that was introduced by Sanov in connection with the theorem for empirical distributions.[27]

We let L_N be the set of all possible empirical distributions of length N, and as before, $P_\mathbf{x}$ is the vector of the fractions of occurrence of state s_i in the sequence, $x_1, x_2, \ldots, x_N$, that is,

$$P_\mathbf{x}(s_i) = \frac{1}{N} \sum_{j=1}^{N} \chi_{s_i}(x_j),$$

---

[26] Vasicek (1980) proved this when $h(a)$ is linear in a.
[27] We follow Dembo and Zeitouni (1993, Sec. 2.1).

where $\chi_s(x)$ is one when $x = s$, and zero otherwise. We use $P_{\mathbf{x}}$ to indicate a random element of the set L_N, where $\mathbf{x}$ is regarded as a random sequence.

We let a random sequence $\mathbf{x} = (x_1, x_2, \ldots, x_N)$ be such that x_j is independent and identically distributed with the distribution function Q, as in the preceding Section 3.7. Reasoning the same way as there, we establish that for every set Γ of the K-dimensional probability vector,

$$
\begin{aligned}
Q(P_{\mathbf{x}} \in \Gamma) &= \sum_{P \in \Gamma \cap L_N} Q(P_{\mathbf{x}} = P) \\
&\leq \sum_{P \in \Gamma \cap L_N} e^{-ND(P;Q)} \\
&\leq |\Gamma \cap L_N| \exp\left[-N \inf_{P \in \Gamma \cap L_N} D(P;Q)\right] \\
&\leq (N+1)^K \exp\left[-N \inf_{P \in \Gamma \cap L_N} D(P;Q)\right],
\end{aligned}
$$

where we use the inequality $(N+1)^{-K} e^{NH(P)} \leq |T(P)| \leq e^{NH(P)}$. Taking the logarithm of both sides, we recover the upper bound of Sanov's theorem:

$$
\begin{aligned}
\lim\left\{\sup_{N \to \infty} (1/N) \ln[Q(P_X \in \Gamma)]\right\} &= -\lim\left\{\inf_{N \to \infty}\left[\inf_{P \in \Gamma \cap L_N} D(P;Q)\right]\right\} \\
&\leq -\inf_{P \in \Gamma}[D(P;Q)],
\end{aligned}
$$

We next relate this $\inf[D(P;Q)]$ to the sample mean of another sequence of random variables, $y_i = f(x_i)$, where f maps the set of states $\{s_1, s_2, \ldots, s_K\}$ into real numbers. Without loss of generality, we assume that $f(s_1) \leq f(s_2) \cdots \leq f(s_K)$, so that the sample mean

$$
m_N = (1/N) \sum_j y_j = \langle f, P_X \rangle
$$

takes its value in the compact interval $[f(s_1), f(s_K)]$. Here, we use the inner-product notation and introduce K-dimensional vectors f with components $f(s_i)$, $i = 1, \ldots, K$, and L_N^y with components $L_N(s_i)$, and write $m_N = \langle f, L_N^y \rangle$.

We fix an arbitrary distribution P in the interior of Γ. Then, for some small enough $\delta \geq 0$, the set $\{P': \sup |P(A) - P'(A)| \leq \delta\}$, where sup is taken over all subset A of the set of states, is contained in Γ, and there is a sequence P_N in $\Gamma \cap L_N$ such that $P_N \to P$ as N goes to infinity. Without loss of generality, we can assume that the support of P_N is contained in that of Q. Then, we have

$$
-\lim_{N \to \infty} \sup\left[\inf_{P' \in \Gamma \cap L_N} D(P';Q)\right] \leq -\lim_{N \to \infty} D(P_N;Q) = -D(P;Q).
$$

This is true for all P in the interior of Γ, hence

$$-\limsup\left[\inf_{P \in \Gamma \cap L_N} D(P;Q)\right] \leq -\inf_{P \in \Gamma^o} D(P;Q).$$

Collecting these two bounds, we have Sanov's theorem:

$$-\inf_{\Gamma^o} D(P;Q) \leq \liminf(1/N)\ln[Q(P_X \in \Gamma)]$$
$$\leq \limsup(1/N)\ln[Q(P_X \in \Gamma)] \leq -\inf_{P \in \Gamma} D(P;Q).$$

For every set A, m_N is in A if and only if

$$P_X \in \{P; \langle f, P \rangle \in A\}.$$

We call this set Γ.

We denote the logarithm of the moment-generating function of the random variable y by

$$\Lambda(\beta) = \ln[E(e^{\beta y})] = \ln\left[\sum_i Q(s_i)e^{\beta f(s_i)}\right].$$

By Jensen's inequality,

$$\Lambda(\beta) \geq \sum_i P(s_i)\ln\left[\frac{Q(s_i)e^{\beta f(s_i)}}{P(s_i)}\right] = \beta\langle f, P \rangle - D(P;Q),$$

where equality holds for

$$P_\beta(s_i) = Q(s_i)e^{\beta f(s_i)-\Lambda(\beta)}.$$

Therefore, for all β and x,

$$\beta x - \Lambda(\beta) \leq \inf_{P:\langle f,P\rangle=x} D(P;Q) = I(x),$$

where the rate function $I(x)$ is defined by the right-hand-side equality.

We differentiate $\Lambda(\beta)$ to note that

$$\frac{d\Lambda(\beta)}{d\beta} = \langle f, P_\beta \rangle.$$

Therefore, we note that

$$I(x) = \sup_{\beta \in R}[\beta x - \Lambda(\beta)]$$

holds for all $x \in \{\Lambda'(\beta) : \beta \in R\}$.

The derivative of $\Lambda(\beta)$ is strictly increasing and $f(s_1) = \inf_\beta[\Lambda'(\beta)]$, and $f(s_K) = \sup_\beta[\Lambda'(\beta)]$. Thus, the rate function is given by the supremum for all x in the interior of the interval $[f(s_1), f(s_K)]$. At the ends [e.g., $x = f(s_1)$], we define $P^*(s_1) = 1$, so that $\langle f, P^* \rangle = f(s_1) = x$. It follows that

$$-\ln[Q(s_1)] = D(P^*; Q) \geq I(x) \geq \sup_{\beta}[\beta x - \Lambda(\beta)]$$

$$\geq \lim_{\beta \to -\infty}[\beta x - \Lambda(\beta)] = -\ln[Q(s_1)],$$

and similarly at the other end.

Cramér's theorem for finite microeconomic states is obtained from Sanov's theorem as

$$- \inf_{x \in A^o} I(x) \leq \lim \, \inf(1/N) \ln[Q(m_N \in A)]$$

$$\leq \lim \, \sup(1/N) \ln[Q(m_N \in A)]$$

$$\leq - \inf_{x \in A} I(x)$$

where A^o is the interior of A for any A on the real axis.

Since A is contained in $\bar{A}^o$, which is in the interval $[f(s_1), f(s_k)]$, we obtain

$$\lim_{n \to \infty} \frac{1}{n} \ln Q(m_n \in A) = - \inf_{x \in A} I(x),$$

for any A on the real axis.

3.8   Conditional-limit theorem

In economic modeling, we frequently want to infer distributions of unobserved states of microeconomic agents, given information on the aggregates of the states, such as averages. This is the way that we use the conditional-limit theorem. For independent and identically distributed random variables, see Cover and Thomas (1991, p. 301) or van Campenhout and Cover (1981) for proofs. There is a corresponding conditional-limit theorem for random vectors that are not independent and identically distributed but are generated by a finite-state Markov chain. See Csiszár, Cover, and Choi (1987) or Dembo and Zeitouni (1993). We take up this topic here since it is very useful in some dynamic discrete-choice models of microeconomic agents in which deviations from desired or ideal situations evolve as finite-state Markov chains.

The simplest version of the theorem is for a sequence of some independent and identically distributed random variables, $X_1, X_2, \ldots, X_N$, with a common probability density function $g(x)$. Given an observed value $(1/N) \sum_i h(X_i) = \alpha$, the theorem states that the probability density of X_1, conditional on the observed value, is given by

$$f_\beta(x) = g(x) \, e^{\beta h(x)},$$

where the parameter β is chosen to satisfy

$$\int h(x) f_\beta(x) dx = \alpha.$$

This shows that the conditional distribution of a given random variable X is the (normalized) product of the maximum entropy distribution and the a priori (initial) distribution.

When the random variable X_1 takes on values from a finite set, we use empirical distributions. We let $Q(x)$ be the common probability mass function (distribution), and A be a closed convex subset of the set of all empirical distributions, denoted by P_{X^N}, where Q is not in A. We denote by P^* the distribution that minimizes the Kullback–Leibler divergence $D(P; Q)$ over the set A. The theorem states that

$$Pr(X_1 = s \mid P_{X^N} \in A) \rightarrow P^*(s),$$

in probability as N goes to infinity. For example, if the set A is defined in terms of the average

$$\frac{1}{N} \sum_i h(X_i) \geq \alpha,$$

then, as we have shown before, the minimizing probability distribution is given by

$$P^*(s) = Q(s) \frac{e^{\beta h(s)}}{\sum_x Q(x) e^{\beta h(x)}},$$

where the first factor is the a priori distribution and the second factor is the maximum entropy distribution where the denominator is the partition function.

When we define a constraint set $\mathbf{C}$ in terms of some macroeconomic variables as

$$\mathbf{C} = \left[P : \sum_s P(s) h_j(s) \geq c_j, \; j = 1, \dots, m \right],$$

the closest distribution to Q in this set is found by minimizing $D(P; Q)$ subject to the constraints defining the set. These constraints are incorporated by the Lagrange multipliers β_j and we derive the conditional distribution as

$$P^*(\mathbf{x}) = \frac{Q(\mathbf{x}) \exp\left[\sum_j \beta_j h_j(x) \right]}{\sum_s Q(s) \exp\left[\sum_i \beta_i h_i(s) \right]}.$$

This is another example of tilted or twisted distributions introduced in the previous section, and which we encounter again later. When Q is uniform, this is the maximum entropy distribution.

CHAPTER 4

Modeling interactions I: Jump Markov processes

This and the next chapter describe applications of a class of stochastic processes, called jump Markov processes,[1] to model evolutionary dynamics of a large collection of interacting microeconomic units that possibly use state-dependent discrete adjustment rules. This class includes branching processes or birth-and-death processes, to which we return in Chapter 5, to model the time evolution of rival technology adoption by firms in an industry.

4.1 Market participation and other discrete adjustment behavior

The economic literature has many examples showing that optimal adjustment behavior by microeconomic units is not always continuous or small. Rather, adjustments are made at some discrete points in time by some finite magnitudes. Similar adjustment behaviors are known to be optimal in several classes of problems in finance, operations research, and control. Many of these reported results show that adjustment or decision (control) rules are of the threshold type: A specific action or decision is chosen or triggered when some key variable, which measures the gap or discrepancy between a desired or ideal value and the actual one, reaches or exceeds (becomes larger or smaller than) some preset threshold or trigger level. Adjustments can be in one direction only, as in the well-known (S, s) inventory holding rule,[2] or they can be more generally bidirectional; that is, adjustments could be upward or downward, as for example in Caballero (1992) where firms hire or fire as the gap between actual and desired levels of employment reach lower or upper bounds. More generally, when state

---

[1] See Hoel, Port, and Stone (1972, Chap. 3) or Breiman (1968, Chap. 15).

[2] Inventory is replenished to level S when the level falls below s, $S \geq s$. Scarf (1960) proved the optimality of this rule under certain technical conditions. See also Blinder (1981) and Blinder and Maccini (1991). Even when the conditions are not met, this rule is often used as a good suboptimal policy or merely as a convenient behavioral rule.

variables of a microeconomic unit are in a certain subset of states, and when the microeconomic unit receives a specific shock or input, the decision of the unit is to choose a particular adjustment from a discrete-choice set.

Microeconomic units following these decision rules, then, act or adjust intermittently. While the variable that represents the gap lies between the thresholds, no action or adjustment is undertaken. For example, firms do not continuously adjust their factors of production or output prices. Srinivasan (1967) and Sheshinski and Weiss (1977, 1983) show that firms in an inflationary environment adjust their output prices intermittently. Similarly, Peck (1974) shows that utility companies facing known exponentially growing demand for electricity expand power-generating capacity at discrete points in time. These examples may not be too realistic, but they are sufficiently suggestive of circumstances under which microeconomic units may engage in discrete adjustment actions over time.

Adjustments of labor forces by firms are also of this type, three examples being Davis and Haltiwanger (1990), Hammermesh (1989), and Caballero (1992). In another class of cash or portfolio management problems, Akerlof and Milbourne (1980), Constantimides and Richard (1978), Frenkel and Jovanovic (1980), and Smith (1989) show that the short-run demand for money, and firms' cash management rules are of the threshold type. Decisions of entry and exit by firms are also of this type. Baldwin and Krugman (1989) and Dixit (1989a,b) show that the problems of foreign firms' entry into and exit from a domestic market in response to foreign-exchange-rate fluctuations are the same kind of discrete decision problems. Similarly, Jovanovic (1982) discusses the entry and exit question for firms in a closed economy in the face of varying output prices.

Another class of examples for which jump Markov processes provide an appropriate framework for modeling is the process of selection of types, as in Conlisk (1980) and Cornell and Roll (1981). There are several types of microeconomic agents: optimizers and imitators, informed and uninformed, purchasers and nonpurchasers of information, or investers and noninvestors. The possibilities are numerous. Furthermore, random encounters of microeconomic agents of several types (see, e.g., Wright 1995) also can be modeled this way with advantage. Although Wright does not treat his problem in such a way, agents clearly can choose their roles or types as parts of their strategy and the problem can be formulated as a jump Markov process, or, more specifically, as a birth-and-death process, especially in situations where the fractions of agents of each type have multiple equilibria.[3]

We propose that all of these and related problems that involve discrete choices made at intermittent time points be formulated as jump Markov processes. Population mixes of agents with alternative decisions will evolve over time

---

[3] Multiple equilibria are discussed in Chapter 5.

according to jump Markov processes. These processes contain probabilistic or stochastic mechanisms for the fractions of agents to change over time.[4]

We call the attention of the readers to the fact that none of the above-mentioned examples, which are drawn from the economics literature, analyzes interaction among microeconomic units.[5] We discuss such interactions in this and the next two chapters. We present a novel aggregation procedure to obtain the macroeconomic dynamics of a large collection of interacting microeconomic units. This is one main motivation for proposing jump Markov processes as a common vehicle by which this and other problems of discrete adjustment behavior can be studied.

This reformulation involves casting the deterministic models into a stochastic framework of jump Markov processes in some of the examples cited above. In some other cases, where the original formulations are already expressed in stochastic terms, there is a need to recognize or reformulate the problems as jump Markov processes. The manner in which these models are reformulated varies from problem to problem. All involve probabilistically specifying interactions of microeconomic units in terms of transition probabilities or transition rates of Markov chains, and all use a version of the Chapman–Kolmogorov equations to derive time evolutions of probability distributions of state variables, suitably defined. See Sections 4.2, 4.7 and 5.1 for further discussion of the basic ingredients for such reformulations.

In a related econometric context, some macroeconomic time series can be modeled by assuming that they are generated as jump Markov processes. See Neftçi (1984) or Hamilton (1989). This aspect is expected to be very important in econometric works related to our reformulation, but it is outside the scope of this book.

4.2   Construction and infinitesimal parameters

We assume a finite or countably infinite set of states, S, for a stochastic process $\{X_t\}$. Although we can identify the set S with a set of positive integers without loss of generality, we use x, y, and z as generic states in this section. At any time $t \geq 0$, $X_t = x$ for some $x \in S$.

Starting from an initial state x, which is not an absorbing state, the process jumps, after an elapse of a random time τ, to a different state, that is, the process

---

[4] In the literature of evolutionary games, one postulates some sort of fitness function to express the idea that better choices win converts. See Conlisk (1980), Cornell and Roll (1981), and Friedman (1991) for examples of this idea. We do not impose deterministic rules but rather examine stochastic processes for this conversion process. See Chapter 5 for details.

[5] For example, as we discuss later, Caballero (1992) and Caballero and Engel (1992) use the Glivenko–Cantelli lemma to deal with the cross-sectional distribution of firms by the discrete choices that they make. This theorem requires that firms' states be independent random variables.

stays at state x for a length of time τ, and then jumps to a different state y, and stays there for a period of time of random duration, then jumps to another state, and so on. Random time intervals between jumps are called holding or sojourn times and are assumed to be exponentially distributed.[6] Such a process is called a jump process.[7] To avoid technical complications, we assume that processes do not jump an infinite number of times in a finite time span.[8]

For each nonabsorbing state x, we associate an exponential density with parameter λ_x and let it govern the time between jumps, that is,

$$P_x(\tau \geq t) = \int_t^\infty \lambda_x e^{-\lambda_x s} ds = e^{-\lambda_x t},$$

where τ is the length of time that the process remains at state x before jumping to a different state, and where $P_x(\cdot)$ denotes the probability of events defined in terms of the process initially at state x, that is, $P(\tau \geq t \mid X_0 = x)$.

We let $W_{x,y}$ be the transition probability from state x to state y, given that a jump occurs. We note that $W_{x,x}$ is zero, and that

$$\sum_y W_{x,y} = 1.$$

Furthermore, we assume that the random variables τ and X_τ are chosen independently of each other, and we let $F_x(\cdot)$ be the distribution function of the random variable τ,

$$F_x(t) = \int_0^t \lambda_x e^{-\lambda_x \tau} d\tau = 1 - e^{-\lambda_x t}.$$

The process is such that whenever and however the jump is made to a state y, state y acts as the initial state of the process from then on. Therefore,

$$P_x\big(\tau_1 \leq s, X_{\tau_1} = y, \tau_2 - \tau_1 \leq t, X_{\tau_2} = z\big) = F_x(s) W_{x,y} F_y(t) W_{y,z},$$

for any x and y, both nonabsorbing. If x is an absorbing state, then we can set $P_x(X_t = y) = \delta_{x,y}, t \geq 0$, which is one when $y = x$, and zero otherwise.

The transition probability $P_{x,y}(t)$ is the probability that the process, starting at x at time zero, will be in state y at time t, that is,[9]

$$P_{x,y}(t) = P_x(X_t = y) = P(X_t = y \mid X_0 = x),$$

---

[6] This assumption is needed to preserve the Markovian property of the stochastic process involved. See Section 4.7 for further detail.

[7] The sample space of this type of processes is the space of right-continuous functions of time with finite left-hand-side limits.

[8] Such processes are called non-explosive, and they are the only processes discussed here.

[9] More generally we have $P_{x,y}(s, t) = P(X_t = y \mid X_s = x)$ of $t \geq s$. We write $P_{x,y}(0, t)$ as $P_{xy}(t)$.

and its sum over y is one:

$$\sum_y P_{x,y}(t) = 1.$$

We note that $P_{x,y}(0) = \delta_{x,y}$. If the initial state x is distributed according to the distribution function $\pi(x)$, then $P_x(X_t = y) = \sum_x \pi(x) P_{x,y}(t)$.

We only discuss an important subclass of jump processes, called time-homogeneous jump Markov processes, which satisfy

$$P(X_t = y \mid X_{s_1} = x_1, \ldots, X_{s_n} = x_n, X_s = x) = P_{x,y}(t - s),$$

for all $0 \le s_1 \le \cdots s_n \le s$, and all x and y in S. A jump process is Markovian if and only if F_x is an exponential distribution for all nonabsorbing states. See Section 4.7.

We let state x be nonabsorbing and show that $P_{x,y}(t)$ satisfies an equation called the backward Chapman–Kolmogorov equation, which is the same as the master equation that will be introduced in Chapter 5. We then derive a useful relationship between the transition probabilities and the parameters of the exponential distributions.

The event in which the process jumps from x to z at some time before t and $X_t = y$ can happen if and only if the first jump occurs at some time $s \le t$ to a state z. Then, the process goes to y in the remaining time $t - s$, that is,

$$P_x(\tau \le t, X_\tau = z, X_t = y) = \int_0^t \lambda_x e^{-\lambda_x s} W_{x,z} P_{z,y}(t - s)\, ds.$$

We sum this expression with respect to z to obtain

$$P_x(\tau \le t, X_t = y) = \int_0^t \lambda_x e^{-\lambda_x s} \left[\sum_{z \ne x} W_{x,z} P_{z,y}(t - s)\, ds \right].$$

The probability that the first jump occurs after t is equal to

$$P_x(\tau \ge t, X_t = y) = \delta_{x,y} P_x(\tau \ge t) = \delta_{x,y} e^{-\lambda_x t}.$$

Since the event $\{X_t = y\}$ can happen in either of these two mutually exclusive ways such that the first jump occurs before or after t, we have

$$P_{x,y}(t) = P_x(\tau \ge t, X_t = y) + P_x(\tau \le t, X_t = y)$$

$$= \delta_{x,y} e^{-\lambda_x t} + \int_0^t \lambda_x e^{-\lambda_x s} \left[\sum_{z \ne x} W_{x,z} P_{z,y}(t - s) \right] ds$$

$$= \delta_{x,y} e^{-\lambda_x t} + \lambda_x e^{-\lambda_x t} \int_0^t e^{\lambda_x u} \left[\sum_{z \ne x} W_{x,z} P_{z,y}(u) \right] du,$$

after substituting the two expressions we derived on the right, and changing the variable of integration from s to $u = t - s$. Next, we differentiate both sides with respect to t to obtain the equation

$$\frac{dP_{x,y}(t)}{dt} = -\lambda_x P_{x,y}(t) + \lambda_x \sum_{z \neq x} W_{x,z} P_{z,y}(t), \tag{4.1}$$

which is valid for all $t \geq 0$. This is usually called a backward equation because the focus is the final state rather than the initial state, and the same final state (y in this case) enters in all terms, according to Cox and Miller (1965, p. 152).

We define the transition rate by setting t to zero in the above, $w_{x,y} = \dot{P}_{x,y}(0)$, and noting that $P_{x,y}(0) = \delta_{x,y}$, and that $W_{x,x} = 0$. We derive the relations among them as

$$w_{x,y} = -\lambda_x \delta_{x,y} + \lambda_x \sum_{z \neq x} W_{x,z} \delta_{z,y} = -\lambda_x \delta_{x,y} + \lambda_x W_{x,y},$$

that is,

$$w_{x,x} = -\lambda_x, \tag{4.2}$$

and

$$w_{x,y} = \lambda_x W_{x,y}. \tag{4.3}$$

These equations relate the parameter of the exponential distribution with the transition rates,

$$W_{x,y} = w_{x,y}/\lambda_x = w_{x,y} \bigg/ \sum_{y \neq x} w_{x,y},$$

where the second equality is obtained by summing Eq. (4.3) with respect to y to derive another relation:

$$\sum_{y \neq x} w_{x,y} = \lambda_x \sum_{y \neq x} W_{x,y} = \lambda_x = -w_{x,x}. \tag{4.4}$$

The parameters $w_{x,y}$ are also called the infinitesimal parameters of jump processes.

Now, we may rewrite the backward Eq. (4.1) using these transition rates to see that

$$\frac{dP_{x,y}(t)}{dt} = \sum_z w_{x,z} P_{z,y}(t),$$

which is called the master equation for the jump Markov process. It is an accounting equation for the probability fluxes. The probability from state x to

y increases by a probability inflow or influx and decreases by an outflow or outflux. Master equations are used extensively in Chapter 5 as well.

Incidentally, a quicker way for deriving the backward equation is to use the Chapman-Kolmogorov equation, Feller (1957, p. 427) or Parzen (1962, p. 291). Start with the Kolmogorov equation, $P(s - h, t) = P(s - h, s)P(s, t)$, where h is a small positive number, and where $P(s, t)$ is the matrix of transition probabilities from state x at time s to state y at time t, $P_{x,y}(s, t) = Pr\{X_t = y \mid X_s = x\}$, and rewrite it as

$$\frac{1}{h}\{P(s, t) - P(s - h, t)\} = \frac{1}{h}\{I - P(s - h, s)\}P(s, t).$$

Letting h approach zero from above, we write the limit as

$$\frac{\partial}{\partial s}P(s, t) = -\omega(s)P(s, t),$$

where

$$\omega(s) = \lim_{h \downarrow 0} \frac{P(s - h, s) - I}{h}.$$

Here, we assume the existence of the indicated limit, see Feller (1957, p. 427), i.e., we assume that

$$\omega_{x,y}(s) = \lim_{h \downarrow 0} \frac{P_{x,y}(s - h, s)}{h},$$

and

$$\omega_x(s) = \lim_{h \downarrow 0} \frac{P_{x,x}(s - h, s) - 1}{h}$$

exist.

In time-homogeneous processes, we have $P(s, t) = P(t - s)$. Then $\partial P(s, t)/\partial s$ is replaced with $-dP(\tau)/d\tau$ with $\tau = t - s$ yielding

$$\frac{dP(t)}{dt} = \omega P(t),$$

where we have used t for τ, and the matrix ω is now a constant since $P(s - h, s) = P(h)$.

Finally, we note that given that the Markov process jumps only once in time interval $(t - h, t)$, the expression

$$\frac{P_{x,y}(h)}{1 - P_{x,x}(h)} \approx -\frac{\omega_{x,y}}{\omega_x}$$

gives the conditional probability of jump from state x to state y in time interval $(t - h, t)$, given that it jumps. We also note that $\omega_x = -\sum_{y \neq x} \omega_{x,y}$ since

$P_{x,x}(s-h,s) + \sum_{y \neq x} P_{x,y}(s-h,s) = 1$. The word backward refers to the points $s-h$ and s which are the points in the past with respect to the current time t.

4.3   Examples

4.3.1   Birth-and-death processes

A birth-and-death process on S, which is a set of positive integers, is such that the transition rate $w_{x,y}$ is nonzero only for $|x-y| = 1$. The transition rate $w_{x,x+1} = v_x$ is called the birth rate, and $w_{x,x-1} = \mu_x$ is called the death rate. From the relations (4.2) through (4.4), we draw important results that

$$-w_{x,x} = \lambda_x = \mu_x + v_x,$$
$$W_{x,x-1} = \frac{\mu_x}{\mu_x + v_x},$$
$$W_{x,x+1} = \frac{v_x}{\mu_x + v_x},$$

and that all other $W_{x,y}$ are zero.

4.3.2   Poisson processes

A Poisson process is a pure birth process with $\lambda_x = \lambda \geq 0$, for nonnegative integer x. The transition rates are such that the only nonzero rate is $w_{x,x+1} = \lambda = -w_{x,x}$.

We start with the master equation for $P_{x,x}(t)$:

$$\frac{d}{dt} P_{x,x}(t) = -\lambda P_{x,x}(t),$$

with the initial condition $P_{x,x}(0) = 1$. Solving this, we derive

$$P_{x,x}(t) = e^{-\lambda t}.$$

The next master equation is for $P_{x,x+1}$

$$\frac{d}{dt} P_{x,x+1}(t) = w_{x,x} P_{x,x+1}(t) + w_{x,x+1} P_{x+1,x+1}(t)$$
$$= -\lambda P_{x,x+1}(t) + \lambda e^{-\lambda t}.$$

Its solution is

$$P_{x,x+1}(t) = \lambda t e^{-\lambda t}.$$

We can continue in this manner. For example, we have

$$\frac{d}{dt}P_{x,x+2} = -\lambda P_{x,x+2} + \lambda P_{x+1,x+2} = -\lambda P_{x,x+2} + \lambda P_{x,x+1},$$

and so on. By induction, we see that

$$P_{x,x+k}(t) = e^{-\lambda t}\frac{(\lambda t)^k}{k!}$$

for positive integer k.

We later introduce some structure to the transition rates by assuming that

$$w_{k,k+l} = f(k, l),$$

where k and l are some positive integers, and we consider a collection of N such jump Markov processes, as in Ethier and Kurtz (1986).

4.4   Equations for averages: Aggregate dynamics

For jump Markov processes, we can derive the differential equations that govern the average of a large collection of microeconomic units, which we can interpret as the differential equation for the aggregate dynamics, that is, the dynamic macroeconomic equation.

When the state space is finite, we speak of the generator of a process by arranging the transition rates in a matrix form:

$$L = [w(x, y)],$$

where we write $w(x, y)$ for $w_{x,y}$ to denote the (x, y) component of the matrix L. When the state space is countably infinite, we assume that the infinite dimensional matrix has only a finite number of nonzero entries in each row, to avoid technicalities. By representing functions on state spaces as column vectors, we have a definition of the generator:

$$(Lf)(x) = \sum_y w(x, y)f(y) = \sum_y w(x, y)[f(y) - f(x)],$$

since $\sum_y w(x, y) = 0$ as we have seen earlier in connection with Eq. (4.4).

Noting that the right-hand side is related to the conditional expectations of f, we define the generator more formally by[10]

$$(Lf)(x) = \lim_{t\downarrow 0} E[f(X_t) - f(x) \mid X_0 = x]/t .$$

---

[10] This generator is also called the infinitesimal generator. For deterministic X_t, the definition shows that the generator is the same as the differential operator.

For jump Markov processes, two or more jumps in a small time interval Δt is of the order $o(\Delta t)$. Hence, only the first jump matters in calculating the expectation. The first jump is exponentially distributed with rate λ_x and we know from Eq. (4.3) that the probability of a jump from state x to a different state y is equal to $w(x, y)/\lambda_x$. Since the probability of exactly one jump in the interval $[0, t)$ is $\lambda_x t e^{-\lambda_x t}$, we have

$$\lim_{t \downarrow 0} E[f(X_t) - f(x) \mid X_0 = x]/t = \lim_{t \downarrow 0} \sum_{y \neq x} [f(y) - f(x)] e^{-\lambda_x t} \lambda_x t \frac{w(x, y)}{\lambda_x t},$$

which, in the limit, yields the generator

$$(Lf)(x) = \sum_{y \neq x} w(x, y)[f(y) - f(x)],$$

where the interchange of taking the limit and summation is valid because the sum is finite. For example, a Poisson process with rate λ_x has its generator as

$$(Lf)(x) = \lambda_x [f(x + 1) - f(x)].$$

For a multidimensional birth-and-death process that we introduce later, the generator is given by

$$(Lf)(x) = \sum_{k=1}^{m} \lambda_k(x)[f(x + e_k) - f(x)],$$

where x jumps to $x + e_k$ at the rate $\lambda_k(x)$, and where the direction of jump is given by e_k. Let X_t^i, $i = 1, \ldots, N$, be a sequence of N independent Poisson processes with the same rate parameter λ. Their sum is also a Poisson process with parameter $N\lambda$. Call this Y_{Nt}. We note first that

$$z_N(t) = Y_{Nt}/N$$

has the generator

$$(L_N f)(z) = \lim_{t \downarrow 0} \frac{1}{t} E[f(Y_{Nt}/N) - f(z) \mid Y_0/N = z].$$

We see that this equation becomes

$$(L_N f)(z) = N\lambda[f(z + 1/N) - f(z)]$$
$$= \lambda f'(z) + O(1/N).$$

We thus are led to define a related generator as N goes to infinity

$$(L_\infty f)(z) = \lambda f'(z),$$

which defines a deterministic function of time $z_\infty(t)$ and the deterministic differential equation

$$\frac{dz_\infty}{dt} = \lambda(z_\infty).$$

To understand this heuristically,[11] recall that the generator acts as a differential operator for deterministic processes, and $Lf = df/dt = (df/dz)(dz/dt)$ for any smooth f. This step is justified by introducing certain martingales as in Kurtz's theorem, which is mentioned below. More generally, with the multidimensional birth-and-death process discussed earlier, the generator for the average $X_N(t)$ is

$$(L_N f)(x) = \sum_{k=1}^{m} N\lambda_k(x)\left[f(x) + \frac{e_k}{N} - f(x)\right]$$
$$= \sum_k \lambda_k(x)\langle \Delta f(x), e_k\rangle + O(1/N),$$

and its limit form is

$$(L_\infty f)(x) = \sum_k \lambda_k(x)\langle \Delta f(x), e_k\rangle,$$

which defines a function $z_\infty(t)$ governed by the differential equation

$$\frac{dz_\infty}{dt} = \sum_{k=1}^{m} \lambda_k(z_\infty)e_k.$$

Here, the rate is a function of x. This is a particular way of introducing interaction or coupling among N processes, and an example of mean-field approximation to which we return in Chapter 5. See also Aoki and Miyahara (1993) for another application of this approximation scheme.

Kurtz (1978) proved that there exist a positive constant c_1 and a function $c_2(\epsilon)$ such that

$$P_x\left(\sup_{0\le t\le T} |z_N(t) - z_\infty(t)| \ge \epsilon\right) \le c_1 e^{-Nc_2(\epsilon)},$$

for all n, and positive ϵ where

$$\lim_{\epsilon\uparrow 0} c_2(\epsilon)/\epsilon = \infty.$$

Thus, as N goes to infinity, we obtain a deterministic differential equation that governs the arithmetic average of the individual jump Markov processes. Given

---

[11] See Shwartz and Weiss (1995) for a martingale justification.

the content of Kurtz's theorem, we know that generators of these processes determine their distributions, and any process whose generator is a first-order differential operator is deterministic in the limit of the number of agents going to infinity. The formula

$$(Lf)(x) = g(x)df(x)/dx,$$

determines the differential equation

$$\frac{dx_t}{dt} = g(x_t),$$

since

$$\int_0^t (Lf)(x_s)ds = \int_0^t g(x_s)\frac{df(x_s)}{dx}ds = \int_0^t \frac{df(x_s)}{ds}ds = f(x_t) - f(x_0).$$

Thus, we have shown how to derive the aggregate equation for the macroeconomic models that arise from a large number of microeconomic agents whose states or decisions are describable as jump Markov processes.

4.4.1   Example

Here is an example of a simple birth-and-death process interpreted as a model of industrywide inventory holding. There are N firms in an industry and each is either "on" or "off." The on firm may represent a firm that is contributing to the increase of the inventory of the industry. Conversely, the off firms do not contribute to the inventory holding of the industry. We assume that the industry as a whole faces demand NC per unit time, where C is some constant. Although this model has two states, we can reduce it to one by working with the fraction of on firms in the industry, which is denoted by x. The transition rates are

$$w_{n,n+1} = N\lambda(1 - x), \ w_{n,n-1} = N\mu x,$$

where λ is the birth rate, that is, the rate at which firms turn on, and μ is the death rate, the rate at which firms cease contributing to inventory buildup. The directions of transitions are simply $e = 1$ for the on direction, and $e = -1$ for the off direction. To ensure stable dynamics, we assume that $\lambda/(\lambda+\mu) \le C \le 1$. If C is larger than 1, then there is no inventory held by the industry. The expression

$$p = \lambda/(\lambda + \mu)$$

gives the stationary state probability that a firm is contributing to industry inventory buildup.

The aggregate equation is

$$\frac{d}{dt}z_\infty(t) = \lambda(1 - z_\infty) - \mu z_\infty.$$

It has a unique solution that shows that from any initial condition it approaches the value p at the exponential rate $\lambda + \mu$.

The level of inventory, denoted by $I(t)$ is given by

$$\frac{dI(t)}{dt} = N[z_\infty(t) - C],$$

if $I(t)$ is positive or if $z_\infty(t)$ is greater than C. What is more interesting is the behavior out of the steady state, which can be examined by applying large-deviation theory.

As discussed in Chapter 3, the logarithm of the moment-generating function is

$$M(\theta) = \lambda(e^\theta - 1) + \mu(e^{-\theta} - 1),$$

and the rate function of the large deviation (see our discussion on Chernoff bounds in Section 3.6.2) involves the Legendre transform

$$h(x, y) = \sup_{\theta \geq 0}[\theta y - M(\theta)].$$

After carrying out this maximization, the rate function is given by $\exp(-NR)$, where

$$R = C \ln(p/C) - (1 - C) \ln\left(\frac{1 - p}{1 - C}\right).$$

In this way, we see that

$$P[z_N(t) \geq C] \approx \left(\frac{p}{C}\frac{1 - p}{1 - C}\right)^N,$$

that is, the probability of inventory buildup is approximately given by the right-hand-side expression. We can calculate many other interesting statistics. See Weiss (1986) for some examples.

4.5   Multidimensional birth-and-death processes

We now describe multidimensional birth-and-death processes. We let M_t^i, $i = 1, \ldots, m$, be independent Poisson processes with parameters μ_i, and e_i be a d-dimensional vector with integer component values. These unit vectors denote the directions of jumps. Changes in states or positions (choices) of a microeconomic agent are represented by

$$X_t = \sum_{i=1}^{m} M_t^i e_i.$$

The total event rate of $\sum_{i=1}^{m} M_t^i$ is given by the sum $\sum_i \mu_i$ of individual processes. Since the sum of Poisson processes is Poisson with the rate parameter given by the sum of the individual rate parameters, the probability that the jump occurs in the direction e_j, conditional on the occurrence of a jump, is given by $\mu_j / \sum_i \mu_i$. The process $\{X_t\}$ is clearly a jump Markov process.

The d-dimensional vectors e_j can be interpreted either as the microeconomic states of agents, or discrete decisions available to these agents. For example, when there are d types of agents, we can assume that, at most, one agent of each type changes his or her type in evaluating the transition rates. The elements of e_j may be either 1, 0, or -1. The word "type" should be broadly interpreted. It may be a cluster of microeconomic agents so that there are d clusters or subsets of agents. Kelly (1979) has several examples of agents forming clusters. We give some examples of this type of model later. Generalizing this, we can consider a general discrete state jump processes with rates depending on state, $\lambda(x)$.

Next, we consider a collection of N such jump Markov processes and define

$$\tilde{X}_N(t) = \frac{1}{N} \sum_j X_t^j,$$

where the superscript j now refers to individual agents. The left-hand side can may be interpreted as the average state of microeconomic agents, or the vector of fractions of choices made by these agents. With N independent Poisson processes with the same rate parameter λ, the sum is Poisson with the rate parameter $N\lambda$.[12] Therefore, the process $\tilde{X}_N(t)$ has the rate parameter $N\lambda$ and jump sizes e_i/N, $i = 1, \ldots, m$.

Expressing the transition rates as before in terms of the state x from which the jump originates and the size of jump l, the duration between jumps of the average process has the parameter

$$\lambda_N(x) = N \sum_l f(x, l),$$

and the transition probability

$$W_{x,x+l/N} = \frac{f(x, l)}{\sum_l f(x, l)}.$$

Kurtz (1970, 1971, 1978) calls these density-dependent Markov chains and discusses examples from ecology, epidemiology and chemical reactions. In all of these examples, the transition rates are linearly homogeneous in the states

---

[12] With Poisson distributions, distributions with rate parameter λ and time scaled as Nt, are the same as the distribution of the sum of N independent Poisson processes each with rate parameter λ and time scaled as t.

and have the form

$$f(x, l) = \sum_k \alpha_k(l) x_k.$$

In Sections 4.5.2 though 4.5.5, we indicate how these frameworks can be applied to model a collection of not necessarily independent microeconomic agents.

4.5.1 Epidemic model interpreted economically

Here is an epidemic model from Kurtz (1971) rendered in economic terms. Suppose there are two groups of firms: Group 1 is a set of firms with poor credit risk records, and group 2 is a collection of firms with good credit records or risks. Firms in group 1 are unable to borrow and may go bankrupt. Firms in group 2 may become bad credit risks by dealing with firms with bad credit risk. We assume that firms' characterizations as to good or bad credit risks are not observable. There are n firms in group 1 and $N - n$ firms in group 2. The only transitions allowed in this model are from $(n, N - n)$ to $(n + 1, N - n - 1)$ or to $(n - 1, N - n)$. We label the former as l_1 and the latter as l_2. The transition l_1 means that a firm with good credit becomes a bad credit risk, and l_2 represents a situation in which a firm with bad credit risk goes bankrupt. The transition rate for l_1 is assumed to be $\lambda(N - n)n/N = N\lambda(1 - n/N)(n/N)$, and that for l_2 given by $\mu n = N\mu(n/N)$. The transition function $f(x, l)$ is therefore specified by

$$f(x, l_1) = \lambda x_1 x_2,$$

and

$$f(x, l_2) = \mu x_1,$$

where x_1 and x_2 are the fractions of firms with good and bad credit ratings.[13]

4.5.2 Open air market linear model I

Let a K-component vector $n = (n_1, \ldots, n_K)$ be associated with a collection of microeconomic agents or units. This vector may represent the composition of microeconomic agents who are classified according to their types, choices or states, i.e., the state vector may consist of some components which refer to

---

[13] We can make an alternative interpretation in that there are N personal computers connected in a network out of which n are infected by a computer virus. By communicating with a computer with a virus, a noninfected computer can become infected. By interpreting the rates for birth and death as those of being infected and being purged of virus, we can use the same machinery described above to describe the time evolution of the status of a population of personal computers in the network.

choices and the rest to "states" in the usual sense of the word. For example, these components may represent alternative strategies they choose, or they may refer to possible categories to which agents belong. To give a simple account, we only consider in this subsection birth-and-death processes with constant or linear transition rates which depend only on departure states.

Suppose that the birth and death transition rates are specified by

$$w(n, n + e_k) = \nu_k,$$

$$w(n, n - e_j) = \mu_j n_j,$$

and

$$w(n, n - e_j + e_k) = \lambda_{jk} n_j.$$

One interpretation of this model is the description of shoppers among the stalls in an open-air market in a city. There are K stalls in total and n_j is the number of customers (or queue size) at stall j. This is an open model in the sense that agents may visit stall k from outside the market, i.e., arrive at the market with the rate ν_k, and may go home with rate $\mu_j / (\mu_j + \sum_k \lambda_{jk})$. Agents may also leave stall j to go to stall k without leaving the market. The transition rates in this model are either constant or linear in n_j, and do not depend on n_k. Later we describe more general forms in which the transition from j to k depends nonlinearly on both n_j and n_k.

This model has been discussed by Kelly (1979, Chapter 2). First, we note the unique existence of a set of positive numbers α_k, $k = 1, 2, \ldots, K$, to solve

$$\alpha_k \left(\mu_k + \sum_m \lambda_{km} \right) = \nu_k + \sum_m \alpha_m \lambda_{mk}.$$

In equilibrium $n_1, n_2, \ldots, n_K$ are independent with

$$\pi_i(n_i) = e^{-\alpha_i} \frac{\alpha_i^{n_i}}{n_i!},$$

for $i = 1, 2, \ldots, K$.

This can be verified by substitution to establish that partial balance equations are satisfied:

$$\pi(n)\{w(n, n - e_j) + \sum_k w(n, n - e_j + e_k)\}$$

$$= \pi(n - e_j)w(n - e_j, n) + \sum_k \pi(n - e_j + e_k) \times w(n - e_j + e_k, n),$$

$$j = 1, 2, \ldots, K,$$

and

$$\pi(n) \sum_k w(n, n + e_k) = \sum_k \pi(n + e_k) w(n + e_k, n).$$

For the process to be reversible, the detailed balance condition must be satisfied, i.e.,

$$\alpha_j \lambda_{jk} = \alpha_k \lambda_{kj},$$

and

$$\alpha_j \mu_j = \nu_j,$$

for $j = 1, 2, \ldots, K$.

4.5.3   Open air market linear model II

Now we keep the total number of shoppers in the market fixed at N by ruling out entry and departure, but allow the transition rate to depend on the destination state as

$$w(n, n - e_j + e_k) = \lambda_{jk} \phi(n_j) \psi(n_k).$$

For a simpler model we still assume linear functions

$$\phi_j(n) = d_j n,$$

and

$$\psi_k(n) = a_k + c_k n,$$

where the coefficients are all positive. We assume that the ratios

$$\frac{a_j}{c_j} = f,$$

and

$$\frac{c_j}{d_j} = g$$

are the same for all $j = 1, 2, \ldots K$ to obtain simple closed form expression for the equilibrium distribution.

We assume that the process is reversible, i.e., there exist positive constants, $\alpha_1, \alpha_2, \ldots, \alpha_K$ satisfying

$$\alpha_j \lambda_{jk} = \alpha_k \lambda_{kj}.$$

It is straightforward to verify that the detailed balance conditions are met with $n_j, j = 1, 2, \ldots, K$ in equilibrium being independent with a negative binomial distribution

$$\pi(n_j) = \binom{f + n_j - 1}{n_j} (1 - g)^f g^{n_j}.$$

The joint density expression is then

$$\pi(n_1, n_2, \ldots, n_K) = \binom{-Kf}{N}^{-1} \prod_j \binom{-f}{n_j}.$$

To be more specific suppose

$$w(n, n - e_j + e_k) = \mu \frac{n_j}{N} \frac{n_k(1 - u) + (N - n_k - 1)u/(K - 1)}{N - 1}.$$

This means that an agent change his mind at rate μ about which stall to visit, i.e., his type changes randomly. Call him A for convenience of reference. A's new type is determined as follows. Among the remaining $N - 1$ agents one of the agent is chosen at random, call him B, and with probability $1 - u$ B's type is the one into which A changes. With probability u A's new type is any one of the other $K - 1$ types, excluding the type of B.

This transition rate is linear, and of the type discussed above with

$$f = \frac{(N - 1)u}{K(1 - u) - 1}.$$

We consider a model in which K is large, and N is also large.

In this situation, it is better to count the number of agents slightly differently. We count the number of stalls with exactly j customers and denote it by β_j, $j = 1, 2, \ldots, K$. Some or most of β's may be zero. By construction we have

$$\sum_{j=1}^{N} \beta_j = K,$$

and

$$\sum_{j=1}^{N} j\beta_j = N.$$

The collection of $\beta's$ describes a pattern of partition of N shoppers among K stalls, and is called random partition by Kingman (1978b). This way of counting is standard in dealing with partitions of a set, and is used also by Hill (1970), Kelly (1979), Watterson (1974) and many others.

Recounting the product in $\pi(n)$ we can write it as the distribution for the β's

$$\frac{K!}{\beta_1!\beta_2!\cdots\beta_N!}\left(\frac{-Kf}{N}\right)^{-1}\prod_{j=1}^{N}\left(\frac{-f}{j}\right)^{\beta_j}.$$

Now, if you let K goes to infinity with u held fixed, then

$$Kf \rightarrow \frac{(N-1)u}{1-u} = \theta,$$

and the equilibrium distribution goes to

$$\pi(\beta) = \left(\frac{\theta+N-1}{N}\right)^{-1}\prod_{j=1}^{N}\left(\frac{\theta}{j}\right)^{\beta_j}\frac{1}{\beta_j!}.$$

See Kelly (1979, p. 148). This formula is known as the Ewens sampling formula. See Ewens (1990).

4.5.4   Nonlinear birth-and-death models

In the next two models transition rates depend on the total population size as well. Suppose that birth and death transition rates are specified by

$$w(n, n+e_j) = g_j(N)\psi_j(n_j),$$

and

$$w(n, n-e_k) = h_k(N)\phi_k(n_k),$$

respectively, where $N = \sum_j n_j$, and where e_j is the d-dimensional vector with 1 in the jth position as the only nonzero elements.[14]
 We verify that the transition rates specified above satisfy the Kolmogorov criterion for the detailed balance[15] by examining the path $n \rightarrow n+e_j \rightarrow n+e_j-e_k \rightarrow n-e_k \rightarrow n$. Along this path, a birth to the jth component occurs first, followed by a death at the kth component, and a death at the jth component. When the appropriate product expressions of the transition rates are compared, we immediately see that the criterion is satisfied; hence, the detailed balance condition holds, that is, there exists a collection of positive numbers $\{\pi(n)\}$, which is the equilibrium distribution of the process:

$$\pi(n)w(n, n+e_j) = \pi(n+e_j)w(n+e_j, n).$$

[14] This example is adapted from Pollett (1986).
[15] See Kelly (1979, p. 21).

By substituting in the expression for the transition rates, we obtain

$$\frac{\pi(n + e_j)}{\pi(n)} = \frac{g_j(N)\psi_j(n_j)}{h_j(N + 1)\phi_j(n_j + 1)}.$$

We can then guess the correct equilibrium distribution to be given by

$$\pi(n) = \prod_{j=1}^{d} \pi_j(n),$$

where

$$\pi_j(n) = \prod_{r=1}^{N} \frac{g_j(r - 1)}{h_j(r)} \prod_{r=1}^{n_j} \frac{\psi_j(r - 1)}{\phi_j(r)}.$$

The equilibrium distribution is the product over the components, that is, each n_j is independently distributed.

We can complicate the previous example by assuming that a death of a component triggers a birth at another component, or an individual agent changes his or her position, choice, or type as the case may be, which is represented by a change of the jth and kth components, which can be expressed as

$$T_{j,k}n = n - e_j + e_k,$$

for $j, k \in S$, where $T_{j,k}$ is defined by this equality.

We verify that the Kolmogorov criteria are met for the transition rate

$$w(n, T_{j,k}n) = \lambda_{j,k}\phi_j(n_j)\psi_k(n_k),$$

where parameter $\lambda_{j,k}$ is a measure of proximity of categories j and k, by examining the paths connecting n to $T_{j,k}n$, then $T_{l,m}n$, $T_{k,j}n$ and returning to n. The detailed balance condition is then given by

$$\pi(n)w(n, T_{j,k}n) = \pi(T_{j,k}n)w(T_{j,k}n, n).$$

We next guess the form of the equilibrium distribution to be

$$\pi(n) = \prod_{j} \pi_j(n),$$

where

$$\pi_j(n) = \alpha_j^{n_j} \prod_{r=1}^{n_j} \frac{\psi_j(r - 1)}{\phi_j(r)},$$

and where α_j satisfies

$$\alpha_j \lambda_{j,k} = \alpha_k \lambda_{k,j}.$$

We can add features to this model, such as dependence on the total numbers of agents, or open the model by allowing entry and exit as in models in Section 4.5.5. This type of entry and exit can be combined with the entry and exit models in the economic literature to reformulate the existing entry and exit models in a more proper stochastic setting. We have more to say on this later in Chapter 5.

4.5.5   Birth-and-death processes for partition patterns

In all the models we discussed so far births and deaths are for agents of particular types or categories. We follow Kelly (1976) to discuss births and deaths of partition patterns $\{\beta\}$. Given a pattern of how N agents are distributed or partitioned among types or classes, we define $B_j\beta$ to indicate that one of the types with j agents now has one more agent. This causes β_j to decrease by one and β_{j+1} to increase by one. Similarly we use $D_j\beta$ to indicate a transition in which β_j decreases by one and β_{j-1} increases by one. This is caused by one agent in a class with j agents leaving the class. When one agent enters the system as a singleton, β_1 increases by one. This is denoted by $B_0\beta$. When a singleton agent leaves the model, then β_1 is reduced by one. This transition is denoted by $D_0\beta$.

The transition rates are defined by

$$q(\beta, B_0\beta) = w(\beta, \beta + e_1) = v\lambda(N),$$
$$q(\beta, B_j\beta) = w(\beta, \beta - e_j + e_{j+1}) = j\beta_j\lambda(N),$$

and

$$q(\beta, D_j\beta) = w(\beta, \beta + e_{j-1} - e_j) = j\beta_j\mu(N),$$

where $e_0 = 0$.

The total population size is also a Markov process with transition rates

$$w(N, N+1) = (v+N)\lambda(N),$$

and

$$w(N, N-1) = Nv(N).$$

The equilibrium distribution is

$$\pi(N) = B\binom{v+N-1}{N}\prod_{r=1}^{N}\frac{\lambda(r-1)}{\mu(r)},$$

where the normalizing constant B is assumed to be finite.

We use the identity noted in Kelly (1976)

$$(1-x)^{-v} = \prod_{j=1}^{\infty}\exp\left(\frac{vx^j}{j}\right),$$

and compare the coefficients of x^N to derive the expression

$$\binom{\nu + N - 1}{N} = \sum_{\sum j\beta_j = N} \prod_{j=1}^{\infty} \left(\frac{\nu}{j}\right)^{\beta_j} \frac{1}{\beta_j!}.$$

The equilibrium distribution for the partition pattern is then given by

$$\pi(\beta) = B \prod_{j=1}^{\infty} \left(\frac{\nu}{j}\right)^{\beta_j} \frac{1}{\beta_j!} \prod_{r=1}^{N} \frac{\lambda(r-1)}{\mu(r)}.$$

By allowing the birth rates to become near zero (small positive ϵ when the population size becomes larger than $M + 1$ for some positive integer M, and letting the death rates to become large when the population size becomes larger than $M + 1$, while maintaing ϵ death rates below the population size M, Kelly shows that the above distribution converges to that given by Ewens as μ becomes large.

4.6   Discrete adjustment behavior

This section describes additional models with a large number of microeconomic units, each of which uses a state-dependent discrete adjustment rule. To them, we apply some of the tools that were introduced earlier in this book. One of the models is similar to that of Caballero (1992) which we outline below. As mentioned at the beginning of this chapter, the main idea of this section is to model adjustment processes of agents as jump Markov processes.

Once we realize that a large collection of microeconomic units, each with a finite choice set or a finite state space, can be modeled thusly, we can apply the resuts of the previous sections and derive aggregate dynamics, that is, the dynamics for the collection. Furthermore, not only the equilibrium behavior but various transient behavior can be analyzed by applying the large-deviation theory of Chapter 3 or, as we do in Chapter 5, by directly analyzing the details of dynamics out of equilibria. Moreover, we can apply Sanov's theorem or the conditional-limit theorem to gain information on the distributions of micro-agents, given some signals on macroeconomic, (aggregate) variables.

There have been several earlier attempts in the economic literature to model a collection of microeconomic agents who make discontinous adjustments in response to changes in their microeconomic states. To quote Caballero and Engel (1992), "There has been a surge in the application of formal microeconomic models of discontinous and lumpy adjustment." They list cash balances, labor demand, investment, entry and exit, prices, durable goods, and technological upgrades as possible applications. They proceed then to attempt to model aggregate economic phenomena based on these models of microagent behavior.

See also Caplin and Leahy (1991, 1995) and references in these two papers for further examples and motivation. Clearly, discrete actions are not limited to inventory holdings of finished goods. Other examples are models of price changes in the presence of so-called menu cost (real resource cost in adjusting nominal prices), and models of durable-goods purchases by consumers, where the ratio of values of durable goods over wealth is the variable that measures the gap between the actual and desired holdings of durable goods. More examples are mentioned at the beginning of Chapter 5.

Dynamics discussed in these seminal attempts were rather specialized and did not use jump Markov processes as vehicles to describe dynamics. These attempts are unsatisfactory in other aspects as well. For example, Caballero and Engel (1992) examined the effects of idiosyncratic shocks and aggregate shocks, but they did not discuss the possibility that some of the aggregate shocks may result from aggregating individual idiosyncratic shocks. Similar remarks can be made about Caplin and Leahy and others in this literature. See our use of Sanov's theorem in this context in Section 4.6.3.

Interactions among microeconomic units were also ignored. The main draw-back of the analysis of this chapter is also that interactions among agents are not adequately treated. We must wait until Chapter 5 for more satisfactory analysis of agent interactions or externalities among agents.

In Section 4.6.1, we reformulate Caballero (1992) who describes firms' behavior of hiring or firing employees as gaps between the desired and actual numbers of workers go above or below desired thresholds. When the gap goes above the firing threshold in response to a bad shock, a firm fires a predeter-mined number of workers, whereas a firm hires another predetermined number of workers when the gap goes below the hiring threshold in response to a good shock. Consider then, a collection of microeconomic agents who have a finite-choice set, say binary. By nature, adjustment processes can be discrete because indivisible variables are involved, or a suitable quantization of deviational variables can make them so. Agents in certain states may always take cer-tain actions or some exogenous signals may trigger specific actions by agents when they are in certain states.[16] In the example that we describe below, the binary decisions are to hire a fixed number of workers or to fire another fixed number of workers when the shortage or excess of workers over some desired numbers of workers triggers job-creation or job-destruction actions by firms. In this example, the magnitude of gaps between the number of workers from the ideal or desired level can be modeled as a finite-state Markov chain or pro-cesses, or can be so embedded. See Parzen (1962) or Cox and Miller (1965) on embedded Markov chains, mentioned in Footnote 4.17.

---

[16] In other words, agents are modeled as cellular automata.

4.6.1   Example of employment adjustment processes I

This example is suggested by Caballero (1992). It is an analysis of firms' hiring and firing decisions that are not continuously carried out, but are enacted only when they experience excess or shortage of employees beyond some preset threshold values. These firms, therefore, have finite-choice sets. Caballero uses a discrete-time framework, which is not really necessary. We can allow the interarrival times of shocks or times between jumps from state to state to be exponentially distributed.[17] We first follow the discrete time description of Caballero to describe the model, and then switch to the description and analysis of the jump Markov process.

The model involves a stochastic process of desired level of employment, which evolves with time according to

$$L_{i,t+1}^* = L_{i,t}^* + l_{i,t}^*,$$

where the adjustment $l_{i,t}^*$ is assumed to be independent and identically distributed and takes on values of ± 1 with probability λ for the increase and $1 - \lambda$ for the decrease in the desired level of employment, in response to a good and bad shock, respectively.

Associated with this is the process of the actual level denoted by $L_{i,t}$, and the gap between the actual and desired level of employment

$$D_{i,t} = L_{i,t} - L_{i,t}^*.$$

It is convenient to define a process $\{\hat{D}_{i,t}\}$ that is the level of gap without personnel action, that is,

$$\hat{D}_{i,t+1} = L_{i,t} - L_{i,t+1}^* = D_{i,t} - l_{i,t}^*.$$

When $\hat{D}_{i,t+1}$ exceeds the job destruction threshold, a predetermined number, F, of people are fired by firm i. When this level falls below the job creation threshold, H number of people are hired, and hence $L_{i,t+1} = L_{i,t} + l_{i,t}$, where $l_{i,t}$ is either $-F$ or H, and

$$D_{i,t+1} = \hat{D}_{i,t+1} + l_{i,t},$$

where $l_{i,t}$ is the personnel action of firm i at time t.[18] Our interest lies in demonstrating a new way to examine the average behavior of a large collection

---

[17] When interarrival times are not exponential, we have non-Markovian processes. They can be rendered Markovian in several ways, as discussed in Cox and Miller (1965, p. 256). See Section 4.7.1 for discussion of one such device.

[18] One of the points made by Caballero is that asymmetrical adjustment by firms does not imply asymmetrical adjustment on the aggregate level. Although this aspect is an important point in his paper, it is not the focus here.

of firms, each with the same rule but possibly subject to idiosyncratic shocks. We just take $H = 1$ and $F = 2$, and set the job destruction threshold at 1 and the job creation threshold at 0.

For example, with $D_{i,t} = 0$, the probability is λ that $\hat{D}_{i,t+1}$ goes below 0, triggering a hiring, since a good shock that increases the desired level of employment occurs with this probability. When $D_{i,t}$ is 1, $\hat{D}_{i,t+1}$ goes above the job destruction threshold with probability $1 - \lambda$. When this happens, $\hat{D}$ is 2, but two people are fired and D is brought down to 0. The process $\{D_{i,t}\}$ is a discrete-time two-state Markov chain.[19] When a firm is in state 0 (D is zero), it hires workers when it is hit with a good shock. When the firm is in state 1 (D is one), it fires workers when is hit by a bad shock. The transition matrix of states of a single firm is

$$W = \begin{bmatrix} \lambda & 1 - \lambda \\ 1 & 0 \end{bmatrix},$$

where the first component refers to state 0. The vector of equilibrium probabilities $p_e = [p_e(0), p_e(1)]$ satisfies

$$p_e = p_e W,$$

which has one independent equation:

$$p_e(0) = \lambda p_e(0) + p_e(1).$$

The equilibrium probabilities are determined by the normalization condition that the probabilities sum to one. We can impose a condition that the average number of employees remains the same per firm, which is $F p_e(1)(1 - \lambda) = H p_e(0)\lambda$. This determines λ, which keeps average employment constant. We can introduce as many states as we wish by changing the threshold levels and H and F suitably. In this example, the equilibrium probability of hiring is $\lambda p_e(0)$ and that of firing is $(1 - \lambda) p_e(1)$. The expected number of people hired is $\lambda p_e(0)$, and that of people fired is $2(1 - \lambda) p_e(1)$.

To keep the average level of employment constant, these two numbers must be equal to each other or, substituting out the probabilities, we note that λ must be a positive number between 0 and 1 which satisfies $\lambda = 2(1 - \lambda)^2$, that is, $\lambda = 1/2$.

It is more instructive to examine the behavior of $\hat{D}_{it}$ for fixed i. We drop subscripts from now on. As soon as state $\hat{D} = -1$ is reached, the state returns

---

[19] This process is discrete-time if the adjustment process $\{l_{i,t}^*\}$ is discrete. By making the timing of the adjustment processes exponentially distributed, we will get a continous-time Markovian process. Alternatively, we can imbed the process to produce Markov chains. See Cox and Miller (1965, p. 88), or Parzen (1962, p. 190).

immediately to $\hat{D} = 0$ with probability 1. Similarly, from $\hat{D} = 2$, the state returns to $\hat{D} = 0$ with probability 1. The transition matrix $\hat{W}$ is given, after arranging states from $-1, 0, 1$, and 2 in that order, by

$$
\hat{W} = \begin{bmatrix} 0 & 1 & 0 & 0 \\ \lambda & 0 & 1-\lambda & 0 \\ 0 & \lambda & 0 & 1-\lambda \\ 0 & 1 & 0 & 0 \end{bmatrix}.
$$

We see that matrix W is a submatrix of this matrix $\hat{W}$.

A slightly more complicated example obtains when the job-creation trigger level is changed to -2 rather than 0, while keeping everything else the same. Now, $\{D_{it}\}$ for any i is a four-state Markov chain, with the state being $\{-2, -1, 0, 1\}$. Again, with $\lambda = 1/2$, the expected number of people hired and fired in the equilibrium process is the same, and the expected number of employees in the model remains constant.

To avoid having equal probability for good and bad shocks, Caballero (1992) assumes that the economy as a whole can be in a good state with probability q, and in a bad state with probability $1 - q$. In good times, good shocks occur with probability λ_g; in bad times, good shocks occur with probability λ_b. A constant level of total employment can be maintained by imposing

$$
q\lambda_g + (1 - q)\lambda_b = 1/2,
$$

that is, by assuming that $\lambda_g = (1 - 1/q)\,\lambda_b + 1/2q$.

The above is a description of a single firm in isolation. If all the firms are independent, with the same probability distributions of desired levels of employment and the trigger levels, then Caballero invokes the Glivenko–Cantelli theorem (Loève 1963, p. 391; Chow and Teicher 1988, p. 266) that the fraction of firms at the upper threshold of job destruction and the fraction of firms at the lower threshold of job creation are the same as the single firm's equilibrium distribution. Firms are assumed to be independent, that is, interactions are not treated.

We can treat a collection of a finite number N of interacting firms explicitly as a special case of jump Markov processes, that is, as a birth-and-death process; see Chapter 5 for details. Not only can we derive the aggregate behavior as the number of firms goes to infinity, we can derive other interesting results such as the average span for industrywide unemployment levels to reach specified levels that cannot be deduced from the Glivenko–Cantelli theorem. Furthermore, by making the transition rates of jump Markov processes suitably nonlinear in the fraction of firms in state 0, for example, we can introduce externality between firms' personnel actions. However, we just discuss the simple birth-and-death example here. A more complicated example is found in Chapter 5.

4.6.2 Example of employment adjustment processes II

We add a little more microeconomic detail to our discussion of the employment adjustment processes of Section 4.6.1 by adding a firm's production function and demand for its goods. Our model is similar to that of Dixit and Stiglitz (1977) or Blanchard and Kiyotaki (1986).[20]

Firm i has the production function in terms of the logarithms of the number of workers (l_{it}), of output (y_{it}), of the number of hours per worker (h_{it}), and of productivity level (u_{it}):

$$y_{it} = a\, l_{it} + b\, h_{it} + u_{it}.$$

Demand is given by

$$p_{it} = -\frac{1}{\eta} y_{it} + v_{it},$$

where p_{it} is the logarithm of the price, η is the price elasticity of output, and v_{it} is the demand shock. Firms are competitive in the labor market, but face a wage curve that is a function of the averge number of hours worked in this industry:

$$w_{it} = g(h_t) + w_t,$$

where h_t is the average number of hours worked, and w_t is the aggregate labor-market shock.

Ideally, firms would like to react to exogenous shocks as if they are known and as if they do not face any adjustment cost. If firms do not face any adjustment cost, then they would keep the same hours per worker and adjust the number of workers each period to maximize one period's net revenue. The result is a linear relation between Δl_{it}^* and Δu_{it}, Δv_{it}, and Δw_t.

Actually, firms face adjustment costs and adjust the number of hours worked as well as the number of workers. Thus, we postulate that

$$\Delta l_{it}^* = \Delta l_{it} + \theta \Delta h_{it},$$

that is, the gap between the actual and desired number of workers is covered by changing the hours worked. Summing this relation over all firms, we have the aggregate relation

$$\Delta L_t^* = \Delta L_t + \theta \Delta H_t,$$

where from the production function

$$\Delta Y_t = a \Delta L_t + b \Delta H_t,$$

---

[20] See also Aoki and Miyahara (1993). Hiring and firing actions of a group of firms in the latter model can be turned into the birth-and-death process of Chapter 5.

on the assumption that the sum of productivity shocks averages out to zero. These two equations can be used to express ΔL_t^* in terms of ΔY_t and ΔH_t.

4.6.3   Example of inferring microstate distribution

We go further with the lumpy adjustment model and apply the conditional-limit theory to infer the behavior of deviations, given the average deviations of the industry, or the aggregate number of people hired and fired in the industry as a whole. This is an improvement on the analysis by Caballero (1992).

We now assume that desired changes in employment are of the form $l_{it}^* = \pm 1$ with probability p, and they equal zero with probability $1 - 2p$, where $p \leq 1/2$.[21] The deviational variable $D_{i,t}$ is described by a two-state Markov chain. We call the state 1 when it is zero; a level below that triggers job-creation action, and one person is hired. State 2 is when D is at one; the upper, or job-destruction, level. Two people are fired when D goes above this level. The variable D_{it} for any i is a Markov chain variable with the transition matrix $[W_{11} = 1 - p, W_{12} = p, W_{21} = 2p, W_{22} = 1 - 2p]$. The equilibrium probabilities are $P_e(1) = 2/3$ and $P_e(2) = 1/3$. At equilibrium, the expected number of people hired is $P_e(1)$ and the number fired is $2P_e(2)$, which are equal to each other.

Suppose now that we have an aggregate signal that is the average number of people hired, that is,

$$\frac{1}{n} \sum_{t=1}^{n} \chi_1(s_t),$$

where χ_1 is the indicator function that is one when s_t is one (i.e, when the deviation $D_{i,t}$ is 0). Here, we keep i fixed. Later we assume that the average over time is approximately equal to the average over the agents i for a fixed t. To avoid results that depend on the initial distribution, we can think of time as being measured after a sufficient time has elapsed from the initial time.

We construct W_β with the entries in the second column modified from those of $W : W_\beta(1, 2) = pe^\beta$, and $W_\beta(2, 2) = (1 - 2p)e^\beta$, for some parameter β to be determined later. The entries in the first column remain the same as in W. We denote its largest eigenvalue by λ_β,

$$\lambda_\beta = (1/2)[1 - p + (1 - 2p)e^\beta] + R,$$

with

$$R = \{[1 - p - (1 - 2p)e^\beta]^2 + 8p^2 e^\beta\}^{1/2}.$$

---

[21] We could assume that $l^* = 1$ with probability p, $l^* = -1$ with probability q, and $l^* = 0$ with probability $1 - p - q$. However, to keep the expected level of employment constant, it is necessary to assume that $p = q$.

We let $l_\beta = [l_\beta(1), l_\beta(2)]$ be the left eigenvector of W_β, and r_β be its right eigenvector, made unique by the normalization condition that their inner product equals one. We can construct the following:

$$p^*(i, j) = \frac{1}{\lambda_\beta} l_\beta(i) W_\beta(i, j) r_\beta(j),$$

for $i, j = 1, 2$.

The marginal distribution is calculated as

$$\bar{p}(1) = p^*(1, 1) + p^*(1, 2) = 2p^2 e^\beta / \{2p^2 e^\beta + [\lambda_\beta - (1 - p)]^2\}.$$

Suppose now that the observed average is α. We choose the parameter β to make this marginal probability equal to α.

For example, if we observe that $\alpha = 0.5$, then we have

$$e^\beta = \frac{1 - p}{1 - 2p}.$$

This can be rewritten as

$$p^*(1 \mid 1) = p^*(1, 1) / \bar{p}(1) = \frac{W_\beta(1, 1) r_\beta(1)}{W_\beta(1, 1) r_\beta(1) + W_\beta(1, 2) r_\beta(2)} = (1 - p) / \lambda_\beta,$$

where $\lambda_\beta = 1 - p + p\sqrt{2(1 - p)/(1 - 2p)}$. Similarly, we have

$$p^*(1 \mid 2) = 2p \frac{1}{2p + \sqrt{2(1 - p)(1 - 2p)}}.$$

The other two conditional densities can be calculated similarly.

The conditional-limit theorem states that the conditional probabilities converge in probability to p^*. Continuing the example then, suppose that $p = 0.4$. Then, we have $W(1, 1) = 0.6$, but $p^*(1 \mid 1) = 0.38$ and $p^*(1 \mid 2) = 0.62$, while $W(2, 1) = 0.8$.

4.7   Generalizations

We note that the preceeding development fails to consider interactions among agents. Agents are distributed in the same way that individual states of an agent are distributed, that is, the fraction of agents in various states is the empirical distribution of this example and it converges to the one dictated by the conditional-limit theorem.

It is more satisfactory if we model interactions among firms more directly. We can consider transition rates, that is, probabilities over a small time interval for the fractions of firms in state 1 to move to state 2 and make it a function of the fractions of firms in states 1 and 2, and so on. This is exactly the way that we model stochastic and dynamic interactions among agents in Chapter 5.

4.7.1   Hazard functions: Age-specific transition rates

Markovian processes are useful to us precisely because probability distributions at different time epochs can be linked by means of transition probabilities or transition rates that are specified fairly directly by modelers. There are several examples of this in Chapter 5. In general, behavior of microeconomic units is simpler to specify than working out the consequences on macroeconomic variables. If specifying these transition probabilities or rates is as complicated as solving the interacting stochastic process as a whole, then our approach that builds up macroeconomic description in terms of specifications of microeconomic units is no longer attractive. This kind of difficulty may be encountered when holding, or sojourn, times of Markov chains are not exponentially distributed. One simple illustration is provided by Cox and Miller (1965, Sec. 6.1), which follows.

Suppose that there are three states $S = \{0, 1, 2\}$, and $X_0 = 0$. The state variable changes into state 1 at $t = T_0$. The state remains at 1 until it reaches state 2 at time $t = T_0 + T_1$, where T_0 and T_1 are independent positive-valued random variables. The holding time of state 0, T_0, is exponentially distributed with mean α. Thus,

$$Pr(X_{t+\Delta t} = 0 \mid X_0 = 0) = (1 - \alpha \Delta t)Pr(X_t = 0 \mid X_0 = 0).$$

Suppose that the holding time in state 1, T_1, has density $\psi(\tau)$ which is not necessarily exponential. We introduce the age- or time-specific transition rate for the event that, conditional on $T_1 > \tau$, is between τ and $\tau + \Delta \tau$, which is given by

$$r(\tau) = \psi(\tau)/\Psi(\tau),$$

where

$$\Psi(\tau) = [1 - Pr(T_1 \leq \tau)] = \int_\tau^\infty \psi(u)\, du,$$

that is,

$$r(t) = -\frac{1}{\Psi(t)}\frac{d\Psi(t)}{dt}.$$

Integrating this, we obtain

$$\Psi(\tau) = \exp\left[-\int_0^\tau r(t)dt\right].$$

If ψ is exponential, then $r(t)$ is constant. In this case, then,

$$Pr(T_1 \geq t + s \mid T_1 \geq s) = \frac{\Psi(t+s)}{\Psi(s)} = \frac{e^{-\lambda(t+s)}}{e^{-\lambda s}} = e^{\lambda t},$$

that is, this conditional probability is independent of the time duration that the system has spent in state 1. Otherwise, it depends on this time.

To evaluate the transition probability

$$P(X_{t+\Delta t} = 1 \mid X_t = 1)$$

with a non-exponential holding-time probability density then, we need to know the time already spent in state 1. We augment the state by this time and use an augmented state $(1, \tau)$, and we consider a related probability that the system is still in state 1 when it was entered in the time interval $I = (t - \tau - \Delta \tau, t - \tau)$. We define

$$w(\tau; t) = \lim_{\Delta \tau \to 0+} \frac{Pr(X_t = 1, X_s = 1, \; s \in I, X_u = 0, u \le t - \tau - \Delta \tau)}{\Delta \tau}.$$

This is the probability that state 1 is still occupied at time t, when it was entered in I. For positive τ, we have

$$w(\tau + \Delta \tau; t + \Delta t) = w(\tau; t)[1 - r(\tau)\Delta \tau] + o(\Delta \tau),$$

and

$$w(0; t + \Delta t) = P(X_t = 0 \mid X_0 = 0)\alpha \Delta t + o(\Delta t).$$

Then, the differential equation for $w(\tau; t)$ is given by

$$\partial w(\tau; t)/\partial \tau + \partial w(\tau; t)/\partial t = -r(\tau)w(\tau; t).$$

with the condition $w(0; t) = \alpha e^{-\alpha t}$.

This is so because the augmented state $(1, \tau)$ is such that state $(1, \tau + \Delta t)$ can be entered only from the state $(1, \tau)$ where τ is positive, and after leaving state 0, the system enters the state $(1, 0)$. State $(1, \tau)$ moves to state 2 where

$$P(X_{t+\Delta t} = 2 \mid X_0 = 0) = P(X_t = 2 \mid X_0 = 0)$$
$$+ \int_0^t w(\tau; t)r(t)d\tau \Delta t + o(\Delta t).$$

Next, we introduce an auxiliary function:

$$W(\tau; t) = w(\tau; t)e\left[\int_0^\tau \psi(u)\,du\right].$$

From the differential equation for w, we derive that

$$\partial W/\partial \tau = -\partial W/\partial t.$$

Namely $W(\tau; t) = W(t - \tau)$. The condition $w(0; t) = \alpha e^{-\alpha t}$ yields the result that

$$w(\tau; t) = \alpha e^{-\alpha(t-\tau)}\Psi(\tau),$$

and

$$P(X_t = 2 \mid X_0 = 0) = \int_0^t \alpha e^{-\alpha(t-u)}[1 - \Psi(u)]\,du.$$

In the above, the notion of age- or time-specific transition rate to a specific state naturally arose. In the reliability literature, this notion is called the hazard (or age- or time-specific, or failure- or death-rate) function.[22] Caballero and Engel (1992) also adapt the notion of hazard function in their modeling.

We let T be a random variable that may represent a lifetime of some item in one interpretation. The hazard function expresses the conditional probability approximately equal to $r(t)\Delta$ that, given that an item has survived up to time t, it will fail in the next Δ time duration. In this sense, $r(t)$ is the transition rate from the state of the item being in working order to that of the item having failed. In a more general context, transition to an absorbing state is at issue, and this rate may depend not only on time but also on the fraction of items that have failed so far, or it may be independent of time.

By appropriately reinterpreting the event failure, Caballero and Engel (1992) use this term by generalizing the function to depend on state, and not just on time. Apparently when they say that the hazard function is $\Lambda(z)$ where z is the gap between actual and ideal values of some choice variable of firms, they mean that only the fraction Λ of firms adjusts when the gap is z. This may create some confusion with the traditional sense of the hazard rate noted above.

[22] See for example, Tijms (1994, p. 352) or Davis (1993, p. 36).

CHAPTER 5

Modeling interactions II: Master equations and field effects

In Chapter 4, we introduced jump Markov processes to pave our way for modeling a large collection of interacting agents. We concentrate here on the types of interactions or externalities that do not lend themselves to modeling with pairwise interaction. We call these externalities "field effects." This term is chosen to convey the notion that interaction with a whole population or class of microeconomic units is involved, that is, aggregate (macroeconomic) effects are due to contributions from a whole population of microeconomic units, or, composition of the whole in the sense that fractions of units in various states or categories are involved. We defer until Chapter 6 our discussion of pairwise interaction or interactions with randomly matched (drawn) anonymous microeconomic units.

A good way to examine field effects – that is, stochastic and dynamic externality – is to study the dynamic behavior of a group of agents who interact through the choices they make in circumstances in which each agent has a set of finite decisions to choose from, and in which they may change their minds as time progresses, possibly at some cost. In such situations, an agent's choice is influenced by the vector of the fractions of agents who have selected the same decisions, because his or her perceived profit or benefit from a decision change will be a function of this vector, namely, the composition of agents with the same decisions in the whole population of agents.

In the economics literature, we find many examples of aggregate variables affecting microeconomic decisions, although they are not called field effects. For example, Becker (1990) examines an individual consumer's demand for some goods which depends on the demand of other customers, such as the demand for popular restaurant seats, theater tickets, and best sellers. What Becker calls the effects of social consumption is an example of what we call field effects; it is discussed further in Section 5.6. In the phenomena examined by Becker there is no reason to think of interactions among agents as pairwise interactions, anonymous or otherwise. Caballero and Lyons (1990, 1992) also discuss the effects of aggregate output on sectoral or other country outputs.

Becker (1974), Schelling (1978), Akerlof (1980), Friedman (1993), Friedman and Fung (1994), and Aoki (1995a) also present examples of field effects. It is interesting to read in Friedman (1991) that biologists used the term "playing the field" to indicate interactions with a whole population.[1]

Here, we present a general framework to model interacting agents in this sense, and we illustrate our procedure on nonlinear birth-and-death processes, which is an important subclass of jump Markov processes introduced in Chapter 4. Two aspects of our modeling approach merit brief mention here. One is the use of nonlinear or state-dependent transition rates to model interactions among agents. This aspect is an important extension or generalization of the types of analysis found in the literature on stochastic dynamic discrete-choice models, surveyed by Eckstein and Wolpin (1989), for example. We provide a way of modeling interactions without the curse of dimensionality associated with the dynamic programming approach commonly used in this literature.

The other is the use of a stochastic dynamic framework and its implication for analysis of models with multiple equilibria. Suppose that a deterministic dynamic macroeconomic model has multiple equilibria with well-defined basins of attraction for each locally stable equilibrium. One important and natural question about such a model is how the model can settle on an economically desirable equilibrium. Because of the deterministic formulation, the only way to reach the desired equilibrium is to be initially in the basin of attraction associated with that equilibrium. This is the issue of history versus perfect-foresight expectations addressed by Krugman (1991), for example. In the stochastic formulation in this chapter, we show that there are positive steady-state or stationary probabilities that the model state is in each basin, and that the state moves from one equilibrium to another with positive probabilities, and mean first-passage times between these equilibria, in principle, can be calculated. The essence of this situation has been captured by the example in Chapter 2 where the expected first-passage time from one equilibrium to another is shown to depend exponentially on the height of the barrier separating the two basins, even though the equilibrium probabilities are independent of the height.

The importance of and the need to cast choice or optimization problems of microeconomic units in a stochastic framework are hinted at in Chapter 4. Briefly, such reformulations involve three ingredients: spaces of states or strategies (decisions), which are called state spaces; transition rates, which specify rates of changes of probabilities of transitions from state to state; and the deterministic equations for the probabilities of states, called master equations.

---

[1] According to Friedman (1993), background environments and prevalence of alternative behavior traits or patterns in a population affect fitness of a particular biological trait or behavioral pattern in biological models.

Unlike the evolutionary game literature, however, it is not the strategy mixes themselves that evolve deterministically.[2] It is the probability distribution of the strategy mixes, not the strategy mixes themselves, that evolves deterministically. Because the states are discrete, we deal directly with sets of probabilities of the states, which we also call distributions. The so-called replicator dynamics in the literature of evolutionary games or the Malthusian dynamics of Friedman are replaced with the master equations. The fitness function of Friedman is replaced with transitions rates that contain some functions, like the fitness function, that affect the rates. When transition rates satisfy the detailed balance conditions, the equilibrium distributions exist in the form of the Gibbs distribution, as discussed by Kelly (1979). See our discussion in Chapters 3 and 4.

Our approach is easier to apply and generally more powerful in circumstances in which specifying transition rates is easier than specifying macroeconomic behavior for the whole. In the applications described in this chapter, the state space is discrete, or agents' choice sets are discrete, and the degree of knowledge of the system is such that the microeconomic states of the system are the vectors of the fractions of agents with the same decisions or microeconomic states, as the case may be. See the examples in Sections 4.5 and 4.6.

At whatever level of detail we wish to describe the stochastic dynamics, the master equation, which is a version of the backward Chapman–Kolmogorov equation, governs the time evolution of the probabilities of the states in the form of probability flows into and out of the states.[3]

This chapter begins with the derivation of the master equation for the state vector composed of the fractions described above and indicates how it is applied in subsequent sections.

5.1   Master equations

The dynamic behavior of a collection of microeconomic units is modeled as discrete-time or continuous-time Markov chains, that is, Markov processes with finite-state spaces. It is described by time evolution of the probabilities of states of Markov chains by accounting for probability flows into and out of (sets of) states. The equations that do this accounting of probabilities are called the Chapman–Kolmogorov equations in the stochastic processes literature (see, e.g., Whittle 1992, pp. 156, 175; or Karlin and Taylor 1981, p. 286). We use a version that is easier to interpret. They are called the master equations in the physics and mathematical sociology literatures, and we use the same name in

---

[2] See the survey of Friedman (1991).

[3] According to Cox and Miller (1965, p. 152), the general characteristic of a backward equation is that in any single equation, the same final state enters in all terms. Our usage of backward is consistent with their characterization. Also we refer the reader to Section 4.2 for an alternate explanation of the term "backward."

this book.[4] The master equations describe time evolution of probabilities of states of dynamic processes in terms of the probability transition rates and state occupancy probabilities. See Kelly (1979, p. 3) or Parzen (1962, Chap. 7) for example. In Weidlich and Haag (1983), we find examples of a birth-and-death stochastic process, which has a simple master equation, being adapted to model the diffusion of opinion or information such as brand choices of consumer goods or voting for political candidates among a population. Recent examples in which master equations are used in economic models are Kirman (1993), Weidlich (1994), and Aoki (1994, 1995a,b).

We let $x(t)$ be a state vector in a finite set S. The initial, condition, $x(0)$, and the state transition probabilities, $Pr[x(t) = s_t \mid x(t - \Delta t) = s_{t-\Delta t}]$, where Δt is the basic time increment and s_t is in S, completely characterize the time evolution of a discrete-time Markov chain. When we treat time as continuous, we write $Pr[x(t') = x']$ as $P(x', t')$. When state spaces are discrete, we have jump Markov processes.[5]

Changes in the conditional probabilities in the small time interval Δt are expressed as

$$P(x', t + \Delta t \mid x, t) - P(x', t \mid x, t) = w(x' \mid x, t)\Delta t + o(\Delta t).$$

Recall our discussion in Chapter 4 on the transition rates. There we conditioned probabilities on $X(0) = x$ and wrote $w_{xx'} = \dot{P}_{xx'}(0)$. Here, we use $w(x' \mid x, t)$ to denote $\dot{P}_{xx'}(t)$. Summing the above with respect to all x', we see that

$$\sum_{x'} w(x' \mid x, t) = 0,$$

that is,

$$w(x' \mid x', t) = -\sum_{x \neq x'} w(x \mid x', t). \tag{5.1}$$

Using the relation

$$P(x', t') = \sum_{x} P(x, t)P(x', t' \mid x, t),$$

we can express the changes in the probabilities as

$$P(x', t + \Delta t) = \sum_{x} P(x, t)P(x', t + \Delta t \mid x, t)$$

$$= \sum_{x} P(x, t)[P(x', t \mid x, t) + w(x' \mid x, t)\Delta t] + o(\Delta t)$$

$$= P(x', t) + \sum_{x} P(x, t)w(x' \mid x, t)\Delta t + o(\Delta t).$$

---

[4] There are many references on master equations; van Kampen (1992, p. 97) tells us the origin of the word "master." See also Kubo (1975) or Weidlich and Haag (1983).
[5] We exclude processes that pass through an infinite number of states in a finite time.

Rearranging the terms, and now treating time as continuous, we let Δt approach zero to see that this relation leads to the equation:

$$\partial P(x', t)/\partial t = \sum_x P(x, t)w(x' \mid x, t).$$

which is known as the master (the backward Chapman–Kolmogorov) equation. See Karlin and Taylor (1981, Chap. 14), for example, for the proof of the existence of the time derivative.

We write the sum of the right-hand side separately for state x' and the rest as

$$\sum_x P(x, t)w(x' \mid x, t) = \sum_{x \neq x'} P(x, t)w(x' \mid x, t) + P(x', t)w(x' \mid x', t),$$

and substitute Eq. (5.1) into $w(x' \mid x', t)$ to rewrite the master equation as

$$\partial P(x', t)/\partial t = \sum_{x \neq x'} P(x, t)w(x' \mid x, t) - \sum_{x \neq x'} P(x', t)w(x \mid x', t). \quad (5.2)$$

This is the usual form in which the master equation is stated. The first term is the sum of the probability flows into state x', and the second is the probability flow out of state x'. When the transition rates are independent of time, the processes are said to be time-homogenous. We discuss processes that are usually time-homogeneous, and so, we drop time arguments from transition rates from now on. In Section 4.7, transition rates are not time-homogeneous.

By setting the left-hand side of the master equation equal to zero, we obtain the condition for a stationary solution. We let $P_e(x)$ denote a stationary probability distribution. In the stationary state or in equilibrium, the probability in- and outflows balance at every state y, and the relation

$$\sum_{x \neq y} w(y \mid x)P_e(x) = \sum_{x \neq y} w(x \mid y)P_e(y)$$

holds for all y. This is the balance condition of probability flows, called the full balance equation (see Whittle 1985, or Kelly 1979, p. 5).

If the probability flows balance for every pair of states, then the equation

$$w(y \mid x)P_e(x) = w(x \mid y)P_e(y)$$

holds for all x and y. This is called the detailed balance condition. See Kelly (1979, Sec. 1.5) for Kolmogorov criteria for stationary Markov chains and processes to satisfy the detailed balance condition. He also shows that the

Kolmogorov criteria are necessary and sufficient for Markov chains or processes to be reversible.[6]

Given an irreducible Markov chain, for any state x_i there is a finite sequence of states that reaches it from some initial state, $x_0, x_1, \ldots, x_i$. If the detailed balance condition holds, we have

$$P_e(x_i) = P_e(x_0) \prod_{k=0}^{i-1} [w(x_{k+1} \mid x_k)/w(x_k \mid x_{k+1})]. \tag{5.3}$$

This probability distribution is a Gibbs distribution since we can express it as an exponential distribution

$$P_e(x) = \text{const } \exp[-U(x)],$$

with

$$U(x_i) - U(x_0) = -\sum \ln\left[\frac{w(x_{k+1} \mid x_k)}{w(x_k \mid x_{k+1})}\right], \tag{5.4}$$

where this expression is independent of paths from x_0 to x_i, because of the Kolmogorov criteria. Therefore $U(x)$ is a potential. Recall our discussion in Sections 3.3 and 3.8.

5.1.1   A collection of independent agents

We describe in this section a benchmark master equation for a system composed of a number of independent agents, each of whom is in one of finitely many microeconomic states. An agent's state evolves with time according to the master equation

$$dp_s/dt = \sum_{s'} (w_{s,s'} p_{s'} - w_{s's} p_s),$$

where $w_{s,s'}$ denotes the transition rates from state s to state s', and $p_s(t)$ is the probability at time t of the agent being in microeconomic state s. We drop the time argument when no confusion is likely.

When N such agents are in a system, the state of the whole system is determined by specifying the microeconomic state of each agent, $s = (s_1, s_2, \ldots, s_N)$. When all of these agents are independent, the probability $P(s)$ is the

---

[6] A stochastic process $X(t)$ is said to be reversible if $X(t_1), X(t_2), \ldots, X(t_n)$ has the same probability distribution as $X(\tau - t_1), X(\tau - t_2), \ldots, X(\tau - t_n)$ for all $t_1, t_2, \ldots, t_n$ and τ. The Kolmogorov criteria mean that, given a starting point, any path in the state space that ultimately returns to it must have the same probability when the path is traced in the reverse direction, in other words, a reversible Markov chain has no net circulation in the state space. See Kelly (1979, p. 25) for a simple necessary and sufficient condition for reversibility.

product

$$P(s) = \prod_{i=1}^{N} p_{s_i}.$$

In Sections 4.5.2 and 4.5.3, we describe collections of Markov processes that are reversible with respect to product-form invariant measures, and indicate how they can be used in modeling interacting microeconomic agents. By weakening the notion of reversibility to that of quasi-reversibility, which roughly corresponds to the notion of partial balance rather than detailed balance, certain interactions among agents can be allowed, as discussed by Pollett (1986).

When agents are exchangeable, one is interested in the occupancy number, $N_1, N_2, \ldots$, that is, the number of the agents in state 1, state 2, and so on. We denote the probability at time t by $P[\{N\}, t]$, where $\{N\}$ refers to $N_1, N_2, \ldots$.

The probability of a particular array of occupancy numbers is

$$P[\{N\}] = \sum p_{s_1} p_{s_2} \cdots p_{s_N},$$

where the summation is over all $s_1, s_2, \ldots, s_N$, which is consistent with the prescribed occupancy number. This probability changes whenever one of the agents changes his or her microeconomic state as in our discussion in Section 4.5.5. Since there are $N_{s'}$ agents in state s', the probability that one of them changes his or her microeconomic state in a small time interval Δt is $w_{s,s'} N_{s'} \Delta t$, since the probability of two or more agents changing their states is of $o(\Delta t)$. Hence, we have

$$dP[\{N\}, t]/dt = \sum_{s,s'} w_{s,s'} z_s^{-1} z_{s'} N_{s'} P[\{N\}, t],$$

where we use the notation $z_s f(s) = f(s+1)$, and its inverse $z_s^{-1} f(s) = f(s-1)$ for any $f(s)$. These notations correspond to those of the lead and lag operators used in the econometrics or time-series literature, and are used as a convenient shorthand. An alternative notation, $T_{j,k}(s_1, s_2, \ldots)$, is also used, as in Section 4.5, to decrease s_j by one and to increase s_k by one.

We let $p_{i,m}(t)$ be the probability of agent i at time t starting from the initial state m. Then, we have

$$P[\{N\}, t] = \frac{N!}{N_1! N_2! \cdots} [p_{1,m}(t)]^{N_1} [p_{2,m}(t)]^{N_2} \cdots.$$

This is the multivariate generalization of the binomial distribution. Recall our discussions of distinguished and nondistinguished agents in counting the configurations compatible with certain macroconditions in Chapters 2 and 3, and see our discussion on exchangeability in the Appendix.

If there is an ensemble of similar systems with N being a random variable from a Poisson distribution with mean $\langle N \rangle$, then the average of the distribution is

$$\langle P(|N|, t) \rangle = \sum_{N=0}^{\infty} \frac{\langle N \rangle^N}{N!} e^{-\langle N \rangle} P[\{N\}, t] = \prod_{i=1} \frac{\langle N_i \rangle}{N_i!} e^{-\langle N_i \rangle}.$$

5.2   Structure of transition rates

This section discusses homogeneity properties of transition rates in the master equations when state spaces are continuous.[7] In our modeling of a collection of N interacting microeconomic units, the variables that are most important in influencing dynamic macroeconomic properties of a model are often not the absolute numbers of agents who occupy particular sets of states of the model, but rather the proportions or fractions of units that are in these sets of states of a model,[8] and possibly N as an indicator of the scale or size of the model.

With a state variable $X(t)$, the probability distribution is governed by the master equation

$$\partial P(X, t)/\partial t = \int [w_N(X \mid X')P(X', t) - w_N(X' \mid X)P(X, t)] \, dX'$$

where we now indicate N explicitly as a subscript to the transition rates from X to X' as $w_N(X' \mid X)$.

We assume that $x(t) = X(t)/N$ behaves as an intensive variable, and that the transition rates depend on X and N through x, except possibly for a scale factor that may depend on N.[9]

We make one additional key assumption in that the change in the state variable, that is, $X' - X$, remains the same for different values of N. This assumption is certainly met in birth-and-death processes since jumps are restricted to be ± 1 from any state regardless of the total number N. This assumption actually is concerned with the scaling properties or homogeneity properties of the transition rates. Loosely put, it means that each of the N microeconomic units may contribute approximately equally to the transition events. (Later, we refine this and consider higher-order transition rates or multiple effects in the transition rates.) To make this explicit, we express the transition rate as a function of the

---

[7] Kurtz (1971, 1978), Kubo, Matsuo, and Kitahara (1973), and Kubo (1975) also note these properties.

[8] This fraction is an example of intensive variables.

[9] Since we keep N fixed in this section, this assumption is innocuous. A fixed function of N can be absorbed into time units as well. If we allow N to vary, there may be situations in which transition rates may depend on N, in addition to x. We can introduce a probability distribution for N and average over the results for fixed N to allow N to be variable. One such example is in Section 4.5.5.

starting state, X', and the jump (vector), $r = X - X'$ as

$$w_N(X \mid X') = w_N(X'; X - X') = w_N(X'; r),$$

and assume that

$$w_N(X'; r) = w_N[N(X'/N); r] = N\tilde{w}_N(X'/N; r) = N\Phi(x'; r),$$

for some function Φ, and where $x' = X'/N$. Using the same function, we can express the transition rate in the opposite direction as

$$w_N(X' \mid X) = N\Phi(x; -r).$$

A scaling property that is seemingly more general is

$$w_N(X'; r) = f(N)\Phi(x'; r),$$

for some positive function $f(N)$. Actually, this factor $f(N)$ can be arbitrary, since it can always be absorbed into the choice of time unit as noted in footnote 9.

More generally, the transition rates may take the form

$$w_N(X \mid X') = f(N)[\Phi_0(x'; r) + N^{-1}\Phi_1(x'; r) + N^{-2}\Phi_2(x'; r) + \cdots],$$

where higher-order terms in N^{-1} may represent higher-order interactions effects among microeconomic units beyond those captured by the leading term.

In terms of these transition rates, the master equation can be rewritten as

$$\frac{\partial P(X, t)}{\partial t}$$
$$= f(N) \int \left[\Phi_0\left(\frac{X - r}{N}; r\right) + N^{-1}\Phi_1\left(\frac{X - r}{N}; r\right) + \cdots \right] P(X - r, t)\, dr$$
$$- f(N) \int \left[\Phi_0\left(\frac{X}{N}; r\right) + N^{-1}\Phi_1\left(\frac{X}{N}; r\right) + \cdots \right] P(X, t)\, dr.$$

In Section 5.3, we discuss two methods for obtaining approximate solutions of this master equation.

5.3 Approximate solutions of the master equations

Only a special class of master equations admits closed-form analytical solutions. Notable among them are generalizations of birth-and-death processes, which are discrete-state Markov chains in which states are integer-valued and jumps are restricted to ± 1. We discuss some examples of this in Section 5.9. See also Aoki (1995b).

When we cannot solve the master equation explicitly, we can approximately solve it by expanding the solution in some parameter in the transition-rate expressions. The parameter should be such that it governs or influences the size of fluctuations of the probabilities by affecting the jumps. As the parameter value approaches a limit, the size of fluctuations should approach zero, so that this solution method produces a macroeconomic (aggregative) equation that is appropriate for a model with a large number of agents.

Here, we discuss two somewhat related methods for approximately solving the master equation. In Section 5.3.1, we describe the method used by van Kampen (1965, 1992). Then, in Section 5.3.2, we describe an alternative method from Kubo et al. (1973) and Kubo (1975).

5.3.1   Power-series expansion

Here, we expand the master equations in N^{-1} retaining terms only up to $O(N^{-1})$.[10] In some models, we anticipate that the probability density, the time evolution of which is governed by the master equation, will show a well-defined peak at some X of $O(N)$ and spread of $O(\sqrt{N})$, if the initial condition is

$$P(X, 0) = \delta(X - X_0).$$

In such cases we change the variable by introducing two variables ϕ and ξ, both of $O(1)$, and, recalling that $x(t) = X(t)/N$, set

$$x(t) = \phi(t) + N^{-1/2}\xi(t).$$

Later we show that ϕ is the mean of the distribution when this change of variable is applicable, that is, $\phi(t)$ keeps track of the mean of $x(t)$, and the spread about the mean is expressed by a random variable $\xi(t)$. This decomposition or representation is expected to work when the probability density has a well-defined peak, and it does, as we soon demonstrate.

We next show that the terms generated in the power-series expansion of the master equation separate into two parts. The first part, which is the largest in magnitude, is an ordinary differential equation for ϕ. This is interpreted as the macroeconomic or aggregate equation. The remaining part is a partial differential equation for ξ with coefficients that are functions of ϕ, the first term of which is known as the Fokker–Planck equation. See Sections 5.4 and 5.13.

Let us solve the master equation with the initial condition, $x(0) = \phi(0) = X_0/N$.[11]

---

[10] When these terms are zero, we may want to retain terms of $O(N^{-2})$. Then we have diffusion-equation approximations to the master equation. Diffusion approximations are discussed in Section 5.14.

[11] We need not be precise about the initial condition since an expression of $O(N^{-1})$ or $O(N^{-1/2})$ can be shifted between the two terms without any consequence. Put differently, the location of the peak of the distribution cannot be defined more precisely than the width of the distribution, which is of $O(N^{1/2})$.

We rewrite the probability density for ξ as

$$\Pi[\xi(t), t] = P[X(t), t],$$

by substituting $N\phi + N^{1/2}\xi$ into X.[12] In rewriting the master equation for Π, we must take the partial derivative with respect to time by keeping $x(t)$ fixed; that is, we must impose the relation

$$\frac{d\xi}{dt} = -N^{1/2}\frac{d\phi}{dt},$$

and we obtain

$$\frac{\partial P}{\partial t} = \frac{\partial \Pi}{\partial t} - \frac{\partial \Pi}{\partial \xi}\frac{d\xi}{dt} = \frac{\partial \Pi}{\partial t} - N^{1/2}\frac{d\phi}{dt}\frac{\partial \Pi}{\partial \xi}.$$

We also note that we need to rescale time by

$$\tau = N^{-1}f(N)t.$$

Otherwise, the random variable ξ will not be of $O(N^0)$, contrary to our assumption, and the power-series expansion will not be valid. But, we also assume $f(N) = N$ in this section. In general, it is the case that $\tau \neq t$. We use τ from now on to accommodate this more general scaling function.

The master equation in the new notation is given by

$$\frac{\partial \Pi(\xi, \tau)}{\partial \tau} - N^{1/2}\frac{d\phi}{d\tau}\frac{\partial \Pi}{\partial \xi}$$

$$= -N^{1/2}\frac{\partial}{\partial \xi}[\alpha_{1,0}(x)\Pi] + \frac{1}{2}\frac{\partial^2}{\partial \xi^2}[\alpha_{2,0}(x)\Pi]$$

$$- \frac{1}{3!}N^{-1/2}\frac{\partial^3}{\partial \xi^3}\left[\alpha_{3,0}(x)\Pi - N^{-1/2}\frac{\partial}{\partial \xi}\alpha_{1,1}(x)\Pi\right] + O(N^{-1}),$$

where $x = \phi(\tau) + N^{-1/2}\xi$, and where we define the moments of the transition rates by

$$\alpha_{\mu,\nu} = \int r^{\mu}\Phi_{\nu}(x; r)\, dr. \tag{5.5}$$

See van Kampen (1992, p. 253) for the terms not shown here.

In this expression we note that the dominant term $O(N^{1/2})$ on both sides is equated. In Section 5.4, we show $\alpha_{10}(\phi)$, the first moment of the leading term of the transition rate $w_N(X \mid X')$, to determine the macroeconomic equation.

---

[12] Following the common convention that the parameters of the density are not carried as arguments in the density expression, we do not explicitly show ϕ when the substitution is made.

Before we discuss the macroeconomic equation in Section 5.4, we describe an alternative method for solving the master equation approximately.

5.3.2   The method of Kubo[13]

Kubo et al. (1973), Kubo (1975), and Suzuki (1978) developed an alternative method to approximately solve the master equation. It involves an asymptotic expression for the probability density of an extensive macrovariable, X, of a large system composed of N microeconomic units, which is expressed as

$$P(X, t) = C e^{N\Psi(x,t)}, \quad x = X/N. \tag{5.6}$$

Although Kubo had physical variables in mind when he developed this asymptotic expression, the approximation can be applied equally well to a macroeconomic variable that depends on a collection of a large number of microeconomic variables, just as the master equations can be so reinterpreted.

To understand this expression heuristically, we can reason as follows: If X is the sum of N microeconomic variables that are normally distributed, and are not interacting, then the probability distribution is Gaussian with the variance proportional to N. So even when microeconomic variables interact, we can write a quadratic approximation of the density function about the most likely value denoted by X_e, as

$$\text{const} \exp[-(X - X_e)^2/2N\sigma^2] = \text{const} \exp[-N(x - x_e)^2/2\sigma^2],$$

where $x_e = X_e/N$, and σ^2 is the variance of X. Thus we expect the expression

$$P(X, t) = C e^{N\Psi(x,t)}$$

to hold, where $\Psi(x, t) \approx (1/N) \ln P(Nx, t)$.

Once we have such an expression, then the most probable value of X at time t is determined by maximizing the exponent of the density, and the most probable evolution of the macrovariable is along the path that maximizes the function Ψ. In general then, we look for an asymptotic evolution of a macrovariable around a deterministic path. An equation that generates this path can be taken as the macroscopic or macroeconomic equation of the model.[14] This approach is similar to the one described above, but details of the expansion differ.

---

[13] The reader is advised to skip this subsection on first reading not to interrupt the main flow of our arguments.

[14] Note the similarity of this path to the reference path in the variational analysis of nonlinear dynamics that produce log-linear models. These models are commonly used in macroeconomics that are variational dynamic models about the reference paths. See, for example, Aoki (1981, p. 14). Here we have fluctuation about the reference path because the model is stochastic.

In this subsection, we follow Kubo and first sketch the derivation of equations that govern fluctuations and decays of macrovariables to an equilibrium value. Then, we describe the behavior of these systems far from equilibria.

We start with the assumed form for the probability density of an extensive macroeconomic variable X of a Markovian system of size N (which is usually the number of agents in the model):

$$p(x, t) = C \exp[N \Psi(x, t)] + O(\epsilon),$$

where

$$p(x, t) = NP(X, t),$$

and we let $\epsilon = N^{-1}$. The constant C is $O(\epsilon^{-1/2})$.

Here, the transition rates are posited to be such that

$$w_N(X; r, t) = Nw(x, r, t).$$

Here, change in state $X' - X$ is denoted by r, and

$$w_N(X - r; r, t) = Nw(x - \epsilon r, r, t).$$

The master equation is rewritten then as

$$\epsilon \frac{\partial}{\partial t} p(x, t) = - \int w(x, r, t) p(x, t) \, dr$$
$$+ \int w(x - \epsilon r, r, t) p(x - \epsilon r, t) \, dr, \tag{5.7}$$

where

$$c_n(x, t) = \int r^n w(x, r, t) \, dr,$$

is the nth moment of the transition rate $w(x, r, t)$.[15] For simpler exposition, we drop the time argument from the transition rates from now on. The convergence of all moments and the formal expansion of the exponential function (known as the Kramers–Moyal expansion[16]) are assumed.

---

[15] Kubo et al. (1973) introduce

$$H(x, q, t) = \int dr (1 - e^{-rq}) w(x, r, t) = \sum_{n=1}^{\infty} \frac{(-1)^{n-1} q^n}{n!} c_n(x, t),$$

and show that the right-hand side of Eq. (5.7) can be compactly expressed as

$$-H[x, \epsilon(\partial/\partial x), t] p(x, t).$$

[16] See van Kampen (1992, p. 199).

Kubo et al. (1973) show that the assumed form of the density propagates over time if it is satisfied initially by solving an equation for the characteristic functions. Here, for convenience of exposition, we assume that this form holds for all $t \geq 0$, and next, we derive an approximate expression for the exponent, Ψ.

We expand the function Ψ as shown:

$$p(x, t) = C \exp[\epsilon^{-1}\Psi_0(x, t) + \Psi_1(x, t) + O(\epsilon)]. \tag{5.8}$$

We substitute this expression into the master equation, and collect terms of $O(1)$ and of ϵ separately to produce

$$\partial\Psi_0(x, t)/\partial t = -\int dr\, w(x, t)\left[1 - \exp\left(-r\frac{\partial\Psi_0}{\partial t}\right)\right],$$

and

$$\partial\Psi_1(x, t)/\partial t = \int dr\left[w(x, r)\left(\frac{r^2}{2}\frac{\partial^2\Psi_0}{\partial^2 x} - r\frac{\partial\Psi_1}{\partial x}\right)\exp\left(-r\frac{\partial\Psi_0}{\partial x}\right)\right],$$

respectively.

We change the variable to

$$x(t) = \phi(t) + z(t),$$

and write $\Psi_0(x, t)$ as $g[z(t), t]$. Then, we obtain

$$\partial g(z, t)/\partial t - \frac{d\phi}{dt}\frac{\partial g(z, t)}{\partial z} = -\int w(\phi + z)dr\left[1 - \exp\left(-r\frac{\partial g}{\partial z}\right)\right].$$

Now, we choose ϕ to be governed by

$$d\phi/dt = c_1(\phi).$$

This is the macroeconomic equation. Terms linear in $\partial g/\partial z$ drop out from both sides of the above. We assume that

$$g(z, t) = a_2(t)z^2 + a_3(t)z^3 + \cdots.$$

Then, the coefficients in this expansion are given by

$$da_2(t)/dt = 2c_2(\phi)a_2^2 - 2c_1'(\phi)a_2,$$

and

$$da_3(t)/dt = 6c_2(\phi)a_2a_3 - \frac{4}{3}a_2^3 - 3c_1(\phi)a_3 + 2c_2'(\phi)a_2^2 - c_1'(\phi)a_2.$$

For a constant ϕ, the equation for a_2 is a Riccati equation and can be solved. In particular, if c_1' is negative, that is, if ϕ is a locally stable equilibrium of the macroeconomic equation, then a_2 approaches $-c_1'/2c_2$ asymptotically. If this power-series expansion of g is truncated at the quadratic term in z, then we reproduce a Gaussian approximation of the solution, by setting $a_2 = -(2v_t)^{-1}$, where v_t is the variance. We note also that this procedure can be easily generalized to a case where x is a vector.

Now, we return to the question of whether the assumed form of the density propagates over time. To show that its form is preserved over time, Kubo et al. (1973) use the characteristic function of x:

$$Q(\xi, t) = \langle e^{i\xi x} \rangle = \int p(x, t)e^{i\xi x}dx,$$

and they show that it is of the form

$$Q(\xi, t) = \exp\left[\frac{1}{\epsilon}\psi(i\epsilon\xi, \epsilon, t)\right],$$

with $\psi(u, t_0) = ux_0$, when the initial condition is given by

$$p(x, t_0) = \delta(x - x_0).$$

Then, initially, the characteristic equation is $Q(\xi, t) = e^{i\xi x_0}$, which is clearly of the form specified.

The function ψ is assumed to have a power-series expansion in ϵ

$$\psi(u, \epsilon t) = \psi_0(u, t) + \epsilon\psi_1(u, t) + \epsilon^2\psi_2(u, t) + \cdots.$$

They show that this assumed form propagates with time, that is, the form is preserved over time. They convert the master equation into that for the characteristic equation which is then solved as a power series in ϵ. The function ψ is assumed to be analytical for all time t. For detail, see the development in Kubo et al. (1973).

5.4 Macroeconomic equation

In Section 5.3.1, we have shown that what remains in the master equation as N becomes large is the equation for the macroeconomic variables. In the expansion of van Kampen, it is[17]

$$d\phi/d\tau = \alpha_{1,0}(\phi), \tag{5.9}$$

[17] Note that

$$\frac{\partial}{\partial\xi}[\alpha_{10}(x)\Pi] = \alpha_{10}(\phi)\frac{\partial\Pi}{\partial\xi} + N^{-1/2}\alpha_{10}'(\phi)\frac{\partial}{\partial\xi}(\xi\Pi) + O(N^{-1}).$$

where $\alpha_{1,0}$, defined in (5.5), is the first moment of the function Φ, which appears in the transition rate expression $w_N(X \mid X') = f(N)\Phi_0(x'; r)$, with respect to r, and in the Kubo approximation, it is

$$d\phi/d\tau = c_1(\phi),$$

where c_1 is the first moment of $w(x, r) = (1/N)w_N(X; r)$. These two expressions are therefore equal, and we write the right-hand side as $g(\phi)$. This is a deterministic aggregate equation for the average, X/N, which is the limiting dynamics as the number of agents goes to infinity.

The zeros of the right-hand side of this function are the equilibria of the macroeconomic model. One should realize that this manner of deriving macroeconomic equations is certainly unknown in the macroeconomic literature.[18]

After the equation for ϕ is determined, the remainder of the master equation governs the density of ξ in van Kampen (1992) or of z in Kubo et al (1973). This equation is called the Fokker–Planck equation when terms of $O(N^{-1/2})$ and smaller are neglected. In Section 5.13, we return to this equation and calculate, among other things, the mean of ξ and show that it remains at zero under certain conditions, that is, that the mean of $x(t)$ is given by $\phi(t)$, and ξ describes the spread about the mean, as we claimed earlier. The variable ϕ can be thought of as the peak (the maximum-likelihood estimate) of the distribution for x in a single peaked distribution, whereas ξ keeps track of the spread of the distribution about the peak.

When $\alpha_{1,0}(\phi)$ or $c_1(\phi)$ is identically zero, then $\phi(\tau) = \phi(0)$ for all non-negative τ, and a small deviation in $\phi(0)$ does not decay to zero. In this case, we need to write the master equation in X/N, expand it in N^{-1}, and redefine τ by $N^{-2}t$. Then, we are led to what is known as the diffusion approximation to which we will return in Section 5.14.

5.5   Specifying transition rates: Examples

Clearly, the transition rates for the states of microeconomic units are the crucial ingredients in our formulation of models for interacting agents with field externality, such as social consumptions, entry-and-exit problems, or other discrete-choice problems for microeconomic units.[19] Here, by modifying examples from Dixit (1989a, b), we illustrate some of the steps that may be involved in specifying transition rates. In Chapter 6, we discuss an additional

---

[18] There is a related way of deriving macroeconomic relations by aggregating hierarchies or trees using the renormalization theory discussed in Chapter 7.

[19] Jump Markov processes can be constructed by specifying infinitesimal conditions, that is, the transition rates. See Breiman (1968, p. 332).

illustration of the transition-rate specification problem, which is based on Little (1974).

5.5.1 Two-sector capital reallocation dynamics

This example reformulates the model in Dixit (1989a) by dropping the assumption that firms are distinguished or identified, and by treating them as exchangeable. There are two sectors in the economy: sector 1 and sector 2. Firms in each sector produce homogeneous goods, good 1 and good 2. They are price takers; good 1 is a numeraire good, and the price of good 2 is a stochasic process P_t, governed by

$$dP_t / P_t = \mu dt + \sigma dB_t,$$

where B_t is a standard Wiener process with $B_0 = 0$. Namely, $\ln(P_t/P_0)$ is equal to $\hat{\mu}t + \sigma B_t$, where $\hat{\mu} = \mu - \sigma^2/2$. See Øksendal (1989, p. 36).

There are a total of N firms, which is fixed. This is the total capital in this economy. Each firm is the same size and indistinguishable from each other. The revenue of the economy as a whole is

$$R(P, n) = PF(n) + G(N - n),$$

where n is the number of firms in sector 2, and F and G are production functions of sectors 2 and 1, respectively. When a firm moves from sector 1 to sector 2, it suffers a down time of production, and its cost is assumed to be

$$h(P, n) = h_0[G(N - n + 1) - G(N - n)],$$

and a firm moving from sector 2 to sector 1 bears a cost

$$l(P, n) = l_0[F(n) - F(n - 1)].$$

We first describe Dixit's (1989a) derivation before we reformulate his model. Let $V(P, n)$ be the value function of the Bellman Dynamic Programming formulation, with a constant discount factor ρ. Since

$$E(dV/dt) + R(P, n) = \rho V(P, n),$$

we obtain a partial differential equation for V:

$$(\sigma^2/2)P^2 V_{PP} + \mu P V_P - \rho V = -R(P, n),$$

where the subscript P indicates partial differentiation.

A particular solution is given by

$$E \int_0^\infty R(P, n)e^{-\rho t}dt = PF(P, n)/(\rho - \mu) + G(P, N - n)/\rho, \quad (5.10)$$

since $E(P_t \mid P_0) = P_0 e^{\mu t}$, and where we assume that $\rho \geq \mu$. The homogeneous part has a solution of the form $V(P, n) = P^\gamma$ where

$$\gamma^2 - (1 - m)\gamma - r = 0,$$

with $m = 2\mu/\sigma^2$ and $r = 2\rho/\sigma^2$. The general form of the homogeneous solution is $A_n P^{-\alpha} + B_n P^\beta$, where $\alpha \geq 0$, and $\beta \geq 1$. We note that $\alpha\beta = r$. The general solution of the partial differential equation is this plus the particular solution Eq. (5.10).

When P becomes sufficiently high, a firm moves from sector 1 to sector 2. This occurs at P_n^+, at which

$$V(P, n - 1) = V(P, n) - h(P, n), \tag{5.11}$$

holds, and the derivative becomes

$$V_P(P, n - 1) = V_P(P, n) - h_P(P, n). \tag{5.12}$$

Similarly, when P drops sufficiently, one firm moves from sector 2 to sector 1. When this happens at P_n^-, we have

$$V(P, n) = V(P, n - 1) - l(P, n) \tag{5.13}$$

and

$$V_P(P, n) = V_P(P, n - 1) - l_P(P, n). \tag{5.14}$$

The first equations of these two sets of equations are merely the value-matching conditions, the right-hand side being the value of the asset acquired minus the exercise prices in the options interpretation by Dixit (1989a). The second equations of the two sets are the gradient-matching conditions. If they do not match, then the assumption that V is the optimal value function is violated. See Merton (1973 n. 60), or Fleming and Rishel (1975, Chap. 6), for example. These four equations determine A_n, B_n, P_n^+, and P_n^-.

It is convenient to define

$$a_n = A_n - A_{n-1},$$
$$b_n = B_{n-1} - B_n,$$
$$f(n) = F(n) - F(n - 1),$$

and

$$g(n) = G(N - n + 1) - G(N - n).$$

The boundary conditions are $A_0 = 0$, and $B_N = 0$. The first condition comes from considering the case of $n = 0$ since $V(P, 0)$ must remain bounded as P

approaches zero. The other condition obtains by considering the case of $n = N$. Then, $V(P, N)$ is approximately given by Eq. (5.10), and cannot include terms of P^β, since β is greater than one. See Dixit (1989a) for further discussion of the boundary conditions.

We can then rewrite the first of the two sets of conditions as

$$a_n(P_n^+)^{-\alpha} - b_n(P_n^+)^\beta + \frac{P_n^+ f(n)}{\rho - \mu} - \frac{g(n)}{\rho} = h_0 g(n),$$

and its derivative with respect to P_n^+. Following Dixit's suggestion,[20] we rewrite these two equations in terms of a dimensionless (pure-number) variable:

$$Q_n^+ = P_n^+ f(n)/g(n).$$

We can obtain approximate linear equations for the price boundary for entry in the cases of very large and very small noise variance σ^2. In the former, the value of α is nearly zero, and the gradient equality equation is approximately given by

$$\beta b_n(Q_n^+)^{\beta-1} = [f(n)/g(n)]^\beta f(n)/(\rho - \mu).$$

This approximation is valid as long as $h_0 + 1/\rho \geq a_n/g(n)$. When this is substituted into the value equalization equation, we derive an explicit expression for the price boundary for entry

$$P_n^+ = \frac{[h_0 + 1/\rho - a_n/g(n)](\rho - \mu)}{(1 - 1/\beta)} \frac{g(n)}{f(n)}.$$

When the variance is very small, the value of the parameter α is approximately given by $2\mu/\sigma^2$, and the gradient equality equation becomes approximately equal to

$$\alpha \frac{a_n}{g(n)} (Q_n^+)^{-\alpha} = \left[\frac{f(n)}{g(n)}\right]^{-\alpha} \frac{Q_n^+}{\rho - \mu}.$$

Substituting this into the valuation equality equation, we obtain

$$P_n^+ = \frac{(h_0 + 1/\rho)(\rho - \mu)}{1 + 1/\alpha} \frac{g(n)}{f(n)},$$

provided this expression is much smaller than $[g(n)/b_n]^{\mu/\rho}$. Proceeding analogously, we derive the expression for the other boundary for exit.

Now, we are ready to reformulate this model. Instead of arranging firms linearly and assuming that marginal firms enter or leave as the case may be, we

---

[20] A. Dixit, Princeton University, 1995, personal communication.

treat each firm as exchangeable[21] and assume that each has a nonzero probability of entering sector 2 to bring the number of firms from $n - 1$ to n, and likewise for n to $n - 1$. These changes are regarded as a birth or a death, and are captured by specifying transition rates of this birth-and-death process, as we show in Section 5.7.

In a continuous-time reformulation, we let $w_{n-1,n}$ be the transition rate from $n - 1$ firms to n firms. Then,

$$w_{n-1,n} = \lambda(N - n + 1)v_{n-1,n},$$

where

$$v_{n-1,n} = \frac{f(t)}{1 - P[T(x) \leq t]},$$

where $x = (1/\sigma)[\ln(P_n^+/P_0) - \hat{\mu}t]$, and $T(x)$ is the first-passage time of a standard Brownian motion to level x, and $f(t)$ is its probability density. See Grimmett and Stirzaker (1992, p. 500) or the Appendix. The probability density $f(t)$ is given by

$$f(t) = \frac{|x|}{\sqrt{2\pi t^3}} e^{-x^2/2t},$$

and the denominator of $v_{n-1,n}$ is given by

$$P[T(x) \geq t] = (1 + e^{-2\beta x})^{-1},$$

where $\beta = (2\pi t)^{-1/2}$. The transition rates are not time-homogeneous, however, unless $\hat{\mu} = 0$. Recall our discussion in Section 4.7 on nontime homogeneous processes.

In a discrete-time framework with a constant interval of time, τ, the probability that $P_{t+\tau}$ exceeds P_n^+ in an interval of length τ is calculated by noting that

$$\ln(P_{t+\tau}/P_t) = \hat{\mu}\tau + \sigma B_\tau \geq \ln(P_n^+/P_t),$$

or

$$B_\tau \geq x,$$

where

$$x = (1/\sigma)[\ln(P_n^+/P_t) - \hat{\mu}\tau].$$

---

[21] See Appendix for discussion of exchangeable random variables.

Then, denoting by $T(x)$ the first-passage time to level x of the Brownian motion process,[22] we have

$$q_{n-1,n} = P[T(x) \leq \tau] = 2P(B_\tau \geq x) = \sqrt{2/\pi\tau} \int_x^\infty e^{-y^2/2\tau} dy.$$

This expression is equal to

$$q_{n-1,n} = \frac{2}{\sqrt{\pi}} \int_{x/\sqrt{2\tau}}^\infty e^{-y^2} dy = \frac{1}{2}\left[1 - \text{erf}\left(\frac{x}{\sqrt{2\tau}}\right)\right],$$

where the error function is defined by

$$\text{erf}(x) = \frac{2}{\sqrt{\pi}} \int_0^x e^{-y^2} dy.$$

We use the approximate formula of Ingber (1982) for the error function:

$$\frac{1}{2}[1 - \text{erf}(x)] \approx (1 + e^{\kappa x})^{-1},$$

where $\kappa = 2/\sqrt{\pi}$. Since each of $N - n + 1$ firms can enter sector 2, the transition probability of the number of firms from $n - 1$ to n is given by

$$W_{n-1,n} = \lambda(N - n + 1)q_{n-1,n} = \lambda(N - n + 1)(1 + e^{2\beta x})^{-1},$$

where $\beta = (2\pi\tau)^{-1}$.

Similarly, any one of n firms can move to sector 1, hence the transition rate from n to $n - 1$ is

$$W_{n,n-1} = \nu n q_{n,n-1},$$

where $q_{n,n-1}$ is defined analogously with $q_{n-1,n}$ by replacing P_n^+ in the definition of x by P_n^-. We then proceed exactly as in Section 5.11.

5.5.2 Exchange-rate pass-through

Similar reformulation is possible for problems with different revenue functions and different entry and exit costs. For example, Dixit (1989b) also discusses the entry and exit problems for foreign firms into domestic markets where the exchange rate is an exogenous stochastic process. Denoting the foreign currency price of domestic currency by R now, denoting by p_n the unit price of the good when n foreign firms are active in domestic market, and denoting by k and l, the costs of entry and exit, respectively, in domestic currency, we can calculate

---

[22] See Appendix.

the threshold levels of exchange rates for entry and exit in much the same way as in the previous example. They are

$$R_n^+ = \frac{w/\rho}{[p_n/(\rho - \mu) - k](1 - 1/\beta)},$$

and

$$R_n^- = \frac{w/\rho}{[p_n/(\rho - \mu) + l](1 - 1/\beta)},$$

where w is the cost to a firm of producing the good.

5.6   Field effects: Stochastic nonlocal and diffuse externalities

As we mention in the introduction of this chapter, there are many economic situations in which a group of microeconomic units interacts through the choices they make. The choices may be influenced partially by the price signals that they observe, but they are not completely decentralized as in the standard-perfectly competitive general-equilibrium approach of the economics literature because the fractions of units making the same choices affect the effectiveness or desirability of the choices.

The literature on stochastic dynamic discrete-choice models does not, by and large, deal with interacting decisions by agents. In the literature of mathematical sociology, Weidlich (1974) was probably the first to treat the problem of interacting agents who have the same choice sets, such as those between two political candidates or between two brands of merchandise. He formulated the dynamic process for the number of agents with the same choice as a birth-and-death stochastic process, and showed the possibility of a bimodal density as an equilibrium density for the fraction of agents with the same choice. See also Weidlich and Haag (1983) or Weidlich (1994) for his recent analysis of the same problem. Glance and Huberman (1993) also discuss a related problem of a group of agents who must decide to cooperate or not. As more people decide to cooperate in their model, it becomes more desirable for others to cooperate as well. Many situations in economics can be similarly modeled as a group of interacting agents with a finite number of alternative choices.

Analysis of externalities in a dynamic context apparently has been non-existent or rather rare until recently in the economic literature.[23] Recently, some works have begun to appear that are based on the adaptation of the Ising models of physics to capture interactions.[24] However, these models assume

---

[23] An example of static analysis can be found in Buchanan and Stubblebine (1962).

[24] See Ellis (1985) for detailed expositions of the Ising models in economics. Many elementary textbooks on physics also treat this model of ferromagnetism. See Brock (1993) and the references cited for economic applications of Ising models.

that agents interact pairwise or only with others in neighborhoods, since the formulation relies on the notion of the Markov random field.[25] See Chapter 6 for our discussion of pairwise or multiple-pair interactions.

Generally speaking, we are interested in modeling weak and diffuse (i.e., nonlocalizable) externalities among agents. Some aspects of environments in which agents choose (e.g., adoption of industry standards, group sentiments, bandwagon effects, herd behavior) and benefits from particular choices cannot be modeled properly as neighborhood effects. More specifically in this chapter, we model interacting agents by a generalized birth-and-death process in which transition rates depend on the fraction of agents who belong to various categories, such as those of agents with the same specific choices or decisions. For easier exposition, we assume that all agents have the same binary decision set, and we deal with a single fraction. The nature of binary choices varies depending on the context of the application: to join or not to join a coalition; to purchase brand X or brand Y of two goods of "apparently" similar quality and prices; to acquire or not to acquire a piece of information in a stock transaction; to adopt a particular strategy or technology of production or not, and so on. At any time each agent has chosen one of the alternatives. We assume that each agent will reevaluate his choice α times per unit time on the average.[26]

Kirman (1992a, 1993, 1994) analyzed the behavior of the group with a binary choice set using the birth-and-death process. He refers to Arthur (1988, 1989), among others, who use some generalized processes such as nonlinear urn models. However, Arthur does not show how such nonlinear processes arise. We relate nonlinearities in transition rates, such as the η in Eqs. (5.16) and (5.17), to (perceived) probabilities of relative advantages of one choice over the other in binary choice situations. See Section 5.7.

5.7   Generalized birth-and-death models

Rather than continue in abstract settings, we focus on a specific situation in which a group of agents has a binary choice set. We let N agents have two choices, strategy 1 or strategy 2. At any given time, n of them are using strategy 1. They reevaluate their choices randomly, and agents act asynchronously. Each agent assesses the probability of the relative merits of alternatives such as profits, costs, or utilities over whatever planning horizon he or she uses, and each has a perceived probability that one choice is superior to the other.

---

[25] There is already much in the literature about when interactions can be modeled utilizing Markov random fields. See, for example, Kindermann and Snell (1980). Brock and Durlauf (1995) are recent economic examples.

[26] In jump Markov processes, time intervals between successive changes of the agents minds are exponentially distributed. Agent's choices thus are not synchronized.

The master equation takes the form

$$\frac{dP_n(t)}{dt} = (z^{-1} - 1)[w_{n,n+1}P_n(t)] + (z - 1)[w_{n,n-1}P_n(t)], \quad (5.15)$$

where $zP_n(t) = P_{n+1}(t)$ is the lead operation, and $z^{-1}P_n(t) = P_{n-1}(t)$ is the lag operation, where the only nonzero transitions are from n to $n \pm 1$. When n is restricted to be nonnegative and bounded from above, as in this section, then obvious changes must be made to this equation at the boundaries of $n = 0$ and $n = N$.

Suppose that the transition rates are such that the number of agents using strategy 1 decreases by one with the transition rate

$$w_{n,n-1} = f(N)[\rho_0(n/N) + (1/N)\rho_1(n/N) + \cdots],$$

and increases by one with the transition rate

$$w_{n,n+1} = f(N)[\gamma_0(n/N) + (1/N)\gamma_1(n/N) + \cdots],$$

where the ellipsis stands for terms of higher order in $1/N$, and n/N is the fraction of agents with strategy 1 and is an intensive variable.

We assume that $f(N)$ is a constant times N. To explain the simplest case, we assume further that

$$\rho_0(n/N) = (n/N)\eta_2(n/N), \quad (5.16)$$

and

$$\gamma_0(n/N) = [1 - (n/N)]\eta_1(n/N), \quad (5.17)$$

with all other order terms such as ρ_1 and γ_1 are being set to zero.

We can repeat the steps leading to the master equation of Section 5.3.1 by noting that $z = 1 + N^{-1/2}(\partial/\partial\xi) + (1/2)N^{-1}(\partial^2/\partial\xi^2) + \cdots$, and that we can write $\Pi(\xi - N^{-1/2}, t)$ for $P_{n-1}(t)$, $\gamma_0[\phi + N^{-1/2}(\xi - N^{-1/2})]$ for $\gamma_0[(n-1)/N]$, and similarly for $P_{n+1}(t)$ and $\rho_0[(n+1)/N]$. Then we find that the expression $\alpha_{1,0}$ in the macroequation defined by Eq. (5.5) is equal to the difference of these nonlinear expressions:

$$\alpha_{1,0}(\phi) = -\rho_0(\phi) + \gamma_0(\phi). \quad (5.18)$$

Next, for the benefit of the reader, we repeat some of the steps here, and derive an approximate equation for $\Pi(\xi, t)$ by retaining terms up to $O(N^{-1/2})$ for the case where the transition rates depend only on ρ_0 and γ_0. To lighten notation, we write α_0 for $\alpha_{1,0}$, and define $\beta_0 = \rho_0 + \gamma_0$.

Noting that the expression $\phi + N^{-1/2}\xi$ always appears in the arguments in α and β, we label it as s. We expand them in the Taylor series. For example, we expand α as

$$\alpha_0(s) = \alpha_0(\phi) + \alpha_0'(\phi)N^{-1/2}\xi + \frac{1}{2}\alpha_0''(\phi)N^{-1}\xi^2 + \cdots .$$

Doing likewise for β_0, substituting them into the master equation, and collecting terms of similar order in N, we derive

$$\frac{\partial \Pi}{\partial \tau} = -\alpha_0'(\phi)\frac{\partial}{\partial \xi}(\xi \Pi) + \frac{\beta_0(\phi)}{2}\frac{\partial^2}{\partial \xi^2}\Pi$$
$$+ \frac{N^{-1/2}}{2}\left[-\alpha_0''(\phi)\frac{\partial}{\partial \xi^2}(\xi^2\Pi) + \beta_0'(\phi)\frac{\partial^2}{\partial \xi^2}(\xi \Pi)\right] + O(N^{-1}).$$

When the expansion is terminated after the first two terms on the right, we obtain the equation up to $O(N^{-1/2})$. The resulting equation is linear in ξ and is called a Fokker–Planck equation. It can be used to obtain a set of ordinary differential equations for the first and second moments of ξ. We return to this equation in Section 5.13.

5.7.1   Mean field approximation of transition rates

The generalized birth-and-death process differs from the simple one only by the fact that extra factors denoted by η_i appear in the transition rates.

But, before we discuss the nature of these factors, we note here that the approximation method known as the mean field method is implicitly employed here. Namely, interactions among agents are removed and replaced with those between agents and a field node with value x,[27] and these interactions are regarded as independent. This explains the presence of the same factors n/N and $1 - n/N$ in the expressions for the transition rates of this more general birth-and-death process as in the simple one for independent agents.

We do not discuss here how agents know or learn x to avoid overlaying expectational dynamics onto the group dynamics and confuse the effects from these two distinct sources of dynamics. We simply remark that, like price variables, knowledge of the field variables serve as (partially) decentralizing variables in the decision processes of agents. Knowledge of a field variable relieves (at least partially) agents of the need for detailed information on interaction patterns. Any macroeconomic variable that serves this decentralizing function can be called a field variable.

---

[27] The concept of mean field has been used in the physics literature for a long time, mainly in connection with models of ferromagnetism. See Griffiths, Wang, and Langer (1966). Fukao (1987) was probably the first to introduce this concept to the systems literature.

We have a statistical description of the behavior of a collection of agents, and this knowledge is embodied in the transition rates. Put differently, we describe the time evolution of a system composed of many interacting microeconomic agents – not deterministically, but rather statistically or probabilistically in the sense that only statistical or probabilistic statements are made. For example, in a given state, we merely know the percentage of microeconomic agents who will switch their decisions over a short time interval in the future. We will know if this is a good assumption or not by a posteriori confirmation or refutation of the theoretical predictions based on this assumption. As we discuss later in this chapter, this approach enables us to predict the probabilities of the system in an equilibrium or expected first-passage time from one equilibrium to another when the system has more than one basin of attraction.

5.8   Expressing relative merits of alternative decisions

We return now to the η factors in the transition-rate expressions (5.16) and (5.17). A key assumption here is that the transition rates are monotonic in the probability that alternative 1 is superior to alternative 2. This probability is denoted by $\eta_1(x)$ and defined by

$$\eta_1(x) = Pr[\pi_1(x) \geq \pi_2(x)],$$

where $\pi_i(x)$, $i = 1, 2$ is a (perceived random) benefit (utility, profit, or payoff) over some unspecified planning horizon of adopting alternative i when fraction x of agents are using it.[28] We note that η_1 (and η_2 which is $1 - \eta_1$) depends only on the differences, $\pi_1(x) - \pi_2(x)$, which we denote by $\Delta\pi(x)$.

Further, we posit that

$$\eta_1(x) = \frac{\exp[\beta\Delta\pi(x)]}{\exp[\beta\Delta\pi(x)] + \exp[-\beta\Delta\pi(x)]},$$

where β is a nonnegative parameter of uncertainty that prevails in the system as a whole. The parameter β stands for the overall uncertainty and can be some complicated functions of individual agents' uncertainty. Put differently, we can say that by interacting with each other, agents spread their degree of uncertainty to the whole system, thus determining the level of uncertainty of the system as a whole, and of individual agents. The extreme case of $\beta = 0$ means that no information about the relative advantages of alternative choices is available.

---

[28] How these functions are specified depends on a more complete microeconomic description of the situations involving the binary choices. The horizon over which the benefits are to be evaluated may depend also on model specifications or some policy variables and so on. These other factors are assumed to be held fixed.

Then $\eta_1(x)$ is equal to $1/2$ for all x in $(-1, +1)$. The larger that β is, the more precisely that the relative merits of alternative choices are known to the agents.

This formulation is similar to the one adopted in the literature of discrete-choice models, although this literature does not discuss time evolution as we do here. See Anderson et al. (1993, p. 50).[29] In dealing with a somewhat related problem, Ceccatto and Huberman (1989) also use a similar expression.

5.9 Equilibrium probability distributions

In Section 5.1, we state that the equilibrium distribution is a Gibbs distribution if the detailed balance condition is met. Now, we show that the detailed balance condition is satisfied by the equilibrium solution of Eq. (5.15) and derive the expression of the exponent, which we call the potential, or Hamiltonian in some cases. Then, we examine the nature of the equilibrium.

Since this demonstration becomes possible without solving the master equation explicitly when the process is a discrete-time birth-and-death process, we discuss only this process in this section. The state space is a set with elements $n = 0, 1, 2, \ldots, N$, for some large positive integer N. We use $n(t)$ to express the state variable.

Instead of Eq. (5.15), the master equation is simply given by

$$P_{t+1}(n) = W_{n-1,n}P_t(n-1) + W_{n+1,n}P_t(n+1) + W_{n,n}P_t(n), \quad (5.19)$$

where $W_{n,n-1}$ is the probability of transition from state n to $n-1$, and where $W_{n,n+1}$ denotes the probability of transition from state n to $n+1$. In the former, the number of microeconomic agents in this subclass is reduced by one (a death), and in the latter, the number of microeconomic agents increases by one (a birth). The probability that the number of agents will remain the same is given by

$$W_{n,n} = 1 - W_{n,n+1} - W_{n,n-1},$$

which is assumed to be positive by taking the unit time step to be small enough.

We denote the equilibrium probabilities by $[P_e(n)]$. Then Eq. (5.19) reduces to[30]

$$P_e(n)W_{n,n+1} = P_e(n+1)W_{n+1,n},$$

which shows that the detailed balance condition is satisfied (Kelly 1979, Sec. 1.5, or Whittle 1992, p. 160). We note that the same equation holds also in the

---

[29] The logarithm of the odds ratio is $\beta \Delta G$. Strauss's model mentioned in Anderson et al. (1993) is exactly the same. Brock (1993) also suggests this connection.

[30] At the edges of $n = 0$ and $n = N$, obvious changes must be made.

continous-time version of the model given by Eq. (5.15). The equilibrium probability distribution is of the Gibbs type.[31]

The equilibrium probabilities satisfy a first-order difference equation, and these probabilities can be obtained by solving it as

$$P_e(n) = P_e(0) \prod_{k=1}^{n} \frac{W_{k-1,k}}{W_{k,k-1}}. \tag{5.20}$$

This corresponds to Eq. (5.3) which is its continuous-time version.

In the simplest birth-and-death process, the transition rates are linear in the state variable. The only nonzero transition rates are from state n to $n-1$, indicating a death, or from n to $n+1$ corresponding to a birth, and they are given by $W_{n,n-1} = \mu n$ and $W_{n,n+1} = \lambda(N-n)$ for some constants μ and λ.[32] We now generalize the transition rates of the basic birth-and-death stochastic processes to include some nonlinear effects:

$$W_{n,n+1} = N \left(1 - \frac{n}{N} \right) \eta_1 \left(\frac{n}{N} \right), \tag{5.21}$$

and

$$W_{n,n-1} = N \left(\frac{n}{N} \right) \eta_2 \left(\frac{n}{N} \right). \tag{5.22}$$

From now on, we set $\mu = \lambda$ without loss of generality.

By substituting into Eq. (5.20) the transition rate expressions Eqs. (5.21) and (5.22), we obtain an explicit expression for the equilibrium probability as

$$P_e(n) = P_e(0)_N C_n \prod_{k=1}^{n} \frac{\eta_1(k/N)}{\eta_2(k/N)},$$

which can be written as

$$P_e(n) = Z^{-1} \exp[-\beta N U(n/N)], \tag{5.23}$$

by introducing a function U, called the potential, by

$$-\beta N U(n/N) - \ln Z = \ln P_e(0) + \ln C_{N,n} + \sum^{n} \ln[\eta_1(k/N)/\eta_2(k/N)],$$

---

[31] This means that the probability distributions belong to an exponential family the exponents of which are called potential functions, that is, of the form: constant $\exp -V(x)$, where $V(x)$ is a potential or a Hamiltonian, namely, it is a function of x and does not depend on the path leading to x.

[32] See Feller (1957, p. 421) or Karlin and Taylor (1981, p. 142). An urn model with these transition rates is equivalent to this simple birth-and-death process and is known as the Ehrenfest model (See Whittle 1992, p. 192).

and where Z is a normalizing constant, called the partition function, which is assumed to be finite, that is,

$$Z = \sum_n \exp[-\beta N U(n/N)] < \infty.$$

Recall our discussion of potentials and partition functions in Chapter 3. We note that the terms in the potential involving the ratios of η disappear from the defining equation for the potential in the case of simple birth-and-death process because when the ratios η_1/η_2 are all ones.

Up to this point, there is no need to identify η with the probability of the perceived advantage of alternative 1 over alternative 2. We could have proceeded by treating η in the transition probabilities as some nonlinear effects. Proceeding this way, we define a function $G(k/N)$, $k = 0, 1, \ldots, N$, by equating the last term, above, with $2\beta \Delta G(k/N)$, that is,

$$\ln[\eta_1(k/N)/\eta_2(k/N)] = 2\beta \Delta G(k/N),$$

where β is a constant of proportionality. In the context of the previous section, ΔG is the same as $\Delta \pi$, the difference of perceived advantage of choice 1 over choice 2. In this context, β is the parameter that represents the degree of uncertainty in the economic environment surrounding agents, or the general level of economic activity, as we have discussed previously.

We divide both sides by N, noting that Z is finite by assumption, and that the logarithm in the above summation is equal to $2\beta \Delta G(k/N)$, and making use of the relation

$$_N C_n = \exp[NH(n/N)] + O(1/N),$$

where H is the base e (Shannon) entropy

$$H(x) = -\frac{1+x}{2} \ln[(1+x)/2] - \frac{1-x}{2} \ln[(1-x)/2],$$

and where we now measure the fraction from the median by variable x defined by

$$(1+x)/2 = n/N,$$

which will be continuous in the limit of N going to infinity, taking on values in the interval $[-1, 1]$.

We obtain the expression for U correct up to $O(1/N)$:

$$U(n/N) = -(2/N) \sum_{k=1}^{n} \Delta G(k/N) - (1/\beta)H(n/N).$$

Since $2/N$ is approximately equal to the differential dx, we replace the above summation by an integral and obtain the expression for the potential as

$$U(x) \approx - \int^x \Delta G(y)dy - (1/\beta)H(x) = -G(x) - (1/\beta)H(x), \quad (5.24)$$

where we write $U(x)$ for $U[(1+x)/2]$, and similarly for $H(x)$. We note in particular that G is a constant in the simple birth-and-death model process since ΔG is zero.

Recall our discussion of maximizing equilibrium probabilities in Chapter 3. The equilibrium probabilities take into account the multiplicity of microconfigurations that produce the same macrovalue, that is, there are $_NC_n$ ways to realize the same n/N.

Since $dH(x)/dx = (1/2) \ln[(1-x)/(1+x)]$, the derivative of the potential function is equal to

$$dU(x)/dx \approx -\Delta G(x) - (1/2\beta) \ln\left[\frac{1-x}{1+x}\right]. \quad (5.25)$$

We set the derivative to zero to obtain the relation

$$2\beta\Delta G(x) = \ln\left[\frac{1+x}{1-x}\right].$$

In the interpretation of the preceding section, ΔG is replaced with $\Delta\pi$. From Eqs. (5.23)–(5.25), we know that an equilibrium of the macroeconomic equation satisfies exactly the same equation with this interpretation. In other words, the critical values of the potential are the critical points of the equilibrium probability distribution $[P_e(n)]$ and are the same as the critical points of the macroeconomic dynamics as seen from Eqs. (5.9), (5.16), (5.17), and (5.18).

When this key relation is solved out for x, we obtain

$$x = \tanh \beta\Delta G(x), \quad (5.26)$$

or designating the right-hand side of Eq. (5.9) as g and using x rather than ϕ, we see that Eq. (5.26) is the same as

$$g(x) = 0,$$

in view of Eqs. (5.16)–(5.18).

The zeros of this equation, $g(x)$, are the critical points of the potential function $U(x)$. In other words, an x that minimizes the potential U, that is, that maximizes the probability $P_e(n)$, satisfies Eq. (5.26) at which point the right-hand side of Eq. (5.6) vanishes. This is the interpretation of the relation between the potential U and the macroeconomic dynamics. In Section 5.10.3 we specialize the functions η_i and examine the nature of the zeros of this function. See also Aoki (1995b).

5.10 Example of multiple equilibria

We discuss an example of the generalized birth-and-death process in order to put the question of existence and selection of multiple equilibria of macroeconomic dynamics in a concrete setting.[33]

5.10.1 Model

There are N firms producing close, substitutable perishable goods.[34]
Each faces a demand schedule

$$p_t = ay_t^{-b}, \quad a \geq 0, 1 \geq b \geq 0.$$

Two technologies of production are available to firms. With technology 1, output is given by

$$y_t = \gamma(x_t)L_t,$$

where x is the fraction of firms using this technology, L is the labor input, and γ is a function that represents a technological externality that is assumed to depend on the fraction of firms using it.[35] It costs to use this technology. It is also possible to introduce a switching cost each time a firm changes over to the other technology. Recall the examples in Section 5.5. The cost is assumed to be the same for all firms adopting it and is given by a constant, F.
  With technology 2, output is given by

$$y_t = L_t.$$

In our model, one-period profit of a firm[36] that adopts technology 1 is

$$\pi_1(x) = \kappa\gamma(x)^\theta - F,$$

where κ is a positive constant[37] and $\theta = (1 - b)/b$. Without loss of generality, we take the wage rate to be one and, for shorter notation, we drop the time subscript from now on.

---

[33] This section is based in part on Aoki (1995a, b).

[34] This assumption is meant to do away with questions of inventories. Alternatively, we can assume that firms using the same production technology are physically the same, but the characteristics and abilities of managers of the firms are distinct and they make independent decisions.

[35] There are other ways to model congestion, learning, or other externalities that depend on x. This seems to be the simplest. This model is similar to the one of Jeong (1993). The nature of analysis and the methodology are different, however. Jeong merely examines the mean and does not discuss the model when it possesses multiple equilibria.

[36] The use of one-period profit function here is purely for illustrative purposes. More generally, each firm will compute profit differences over its own planning horizon.

[37] $\kappa = a^{1/b}(1 - b)^{(1-b)/b}b$.

Use of technology 2 yields the one-period profit of

$$\pi_2(x) = \kappa.$$

For later discussion it is more convenient to redefine the technology externality factor as $\mu(x) = \gamma(x)^{1/\theta}$. There is no loss of generality because γ is arbitrary at this point. With this redefinition, the profit differential is given by

$$\Delta\pi_t(x) = \pi_1(x) - \pi_2(x) = \kappa[\gamma(x) - 1] - F.$$

We define a new function

$$\omega(x) = \frac{\gamma(x)}{\gamma(0)} - \frac{1 + F/\kappa}{\gamma(0)}, \tag{5.27}$$

and rewrite the expression for the one-peirod profit difference as

$$\Delta\pi_t(x) = \kappa\gamma(0)\omega(x). \tag{5.28}$$

Actually, the expressions for the profits and the underlying equations for demands and outputs and the like are not precise relations. Rather, they should be interpreted as some sorts of average or typical relationships that serve as guides rather than exact mathematical relations.[38] In this sense, we regard Eq. (5.28) as an average or perceived relation with some ambiguity about it or some unknown or imprecisely known distributions associated with it. This perceived profit difference affects the firms' switching between the two alternative technologies.

Assuming without loss of generality that $\gamma(0)$ is positive,[39] the equilibrium is stable if and only if

$$\beta\omega'(x)(1 - x^2) \leq 1.$$

If the derivative of ω is nonpositive, then this condition is always satisfied. One simple example of this is when the difference $\Delta\pi$ is a constant. When β is large, and if ω' is positive, then this inequality may be violated, and we then have an unstable equilibrium.

5.10.2 Solutions

We denote $\Delta\pi(x)$ as $\omega(x)$ for short. Then Eq. (5.26) becomes

$$\omega(x) = \frac{1}{2\beta} \ln\left(\frac{1+x}{1-x}\right),$$

where $|x| \leq 1$. Depending on the specification of ω, this equation may have more than one solution.

---

[38] Alternatively, we can think of F as a random variable.

[39] The locations of zeros of the macroeconomic dynamics are symmetric with respect to the origin.

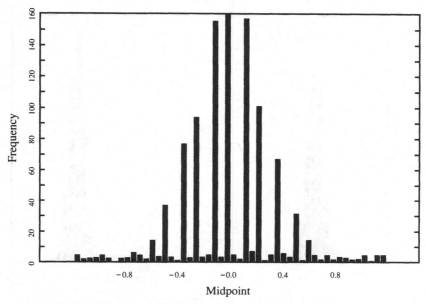

Fig. 5.1. Histogram of 500 runs with $N = 200$ firms with $\beta = 0.001$ and one stable equilibrium.

5.10.3 *Some simulation results*

A model with the relation (5.27) specified by

$$\omega(x) = 1 + 64x - 100x^3/3$$

has been used[40] with several values of β to produce a single stable and unstable equilibrium and three equilibria, one of which is unstable: with $\beta = 1.0$, one unstable equilibrium; with $\beta = 0.001$, one stable equilibrium; with $\beta = 0.03$, two stable equilibria at $x = \pm 0.95$, and one unstable equilibrium near zero.

When we run two cases, where the total number of firms, N, is 20 or 200, the general picture that we obtain is the same. Even the case with a small number, $N = 20$, reproduces the general characteristics that the case with the large number, $N = 200$, exhibits. In Figs. 5.1–5.3, we show the results of 500 replications of firms choosing technologies with the prescribed probabilities and the histograms of the values of x after 20 transitions. With two stable equilibria we clearly see bimodal histograms. With a single stable equilibrium at $x = 0$, we observe clustering of $x(t)$ around zero.

---

[40] This function could arise from π_1 and π_2 which are both quartic with the same fourth-power term.

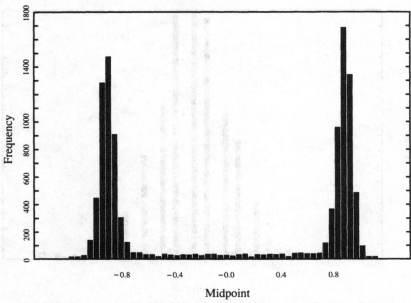

Fig. 5.2. Histogram of the same with two stable equilibria with $\beta = 0.03$ and one unstable equilibrium.

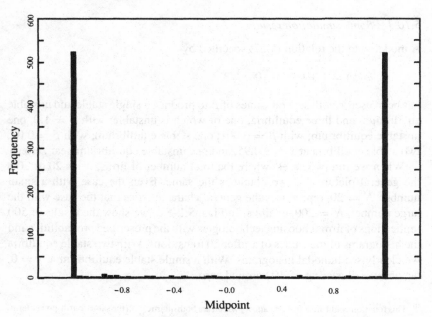

Fig. 5.3. Histogram of the same with $\beta = 1.0$ and one unstable equilibrium.

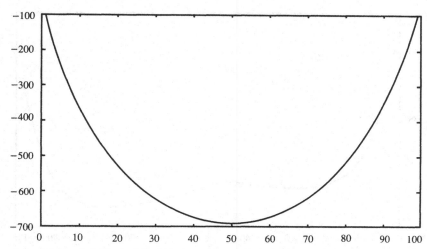

Fig. 5.4. Potential with one stable equilibrium with $\beta = 0.001$. See the text for the expression of the potential.

See Aoki (1995b) for examinations of the critical points as functions of β and N. We observe that small values of β mean that the potential benefits of a choice are not clear, that roughly equal numbers of firms switch their choices, and that the fraction of approximately one-half is stable. Large values of β imply that the perceived benefit of one alternative over the other is so convincing that a large number of firms respond to even a small perceived benefit of one choice hence the fraction of one half is unstable. For β with values in between these two extremes, just the right fraction of firms switch their decisions so that both a small fraction and a large fraction are stably maintained.

Figures 5.4–5.7 show how the potential $U(x)$ defined by Eq. (5.24) behaves qualitatively differently in this example for different values of β with $N = 100$. Figure 5.4 has one stable equilibrium and Fig 5.7 has an unstable equilibrium. Figures 5.5 and 5.6 show how two locally stable and one locally unstable equilibria develop as the values of β increase. Values of β that are too large produce only unstable equilibria in the relevant range of x. This example and the figures clearly demonstrate the importance of the entropy terms for small values of β, that is, the importance of the multiplicity of microeconomic states consistent with a given macroeconomic state.

5.11 First passage times

In Chapter 2, we discuss the first-passage time between two equilibria of a simple two-state Markov chain. We now calculate the first-passage probabilities

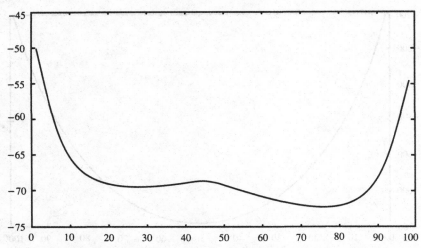

Fig. 5.5. Potential with two locally stable and one unstable equilibrium, small β, $\beta = 0.01$.

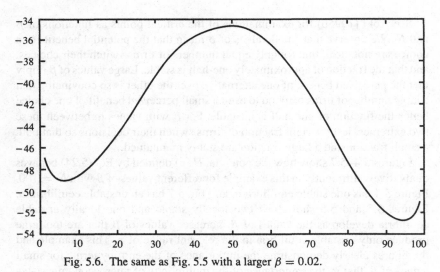

Fig. 5.6. The same as Fig. 5.5 with a larger $\beta = 0.02$.

and mean first-passage times for the generalized birth-and-death process that we have been discussing. We shall see that the essence of the problem is captured by the simple example in Chapter 2. We discuss the first passage between two locally stable equilibria when they are on both sides of a locally unstable equilibrium, a possibility that we did not encounter in Chapter 2. The method for calculating first-passage probabilities or mean first-passage time is well known

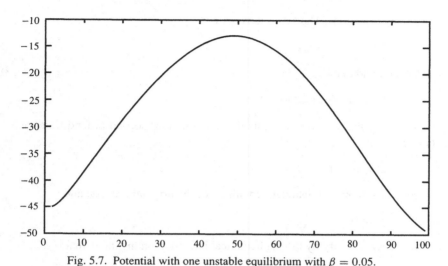

Fig. 5.7. Potential with one unstable equilibrium with $\beta = 0.05$.

(see, e.g., Parzen 1962, Chap. 6; Cox and Miller 1965, Sec. 3.4; Grimmett and Stirzaker 1992, Sec. 6.2); or van Kampen (1992, Chap. XII)

To lighten notations, we use r_n for $w_{n,n-1}$, and g_n for $w_{n,n+1}$. Using this new notation, we repeat the generic equation of the birth-and-death process (5.15) here, where we now write $p_n(t)$ rather than $P_n(t)$ for the probability of n at time t,

$$\frac{dp_n}{dt} = (z - 1)r_n p_n + (z^{-1} - 1)g_n p_n. \tag{5.29}$$

Also, from now on, we use $p_{n,m}$ to indicate the solution of this master equation with the initial probability concentrated at state m, that is, $p_{n,m}(0) = \delta_{n,m}$, where δ is the Kronecker delta.

To calculate the probability distribution of time for a state of a Markov chain to reach state c for the first time from initial position m, we treat state c as an absorbing state. We define τ_m as the mean first-passage time from state m to state c. It is governed by

$$\tau_m - \Delta t = (g_m \Delta t)\tau_{m+1} + (r_m \Delta t)\tau_{m-1} + [1 - (g_m + r_m)\Delta t]\tau_m,$$

for any m in $\{a + 1, a + 2, \ldots, c - 1\}$.

This equation gives rise to the next second-order difference equation:

$$-1 = g_m(\tau_{m+1} - \tau_m) - r_m(\tau_m - \tau_{m-1}).$$

This equation can be solved conveniently by converting it into two first-order difference equations. The first one is defined by

$$\delta_m = \tau_{m+1} - \tau_m,$$

and the second one by

$$\delta_m = (r_m/g_m)\delta_{m-1} - (1/g_m).$$

The two conditions needed to fix the solution of the second-order difference equation are:

$$g_a\delta_a = -1,$$

since r_a is zero by the boundary condition of the original process, and

$$\tau_c = 0.$$

It is easy to verify by the mathematical induction on the index that

$$\delta_k = -(1/g_k p_k^e)(p_a^e + \cdots + p_k^e),$$

for $k = a, a+1, \ldots$, after we rewrite the ratio r_n/g_{n-1} by p_{n-1}^e/p_n^e by using the detailed balance condition.

Summing the expression for δ_k we obtain

$$\tau_m = -\sum_{k=m}^{c-1} \delta_k.$$

By selecting a as the initial condition we arrive at the expression for the mean first passage time from state a to state c as

$$\tau_{a,c} = \sum_{k=a}^{c-1} \frac{1}{g_k p_k^e} \sum_{\mu=a}^{k} p_\mu^e.$$

Reasoning analogously in the case where state a is treated as absorbing, we obtain the mean first passage time from state c to state a

$$\tau_{c,a} = \sum_{k=a}^{c-1} \frac{1}{g_k p_k^e} \sum_{\mu=k+1}^{c} p_\mu^e.$$

5.11.1 *First-passage times of unstable dynamics*

We apply the result of the previous section to a situation in which the macroeconomic Eq. (5.9) has two stable and one unstable equilibria, as in one of our simulation studies.

Suppose that there are three critical points in the macroeconomic equation:

$$\phi_a \leq \phi_b \leq \phi_c,$$

where we write state a as ϕ_a, and so on, to conform with the notation used in the macroeconomic Eq. (5.9). Suppose that the middle state is locally unstable and the other two states are locally stable.

To calculate the probability of reaching a vicinity of ϕ_c from the domain of attraction of ϕ_a, the exact positions of the initial and final states are not important, because the system runs through all of the states in the vicinity of these two stable points in a time much shorter than the transition time between these two states. We take ϕ_a as the initial state and ϕ_c as the final state. Therefore, we make ϕ_c an absorbing state and calculate the first-passage probability from ϕ_a.

If the system starts out at a state near the boundary of the domain of attraction of ϕ_a −, that is, close to ϕ_b − any probability distribution originally peaked near ϕ_b evolves over time and does not remain localized. To paraphrase van Kampen (1992, p. 330), evolution occurs as follows:

(1) The density broadens rapidly, but fluctuations across ϕ_b are possible.
(2) Two peaks develop, separated by a low peak at ϕ_b. Practically no probability is exchanged across ϕ_b. Consequently, total probabilities contained in each peak are practically constant over time.
(3) Peaks reach local equilibrium shapes. This density is metastable. On a very long time scale, fluctuations across ϕ_b transfer probability between the two peaks.

We can summarize or capture the essence of the behavior in a way analogous to that of the example in Section 2.4.1. We let $p(x, t)$ be the probability density function for a real variable x.[41] Let

$$\pi_a = \int_{-\infty}^{\phi_b} p(x, t) dx,$$

and

$$\pi_c = \int_{\phi_b}^{\infty} p(x, t) dx$$

be the probabilities to the left and right of the unstable equilibrium state ϕ_b. These probabilities are governed by the master equation

$$d\pi_a/dt = -w_{a,c}\pi_a + w_{c,a}\pi_c = -d\pi_c/dt.$$

---

[41] In our example of Sections 5.9 and 5.10, x ranges from −1 to 1. In that case, we replace the lower l imit of integration by −1 and the upper limit by 1.

If we set up an absorbing barrier at ϕ_c, then the equation changes to

$$d\pi_a/dt = -w_{a,c}\pi_a.$$

The mean time before absorption by ϕ_c is

$$-\int_0^\infty t\frac{d\pi_a}{dt}dt = 1/w_{a,c},$$

where we use the notation $\tau_{a,c} = 1/w_{a,c}$ presented in the introduction to Section 5.11.

Because these two probabilities sum to one, we can solve for

$$\pi_a(\infty) = \frac{\tau_{a,c}}{\tau_{a,c} + \tau_{c,a}}.$$

Substituting out the expressions for the mean first-passage times obtained earlier, we note that

$$\pi_a(\infty) = \frac{\sum_{k=a}^{c-1} \frac{1}{g_k p_k^e} \sum_{\mu=a}^{k} p_\mu^e}{\sum_{k=a}^{c-1} \frac{1}{g_k p_k^e}}.$$

In this expression, if $\sum_a^\mu p_\mu^e$ is approximated by the maximum term p_a^e, then $\pi_a(\infty)$ is equal to p_a^e.

Using the discrete-time formulation, we can calculate this absorption probability as follows: We let $f_m(t)$ be the probability density of being absorbed by state c in the next t time unit when the initial condition is state m. Then,

$$\pi_m = \int_0^\infty f_m(t)dt$$

is the probability of being absorbed by state c from the initial state m. From the expression for the Laplace transform for f_m, we note that

$$\pi_m = \hat{f}_m(0),$$

where $\hat{f}_m$ is the Laplace transform of f_m.

From the recursion relationship

$$f_m(t) = g_m\Delta t f_{m+1}(t - \Delta t) + r_m\Delta t f_{m-1}(t - \Delta)$$
$$+ \{1 - (g_m + r_m)\Delta t\}f_m(t - \Delta t),$$

we derive the differential equation for f_m as

$$\frac{df_m}{dt} = g_m(f_{m+1} - f_m) - r_m(f_m - f_{m-1}).$$

The initial condition is $f_m(0) = 0$.

We take the Laplace transform of this differential equation and set s to zero to obtain

$$(g_m + r_m)\pi_m = g_m\pi_{m+1} + r_m\pi_{m-1}.$$

This second order difference equation for π_m is solved in two steps as before. Let

$$\Delta_m = \pi_m = \pi_{m+1} - \pi_m.$$

The two conditions are $\pi_c = 1$, and $\pi_a = 0$. The first follows because the system is already at the absorbing state, and the second states that state a is another absorbing state from which there is no possibility of escaping to state c. Solving the first order difference equation

$$\Delta_m = (r_m/g_m)\Delta_{m-1},$$

we obtain

$$\Delta_k = \frac{g_a p_a^e}{g_k p_k^e}\Delta_a,$$

where, as before, we replace the ratio $r_\mu/g_{\mu-1}$ with $p_{\mu-1}^e/p_\mu^e$. Next, we use $\pi_c = 1$ to eliminate Δ_a. The result is

$$\pi_m = \left(\sum_{k=a}^{m-1}\frac{1}{g_k p_k p_k^e}\right)\left(\sum_{k=a}^{c-1}\frac{1}{g_k p_k^e}\right)^{-1}.$$

We write this as $\pi_{c,m}$.

Proceeding exactly analogously, we can obtain the expression for the probability of being absorbed by state a from the initial state m,

$$\pi_{m,a} = \left(\sum_{k=m}^{c-1}\frac{1}{g_k p_k p_k^e}\right)\left(\sum_{k=a}^{c-1}\frac{1}{g_k p_k^e}\right)^{-1}.$$

It is reassuring to verify that $\pi_{m,a} + \pi_{m,c} = 1$.

Recalling that $g_k = W_{k,k+1}$ and the expression for $p_e(k)$, we see that

$$\tau_{c,a} \approx \text{const} \exp[\beta N\{U(b) - U(a)\}],$$

after we recall the equation which determines the critical points,

$$2\beta\Delta G(b) = \ln\frac{1+b}{1-b}$$

and that

$$\beta\left[U\left(\frac{1+n}{N}\right) - U\left(\frac{n}{N}\right)\right] \approx 0.$$

On the average, it takes the time given by

$$\tau_{c,a} = \text{const}\exp(\beta N V),$$

for N agent to cross over from state a to state c, where V is the height of the potential barrier from state a to state b. This could be a very long time.[42] This result is essentially the same as that captured by the simple example in Chapter 2.

5.12   The master equation for hierarchical dynamics

This section continues the discussion of dynamics with hierarchically structured state spaces mentioned at the end of Chapter 2. There are N agents. With binary choices, there are 2^N possible configurations in the state space of this model. If each agent can choose from α alternatives, then there are α^N points in the state space. As we discuss in Section 2.5.1, we can organize these states into a K-level tree as follows: The state space is first divided into m_1 clusters. Each cluster is then subdivided into m_2 clusters at the second level of hierarchy. At the bottom, there are $m_1 m_2 \cdots m_K$ clusters or nodes in total.

The master equation is given by

$$\frac{dp_a}{dt} = \sum_{b \neq a}[w_{ba}p_b(t) - w_{ab}p_a(t)],$$

where $p_a(t)$ is the (occupancy) probability at time t of the system being in state a, identified with a particular cluster, that is, a leaf of the tree, and where the transition probability rate from state a to state b is denoted by w_{ab}. We discussed a simple example in Section 2.5.3.

We first assume that the transition rate w_{ab} depends only on the tree distance between a and b. Recall that this distance is the minimal number of levels retraced toward the root until a common node is located that is shared by nodes a and b. We denote the transition rate between two nodes with tree distance k by w_k, that is, $w_{ab} = w_k$ when $d_{a,b} = k$, where d is tree distance.

Because this distance is symmetric, $w_{ab} = w_{ba}$. Namely, the detailed balance condition is met with equal equilibrium probabilities for all states.

In Section 2.5.4, we illustrate how dynamics with tree-structured state space can be aggregated. In this model, we aggregate states in the same way. When the probabilities of the states being in a cluster at the lowest level of the hierarchy are (nearly) equalized, these states can be lumped together and the number of the system states is reduced by a factor m_K to form a $(K - 1)$ level tree, and so on.

---

[42] Ceccatto and Huberman (1989) reach a similar conclusion in a somewhat different context.

To convey this idea simply, we set K to 2 in the next example. Each cluster is indexed by (j_1, j_2), where the first index refers to the cluster at level 1, and the second to the cluster in the bottom level of the hierarchy. We define

$$p_{j_1}(t) = \sum_{j_2=1}^{m_2} p_{j_1, j_2}(t), \quad j_1 = 1, \ldots, m_1. \tag{5.30}$$

These probabilities are normalized by

$$\sum_{j_1=1}^{m_1} p_{j_1}(t) = 1.$$

Given a particular node denoted by (j_1^*, j_2^*), we note that

$$\sum_{j_2 \neq j_2^*} p_{j_1^* j_2} = p_{j_1^*} - p_{j_1^* j_2^*}.$$

We also have

$$\sum_{j_1 \neq j_1^*} p_{j_1} = 1 - p_{j_1}^*.$$

In this notation the master equation becomes

$$\frac{dp_{j_1 j_2}(t)}{dt} = w_2 + (w_1 - w_2)p_{j_1} - [m_1 m_2 w_2 + m_2(w_1 - w_2)]p_{j_1 j_2},$$

where we define a time constant τ_2 by $1/\tau_2 = m_1 m_2 w_2 + m_2(w_1 - w_2)$.

Summing the master equation with respect to the second index, we obtain

$$dp_{j_1}(t)\, dt = m_2 w_2 - m_1 m_2 w_2 p_{j_1},$$

where we define another time constant τ_1 by $1/\tau_1 = m_1 m_2 w_2$.

The solution of this differential equation is

$$p_{j_1}(t) = m_1^{-1} + e^{-t/\tau_1}[p_{j_1}(0) - m_1^{-1}].$$

Substituting this in the differential equation for $p_{j_1 j_2}$, and integrating it, we obtain

$$p_{j_1 j_2}(t) = \frac{1}{m_1 m_2} + m_2^{-1} e^{-t/\tau_1}[p_{j_1}(0) - m_1^{-1}]$$
$$+ e^{-t/\tau_2}[p_{j_1 j_2}(0) - m_2^{-1} p_{j_1}(0)].$$

This equation clearly shows that deviation from the equilibrium at level 1 is eliminated with time constant τ_1 and at level 2 with time constant τ_2. These are the two time constants of these dynamics.

We assume that transitions between states at small distances from each other are easier than those at large distances, that is, $w_1 \gg w_2$ and $\tau_1 \gg \tau_2$, because, by assumption, a transition between two states in the same cluster is much more likely to occur than a transition between states in different clusters. After a time elapse of $O(\tau_2)$, the probabilities become

$$p_{j_1 j_2}(t) \approx (m_1 m_2)^{-1},$$

that is, the states in the same cluster at level 2 have nearly the same probabilities. After an elapse of time of $O(\tau_1)$, states in the clusters on level 1 have nearly equal probability, $1/m_1$, and the system is in equilibrium.

In this example the equilibrium probabilities are the same for all states because of our assumption that the transition rates depend only on the tree distance between the states. If they are not the same, we redefine the transition rate w_{ab} to be $w_k e^{-0.5\beta(U_b - U_a)}$ and similarly for w_{ba}, where U_b is the value of a potential in state b, and β is some nonnegative constant. Then, the detailed balance condition is satisfied with the equilibrium probabilities defined by

$$p_e(a) = e^{-\beta U_a}/Z,$$

where we write the equilibrium probability of state a as $p_e(a)$, and Z is the normalizing constant. This is a Gibbs distribution, and it is essentially the same as the example in Section 2.5.

The master equation becomes

$$dp_a dt = e^{-\beta U_a} \sum_{b \neq a} w_{ba} p_b(t) - \left(\sum_{b \neq a} e^{-\beta U_b} w_{ab} \right) p_a(t).$$

We redefine the time constants by

$$1/\tau_1 = w_1 Z,$$

and

$$1/\tau_2 = w_1 Z + (w_1 - w_2) Z_{j_1},$$

where

$$Z_{j_1} = \sum_{j_2} e^{-\beta U_{j_1 j_2}},$$

and

$$Z = \sum_{j_1} Z_{j_1}.$$

More generally, with a K-level tree, we have

$$p_{j_{r+1},\ldots,j_K}(t) = \sum_{j_r=1}^{m_r} p_{j_r,\ldots,j_K}(t).$$

The solution of this master equation is

$$p_{j_1\cdots j_K}(t) = \sum_{r=1}^{K} e^{-t/\tau_r}\left[\frac{p_{j_r\cdots j_K}(0)}{N_{r-1}} - \frac{p_{j_{r+1}\cdots j_K}(0)}{N_r}\right] + 1/N_K,$$

with

$$1/\tau_r = \sum_{j=r}^{R} N_i(w_i - w_{i+1}),$$

where $w_{K+1} = 0$, and $N_i = \prod_{j=1}^{i} m_j$.

When m_i is the same for all i, the autocorrelation function is given by

$$p_0(t) = (m-1)\sum_{r=1}^{K} m^{-r} e^{-t/\tau_r} + m^{-K},$$

with

$$1/\tau_r = \sum_{i=r}^{K} m^i(w_i - w_{i+1}).$$

When the transition rate is

$$w_k \approx e^{-\beta\delta_k},$$

and when δ_k is linear in k with the constant of proportionality, δ, Ogielski and Stein (1985) showed that the initial state moves a distance $d(t)$ in time t given by

$$\langle d(t)\rangle \approx (\beta\delta)^{-1}\ln t,$$

and the correlation becomes

$$p_0(t) \approx m^{-d(t)} \approx t^{-\ln(m/\beta\delta)}.$$

We discuss their model in Chapter 7.

5.13 The Fokker–Planck equation

5.13.1 *Power series expansion*

We return in this section to the power series expansion of the master equation discussed in Section 5.3.1. After removing the macroeconomic terms from the power-series expansion of the master equation, the remaining terms yield the equation that has terms of $O(N^0)$ as the largest remaining terms:

$$\frac{\partial \Pi(\xi, \tau)}{\partial \tau} = -\alpha'_{1,0}(\phi)\frac{\partial(\xi \Pi)}{\partial \xi} + \frac{1}{2}\alpha_{2,0}(\phi)\frac{\partial^2 \Pi}{\partial \xi^2},$$

which is called a linear Fokker–Planck equation.

As for stochastic fluctuations about the mean, we apply the results obtained for the moments. For shorter notation, we call $\alpha_{1,0}$ and $\alpha_{2,0}$ by g and h, respectively. For example, we have $g = -\rho_0 + \gamma_0$ and $h = \rho_0 + \gamma_0$, in the case of the generalized birth-and-death process of Section 5.7. By repeated integrations by parts, we obtain

$$\frac{\partial \langle \xi \rangle}{\partial \tau} = g'(\phi)\langle \xi \rangle,$$

and

$$\frac{\partial \langle \xi^2 \rangle}{\partial \tau} = 2g'(\phi)\langle \xi^2 \rangle + h(\phi).$$

In the above, we impose the boundary conditions

$$\xi^2 \Pi|_{-\infty}^{\infty} = 0,$$

$$\xi \partial \Pi/\partial \xi|_{-\infty}^{\infty} = 0,$$

and

$$\Pi|_{-\infty}^{\infty} = 0.$$

From these two, we note that the differential equation for the variance of ξ is the same as that for the second moment $\langle \xi^2 \rangle$.

We let the initial conditions be given by

$$\langle \xi \rangle_0 = 0, \ \langle \xi^2 \rangle_0 = 0.$$

With the zero initial condition, $\langle \xi \rangle_\tau$ is identically zero if $g'(\phi)$ is negative. This establishes our earlier claim that the expected value of n/N is equal to ϕ.

Therefore, the first moment of x is governed by

$$\frac{\partial \langle x \rangle}{\partial \tau} = g(\langle x \rangle) + O(N^{-1}).$$

In a stationary state, the correlation is given by

$$\langle x(0)x(t) \rangle = \frac{h(\phi^s)}{2N|g'(\phi^s)|} \exp[-|g'(\phi)|\tau],$$

in locally stable regions, where $g(\phi^s) = 0$. See van Kampen (1992, p. 259).

When there is a locally unstable region, the assumption of a single peak in the set of probabilities no longer holds.

The partial differential equation for the characteristic equation

$$G(k, \tau) = \langle e^{ik\xi} \rangle$$

is given by

$$\frac{\partial G(k, \tau)}{\partial \tau} = ak(\partial G/\partial k) - \frac{1}{2}bk^2 G,$$

where we set $\alpha'_{1,0} = a$, and $\alpha_{2,0} = b$ for shorter notation. This linear partial differential equation can be solved by the method of characteristics (see, e.g., Sommerfeld 1949).

The characteristics are determined by

$$dk/d\tau = -ak,$$

and along the characteristics, $k = ce^{-a\tau}$, the function G is

$$\frac{d \ln G}{d\tau} = -\frac{1}{2}bk^2.$$

Hence we see that the characteristic equation for ξ is that of a Gaussian random variable, and its distribution is determined by the first two moments. These moments are the same as the ones we calculated above. We thus conclude that the solution of this Fokker–Planck equation is a Gaussian distribution.

Often, the Fokker–Planck equation is stated as

$$\frac{\partial P(x, t)}{\partial t} = -\frac{\partial[K(x)P(x, t)]}{\partial x} + (\epsilon/2)\frac{\partial^2[Q(x)P(x, t)]}{\partial x^2},$$

where we have seen earlier that these coefficients have the interpretation

$$K(x_0) = \lim_{t \downarrow 0}\langle x(t) - x_0 \rangle/t,$$

and

$$\epsilon Q(x_0) = \lim_{t \downarrow 0}\langle x(t) - x_0 \rangle^2/t,$$

that is, it is the average change of x per unit time at x_0 and the average squared change per unit time. The coefficient $K(x)$ is called the drift coefficient, and $Q(x)$ is the diffusion coefficient. By defining a probability flow function

$$I(x, t) = K(x)P(x, t) - (\epsilon/2)\frac{\partial[Q(x, t)P(x, t)]}{\partial x},$$

the Fokker–Planck equation is expressible as

$$\frac{\partial P(x, t)}{\partial t} = -\frac{\partial I(x, t)}{\partial x},$$

with the boundary condition $I(x, t) = 0$ as $|x|$ approaches infinity.

We obtain a stationary solution $P_e(x)$ of the Fokker–Planck equation by setting the right-hand side to zero and solving $I(x) = 0$, subject to boundary conditions, that is, solving

$$K(x)P_e(x) = (\epsilon/2)(\partial/\partial x)[Q(x)P_e(x)].$$

We can write

$$P_e(x) = \text{const } Q(x)^{-1} \exp\left[\frac{2}{\epsilon} \int \frac{K(y)}{Q(y)} \, dy\right].$$

5.13.2   The Kubo method

By inverting the transform of the characteristic equation derived in Section 5.3.2, we derive

$$p(x, t) = \frac{1}{2\pi} \int Q(\xi, t)e^{-i\xi x}d\xi = \frac{1}{2\pi} \int \exp\left[\frac{1}{\epsilon}\psi(i\epsilon\xi, \epsilon, t) - i\xi x\right]d\xi.$$

This equation is used by Kubo et al. (1973) to justify the asymptotic form that we use.

By specifying the functional form of w, we can evaluate fluctuations and movements of macrovariables. The transition probability density from x_0 to x in a time interval t_0 to t is given by

$$p(x, t \mid x_0, t_0) = \frac{1}{2\pi} \int \exp\left[\frac{1}{\epsilon}\psi(i\epsilon\xi, t \mid x_0, t_0) - i\xi x\right]d\xi.$$

Asymptotic evaluation of this integral yields an expression

$$p(x, t \mid x_0, t_0) = [2\pi \Delta(x, t \mid x_0, t_0)]^{-1/2} \exp\left[\frac{1}{\epsilon}\phi(x, t \mid x_0 t_0)\right],$$

where Δ is of $O(\epsilon)$.

If we write the average of $x(t)$ as

$$\langle x_t \rangle = E[x(t)] = y(t) + \epsilon u(t) + O(\epsilon^2),$$

then $y(t)$ is the most likely path of $x(t)$ up to $O(1)$, and the variance

$$\langle [x(t) - \langle x_t \rangle]^2 \rangle = \epsilon v(t) + O(\epsilon^2),$$

and the deviation of the average path from $y(t)$ comes from the nonlinearity of the first moment of the cumulant $c_1(y)$. It can be shown that they are given by

$$dy(t)/dt = c_1(y),$$
$$dv(t)/dt = 2c_1'(y)\sigma + c_2(y),$$

and

$$du(t)/dt = c_1'(y)u + \tfrac{1}{2}c_1''(y)\sigma.$$

The simplest case is that of Brownian motion for which we put

$$c_1(y) = -\gamma y,$$

and

$$c_2(y) = c = \text{constant}.$$

We have $y(t) = y_0 e^{-\gamma t}$, and

$$v(y) = v_e + (v_0 - v_e)e^{-2\gamma t},$$

with $v_e = c/2\gamma$.

The equilibrium density function is a Gaussian distribution:

$$p_e(x) = (2\pi\epsilon v_e)^{-1/2}\exp(-x^2/2\epsilon v_e).$$

The non-equilibrium density has the mean $y_0 e^{-\gamma t}$ and standard deviation $\sigma(t)$, where y_0 is the mean of $p_e(x, 0)$.

The correlation is given by

$$\langle x(t_1)x(t_2)\rangle = \langle x(t_1)^2\rangle\exp[-\gamma(t_2 - t_1)],$$

for $t_2 \geq t_1$.

Returning to the transition probability rates, suppose that the detailed balance condition is satisfied. Then we have

$$P_e(X)W(X' \mid X) = P_e(X')W(X \mid X'),$$

where $P_e(X)$ is the equilibrium probability density. We can express the transition probability rates as

$$W(X' \mid X) = \bar{W}(X' \mid X)[P_e(X')/P_e(X)]^{1/2},$$

where $\bar{W}(X \mid X') = \bar{W}(X' \mid X)$, since this expression certainly satisfies the detailed balance condition.

Since $P_e(X)$ is of the exponential type,

$$P_e(X) = \text{const}\,\exp[\Psi_e(X)],$$

we have

$$W(X' \mid X) = \bar{W}(X' \mid X) \exp\{(1/2)[\Psi_e(X') - \Psi_e(X)]\}.$$

Suppose further that

$$(1/N)\Psi_e(X) = -\beta f(x).$$

Then the normalized transition probability rate is given by

$$w(x,r) = \bar{w}(x,r) \exp[-(1/2)\beta r (\partial/\partial x) f(x) + O(\epsilon)],$$

where

$$\bar{w}(x,r) = \bar{w}(x + \epsilon r, -r) = \bar{w}(x, -r) + O(\epsilon).$$

The odd moments of $\bar{w}$ are evaluated as

$$c_n(x) = 2 \int dr r^n \bar{w}(x,r) \, \sinh[-(1/2)\beta \partial f(x)/\partial x] + O(\epsilon),$$

and the even moments are

$$c_n(x) = 2 \int dr r^n \bar{w}(x,r) \cosh[-(1/2)\beta \partial f(x)/\partial x] + O(\epsilon),$$

where the integrals are over $r \geq 0$.

An equilibrium state x_e is defined by

$$c_1(x_e) = 0.$$

Here, an equilibrium is meant to say that x_e is a constant. By defining $\Delta\phi$ to be $\phi - \phi_e$, and so on, we see that

$$\frac{d}{dt}\Delta\phi = -\gamma_e \Delta\phi + O(\Delta\phi),$$

where

$$\gamma_e = -\partial c_1(x)/\partial x,$$

evaluated at x_e. Deviation Δx has a normal density with mean zero and variance ϵv_e where

$$v_e = (1/2)c_2(x_e)/\gamma_e.$$

If the transition probability rates are given by the above equation, then

$$\gamma_e = \beta f''(x) \int_{r \geq 0} dr r^2 \bar{w}_0(x_e, r),$$

and

$$c_2(x) = 2\gamma_e/\beta f''(x_e) + O(\Delta x^2),$$

which yields

$$v_e^{-1} = \beta f''(x_e).$$

We discuss situations with multiple equilibria in Section 5.10.

So long as a system time path does not pass through unstable equilibrium in the course of its time evolution, deviation of the path about the most likely deterministic path $\phi(t)$ can be described as a normal distribution. (See Section 5.11 for discussion of unstable equilibria.)

Integrating over a short time span Δt of the set of three equations for ϕ, u, and σ, we express

$$y(t + \Delta t \mid x, t) = x_t + c(x_t)\Delta t + O(\Delta t^2),$$
$$v(t + \Delta t \mid x_t, t) = c_2(x_t)\Delta t + O(\Delta t^2),$$

and

$$u(t + \Delta \mid x_t, t) = O(\Delta t^2).$$

For multistage probability densities, we have the representation as a path integral:

$$p(x_1, t_1, \ldots x_n, t_n) = \int \exp\left\{-\int_{t_1}^{t_n} \frac{1}{2\epsilon c_2(x_t)}[dx_t/dt - c_1(x_t)]^2 \, dt\right\} dD,$$

where dD stands for integration with respect to all the arguments. And, the right-hand side of this becomes

$$\frac{1}{2\epsilon} \sum \frac{1}{2c_2(x_t)}[x_{t+\Delta t} - x_t - c_1(x_t)]^2 \Delta t + O(\Delta t^2).$$

5.14   The diffusion-type master equation

In the macro equation, we have tacitly assumed that $\alpha_{1,0}(\phi)$ or $c_1(y)a$ is not zero. If it is zero, then there is no corresponding macroeconomic equation. We also see from the moment relations that the variance term grows linearly

$$\langle \xi^2 \rangle = \alpha_{2,0}(\phi)\tau.$$

Starting from a delta function as the initial distribution, the fluctuations become of the same order as the macroeconomic variable after the elapse of time of $O[N/\alpha_{2,0}(\phi)]$.

If we now assume that an extensive variable X has an intensive variable $x = X/N$ and a width, that is, fluctuation of $O(N)$, and expand the master equation in $1/N$, dropping the assumption that the probability distribution is sharply peaked about some X, we extract from the power-series expansion

$$\frac{\partial P(x, \tau)}{\partial \tau} = -\frac{\partial(\alpha_{1,1}P)}{\partial x} + \frac{1}{2}\frac{\partial^2[\alpha_{2,0}(x)P]}{\partial x^2},$$

where we redefine the rescaled time τ by

$$\tau = N^{-2}f(N)t.$$

We do not approximate α_{ij} about a peak as before, but must leave them as nonlinear functions of x. This equation is called the diffusion approximation of the master equation. See van Kampen (1992, Chap. XI).

A diffusion process is a continuous-time stochastic process with the (strong) Markov property, and with (almost always) continuous sample paths. Its state space is an interval on the real line, including the entire $(-\infty, \infty)$. Some economic processes can be modeled by diffusion processes, or are approximated by such, as we describe in this section.

We let $X(t)$, $t \geq 0$, be a diffusion process[43] and let $\Delta_h X(t) = X(t + h) - X(t)$. The first two infinitesimal moments that are assumed to exist are defined by

$$\lim_{h \downarrow 0}(1/h)E[\Delta_h X(t) \mid X(t) = x] = \mu(x, t),$$

which is called the drift parameter, and

$$\lim_{h \downarrow 0}(1/h)E\{[\Delta_h X(t)]^2 \mid X(t) = x\} = \sigma(x, t),$$

which is called the diffusion parameter.

Higher moments are usually zero.

Vector-valued diffusion processes have analogs of these infinitesimal relations. Analysis of many discrete-time stochastic models are made easier by approximating with analogous diffusion models. We show this by several examples.

5.14.1   Ornstein–Uhlenbeck model

A well-known diffusion process is the Brownian motion and the Ornstein–Uhlenbeck processes, which have the entire real line as the state space. The

---

[43] If diffusion processes are terminated at possibly random times, then they are called diffusions with killing.

drift and diffusion parameters, respectively, are

$$\mu(x) = -\alpha x$$

and

$$\sigma^2(x) = \sigma^2 = \text{constant}.$$

For a Brownian motion, α is zero.

A discrete version of the Ornstein–Uhlenbeck process is the Ehrenfest urn model. There are two urns, A and B, containing a total of $2N$ (indistinguishable) balls. When there are i balls in urn A, there will be $i + 1$ balls with probability $1 - i/N$ next time (that is, Δt instant later), and $i - 1$ balls with probability $i/2N$. Letting $X_N(t)$ denote the number of balls in urn A at time instant t, we can express this as

$$Pr[\Delta X_N = \pm 1 \mid X_N(t) = x] = 1/2 \pm (N - x)/2N.$$

We rescale this process both in time and state space by

$$Y_N(\tau) = \frac{X_N([N\tau]) - N}{\sqrt{N}},$$

where $[N\tau]$ is the integer part of $N\tau$, and we let $N \to \infty$, and $\Delta t \to 0$, while keeping the product fixed, $\Delta t = 1/N$.

In the above, N in the numerator is a centering constant, $1/\sqrt{N}$ scales the state variable, and N in $N\tau$ rescales time. A unit of time for Y_N process is roughly equal to N transitions of the original X_N process because $\Delta t = 1/N$.

We define ΔY as $Y_N(\tau + 1/N) - y_N(\tau)$. Then, noting that $Y_N(\tau) = y$ is $X_N([N\tau]) = N + y\sqrt{N}$, we get

$$Pr[\Delta Y = \pm 1/\sqrt{N} \mid Y_N(\tau) = y] = (1/2) \mp y/2\sqrt{N}.$$

Using the above, we calculate the first two infinitesimal parameters of the Y_N process as

$$(1/\Delta t)E[\Delta Y_N \mid Y_N(0) = y] = -y,$$

and

$$(1/\Delta t)E[(\Delta Y_N)^2 \mid Y_N(0) = y] = 1,$$

and we verify that

$$(1/\Delta t)E[(\Delta Y_N)^4 \mid Y_N(0) = y] = 1/N,$$

which goes to 0 as $N \to \infty$.

This last condition is sufficient for the existence of a process, called a standard process, and it is also a diffusion process (see Karlin and Taylor 1981, Chap. 15, for detail).

5.14.2   *Wright–Fisher model: A binary-choice model*

This example restates the genetic models of Karlin (1966, pp. 197–200) in economic language. It is an example of birth-and-death processes as well. This model can be used to describe a population composed of agents of two types: For example, there are N agents type a and type b. These types could be a number of things: state of expectations, optimistic versus pessimistic; adopting one or the other strategy in advertising, production, or investment; buying or not buying particular assets or pieces of information; employed and unemployed and searching for jobs; and so on.

An extensive macrovariable is the number of agents of type a. An intensive variable is $y = X/N$. This example is first described in terms of X and later transformed in terms of y. The value of X describes the state of this model. The state changes its value at discrete time instants by having a randomly selected agent changing its type with nonzero probability. Suppose that $X(t) = j$. Then, a randomly selected agent is of type a with probability j/N, and type b with probability $1 - j/N$. We let α be the probability that type a changes to type b at the next time instant, and we let β denote the probability that type b is changing into type a. Then,

$$p_j = (j/N)(1 - \alpha) + (1 - j/N)\beta$$

is the probability that a randomly selected agent is type a.

The process $X(t)$ evolves as a Markov chain governed by the transition probability matrix with elements

$$p_{ij} = C_{N,j} p_i^j (1 - p_i)^j.$$

We assume that α and β go to zero in such a way that $\alpha N \to \kappa_1$ and $\beta N \to \kappa_2$.

We define $Y_N(\tau) = X([N\tau])/N$, and let $\Delta t = 1/N$. Thus,

$$\Delta Y_N(\tau) = Y_N(\tau + 1/N) - Y_N(\tau),$$

is such that its first two infinitesimal parameters are

$$\lim_{h\downarrow 0+} (1/h) E[\Delta Y_N(\tau) \,|\, Y_N(\tau) = y] = -\alpha y + (1 - y)\beta,$$

and

$$\lim_{h\downarrow 0+} (1/h) E\{[\Delta Y_N(\tau)]^2 \,|\, Y_N(\tau) = y\} = y(1 - y).$$

The fourth infinitesimal moments are shown to vanish in the limit.

In some cases, it is better to modify the definition of p_i by including effects to indicate that one of the two choices is better. For example, if it is somehow better for type a to survive than type b, then this factor is included by assuming that the ratio of type a and type b agents surviving to the next time is $1 + s$. Then, we redefine p_i by

$$p_i = \frac{(1+s)[i(1-\alpha) + (N-i)\beta]}{(1+s)[i(1-\alpha) + (N-i)\beta] + [i\alpha + (N-i)(1-\beta)]}.$$

Karlin and Taylor (1981) show that setting s to be σ/N, the drift and diffusion parameters are

$$\mu(y) = \sigma y(1-y),$$

and

$$\sigma^2(y) = y(1-y),$$

respectively.

Since the type a individual is increased only if the type b agent dies, the conditional probability that $X(t+) - X(t) = 1$, given that $X(t) = j$, is

$$(1 - j/N)[(j/N)(1-\alpha) + (1 - j/N)\beta].$$

Similarly, the conditional probability that $X(t+) - X(t) = -1$, given that $X(t) = j$, is

$$(j/N)\{(1 - j/N)[1 - \beta + (j/N)\alpha]\}.$$

Then, assuming that the probability that the state changes during the time interval $(t, t+h)$ is $\lambda h + o(h)$, we obtain λ_j by multiplying the first conditional probability by λ, and μ_j is equal to λ times the second conditional probability, for j ranging from 0 to N.

To examine what happens to the stationary distributions as $N \to \infty$, we assume that α and β go to zero in such a way that $\alpha N \to \kappa_1$ and $\beta N \to \kappa_2$. Then, following Karlin and Taylor (1981) and defining $k = [xN]$ as the greatest integer less than or equal to xN, we obtain

$$\pi_k \sim c\kappa_2 N^{\kappa_2 - 1} x^{\kappa_2 - 1}(1-x)^{\kappa_1 - 1}.$$

We have

$$\pi_k \Big/ \sum_i \pi_i \sim \frac{x^{\kappa_2 - 1}(1-x)^{\kappa_1 - 1} dx}{\int_0^1 x^{\kappa_2 - 1}(1-x)^{(\kappa - 1)} dx}.$$

5.14.2.1 Unemployment-rate model

We can think of type a in the previous example as the unemployed, and let $X(t)$ be the number of unemployed in a population of size N.[44] Then, the intensive

---

[44] This model is based on Aoki (1989b).

variable $Y_N(t)$ is the rate of unemployment of this population. We use the factor $1 - s$ with $s = \sigma/N$ to incorporate the effects that the unemployed are more disadvantaged than the employed in surviving or staying in job-search activities. Following the same procedure as above, we find that the first infinitesimal parameter is reduced by a factor proportional to σ times the second infinitesimal parameter:

$$\mu(y) = -\kappa_1 y + \kappa_2(1 - y) - \sigma y(1 - y).$$

The second infinitesimal parameter remains the same:

$$\sigma^2(y) = y(1 - y).$$

We use the connection between the Ito diffusion and the generator of the diffusion, see Øksendal (1989, Chap. VII). The Ito stochastic differential equation with these infinitesimal parameters is

$$dy_t = \mu(y)\,dt + \sqrt{y(1 - y)}\,dW_t,$$

where W_t is a standard Brownian motion.

We expand the drift and diffusion parameters around $y_{t_0} = y_0$, and consider an approximate stochastic differential equation

$$du_t = (a - bu_t)\,dt + (c + eu_t)dW_t,$$

where $u_t = y_t - y_0$; $a = \kappa_2(1 - y_0) - \kappa_1 y_0 - \sigma y_0(1 - y_0)$; $b = \kappa_1 + \kappa_2 + \sigma(1 - y_0) - \sigma y_0$; $c = \sqrt{y_0(1 - y_0)}$; and $e = (1 - 2y_0)/[2\sqrt{y_0(1 - y_0)}]$.

To solve this differential equation, we recall Ito's theorem (Arnold 1974, p. 90) and the result in Arnold (p. 136): The solution u_t can be written as

$$u_t = f(Y_t, Z_t),$$

with $f(x, y) = e^x y$, where

$$Y_t = \ln \phi_t,$$

and

$$\frac{d\phi_t}{\phi_t} = -b\,dt + e\,dW_t,$$

and

$$Z_t = \int_{t_0}^{t} \phi_s^{-1}(a - ce)\,ds + \int_{t_0}^{t} \phi_s^{-1}c\,dW_s.$$

We note that

$$\phi_t = \exp(-\gamma t + eW_t),$$

where $\gamma = b + e^2/2$. Hence, the solution is

$$u_t = \exp(-\gamma t + eW_t)\left[u_0 + \int_{t_0}^t (a - ce)\exp(\gamma s - eW_s)\,ds \right.$$
$$\left. + c\int \exp(\gamma s - eW_s)\,dW_s \right],$$

where the initial condition u_0 is zero in this case, but in general it may not be.

We next calculate the conditional expectation of the unemployment rate, $E(u_{t+s} \mid u_t)$ to see how different model parameters affect this expectation. We need the following fact.

We let $Z_t = \exp(at + bW_t)$. Then,

$$E(Z_t) = \exp(a + b^2/2)t.$$

To see this, we apply Ito's lemma to Z_t

$$dZ_t = aZ_t dt + bZ_t dW_t + (b^2/2)Z_t(DW_t)^2 = (a + b^2/2)Z_t dt + bZ_t dW_t.$$

Integrating this, we have

$$Z_t - Z_0 = (a + b^2/2)\int_0^t Z_s ds + b\int_0^t Z_s dW_s.$$

We take the expectation of the above (conditional on the sigma algebra at time t=0), recalling that $E(\int^t Z_s dW_s) = 0$. The result is

$$EZ_t = Z_0 + (a + b^2/2)\int_0^t EZ_s ds,$$

or differentiating it with respect to t

$$dEZ_t/dt = (a + b^2/2)EZ_t,$$

that is, the result we want after integrating this with respect to t.

Now, we apply this fact to the expectation of u_{t+s} conditional on u_t. Thus,

$$E(u_{t+s} \mid u_t) = e^{-bs}u_t + (a - ce)\int_0^s e^{-bv}\,dv$$
$$= e^{-bs} + [(a - ce)/b](e^{-bs} - 1),$$

because of the definition of γ. As $s \to \infty$, it approaches a rate $(ce - a)/b$, which in the original model parameters is

$$\frac{(1 - 2y_t)/2 + \kappa_1 y_t - \kappa_2(1 - y_t) + \sigma y_t(1 - y_t)}{\kappa_1 + \kappa_2 + \sigma(1 - 2y_t)}.$$

Since y_t is small, at most of $O(0.1)$, we can approximate it by

$$\frac{0.5 - \kappa_2}{\kappa_1 + \kappa_2 + \sigma}.$$

5.14.3   Logistic model

In this model, the population size ranges from N_1 to N_2 $(N_2 \geq N_1)$. Very often the birth and death rates are proportional to the population size. We assume that, given the population size $X(t)$,

$$\lambda = \alpha[N_2 - X(t)],$$

and

$$\mu = \beta[X(t) - N_1].$$

We can put a number of possible interpretation on the terms "birth" and "death" in this example as well. When the population size is n, each of n agents has an infinitesimal birth rate λ, and $\lambda_n = \alpha n(N_2 - n)$. Similarly, the relation $\mu_n = \beta n(n - N_1)$ obtains. We note that

$$\pi_{N_1+m} = \frac{\prod_0^{m-1} \lambda_j}{\prod_1^m \mu_i},$$

which simplifies to

$$\frac{N_1}{N_1 + m} C_{N_2-N_1, m} (\alpha/\beta)^m.$$

Hence, after normalizing it by the sum,

$$p_{N_1+m} = \frac{c}{N_1 + m} C_{N_2-N_1, m} (\alpha/\beta)^m,$$

where the constant c is appropriately scaled.

CHAPTER 6

Modeling interactions III: Pairwise and multiple-pair interactions

So far, we have concentrated on modeling a large collection of microeconomic agents subject to field-effect externality. We have shown that we can specify the transition rates for microeconomic units in such a way that they satisfy the detailed balance conditions, and that we establish Gibbs distributions as equilibrium distributions for the state of finite-state Markov chains, and we have investigated the implications of multiple equilibria for the resulting macroeconomic dynamics.

In this chapter, we discuss another circumstance under which Gibbs distributions arise by modeling pairwise externality or interaction among microeconomic units. Unlike field effects, unit i is assumed to interact with unit j, which can be specified as one of i's neighbors or can be anonymous, as in Cornell and Roll (1981). When more than a single pair is involved in interaction, then we have multiple-pair interactions. A history of past interaction patterns may affect the current interaction coefficients, causing complex patterns of interactions to evolve over time.

6.1 Pairwise or multiple-pair interactions

6.1.1 Ising model

Ising used interaction among magnetic dipoles located at neighboring sites to model phase transitions and spontaneous magnetization in 1925. See Ellis (1985, p. 131). He put magnetic dipoles at d-dimensional regular lattice sites. Later this regular lattice structure was relaxed and a graph structure was introduced with dipoles located at nodes of the graph. This type of neighborhood interaction was later formalized as a Markov random field which has a well-developed literature. Markov random field models have many applications outside physics, including sociology and economics. See Spitzer (1975) and Kindermann and Snell (1980).

Two important contributions by Ising are: (1) The notion of interaction between neighboring sites was formalized by a Hamiltonian in which quadratic terms of the dipole variables were summed only over neighborhoods; and (2) probabilities were assigned to configurations of spin dipoles as Gibbs distributions.

The Ising model is the best-known example of local or short-range inter-action. Only agents located at sites of a well-defined neighborhood of a given site or agent are assumed to interact pairwise. There are many examples in a variety of disciplines that have adapted the Ising modeling scheme in various guises to deal with local interaction. A given unit interacts with other units with short-range forces or effects of some sort, or with units of similar characteristics in some metric. Behavior of a large collection of basic units is then shown to exibit some group reinforcement or other collective or mass effect, that is, externalities due to some type of neighborhood interaction. Opinion, preference, or network formations of a political or economic nature in sociology or economics, and even the question of how schools of fish manage to swim in the same direction, (see Callen and Shapero 1974) have been explained using models that have basically the same mathematical structures as the Ising model.

Weidlich was probably the first who used Ising model to explain the polarization (or dichotomy) phenomena in sociology (Weidlich 1974, Weidlich and Haag 1983). Events or instances in which one particular brand out of several brands of similar qualities and price ranges dominates the market have been explained as critical or phase-transition behavior, in analogy to spontaneous magnetization in the original Ising model.[1]

In economics, the Ising model has been adapted to explain diffusion of technical innovations by modeling the process of adoption of new technology as the result of interaction with neighboring firms. The notion of neighborhood is somewhat forced or artificial in this and some other economic applications, however. Föllmer (1973) introduced the Ising model into general equilibrium economics, using the framework introduced by Hildenbrand (1971). In this setup, he needed a certain ergodicity result. As we see in Chapter 5, however, this ergodicity property does not hold in more interesting economic problems that have multiple equilibria, because they call for the framework of ergodic decompositions. Since Föllmer, there have been a few economic models patterned after the Ising model, or its generalized version called the Curie–Weiss model. See Brock (1993) or Durlauf (1991), among others.

6.1.1.1 Long-range pairwise interactions
The Curie–Weiss model is a simple modification of the Ising model. It allows all agents in the system to interact with each other with a constant strength that

---

[1] Arthur (1989) describes several such historical instances. He is apparently unaware of the work by Weidlich and proposes an ad hoc nonlinear urn model to explain the dominance of market by a single brand. Liebowitz and Margolis (1994) are somewhat critical of Arthur's historical accounts.

descreases at the rate of $1/N$ as N becomes large. Interaction is long-range because every pair in the system interacts with the same strength.

The spin-glass models modify the Curie–Weiss model by allowing the interactions between pairs of agents to be random. These models may be more general in that higher-order multiple-agent interactions terms can be included. One such example is from van Hemmen, van Enter, and Canisius (1983).

6.2   A model of pairwise externality

In Chapter 5, we use a generalized birth-and-death process to model a collection of interacting microeconomic units that use discrete or lumpy adjustment rules. There, externality is of the field-effect variety, and no specific pairwise interaction or interconnection pattern among units is assumed.

In this section, we go beyond Ising models and utilize recent developments in the literature of neural networks to develop a model of a collection of microeconomic agents who interact pairwise. We draw an analogy between the dynamics of a large collection of microeconomic units that have discrete-choice sets and the dynamics of a large collection of neurons.

Neuron i's membrane potential builds up as a result of the activities of neurons to which it is connected in the upstream of impulse propagation. The state of a neural assembly is fully described by the set of electrical voltages of its individual neurons. When the membrane voltage of a neuron exceeds its threshold, it emits an electrical impulse, and the membrane voltage is reduced to its resting level. Except for a sign change, the inventory depletion process and the process of membrane voltage buildup are statistically and analogously describable. We can think of the voltage buildup as the negative of the inventory depletion as orders are filled. When the inventory drops to a level s, then, discontinuously, the level is increased to a level S. When the membrane voltage reaches a threshold, it drops to its resting value.

In economic models, we face a familiar and largely unresolved problem of how to introduce dynamics by which equilibrium states are reached in models composed of a large number of interacting agents, even when we manage to define and characterize equilibria of such models. Needless to say, we do not wish to resort to the traditional but unsatisfactory device of tatônnement processes mediated by auctioneers, or some other artificial devices, such as representative agents, to avoid dynamics. This is the main reason why we propose the use of jump Markov processes to describe interaction dynamics.

The same kind of indeterminacy exists in describing dynamic behavior and equilibria of neural networks. Unlike economic models, one looks to biological factors for the clues in modeling the dynamics of networks of neurons. More specifically, Little (1974) and Hopfield (1982) provide two dynamic mechanisms for artificial neural networks. We describe the Little model since he bases his development on the master equation, which is also our basic dynamic equation in this book, and since he derives nonquadratic and other forms of Hamiltonians. Later in this section, we relate the Little model to economic models.

6.2.1   Potentials and equilibrium probability distributions

In Chapter 5, we introduce potentials as the exponents of equilibrium Gibbs distributions, and observe that the potentials are the sum of two components: a term representing objective functions such as cost or utility and another term which is an entropy term that measures multiple ways of achieving the same macroeconomic configuration. Here, we provide further characterization of potentials in the exponents of Gibbs distributions.

Since we want to model a large collection of agents, we begin by reviewing how potentials arise in our models. This is a useful way to proceed because once potentials are found we can describe the equilibria of the models by the Gibbs distribution. Generally, no obvious extensive quantity exists that can serve as a potential for our economic model. We focus on reversible Markovian systems, that is, Markov processes that satisfy the detailed balance conditions. Then we can construct potentials for them. Recall that stationary Markovian processes are reversible if and only if the detailed balance condition is satisfied.[2] The exponential part of a Gibbs distribution becomes path independent because of the Kolmogorov criterion, that is, it is a potential, and is called a Hamiltonian by physicists. See Peretto (1984). Once we have the Gibbs distribution, we can utilize all the tools for macroscopic adjustment dynamics that we introduce in our discussion of master equations in Chapter 5.

In a Markovian system, probabilities of certain states being occupied evolve, adopting a discrete-time formulation for now, according to

$$P(Y, n+1) = \sum_X W(Y \mid X) P(X, n),$$

where states for the collection of agents are denoted by uppercase letters X, Y, Z, to distinguish them from those of individual agents which are labeled by lowercase letters, x, y, z, or by i, j, k, and where the one-step transition probability from state X to Y is denoted by $W(Y \mid X)$, on the assumption that the process is time-homogeneous, that is, the transition probabilities are independent of time. In more detail, we mean by $P(X, n)$ the probability of the model being in state X at time $n\Delta$, where Δ is a small positive time unit, and we write the one-step transition probability $W(Y, \Delta \mid X, 0)$ as $W(Y \mid X)$ for short. We arrange these transition probabilities into matrix W which has $W(Y \mid X)$ for

---

[2] See Chapter 4 in this volume, or, Kelly (1979) or Pollett (1986) for reversible Markov processes.

fixed X, and Y ranging over all possible configurations arranged as a column vector $\mathbf{X}$. Thus, the elements of each column sum to one.

The Perron–Frobenius theorem tells us that all the eigenvalues of this matrix W are not greater than one in magnitude, and that there is a unique eigenvalue $\lambda_1 = 1$ with its left eigenvector having all elements equal to one, that is, $v(X) = 1$, for all $\mathbf{X}$. We denote the components of the right eigenvectors by $u(Y)$ for this eigenvalue.

We know that the stationary or equilibrium probability distribution exists in the form

$$P_e(X) = \Xi^{-1} e^{-\beta H(X)}$$

for some function $H(X)$ which is an extensive quantity, called the potential or Hamiltonian, if and only if the detailed balance condition is met, that is,

$$w(Y \mid X) e^{-\beta H(X)} = w(X \mid Y) e^{-\beta H(Y)}.$$

Recall Section 3.3.

We can write the limiting expression for the equilibrium probability as

$$P_e(Y) = \lim_{n \to \infty} P(Y, n).$$

Using the polar decomposition of W,[3] we know that only the left and right eigenvectors of the largest eigenvalue $\lambda_1 = 1$ remain in the limit, that is,

$$P(Y, n) = \sum_Y W(Y \mid X)^n P(X, 0) \to \sum_X v(X) u(Y) P(X, 0),$$

as $n \to \infty$. Since $v(X) = 1$ for all X, and $P(X, 0)$ sums to 1, we obtain

$$P_e(Y) = u(Y).$$

Therefore, if $u(Y)$ is positive for all Y,[4] then we can define a potential or a Hamiltonian as

$$H(Y) = H_0 - (1/\beta) \ln[u(Y)],$$

and

$$P_e(Y) = \Xi^{-1} e^{-\beta H(Y)},$$

where $\Xi = \sum_X e^{-\beta H(X)}$ is assumed to be finite.

---

[3] See Aoki (1989, p. 10) on polar decomposition.
[4] Markov processes that satisfy the detailed balance conditions also satisfy this condition.

Returning to a continuous-time description, the probabilities evolve according to the master equation given by

$$\frac{\partial P(X, t)}{\partial t} = \sum_{Y \neq X} [w(X \mid Y) P(Y, t) - w(Y \mid X) P(X, t)], \qquad (6.1)$$

where $w(X \mid Y)$ is the time-homogeneous transition rate from state Y to state X that is introduced in Chapter 4 and used extensively in Chapter 5 and elsewhere. We assume that the Markov chain is stationary.

The Kolmogorov criteria is shown to be satisfied (Kelly 1979, p. 21, and Exercise 1.5.2). We let X be a state from which transitions to all other states are possible, that is, $W(S \mid X)$ is positive for all states $S \neq X$. Then, for any other two states, Y and Z, we have

$$W(X \mid Z) W(Z \mid Y) W(Y \mid X) = W(X \mid Y) W(Y \mid Z) W(Z \mid X). \qquad (6.2)$$

6.2.2   Analogy between economic agents and neurons

We give a slightly different version of the example in Chapter 5 to illustrate a loose analogy of the Little model dynamics to economic dynamic systems composed of a large number of agents who use the well-known (s, S) policy for inventory holding, where the bounds s and S may vary from agent to agent. Examples may be storekeepers who stock and sell items (intermediate goods) that are bought and possibly supplied by other storekeepers in the model. They also may buy and sell with outside consumers (final demands) as well. Customers (including other storekeepers) place orders of random magnitude at random times to a given owner i with whom they transact. Thus owner i's inventory level then behaves like the (negative) membrane voltage in the Little model, except that they are being reduced by a random amount at random times rather than being built up at random times by random amounts as in membrane potentials, until it reaches a threshold (lower bound s) θ_i, at which time storekeepers i order up to an upper bound S. The average inventory level of owner i then is analogous to the average membrane potential $\bar{a}_i$ as we described earlier

$$\bar{a}_i = \sum_j C_{ij} s_j,$$

where s_j stands for the state of owner j (such as ordering or not ordering). His or her ordering activities can be distributed among other agents with whom he or she conducts business, and the amounts are captured by the random coefficients C_{ij}. Admittedly this is crude, but it is sufficient to characterize Markov chain models (in synchronous version) or continuous-time Markov chains (in asynchronous version) to capture macroeconomic features of this type of interaction by focusing on the fraction of agents who are ordering at any given time.

Into this basic framework, we can build in the effects of past experience or policy actions by making the coefficients or thresholds functions of past histories of transactions or policy actions. We illustrate this in Section 6.4 when we discuss the time evolution of patterns of interaction and how they depend on the precise specifications of these model parameters.

Kelly (1979) and Whittle (1986) discuss interactions or dynamics of social groups. By endogenizing some of the parameters that characterize the rates of birth, death, migration, or formation and breakup of groups of various sizes, we can introduce dynamics into social interactions, just as we can for economic interactions. Pollett (1986) discusses a framework in which a collection of inter-acting stationary Markov processes that satisfy the detailed balance conditions are still describable by product-form invariant measures with respect to which the whole process satisfies the detailed balance conditions. These processes may thus provide useful devices for modeling interacting microeconomic agents be-yond the kind we have discussed. See our discussion in Section 4.5. For a model of agents with heterogeneous beliefs, for example, rates of arrivals of new infor-mation from exogenous sources ultimately will influence collective dynamics. See Aoki (1975b) or Friedman and Aoki (1992) for such examples.

6.3 Example of information-exchange equilibrium distribution

This is an illustration of a way of deriving transition rates or in this case transition probabilities since we use the discrete time formulation for easy illustration. We adapt the Little model[5] to derive the transition probabilities and the equilibrium distribution of a large number of agents who exchange information with each other. The basic scheme is similar to that of the opinion formation model of Weidlich and Haag (1983). We modify it by introducing a threshold level or reservation level. We let agent i exchange information with other agents. Agent i changes his or her mind only when the net effect of the signals received exceeds his or her reservation level.

This basic framework can be interpreted in several ways, such as agents being bullish or bearish, or in the market or not in the market in financial applications, buying or not buying additional pieces of information in decision making, or more generally being optimistic or pessimistic. The threshold level can be called agent i's skepticism or mood, for example. Thus, each agent can be in one of two states, which are denoted by state variable $s_i = \pm 1$. The state of the model, also called configuration, is denoted by uppercase letters X, Y, Z,

---

[5] Little (1974).

and so on, where $X = \{s_1, s_2, \ldots, s_N\}$, and N is the total number of agents in the model. The total number of configurations is 2^N.

We assume that the net effect of these interactions is represented by a net random signal received by agent i, $a_i(X)$, when the system as a whole is in configuration X. The signal is normally distributed with mean

$$\bar{a}_i(X) = \sum_j C_{i,j} s_j(X), \tag{6.3}$$

where $s_j(X)$ means agent j's state when the configuration is X. We assume that the variance is the same for all agents, and is denoted by ϕ. For simpler exposition, the coefficient C_{ij} is taken to be a constant.[6] It may reflect the precision of agent j's information or frequency of contact with agent j in some sense. Agent i's reservation level is denoted by θ_i.

The probability that agent i will be in the market next period, given the current configuration X (i.e., the transition probability in the discrete-time formulation) is then given by

$$W[s_i(n+1) = 1 \mid X(n)] = Pr(a_i \geq \theta_i) = 1 - Pr(a_i \leq \theta_i),$$

where

$$Pr(a_i \leq \theta_i) = \int_{-\infty}^{\theta_i} p(a_i) da_i,$$

where $p(\cdot)$ is the Gaussian density with mean $\bar{a}_i$ and variance ϕ. We change the variable of integration to $y = (a_i - \bar{a}_i)/\sqrt{2\phi}$. Then, we see that this probability is expressible using the error function as

$$(1/2)\left\{1 - \mathrm{erf}\left[\frac{h_i(X)}{\sqrt{2\phi}}\right]\right\},$$

where $h_i(X)$ is defined by[7]

$$h_i(X) = -\bar{a}_i + \theta_i,$$

and where the error function is defined by

$$\mathrm{erf}(x) = \frac{2}{\sqrt{\pi}} \int_0^x e^{-y^2} dy.$$

We note that $W[s_i(n+1) = -1 \mid X(n)] = 1 - W[s_i(n+1) = 1 \mid X(n)]$.

---

[6] We later refer to the work of Little and Shaw (1978) in which the coefficients are averages of some past interaction history.

[7] An exogenous influence on the agents by some aggregate or exogenous signals such as optimism or pessimism of individual agents may be included to affect the threshold levels of agents.

Since $s_i = \pm 1$, and noting that the error function is an odd function, we can write both cases concisely as

$$W[s_i(n+1) \mid X(n)] = (1/2)\{1 - \mathrm{erf}[s_i(n+1)u_i]\}, \tag{6.4}$$

where $u_i = h_i[X(n)]/\sqrt{(2)}\phi$. Larger θ_i means smaller transition probability $W(s_i \mid X)$. Larger variance means that the transition probabilities approach $1/2$.

Using the approximation[8]

$$(1/2)[1 - \mathrm{erf}(u_i)] \approx (1 + e^{\kappa u_i})^{-1},$$

where $\kappa = 4/\sqrt{\pi}$, and by assuming that agents conditionally act independently given configuration, we can write the one-step transition probability from configuration X to configuration Y where Y is made up of $s_i(n+1)$, $i = 1, \ldots, N$, as

$$W(Y \mid X) = \prod_{i=1}^{N} W[s_i(Y) \mid X] = \prod_i \frac{e^{\beta s_i(Y)h_i(X)}}{e^{\beta s_i(Y)h_i(X)} + e^{-\beta s_i(Y)h_i(X)}}, \tag{6.5}$$

where $\beta = \sqrt{2/\pi}\phi^{-1}$, and where we now write $s_i(Y)$ for $s_i[Y(n+1)]$ and $s_i(X)$ for $s_i[X(n)]$.

The numerator of Eq. (6.5) can be written as $\exp[-\beta H(Y \mid X)]$, where

$$H(Y \mid X) = -\sum_i s_i(Y)h_i(X) = \sum_{ij} C_{ij}s_i(Y)s_j(X) - \sum_i \theta_i s_i(Y). \tag{6.6}$$

The denominator is the normalizing constant which is equal to the sum of the numerator over all configurations. To write the denominator explicitly, we note that $\prod_{i=1}^{N}(e^{z_i} + e^{-z_i}) = \sum_Z \exp(\sum_{i=1}^{N} \sigma_i z_i)$ for any z_i sequence, where configuration Z is made up of $\sigma_i = \pm 1$, $i = 1, \ldots, N$.[9] We can write the denominator as $\prod_i 2\cosh[\beta s_i(Y)h_i(X)]$, where cosh is the hyperbolic cosine. This expression for the denominator is also equal to $2\cosh[\beta h_i(X)]$ since cosh is an even function of $s_i(Y) = \pm 1$.

Hence we have the expression for the transition probability from configuration X to configuration Y as

$$W(Y \mid X) = \frac{e^{-\beta H(Y \mid X)}}{\sum_Z e^{-\beta H(Z \mid X)}} = \frac{e^{-\beta H(Y \mid X)}}{\prod_i 2\cosh[\beta h_i(X)]}. \tag{6.7}$$

The higher the noise level, the higher the variance ϕ, and the lower the parameter β.

---

[8] Ingber (1982) shows that this is indeed a good approximation.

[9] For example, with $N = 2$, we have $(e^{z_1} + e^{-z_1})(e^{z_2} + e^{-z_2}) = \Sigma_{\sigma_1 = \pm 1, \sigma_2 = \pm 1} e^{\sigma_1 z_1 + \sigma_2 z_2}$.

We know from Kelly (1979, pp. 5, 21, and Exercise 1.5.2) that a Gibbs distribution exists as an equilibrium distribution

$$P_e(X) = \Xi^{-1} e^{-\beta H(X)}$$

for some function $H(X)$, where Ξ is the normalizing constant, if and only if the detailed balance condition holds, and that the detailed balance condition holds if and only if the Kolmogorov criterion is met. We next show that these transition probabilities satisfy the Kolmogorov criterion, hence the detailed balance condition. Here, we use the criterion in the form given in Eq. (6.2), for any three configurations X, Y, Z of any irreducible Markov chain:

$$W(X \mid Y) W(Y \mid Z) W(Z \mid X) = W(X \mid Z) W(Z \mid Y) W(Y \mid X).$$

For shorter exposition, we assume that θ_i is zero for all i from now on. When Eq. (6.5) is substituted into this relation, the left-hand-side expression is

$$\prod_{X,Y,Z} \frac{\exp\left[\beta \sum_{ij} C_{ij} s_i(X) s_j(Y)\right]}{\prod_i 2\cosh\left[\beta \sum_{ij} C_{ij} s_j(Y)\right]},$$

and similarly for the right-hand side. We note in particular that the denominators of both sides are the same. The numerators are equal only if $C_{ij} = C_{ji}$. Suppose that this holds, and we consider the ratio $W(X \mid Y)/W(Y \mid X)$. From Eq. (6.5), using the cosh expression for the denominator, we obtain

$$\frac{W(X \mid Y)}{W(Y \mid X)} = \frac{\exp\left[\beta \sum_{ij} C_{ij} s_i(X) s_j(Y)\right] \prod_i 2\cosh\left[\beta \sum_j C_{ij} s_j(X)\right]}{\exp\left[\beta \sum_{ij} C_{ij} s_i(Y) s_j(X)\right] \prod_i 2\cosh\left[\beta \sum_j C_{ij} s_j(Y)\right]}.$$

If C_{ij} is symmetric, then we see that the ratio is expressible as

$$W(X \mid Y)/W(Y \mid X) = F(X)/F(Y),$$

where

$$F(X) = \prod_i \cosh\left[\beta \sum_j C_{ij} s_j(X)\right].$$

Therefore, by the detailed balance condition, the equilibrium distribution is the Gibbs distribution with the exponent

$$H(X) = -(1/\beta)\ln F(X).$$

This is the potential (Hamiltonian) for the collection of symmetrically interacting microeconomic units.

In the case of small β (high-noise-level case), we can use an approximate expression:

$$\ln \cosh \beta x \approx \ln(1 + \beta^2 x^2/2) \approx \beta^2 x^2/2,$$

that is, the Hamiltonian is approximately given by

$$H(X) = -\frac{\beta}{2} \sum_{i,j=1}^{N} K_{i,j} s_i(X) s_j(X),$$

with $K_{i,j} = \sum_k C_{i,k} C_{k,j}$.

With a large β (a small-noise case), we use the relation

$$\ln \cosh \beta x \approx \beta |x|,$$

and hence

$$H(X) \approx -\sum_{i=1}^{N} \left| \sum_{j=1}^{N} C_{i,j} s_j(X) \right|.$$

It is interesting to observe that a quadratic Hamiltonian obtains as a large noise-limiting case, and for a small-noise case, the Hamiltonian is not quadratic.

For small β, Eq. (6.5) is approximated by

$$W(Y \mid X) \approx [1 - \beta H(Y \mid X)]/2^N,$$

since the denominator becomes approximately equal to $\sum_Z[1 - \beta H(Z \mid X)] \approx \sum_Z 1 = 2^N$. This shows that, for small β, each configuration becomes approximately equiprobable. The denominator is exactly 2^N if $\sum_Z s_i(Z) = 0$.

Since the Little model, on which the above derivation is based, is a discrete-time model, agents make decisions in lock-step manner. It is better to treat decisions by microeconomic units as asynchronous, and their dynamics as governed by the continuous-time jump processes.[10]

6.4   Time evolution of patterns of interaction

As an illustration of how past experience can be built into the interaction coefficients and how they can affect time evolution of interactions among microeconomic units, we use the model of Little (1974) and follow Little and Shaw

---

[10] Rather than the lock-step dynamics of discrete-time Markov chains, it is well known that we can introduce continous-time Markov chains in which times between transitions are exponentially distributed. See Chapter 4. Except for some technical conditions to exclude explosive behavior, nothing new arises. See Karlin and Taylor (1981, Sec. 14.4) for the conditions. Alternatively, we can allow processes to proceed asynchronously but time aggregate events within a given time interval to produce discrete-time processes.

(1978) to describe how interaction patterns can evolve over time for specific forms of interaction coefficients C_{ij}.

We treat $s_i(X)$ such that

$$\sum_X s_i(X)s_j(X) = 2^N \delta_{i,j}.$$

This assumption means that when states of microeconomic units are averaged over all possible configurations, they are uncorrelated. Later manipulations become simpler if we introduce a vector of states for unit i in all possible system configuration by an 2^N-dimensional column vector

$$S^i = [s_i(C_1), s_i(C_2), \dots, s_i(C_{2^N})]',$$

where we denote a configuration from 1 to 2^N by $C_1, \dots, C_{2^N}$, and define a matrix $S = (S^1, \dots, S^N)$. We introduce a normalized vector ψ^i which is a vector of state of microeconomic unit i over all possible configurations with component

$$\psi^i_X = 2^{-N/2} s_i(X).$$

We define a matrix

$$\Psi = (\psi^1, \psi^2, \dots, \psi^N),$$

which is $2^N \times N$, and note that $\Psi'\Psi = I_N$.

We first assume that θ_i is zero for all i. The transition probability is

$$W(Y \mid X) \approx \frac{1 - \beta \sum_j C_{ij} s_i(Y) s_j(X)}{2^N},$$

where we assume that the coefficients C_{ij} are determined from past experience of interactions by

$$C_{ij} = \left[\sum_{A,B} U_{A,B} s_i(A) s_j(B) \right] b_i b_j,$$

where $U_{A,B} = U_{B,A}$, and b_i are all nonnegative. Effects of past history of interaction are embedded into the matrix U. This means that past interactions in which units i and j may be in different configurations are averaged over all configurations. The factors $b_i b_j$ can indicate some predilection for interaction. We can consider the effects of different specifications as well.

We can express $H(Y \mid X)$ hence $W(Y \mid X)$ compactly using these matrices. First, we define

$$T_{A,B} = \sum_i s_i(A) s_i(B) b_i,$$

and define matrix $T = (T_{A,B})$ which is $2^N \times 2^N$, and note that the matrix T is expressible as

$$T = SBS',$$

where $B = \mathrm{diag}(b_1, \ldots, b_N)$, and

$$H(Y \mid X) = \sum_{A,B} U_{A,B} T_{X,A} T_{Y,B} = (T\,U\,T')_{Y,X}.$$

Matrix T has ψ's introduced earlier as eigenvectors. There are only N nonzero eigenvalues, the rest being all zeros. The nonzero eigenvalues are

$$\lambda_i = 2^N b_i,$$

for $i = 1, 2, \ldots, N$.

With nonzero θ_i, we can suppose that the ratio $\theta_i / \sum_j C_{ij}$ is the same for all i. We denote this common value by c. Then,

$$H(Y \mid X) = -\sum_i s_i(Y) \sum_j C_{ij}[s_j(X) + c].$$

Now, if we suppose that

$$C_{ij} = \sum_{A,B} U_{A,B} s_i(A)[s_j(B) + c] b_i b_j,$$

then

$$H(Y \mid X) = -\sum_{A,B} U_{A,B} \left[\sum_i b_i s_i(Y) s_i(A) \right] \left[\sum_j v_j [s_j(X) + c] \right] [s_j(B) + c].$$

We can proceed as before, now defining $T_{A,B} = \sum_i [s_i(A) + b][s_j(B) + b]$. This newly defined matrix T has one large eigenvalue $(b^2 N + 1)2^N$, eigenvalue 2^N of multiplicity $N - 1$, and all remaining eigenvalues are zero. This implies that one pattern of activity dominates all others in this model.

CHAPTER 7

Sluggish dynamics and hierarchical state spaces

This chapter discusses dynamics on state spaces that are hierarchically structured. As the examples in Sections 2.5.3 and 5.12 suggest, dynamics with such structured state spaces may exhibit sluggish responses, much slower than the exponential decays associated with ordinary dynamics.

In this chapter, we introduce the notion of the "renormalization group" into hierarchically structured state spaces as a method of aggregation, that is, as a procedure for trimming the level of branches of tree hierarchies. This aggregation scheme is different from the one we introduced via the master equation in Chapter 5, and potentially useful, but not standard in the macroeconomic literature.

We also address the question of sensitivity of macromodels with respect to details of microeconomic unit specification. By means of several examples, we show that the sluggishness of dynamic responses of hierarchically structured systems is robust, or insensitive to details of micromodel specifications.

7.1   Examples of hierarchically structured state spaces

Some examples of hierarchically structured models are presented in Chaper 2. Here are some more examples to serve as additional evidence of the relevance of hierarchically structured models in macroeconomic modeling.

Further discussion of the notion of ultrametrics, and dynamics with transition rates (probabilities) that are functions of ultrametrics follow this section.

7.1.1   Correlated patterns of macroeconomic activity

Suppose that a dynamic model composed of N microeconomic units has M locally stable equilibria, and we use a superscript to designate the equilibrium, for example, $x_i^\mu, i = 1, \ldots, N$, and $\mu = 1, \ldots, M$. Suppose further that we classify these equilibria into a finite number of categories by the magnitudes of pairwise correlations of state variables in these equilibria. The correlations are calculated by

$$q_{\mu,\nu} = (1/N) \sum_{i=1}^{N} x_i^{\mu} x_i^{\nu},$$

between, say, two local equilibria, μ and ν.[1]

Suppose that $M = 24$, and we classify 24 local equilibria, denoted by s_i, $i = 1, \ldots, 24$, into a three-level tree with $B_1 = 3$, $B_2 = 2$, and $B_3 = 4$, where B_i is the number of branches emanating from node i. At level 3 (bottom of the tree), each leaf corresponds to one of $3 \times 2 \times 4 = 24$ local equilibria of this macroeconomic model.

Suppose we prune the tree back to two levels by lumping four leaves at level 3 into one leaf, that is, each leaf of this two-level tree contains four leaves of the original three-level tree. There are now 3×2 leaves (clusters) at the bottom, each of which contains four locally stable equilibria of the model. For example, node 1 on level 2 contains equilibria s_1 through s_4, and node 6 contains equilibria s_{21} through s_{24}.

Suppose further that the pairwise correlations of these equilibria within the same node on level 2 are the same, which is denoted by ρ_1. If we denote the correlation between equilibria s_i and s_j by $q_{i,j}$, then we have $q_{1,2} = q_{17,20} = \rho_1$. Those pairwise correlations between equilibria belonging to two distinct clusters with the common node on level 1 are denoted by ρ_2. For example, $q_{3,8} = q_{20,21} = \rho_2$, and those between two states with the root as the common node are ρ_3, such as $q_{1,9} = q_{1,13}$, where $\rho_1 \geq \rho_2 \geq \rho_3$. See Fig. 7.1. In Section 7.1.9 we give an example of a branching process that possesses properties such as those hypothesized here.

In this way, we can classify local equilibria into a tree structure. When x is a vector, and if we calculate correlations for each component of the vectors separately, then we have vectors of correlations. We may encounter difficulty in classifying these vectors uniquely into clusters as the next example illustrates.

7.1.2   *Vectors in an infinite dimensional space*

The notion of ultrametric distance is introduced in Chapter 2. As a simple example of spaces with ultrametric distances, we consider a set composed of M N-dimensional vectors in which each component is chosen independently, with a finite mean v and second-order moment s^2. Vectors are denoted with superscripts. The correlation between two vectors x^a and x^b is

$$\lim_{N \to \infty} (1/N) \sum x_i^a x_i^b = v^2 (1 - \delta_{ab}) + s^2 \delta_{ab}.$$

[1] At the moment we assume that we can do this unambiguously. In Chapter 2, we have seen an example that suggests that such a classification does not always work.

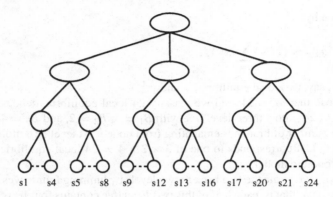

Fig. 7.1. A three-level tree.

If we define the distance $d_{a,b}$ in this space by the above, then all triangles formed by three arbitrary points are equilateral, that is, special isosceles triangles. This space is an example of an ultrametric space in which all triangles are isosceles (Schikhof 1984, p. 47).

7.1.3   Cost barriers as ultrametrics

This example shows that the notion of ultrametrics naturally arises in optimization problems. We consider a deterministic cost minimization problem for some unspecified dynamic system with a state vector of several – actually many – dimensions, and suppose that the cost index admits several local minima. In other words, suppose that functions to be minimized have complicated cost landscapes.

We denote by $C_{a,b}$ the largest cost in going from a local minimum a to another local minimum b via paths connecting these two. This notion captures a feature of the cost landscape in which a barrier separates the basin in which a local minimum a is located from that in which b is located. For definiteness, we suppose that a path is a sequence of state vectors in which two successive vectors differ by a change in a single component of the vector that defines a configuration. This type of transition between microstates arises in many optimization problems: For example, in going from point A to point B in a city where streets are layed out in checkered patterns, you cannot go straight from A to B but must go along city blocks and change directions. Similarly, in a model composed of several microeconomic agents with binary-valued microstate variables, a change in configurations is produced by some agent i changing its state if we take a time interval small enough to ensure that the probability of several agents changing their states in the same time interval is a higher order of smallness.

By definition, the barrier separating locally stable state a from b is the smallest of the largest cost

$$C_{a,b} = \min_{a \to b}[\max \ C],$$

where $a \to b$ indicates all paths from a to b and the maximization is taken over all paths from a to b.

The barriers are ultrametric because they satisfy the strong-triangle inequality

$$C_{a,b} \leq \max_{c}[C_{a,c}, C_{c,b}].$$

More generally, the minimal spanning tree method[2] can be used to construct a particular kind of ultrametric, called a subdominant ultrametric. See Jardine and Sibson (1971) or Rammal and Toulouse (1986).

7.1.4   Voter preference patterns among alternatives

In this example, N voters are divided over three alternatives, A, B, and C, say, and are clustered into six categories over their preference orders of the three alternatives. They are: $A > B > C$, $A > C > B$, $B > A > C$, $B > C > A$, $C > A > B$, and $C > B > A$, where '$>$' means "preferred to." We number these preference patterns from 1 to 6 for convenience. The distribution of voters among these six categories can be organized as a two-level tree. The first level has three categories, depending on what is most preferred. C_1 contains voters who prefer A to B or C. C_2 contains those who prefers B above all others, and voters belong to C_3 if they prefer C most of all. Each of these categories is further divided into two subcategories, depending on what voters prefer as their second choice, given their first choice. See Fig. 7.2. Let $N_i, i = 1, \ldots, 6$ be the number of voters in subcategory i. As Berg (1985) discusses, the joint distribution of these six numbers is given by the Bose–Einstein statistics under certain assumptions on voter homogeneity of preferences.[3]

Here, we introduce the distance between the six patterns. If we wish to introduce dynamics into the problem by assuming that voters may switch randomly from one preference to another over time, then we may construct a Markov chain on the state space composed of these six patterns. The transition probabilities are introduced between the patterns, presumably as functions of the distances between them. Chapters 4 and 5 have examples of this type of dynamics on trees.

---

[2] See, for example, Murtagh (1983).
[3] See Chapter 3 and the Appendix for discussion of the Bose–Einstein allocations.

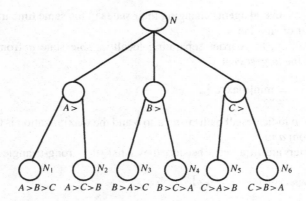

Fig. 7.2. A two-level tree with six preference patterns.

From symmetry considerations, we have $d_{1,2} = d_{3,4} = d_{5,6}$. We can set these distances to one. Also, by symmetry we have $d_{1,3} = d_{2,5} = d_{4,6}$, and $d_{1,6} = d_{2,4} = d_{3,5}$. For example, a voter changing his mind about his first preference between A and B is moving from pattern 1 to pattern 3. Those whose first preference changes from A to C are moving between pattern 1 and pattern 6, and so on. These distances should be larger than one because the moves involve changes in the first preferences and not the second preferences. We can assume that $d_{1,6} = d_{2,4}$ because both involve interchanges of the preferred alternatives in the first and the third positions, while keeping the second preference invariant. This means that all of these moves involve the same distance, call it two. With these assignments of distances, the nodes of a tree have ultrametric distances defined for them.

7.1.5   Champernowne's income distribution model

Pareto is generally credited with the discovery that the number of persons with incomes that exceed the rth category, when ranked by size, are distributed by $r^{-\rho}$, where ρ is close to one (Zipf 1949, Chaps. 9, 10).

Here, we describe a model of income distributions by Champernowne (1953), which has the equilibrium distribution of the Pareto type, as an example of a hierarchical system with the ultrametric distance defined on it.

He divides personal income into categories of equal proportionate width, starting from the minimum income level, $\underline{i}$, into $a\underline{i}$, $a^2\underline{i}$, and so on for some constant a greater than one. Category g thus covers the income range from $a^{g-1}\underline{i}$ to $a^g\underline{i}$, $g = 1, 2, \ldots$. Next he introduces the transition probability $p_{g,h}$ in which a person who is in category g at time t goes to category h at the next (discrete) time instant, and assumes that this probability is a function

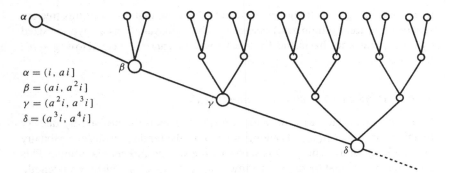

$\alpha = (\underline{i}, a\underline{i}]$
$\beta = (a\underline{i}, a^2\underline{i}]$
$\gamma = (a^2\underline{i}, a^3\underline{i}]$
$\delta = (a^3\underline{i}, a^4\underline{i}]$

Fig. 7.3. Champernowne's logarithmic income scale as a tree structure.

of $g - h$ only, that is, the transition probabilities are assumed to be time homogenous.

We will see how this scheme of transition probabilities can be constructed or understood from the viewpoint of a hierarchy with ultrametric distances. Before we do this, however, we note that a person in category g now expects his or her income at the next period to be about

$$\sum_h p_{g,h} i_h = \sum_{g-h} a^{g-h} i_g = \text{const } i_g,$$

namely, some constant times his or her current average, which we denote by i_g, the average income of persons in category g, since the average income of category g is about a^{g-h} times that of category h. For p_n sufficiently small for positive and large n, he or she assumes that this constant is less than one.

To recognize that this scheme is a hierarchy, see Fig. 7.3, where the tree is shown with leaves as level 1. (It is convenient here to show trees not as an upside-down tree with roots on top.) The leftmost node (leaf) is associated with catgory 1, that is,

$$C_1 = \{i; \ \underline{i} \le i \le a\underline{i}\}.$$

The second and the third nodes from the left contain incomes in category 2,

$$C_2 = \{i; \ a\underline{i} \le i \le a^2\underline{i}\}.$$

To be concrete, we think of the case $a = 2$. Since the width of C_2 is twice that of C_1, it is natural to use two leaves to represent C_2. Proceeding this way, C_3 is represented by four leaves together, and so on.

As seen in Fig. 7.3, C_2 may be identified with a node on level 2, C_3 as a node on level 3, and so on. In general, category C_g is a node on level g of this tree. Then, categories are nodes of the tree. We note that nodes of this tree are separated by tree (ultrametric) distances, which are functions as hypothesized by Champernowne, that is, the distance between C_g and C_h is equal to $\phi(g - h)$, for some function ϕ.

7.1.6   *Random walks on a logarithmic scale*

Hierarchies naturally arise in random walks in which the probability density function for step x, $p(x)$, has a long tail, that is, the random walks occasionally execute long jumps, and $p(x)$ is such that the second moment is infinite. This condition means that there is no natural scale to measure a typical jump length. Jumps or walks of all sizes occur and they form self-similar sets of clusters in a probabilistic sense (not in the literal geometric sense) as we describe later.

In this section, we use the Champernowne model of income distributions. This model can be interpreted as income following random walks on a logarithmic scale. We also show that the model can be thought of as a random walk on a hierarchy. We later discuss how hierarchies arise in general following Montroll and Shlesinger (1984). Here we have a simple example of random walks on a tree. We merely make the transition probabilities functions of ultrametric distance:

$$p_{i,j} = \rho(d_{i,j}) = p_0 / \left(a^{d_{i,j}-1} \right),$$

with $a \geq 1$, where $d_{i,j}$ is the tree distance between node i and node j. Thus, in Fig. 7.3, the distance $d_{1,2} = 1$, and the transition probability $p_{1,2} = p_0$. The distance between nodes 1 and 4, however, is three, and the corresponding transition probability is p_0/a^2.

Suppose we now change the structure of the tree slightly by defining states on leaves, 1, 2, 4, 16, 256, and so on, that is, starting from leaf 1, and at 2^{2^k} th leaves, $k = 1, 2, \ldots$. Then, starting from leaf 1, the distance to state 2, 3, $\ldots$ increases in the powers of 2; $d_{1,2} = 1$, $d_{1,3} = 2$, $d_{1,4} = 4$, $d_{1,5} = 8$, and so on.

To make the walk symmetric so that the mean is zero, we suppose the mirror image of the leaves extend to the negative direction of the x axis. The probability of a given jump x is

$$p(x) = \frac{a-1}{2a} \sum_{j=0}^{\infty} a^{-j} (\delta_{x,2^j} + \delta_{x,-2^j}).$$

For $a \leq 4$, the expression for the second moment

$$\langle x^2 \rangle = \frac{a-1}{a} \sum (4/a)^j,$$

diverges. As explained in Montroll and Shlesinger (1984, p. 81), the fractal dimension of the clusters of the random walks is

$$F = \frac{\ln a}{\ln 2}$$

in this model, and the effective dimension is $e = 1 + (2 - F)$ (see Montroll and Shlesinger 1984, p. 86), which is greater than 2 if a is less than 4. This effective dimension of the random walk ensures that the probability of the walk returning to the starting point is less than one. The two conditions that $\langle x^2 \rangle = \infty$, and that $e \geq 2$ are necessary for the random walk trajectories to generate a set of self-similar clusters of points. See also Huges, Montroll, and Shlesinger (1982).

7.1.7   Random multicomponent cost

Suppose we write two as the product of three factors α_i, $i = 1, 2, 3$, none of which is less than one. For example, we can make them all equal to $2^{1/3}$ which is about 1.44. Then, with $N = 20$, $2^{N/3} = 101.59$, or approximately 10^2. Thus with $N = 20$, approximately 10^6 configurations are divided into about 10^2 clusters or subsets, each of which contains about 10^4 configurations. Each such cluster can be further subdivided into another 100 clusters, each with about 100 configurations. We associate a two-level tree (omitting the root from the count of levels). Each leaf of this tree contains about 100 configurations on level 2, that is, at the bottom of the tree.

When the number of agents is 100, with three equal factors as in the case of 20 agents, the total number of configurations is split into 10^{10} clusters, each containing 10^{20} configurations. At the bottom level of the tree, each cluster contains about 10^{10} configurations, implying that there are about 10^{20} leaves! Even with only 100 agents, there are an incredible number of possible configurations.

As a more concrete example, we suppose that agents incur a cost in their activities that consists of two components. The first component, c_1, represents that part of the cost generally shared by all the agents in the model whereas the second, c_2, is more agent-specific. We measure the costs from some reference level, so that the c_i are random deviational cost components. We assume that the c_i are all independent and that their means are zero. See Section 7.1.8 where we characterize these variables as martingales.

Each agent in this model is assumed to have this cost decomposition. The total cost is the sum of the two for each agent,

$$c = c_1 + c_2,$$

and the economywide average cost is the average of the above over all agents. For simplicity, we assume that each component is binary valued, $c_1 = \pm\alpha$, and $c_2 = \pm\beta$, for example.

To illustrate with a small example, we suppose that there are three agents. Since there are $2^3 = 8$ ways for the three agents to incur each component of the costs, there are 8^2 configurations in total. The set of configurations is partitioned into eight subsets represented by eight nodes on level 1 of a tree. Then, each node contains, all possible realizations of the second component for a given realization of c_1 for the three agents. Each of these subsets is further partitioned into eight subsets, each of which now contains a single configuration, which is a particular realization of the second cost component for the three agents. Namely, on level 2, the set of configurations associated with each node on level 1 is further partitioned into two subsets, depending on the realized value of c_2, either β or $-\beta$.

In a more general setting, we can speak of a K component or factor decomposition of the cost of doing business or conducting some economic activity by agents such as firms or households.[4] With N agents, there are 2^{NK} number of configurations in total. If these configurations are partitioned on the basis of patterns of the first component, then there are 2^N clusters at level 1, each containing $2^{N(K-1)}$ numbers of configurations. Each cluster at level 1 is further partitioned into 2^N subclusters, and so on, until at level K, each leaf contains a single configuration.

The integer K is dictated by the degree of disaggregation used by the modeler, and of course varies according to the particular modeling context and needs. Typically, it is much smaller than the number N of agents in the system; still, it could be quite large, for example, $K = O(N^a)$, with a some number less than one.

7.1.7.1 *Example of a two-level tree*
We next calculate the joint probability that configurations 1 and 2, which are two leaves at level K of a tree, have cost c_1 and c_2, respectively, assuming that cost components are normally distributed.

We suppose that r is the closest common level to level K from which the two configurations separate. We can decompose the costs into the common part and the idiosyncratic part:

$$c_i = \phi + \phi_i, \quad i = 1, 2,$$

where

$$\phi = \sum_{j=1}^{r} c_j^i,$$

---

[4] We could equally speak of the policy effects or impacts on agents, and decompose them into economywide, sectorwide, and agent-specific effects.

and

$$\phi_i = \sum_{j=r+1}^{R} c_j^i, \quad i = 1, 2.$$

From our independence assumption of the deviational costs, it follows that ϕ, ϕ_1, and ϕ_2 are independent random variables. We separate the variance of c's into two components: var $\phi = NJ^2 v/2$, and var $\phi_i = NJ^2 (1 - v)/2$, for some v between zero and one. We write the joint density for the three independent random variables ϕ, $c_1 - \phi_1$, and $c_2 - \phi_2$, and integrate ϕ out to derive

$$P(c_1, c_2) = \text{const} \exp\left[-\frac{(c_1 + c_2)^2}{2N(1 + v)J^2} - \frac{(c_1 - c_2)^2}{2N(1 - v)J^2} \right].$$

The random variables c_k, $k = 1, \ldots, K$, are all normally distributed with zero mean, and variance σ_k, to be specified further below. We note that the partial sums of the cost expressions that can be naturally associated with nodes of the tree become martingales with these assumptions.[5]

Because K is much smaller than the total number of states for any reasonable size N, a large number of states will have costs nearly equal to each other. Given a state, the number of states that share the same node with it at level r but belong to a different cluster of states at level $r + 1$ is given by

$$\left(\prod_{j=r}^{K} \alpha_j \right)^N - \left(\prod_{j=r+1}^{K} \alpha_j \right)^N.$$

We write this expression as e^{Nu} to define the number u. As N goes to infinity, it approaches

$$u \to \sum_{j=r}^{K} \ln \alpha_j.$$

This is used to define the probability density of the cost levels. Since $(\alpha_K)^N$ can be large for large N, we can think of each cluster at the bottom as representing a set of microeconomic states with equilibrium as the average of the costs of these configurations. As we see in Chapter 5, the states in a given cluster can be thought to be distributed according to a Gibbs distribution.

---

[5] This assumption is not as arbitrary as it may appear on the first reading. Recall that all N agents contribute to each term in the cost decomposition expressions. It is thus natural to assume that the variance is proportional to N, given our assumptions on independence of agents' costs.

7.1.8   *Martingales*

Recall our discussion on tree metrics and martingales in Chapter 2. As before, we label the nodes of a tree by a superscript to indicate the path (branches) traced from the root to that particular node. For example, superscript $\mu = (\mu_1, \ldots, \mu_r)$ indicates the path from the root to a node at level r, where μ_j indicates the μ_jth node at level j (counting from the left).[6]

We can concatenate two superscripts, μ and ν, to denote a joint path indicated by superscript μ followed by that of ν. Therefore, two paths with superscripts (ρ, μ) and (ρ, ν) with distinct μ and ν share a common path denoted by ρ and then separate into two distinct paths denoted by μ and ν.

In the example of a system composed of three agents with two-component cost decomposition, we number the node on level 1 from the left as $\mu_1 = (1, 1, 1)$, $\mu_2 = (1, 1, -1)$, $\mu_3 = (1, -1, 1)$, and so on, where ± 1 stand for c_1 being $\pm \alpha$ for each of the three agents, for example, $(1, -1, 1)$ means that c_1 is α for agents 1 and 3, and is $-\alpha$ for agent 2. According to this convention, $C^{(2)}$ is the second cluster from the left on level 1, namely $c_1 = -\alpha$ for agent 3, and it is α for agents 1 and 2. There are eight configurations in this particular cluster. $C^{(1,3)}$ means that $c_1 = \alpha$ for all three agents, but $c_2 = -\beta$ for agent 2.

Now we consider any two paths of a K-level tree and the associated costs, $C^{(1)}$ and $C^{(2)}$. By considering the cost expressions to be deviational variables from some averages, and assuming independence of the additive cost components, we ensure the equality of the conditional expectation

$$E\left[C^{(\rho, \mu)} \mid C^\rho\right] = C^\rho,$$

that is, the deviational costs are martingales. We also note that costs associated with two distinct paths are independent, conditional on the cost associated with the node that is the closest common part of the two paths. In other words, if the common node is at level r, then conditional on the cost associated with the path from the root to that particular node on level r, $\sum_{i=1}^r c_i$, the additional costs from that level to whatever the level at the end of the paths are conditionally independent and have zero conditional mean. In this way, we can associate a set of martingale random variables with each node of the tree. Now, we consider the two costs associated with any two paths (ρ, μ) and (ρ, ν) branching out from the common node. We have

$$E\left[C^{(\rho, \mu)} C^{(\rho, \nu)} \mid C^\rho\right] = (C^\rho)^2,$$

and taking expectation again,

$$E\left[C^{(\rho, \mu)} C^{(\rho, \nu)}\right] = E(C^\rho)^2.$$

---

[6] With binary trees, the construction is identical to the coin-tossing space we discussed in Section 2.5.1.

This shows that the tree we have constructed above is not just any tree. It is characterized by the equality of the correlation of any two costs in the same node, conditional on the partial cumulative cost component at the closest common node, because costs are martingales as we have noted above.

The tree classification described above collects into a node all configurations that have the same correlation coefficient between any two of them. This partition is not always possible using correlations as we have shown by a counterexample of Feigelman and Ioffe (1987). Partitions are possible for this tree classification because we build the martingale properties into costs. See Section 7.1.9.

7.1.9   Branching processes

Consider a K-step Markov chain to generate y_k, $k = 1, \ldots, K$, by the transition probabilities $P_k(y_k \mid y_{k-1}, \ldots, y_1)$, where y_k takes on discrete values for simpler exposition. The value of K determines the level of hierarchy. Draws of y_k are independently repeated B times, where B is the number of branches of the tree, $k = 1, \ldots, K$. At the end (bottom of the hierarchy), we have B^K realizations of y_K associated with B^K branches. We can label them by the K-dimensional vector $\alpha = (\alpha_1, \ldots, \alpha_K)$ as y^α. We can associate a binary-valued random variable, s_i^α, by repeating the process for all N agents independently, $i = 1, \ldots, N$, and defining $s_i^\alpha = \text{sgn}(y_i^\alpha)$.[7]

We consider a set of vectors that is to be partitioned into a hierarchy. At the ith step, the tree has been generated up to the $(i-1)$th level. At the end of each branch, there is a cluster or partitioned subset. In the case of B branches per node, we draw B times a component of a stochastic vector, y_j^i, with a probability distribution conditioned by the values of the already-drawn vectors on that branch (the ancestors) $y^{i-1}, y_j^{i-2}, \ldots, y_j^1$. This branching process is defined by the distribution of $P_i(y^i \mid y^{i-1}, \ldots, y^1)$. At each level of the tree, such conditional distributions are specified.

The correlation between two vectors depends only on their ancestry and is larger, the closer they are in parenthood. In the limit of infinite levels of trees, this set of vectors becomes ultrametric. Using the chain rule of conditional

---

[7] Tree structures also can be associated with branching processes for k types of particles or agents, as pointed out by Moore and Snell (1978) and by Rammal and Toulouse (1986). From the root, each of k types of agents is generated with appropriate probabilities. Levels of trees correspond to generations in branching processes. An agent of a given type can produce agents of all types for the next generation with probability $p_{a,b}(i)$ which is the probability of a type a agent generating i agents of type b, for example. After K levels are generated, then we go back to the root and repeat the process N times to generate an N-agent tree.

probability densities,

$$p(a, b \mid c) = p(b \mid c)p(a \mid b, c),$$

and its integrated version

$$p(a \mid c) = \int p(b \mid c)p(a \mid b, c)\, db,$$

we write the joint density as the product of conditional densities:

$$p(y^1, y^2, \ldots, y^j) = p(y^{k+1}, y^{k+2}, \ldots, y^j \mid y^k, y^{k-1}, \ldots, y^1)$$

$$= \prod_{l=k+1}^{j} p(y^l \mid y^{l-1}, \ldots, y^1),$$

for $j \geq k$. In general, we have

$$E\big[y^{(\mu,\nu)} y^{(\mu,\nu')}\big] = E\big[E\big(y^{(\mu,\nu)} y^{(\mu,\nu')} \mid y^{(\mu)}\big)\big].$$

By the assumed conditional independence, the above equals $E[(y^{(\mu)})^2]$.

To illustrate, we let $K = 3$, and let the transition probability be given by $P_k(y_k \mid y_{k-1})$. Then, for the paths $\alpha = (\alpha_1, \alpha_2, \alpha_3)$ and $\beta = (\alpha_1, \alpha_2, \beta_3)$, the largest correlation is q_3, given by (now treating y's as continuous)

$$q_3 = \int P_1(y_1)dy_1 \int dy_2 P_2(y_2 \mid y_1) \left\{ \int P_3(y_3 \mid y_2)[\mathrm{sgn}(y_3)]^2 dy_3 \right\} = 1.$$

For a path $\beta = (\alpha_1, \beta_2, \beta_3)$, that is, when α and β share only α_1, we have

$$q_2 = \int P_1(y_1)dy_1 \int dy_2 P_2(y_2 \mid y_1)[P_3(y_3 \mid y_2)\,\mathrm{sgn}(y_3)]^2,$$

and finally, when paths α and β share only the root, then

$$q_1 = \int dy_1 P_1(y_1) \left[\int P_2(y_2 \mid y_1)\, dy_2 \int P_3(y_3 \mid y_2)\, \mathrm{sgn}(y_3) dy_3 \right]^2.$$

There are many different Markov processes that generate the same tree with the same correlations. Higher-order correlations need to be used to differentiate them. In the above example, at level 2 of the hierarchy, the local state variable is defined by

$$m(y_2) = \int P_3(y_3 \mid y_2)\, \mathrm{sgn}(y_3) dy_3.$$

We let $m_i(\alpha)$ be the value of the local average of the microstate at site i when the configuration is α. We define the overlap of two macrostates, or configurations

α and β, by

$$q(\alpha, \beta) = N^{-1} \sum_{i=1}^{N} m_i(\alpha) m_i(\beta).$$

In the case when the interactions between sites are random, the overlap is taken first with the fixed interaction pattern, and later averaged over random interactions.

We take any three macroscopic states, α, β, and γ, say. Then, of the three overlap measures, $q(\alpha, \beta)$, $q(\beta, \gamma)$, and $q(\gamma, \alpha)$, at least two of them are the same in a macroscopic state space with an ultrametric topology. For any value of q, we can partition the whole macrostate space by grouping all macrostates with correlation q or greater. Since this process can be repeated for any one of the partitioned subsets, we see that the macrostate space has a hierarchical structure.

7.2   Dynamics on hierarchical state spaces

To build or analyze a model composed of a large number of agents, we start with the set of all possible configurations of the agents' (discrete) microstates, the set of their (discrete) microeconomic state variables and/or choice variables, types of agents, and so on. We use state space or configuration space in this enlarged sense. We may introduce some performance index or cost index on the configuration space to express our preference for some configurations over others. Then, we speak of a performance or cost landscape that parallels the phrase "energy landscape" used by physicists.

If the model possesses only one locally stable equilibrium in the state space, then life is simple. In general, the landscape contains many locally stable or metastable, that is, locally stationary equilibria, as well as some locally unstable equilibria. In the case of deterministic dynamics, we can work with basins of attractions, barring dynamics with strange attractors, since these stationary states are located in basins of attraction, separated by barriers of varying heights. In stochastic dynamics, states do not necessarily stay in one basin, but may move around in different basins of attractions, as we see in Chapter 5.

Using a measure of distance, that is, a measure of dissimilarity, we partition or organize the state space into a hierarchical or tree structure. We see some preliminary examples in Chapters 2 and 5. This section is a further elaboration of the notion of constructing or analyzing Markov chains with their states organized into tree or hierarchical form. An alternative treatment of large Markov chains as jump processes is mentioned in Chapters 4 and 5.

7.2.1   Ultrametrics: Hierarchical distance

A metric space X is an ultrametric space if the metric d satisfies a strong triangle inequality, rather than the usual triangle inequality,

$$d(x, z) \leq \max[d(x, y), d(y, z)],$$

for all $x, y, z \in X$.

Ultrametric spaces have some unusual properties. For example, triangles are isosceles triangles, that is, at least one pair of distances, $d(x, y), d(y, z)$, and $d(z, x)$, are the same (Schikhof, 1984, Prop. 18.2). We define a closed ball of radius r and center $a \in X$ as the set

$$B_a(r) = [x \in X : d(a, x) \leq r],$$

and an open ball by replacing $\leq$ with a strict inequality sign. However, each ball in X is both open and closed (Schikhof 1984, Prop. 18.4).

What is important for our classification schemes is the following fact.

Fact.   *We let B_1 and B_2 be balls in X. Then either they are ordered by inclusion, that is, either $B_1 \subset B_2$ or $B_2 \subset B_1$, or they are disjointed. In the latter case for all $x \in B_1$ and $y \in B_2$, we have $d(x, y) = d(B_1, B_2)$.*

See Schikhof (1984, Prop. 18.5).

In our usage, balls are clusters or tree nodes. Another unusual fact is that every point of a ball can serve as a center.

Ultrametric distances are associated with hierarchy and conversely. See Rammal and Toulouse (1986). Trees with ultrametrics are such that points or patterns belonging to the same node have the same correlation measures, whereas nonultrametric trees do not have this property.

A set of points with an ultrametric distance has the set partitioned into non-overlapping clusters such that, given a measure of distance d, if two points belong to the same cluster, then their distance is d, two states belonging to two separate clusters have a distance greater than d. With $d' \leq d$, the clusters induced by d' are subclusters of those at scale d.

We want to speak of approximations in ultrametric spaces. An important notion in approximation is that of spherical completeness. An ultrametric space is spherically complete if each nested sequence of balls has a non-empty intersection. Then, a subset Y of X has a best approximation of $a \in X$ in Y in that $d(a, b) = d(a, Y) = \inf[d(a, y) : y \in Y]$. See Schikhof (1984, Sec. 21), our use of subdominant ultrametrics, and the measure of ultrametricity discussed in Rammal and Toulouse (1986).

To summarize, we need a stronger notion of ultrametrics in order to partition sets of patterns and subpartition the partitioned subsets further and further. We use this notion to quantify situations in which points within a given cluster are closer to each other than to points not in the same cluster.

We have shown how martingales are introduced onto trees and how their correlations naturally fall into the ultrametric structures. This also holds in the example of the random cost model.

States of the macroeconomy are numerous. The macroeconomy can find itself in many conditions of economic health, measured by a large number of indicators, such as the rates of real GNP growth, capital investment, changes in unemployment, inventory accumulation or decumulation, money stock growth, government deficit change, changes in short-term interest rate, or stock indexes. We can think of the realizations of these measures of economic states as being locally stable, that is, economy in a similar state of economic health will eventually lead to the same equilibrium or long-run situations as measured by these indicators.

Thus, the macroeconomy is capable of residing near a number of possible equilibria. They may range from very good times to very severe recessions and a number of intermediate states. We can think of the macroeconomy in one of these states or near them or in the process of moving from one such equilibrium to another. Sets of equilibria are therefore sets of locally stable patterns as are the patterns stored in associative memory devices. Hierarchies are useful in representing or storing categorical information, or sets of information to be classified first by gross features and then refining them further into finer details, in precisely the same way that associative or content-addressable memories in computer science or neural networks use tree structures.

Our random cost model illustrates the idea. In this way, we organize sets of equilibria into hierarchies or trees. Trees partition sets of equilibria into non-overlapping subsets. The point is to use a set of indices to partition macroeconomic states of the economy by employing some ultrametric measure of similarity or dissimilarity.

We specify a pattern or an equilibrium by a set of K indices or attributes, or we can speak of encoding equilibria by K-bit words, in which each attribute represents a "yes" or "no" answer to such questions as the signs of the growth rate of investment. To organize them into a binary tree, we first partition these equilibria into two sets, based on the first coordinate or attribute; then, each subset is further partitioned by the second attribute, and so on.

Equilibria belonging to the same node or cluster have the same degree of correlation or overlap. We see in Chapter 2 and in Section 7.1 that this can be achieved by associating sets of random variables, which are martingales, with nodes of trees.

In the classification of the three patterns in the example in Section 2.5.1.3, if we regard the patterns as being encoded by 4-bit words, then all three patterns belong to the same nodes at the first two levels, or bits; on the third level, pattern ξ^3

separates from the rest; and on the fourth level, ξ^2 separates from the first. Thus, when three patterns are partitioned into two sets, based on the first two attributes, all three belong to the same set. When this set is partitioned further depending on the third attribute, then ξ^3 belongs to a different partitioned subset than the other two, and so on. Two equilibria belonging to two different nodes have less overlap than those beloging to the same node. These overlaps are functions of the minimum number of levels of the hierarchy that we have to trace branches of the tree back to the root before we find the common node to the two equilibria. This distance defines the ultrametric distance between the two equilibria.

At least two types of tree structures are useful in macroeconomic modeling: one to organize sets of (quasi) equilibria, and the other to aggregate sets of participants in a number of different equilibria or basins of attractions. Both are illustrated in Chapter 2 and in Section 7.1.

7.2.2   Ogielski–Stein model

Ogielski and Stein (1985) analytically solved a master equation for a finite-state Markov chain with ultrametric hierarchical state structure, that is, random walk models on symmetric trees with ultrametric distance.[8]

We can associate states of a Markov chain with the leaves at the bottom of a binary tree with n levels. Let $P_i(t)$ be the probability that the system is in state i at time t. We assume that the transition probability rates between any two states depend only on the ultrametric distance between these states. We denote the rate by ϵ_i when the distance is i: For example, the rate is ϵ_1 between two states of distance 1, the rate is ϵ_2 between two variables of hierarchical distance 2, and so on. Fortunately, we can calculate the eigenvalues and eigenvectors of this transition rate matrix analytically.

The master equation is

$$\frac{dP}{dt} = WP,$$

where the matrix W is symmetric and has the structure

$$W = \begin{pmatrix} W_1 & W_2 & & & & \\ W_2 & W_1 & & W_3 & & \cdots \\ & & & W_1 & W_2 & \\ & W_3 & & W_2 & W_1 & \cdots \\ & \cdots & & & \cdots & \cdots \end{pmatrix},$$

---

[8] In the physics literature, there are related works. See Bachas and Huberman (1987), for example. They treated nonsymmetric trees and showed the importance of tree silhouette, which they defined to indicate how fast the number of branches grow as you move from the root into hierarchical levels.

with the submatrices specified by

$$W_1 = \begin{pmatrix} \epsilon_0 & \epsilon_1 \\ \epsilon_1 & \epsilon_0 \end{pmatrix},$$

where $\epsilon_0 = -\sum_i \epsilon_i$, $W_2 = \epsilon_2 e_2 e_2'$, $W_3 = \epsilon_3 e_4 e_4'$, and so on, where e_k is the k-dimensional vector with all elements equal to one, that is, $e_k = [1, \ldots, 1]'$: $k \times 1$.

Since the elements of each row of W represent the transition probability rates, the row sums are all zero. For example, with $n = 3$, the matrix W is 8×8, and we have

$$\epsilon_0 + \epsilon_1 + 2\epsilon_2 + 4\epsilon_3 = 0.$$

In the n-level binary tree structure, there are 2^n states since there are that many leaves at the bottom. States $2k - 1$ and $2k$ are aggregated at the next level up, $k = 1, \ldots, 2^{n-1}$, and so on. For example, state 5 is one distance away from state 6, but two distances away from states 7 and 8, and three distances away from states 1, 2, 3, and 4. The composite or superstate $(1, 2)$ which combines states 1 and 2 is one distance away from superstate $(3, 4)$, and two distance away from superstates $(5, 6)$ and $(7, 8)$, and so on.

The eigenvectors of the matrix W have a structure that groups the vectors into subvectors of dimension 2^k. To be concrete, we describe a tree with eight states. With eight states in the system, the first eigenvector is e_8, the second $(e_4', -e_4')'$, the third is $(e_2', -e_2', z_4')'$, the fourth is $(z_4', e_2', -e_2')'$, the fifth is $(1, -1, z_6')'$, the sixth is $(0, 0, 1, -1, z_4')'$, and the last two are $(z_4', 1, -1, 0, 0)'$ and $(z_6', 1, -1)'$, where z_k denotes the k-dimensional vector with all-zero elements.[9]

Since W is symmetric in this example, eigenvectors with distinct eigenvalues are orthogonal. We note that eigenvectors with the same eigenvalues also can be chosen to be orthogonal so that all eigenvectors are orthogonal to each other. Later, we show an example of a nonsymmetric tree and dynamics with a nonsymmetric matrix W.

The first eigenvector has the eigenvalue 0, indicating that this vector represents the long-run equilibrium state of the system, in which all states are equally probable. The second has the eigenvalue $\epsilon_0 + \epsilon_1 + 2\epsilon_2 - 4\epsilon_3$, which is equal to $-8\epsilon_3$, which corresponds to the escape probability rate from a cluster composed of four neighboring states into another with four neighboring states. The third one has the eigenvalue $\epsilon_0 + \epsilon_1 - 2\epsilon_2$. This eigenvalue has multiplicity two because the fourth eigenvector also has this eigenvalue. This eigenvalue corresponds to the escape probability rate from a cluster composed

---

[9] With nonsymmetric trees where the number of branches may not be the same for all nodes at a given level, the expressions of eigenvectors are somewhat more complicated but are describable analytically. See Bachas and Huberman (1987) for example.

of two neighboring states into another composed of two neighboring states. The eigenvalue $\epsilon_0 - \epsilon_1$ has multiplicity four corresponding to the fifth through eighth eigenvectors. These eigenvalues represent the escape probability rate from a single state, and all are negative, this is, the dynamics are asymptotically stable.

Taking another look at the dynamics, we can express W in the polar decomposition form

$$W = \sum_i \lambda_i u_i u_i',$$

where u_i is now normalized, that is, $\langle u_i, u_j \rangle = \delta_{i,j}$, which is the Kronecker delta notation.

Then, the master equation can be rewritten as

$$dP/dt = \sum_i \lambda_i \langle u_i, P \rangle u_i,$$

that is, the dynamic modes decouple, the master equation simplifies, and decomposes into eight first-order differential equations:

$$\frac{d\langle u_i, P \rangle}{dt} = \lambda_i \langle u_i, P \rangle, \quad j = 1, \ldots 8.$$

Integrating the above, we obtain the expression for the modes as

$$\langle u_i, P \rangle(t) = \langle u_i, P \rangle(0)e^{\lambda_i t}, \quad i = 1, \ldots 8,$$

and the probability vector can be written as

$$P(t) = \sum_i \langle u_i, P(t) \rangle u_i.$$

These equations show that the ith component of the probability vector in the coordinate system with the u's as basis vectors returns to zero at the exponential rate dictated by the eigenvalue λ_i. Starting from the initial condition $P_1(0) = 1$, the autocorrelation of $P_1(t)$ is given by

$$P_1(t) = 2^{-3} + 2^{-1}e^{-\lambda_1 t}v_1 + 2^{-2}e^{-\lambda_2 t}v_2 + 2^{-3}e^{-\lambda_3 t}v_3,$$

where the first two components of v_1 are 1 and -1, and the rest are all zero; the first two components of v_2 are ones, the next two components are -1, and the rest all zero; and the first four components of v_3 are all ones, and the rest are all -1.

We now specialize the forms of these ϵ_i so that the barriers of escape between combined clusters increase with the distance. We denote $2^{k-1}\epsilon_k$ by R^k, where $R = e^{\beta\delta}$ for some β and δ. This quantity is the probability rate of jumping from a given site to any of 2^{k-1} sites that are k distances away. This assumption is that the escape probability barrier grows linearly with the distance. This system then has time scales of R, R^2, and R^3 corresponding to time horizons involved in moving between neighboring states, and to states of one to three distances away. In the long-run equilibrium, all eight sites have the same probability of 1/8 of being occupied.

Then, within a time span of $O(R)$, all sets of neighboring states reach equilibrium and become indistinguishable. Hence, by scaling time by R^{-1}, we can aggregate the bottom level and we are left with a hierarchical structure with one fewer level. This means that the ultrametric distance is reduced by one. This is the essence of the renormalization group theory argument described in Section 7.3. This leads to the expression of the correlation coefficient for large t of the form

$$\lim_{t \to \infty} \langle d(t) \rangle \sim (\ln t)/\beta\delta.$$

Recall the example in Sections 2.4.2 and 2.5.4.

The transition probability rate matrix can be specified slightly differently, without ultrametricity, and may still possess the multiple-time-scale feature as in the example above. Such an example is in Huberman and Kerszberg (1985).

7.2.2.1 *An example of aggregation of hierarchical dynamics*

We have suggested how hierarchical systems can be aggregated using renormalization theory. In simple cases such as the present example, we can aggregate states directly, by taking advantage of the regular structure of the matrix of probability transition rates. Here, we illustrate the method for an eight-state model.

We have shown that this model has four distinct eigenvalues: $\lambda_1 = 0 \geq \lambda_2 \geq \lambda_3 \geq \lambda_4$, and that two states on the bottom level coalesce into one after elaspse of time proportional to $1/\lambda_4$.

We note earlier that all eight eigenvectors are chosen to be orthonormal. To eliminate the fastest dynamic mode, that is, the one due to the eigenvalue λ_4, we project the probability vector on the subspace spanned by eigenvectors 1 through 4, since eigenvectors 5 through 8 have eigenvalue λ_4. Although we can discuss aggregation in terms of these original eigenvectors, it is more convenient to proceed as follows.

We define matrix S by

$$S = \begin{pmatrix} S_1 & 0 \\ 0 & S_1 \end{pmatrix},$$

where the submatrix is defined by

$$S_1 = \begin{pmatrix} 1 & 1 & 0 & 0 \\ 0 & 0 & 1 & 1 \end{pmatrix}.$$

We define the aggregated matrix W^* of the original transition probability rates by

$$SW = W^*S,$$

where $W^* = (1/2)SWS'$. Then, the master equation for the aggregated system becomes

$$\frac{dq}{dt} = W^*q$$

with $q = SP$, that is, $q' = (P_1 + P_2, P_3 + P_4, P_5 + P_6, P_7 + P_8)$.

This aggregated matrix is given by

$$W^* = \begin{pmatrix} W_1^* & W_2^* \\ W_2^* & W_1^* \end{pmatrix},$$

where submatrix W_1^* has the diagonal elements $\epsilon_0 + \epsilon_1$ and the off-diagonal elements $2\epsilon_2$, and all elements of submatrix W_2^* are equal to $2\epsilon_3$.

This matrix has zero row sums; hence, it is a matrix of transition probability rates. Its eigenvalues are λ_1, λ_2, and λ_3, as we indicate earlier, and can be verified easily. The eigenvectors are e_4, $(e_2', -e_2')'$, $(1, -1, 0, 0)'$, and $(0, 0, 1, -1)'$.

After an elapse of time of $O(1/\lambda_3)$, the equilibrium states of the aggregated hierarchical system are further coalesced into two states. The master equation now becomes

$$\frac{dr}{dt} = W^{**}r$$

with the aggregated vector $r = Tq = TSP$, with the matrix

$$T = \begin{pmatrix} 1 & 1 & 0 & 0 \\ 0 & 0 & 1 & 1 \end{pmatrix}.$$

The elements of the matrix TS show that the first component of r is the sum of the first four components of the vector P, and the second is the sum of the last four components of P. The $(1, 1)$ element of the matrix W^{**} is $\epsilon_0 + \epsilon_1 + 2\epsilon_2$, which is also the $(2, 2)$ element. The $(1, 2)$ and $(2, 1)$ element of W^{**} is $4\epsilon_3$. The eigenvalues of this matrix are λ_1 and λ_2.

After an elapse of time proportional to $1/\lambda_2$, the entire set of the original eight equilibria collapses into one, that is, the whole system is in equilibrium and all eight states are aggregated into one.

7.2.2.2   A nonsymmetric tree

We next describe a hierarchy represented by a simple nonsymmetric tree. To illustrate, we use a two-level system with three equilibrium states. The matrix of transition probability rates is given by

$$W = \begin{pmatrix} -(\epsilon_1 + \epsilon_2) & \epsilon_1 & \epsilon_2 \\ \epsilon_1 & -(\epsilon_1 + \epsilon_2) & \epsilon_2 \\ \epsilon_2 & \epsilon_2 & -2\epsilon_2 \end{pmatrix}.$$

The eigenvalues are: $\lambda_1 = 0$, $\lambda_2 = -3\epsilon_2$, and $\lambda_3 = -(2\epsilon_1 + \epsilon_2)$. The corresponding eigenvectors are $(1, 1, 1)$, $(1, 1, -2)$, and $(1, -1, 0)$. After one level of aggregation, the probability vectors are given by the aggregation matrix

$$S = \begin{pmatrix} 1 & 1 & 0 \\ 0 & 0 & 1 \end{pmatrix}.$$

The master equation for the aggregated vectors is given by

$$\frac{dq}{dt} = W^* q,$$

where $q = Sp$, and the matrix of transition probability rates is given by

$$W^* = \begin{pmatrix} -\epsilon_2 & 2\epsilon_2 \\ \epsilon_2 & -2\epsilon_2 \end{pmatrix},$$

which inherits the eigenvalues λ_1, and λ_2, after an elapse of time of $O(1/\lambda_3)$.

7.2.3 *Schreckenberg's model*

Unlike the previously discussed models of random walks on trees in which only the transitions to the nearest neighors are allowed, Schreckenberg (1985) examined a random-walk model on trees in which all possible transitions to other states are allowed.

There are N number of microstates in total. Here, it is convenient to count the levels from the bottom up. At the root of a $K + 1$ level tree, there is one cluster with N microstates. We let $m_{K+1} = N$. At the next level down, there are N/m_K clusters, each with m_K microstates. In general, on level $l + 1$, there are N/m_l clusters, each containing m_l microstates. At the bottom, level 1, there are N clusters, each with a single microstate, that is,

$$N = m_{K+1} \geq m_K \geq \cdots \geq m_1 \geq m_0 = 1.$$

We fix one microstate at the bottom and call it state a. We define the set of microstates that are exactly at an ultrametric distance k from state a:

$$S_k = [x : d(a, x) = k].$$

We note that $|S_k| = m_k - m_{k-1}$, $k = 1, \ldots, K$. The transition probability rate from state a to any state $x \in S_k$ is ϵ_{k-1}.

For example, there are $m_1 - 1$ microstates from a to which the transition probability rate is ϵ_0. The transition probability rates are only a function of the ultrametric distance. We have

$$\epsilon_0 \geq \epsilon_1 \geq \cdots \geq \epsilon_K \geq \epsilon_{K+1} = 0.$$

We define $P_l(t)$ as the probability that the microstate starting from state a at time 0 is in a cluster at level $L + 1$ at time t. Denoting this by x_t, we have

$$P_0(t) = Pr(x_t \in C_1),$$

where C_1 is a cluster at level 1 for which the master equation is written as

$$\frac{dP_0(t)}{dt} = -\sum_{i=0}^{K} (m_{i+1} - m_i)\epsilon_i P_0(t) + \sum_{i=0}^{K} \epsilon_i Q_i,$$

where

$$Q_i = P_{i+1} - P_i = Pr[x_t : d(a, x_t) = i + 1].$$

At level $l + 1$, there are m_l microstates per cluster. Hence, we write the master equation for P_l/m_l as

$$\frac{d(P_l/m_l)}{dt} = -\sum_{i=l}^{K} (m_{i+1} - m_i)\epsilon_i (P_l/m_l) + \sum_{i=l}^{K} \epsilon_i Q_i.$$

We are assuming that microstates in a cluster are equally likely, that is, indistinguishable as in the Bose–Einstein statistics.

This master equation can be rewritten as

$$\frac{d}{dt}(P_{l+1}/m_{l+1} - P_l/m_l) = -\sum_{i=l}^{K} (m_{i+1} - m_i)\epsilon_i (P_{l+1}/m_{l+1} - P_l/m_l)$$
$$+ (m_{l+1} - m_l)(\epsilon_l P_{l+1}/m_{l+1}) - \epsilon_l Q_l.$$

Substituting the definitional relation for Q_l, we obtain

$$\frac{d}{dt}(P_{l+1}/m_{l+1} - P_l/m_l)$$
$$= -\left[\sum_{i=l}^{K} (m_{i+1} - m_i)\epsilon_i + m_l \epsilon_l \right](P_{l+1}/m_{l+1} - P_l/m_l).$$

We define the time constant τ_l by

$$\tau_l^{-1} = \sum_{i=l}^{K} (m_{i+1} - m_i)\epsilon_i + m_l \epsilon_l$$

At time 0, state a belongs to a node at all levels; hence, we have the uniform initial condition $P_i(0)/m_i = 1/m_i$. Recalling that $P_{K+1}(t) = 1$, we can write the solution of the master equation as

$$P_l(t)/m_l = \sum_{i=l}^{K}(1/m_i - 1/m_{i+1})e^{t/\tau_i} + 1/N.$$

We also note that

$$\frac{Q_l}{m_{l+1} - m_l} = \sum_{i=l}^{K}(1/m_i - 1/m_{i+1})e^{-t/\tau_i} - (1/m_l)e^{-t/\tau_i} + 1/N.$$

To examine a simple case, we assume that the number of branches per node is a constant at every level of the tree, that is, the ratio m_{i+1}/m_i is a constant m. Then $m_l = m^l$. We suppose further that the time constants are such that

$$\tau_{l+1}^{-1} = \kappa\tau_l^{-1}$$

for a small constant κ. This is compatible with the ratio of the transition rates $\epsilon_{l+1}/\epsilon_l$ being about κ/μ. We have

$$P_0(t) = (1 - 1/m)\sum_{l=0}^{\infty}(1/m)^l e^{-\alpha/\beta}t,$$

for some constants α and β.

Schreckenberg (1985) shows then that for large t this expression is

$$P_0(t) \sim (1 - 1/m)h[\ln(\alpha t)](\alpha t)^{\ln(m/\ln\beta)},$$

where h is a periodic function $h(x + \ln\beta) = h(x)$, for all x.

The oscillations are a consequence of the self-similarity of the different levels of the hierarchy. The set of time constants does not change when the time scale is muliplied by a factor β.

7.3   Pruning trees: Aggregation of hierarchical dynamics

In Chapter 5, we see that macroeconomic equations are identified from the power-series expansion of the master equations as the first term of expansion in $O(1/N)$, where N is the number of agents in the model. In describing the model of Ogielski and Stein, we introduced another aggregation scheme for Markov chains with a tree-structured state space. This section provides further theoretical development along this line as well as two specific examples for aggregating Markov chains via renormalization theory.

7.3.1   *Renormalization group theory*

The renormalization group theory is quite useful for studying interactive or cooperative behavior of agents in a model with many degrees of freedom, and with regular structure in the sense analogous to that of self-similar structures in fractals.

The method consists of studying the behavior of economic models under changes of scale in time and the state variables. As examples, we describe the models of Collet and Eckmann (1978) and Idiart and Theumann (1990) in order to discuss how a model with $2N$ agents can be aggregated to build a model for N agents. In fact, aggregation can be put on a firm footing when the renormalization group theory can be brought to bear in tree models with a large number of levels, because the structure per level of the models are similar in much the same sense that certain segments of fractals are self-similar. For such self-similarly structured models, the theory tells us exactly what changes of scale in variables and in time are needed to aggregate microvariables to more coarse-grained, or macrovariables, that is, in forming a suitable weighted average of lower-level variables to replace the lower-level variables. Recall our discussion of aggregation of tree dynamics in Section 2.5.4.

The basic step in applying the theory is similar to constructing stable laws in probability theory, as is emphasized by Jona-Lasinio (1975) in the physics literature. The limiting behavior is, to a large extent, independent of the details of the underlying probability distributions.

Here, we only sketch a simple case. We consider a Hamiltonian

$$H = \frac{-1}{2|\Lambda|}\left(\sum_{i \in \Lambda} s_i\right)^2,$$

and, defining $S(\Lambda)$ to be the sum $\sum_i s_i$, the probability density function is given by

$$p_\Lambda(s_1, \ldots, s_{|\Lambda|}) = \text{const} \exp\left[\frac{\beta}{2|\Lambda|}S(\Lambda)^2\right].$$

We consider the case where $\sum_i s_i = m$, and define $Y(\Lambda) = S(\Lambda)/|\Lambda|^{\rho/2}$. Then, the probability density is given by

$$p[Y(\Lambda) = y] = Z_\Lambda^{-1}C_{|\Lambda|,m} \exp\left[\frac{\beta}{2}y^2|\Lambda|^{\rho-1}\right],$$

where

$$Z_\Lambda = \sum_{k=0}^{|\Lambda|} C_{|\Lambda|,k} \exp\left[\frac{\beta k^2}{2|\Lambda|}\right],$$

with $|\Lambda| - 2m = y|\Lambda|^{\rho/2}$.

Using the Stirling formula, we obtain a nontrivial limit as $|\Lambda|$ goes to ∞ only when ρ is equal to one if β is not equal to one,

$$\lim_{|\Lambda|\to\infty} p(y) = \text{const} \exp\left[\frac{(1-\beta)}{2}y^2\right].$$

With $\beta = 1$, the limit becomes

$$\lim p(y) = \text{const} \exp(-y^4/2),$$

for the case of $\rho = 3/2$.

More generally, with $m = m_1 + m_2$, and noting that

$$C_{|\Lambda|,m} = \sum_{m_1,m_2} C_{|\Lambda|/2,m_1} C_{|\Lambda|/2,m_2},$$

we obtain the relations between the probability density functions:

$$p_{|\Lambda|}(m) = \sum_{m_1,m_2} p_{|\Lambda|/2}(m_1) p_{|\Lambda|/2}(m_2) \exp\left[-\frac{2\beta}{|\Lambda|}(m_1-m_2)^2\right].$$

We let $u = (m_1 - m_2)/|\Lambda|^{\rho/2}$. Then, we can express the probability density function for y as

$$p_{|\Lambda|}(y) = \text{const} \int \exp(-|\Lambda|^{\rho-1}u^2) p_{|\Lambda|/2}[y/2^{1-\rho/2} + u)]$$
$$\times [p_{|\Lambda|/2}[y/2^{1-\rho/2} - u)]du.$$

As we let $|\Lambda|$ go to infinity, the limiting density functions satisfy

$$p_\infty(y) = [p_\infty(y/2^{1-\rho/2})]^2.$$

There is therefore a two-parameter family of fixed points of the transformation,

$$\exp(-\lambda|y|^\mu),$$

where $\mu = 1/(1 - \rho/2)$, and λ is an arbitrary constant.

Dyson (1969) introduced a hierarchical structure to random fields by defining a Hamiltonian by

$$H(\sigma) = -\sum_{i,j \in S} U_{i,j}\sigma_i\sigma_j,$$

where S is a lattice, and where $U_{i,j}$ is chosen to be $d_{i,j}^{-a}$, where the hierarchical or ultrametric distance is defined by

$$d(i,j) = 2^{n(i,j)-1},$$

if i and j are not the same, and $d(i, i) = 0$, where $n(i, j)$ is the smallest n such that i and j belong to the same cluster. We refer the reader to Bleher and Major (1987) for analysis of hierarchical dynamic model originally proposed by Dyson (1969) which is also discussed by Collet and Eckman (1978).

7.3.2   Collet–Eckman model

Collet and Eckman (1978) discuss a simple hierarchical model with M levels with $N = 2^M$ number of sites or microeconomic units. The Hamiltonian is given by

$$H_{N,f} = H_N + \sum_{j=0}^{N} f(s_j),$$

where

$$H_N = -\frac{1}{2} \sum_{k=1}^{M} (c/4)^k \sum_{j=0}^{2^{M-k}-1} S_{j,k}^2,$$

and where we define

$$S_{j,k} = \sum_{l=1}^{2^k} s_{j2^k+l}.$$

By construction, $S_{j,k}$ variables are the sums of all s_i belonging to the same cluster.[10]

The Hamiltonian H_N represents the interactions among these variables. The interaction between the variables s_i and s_j is $-(c/4)^k$, where k is the lowest level at which s_i and s_j lie in the same cluster. In other words, the interaction is a function of the ultrametric distance. In their model, levels are labeled from the bottom. At level 1, two of the sites are aggregated to form $S_{j,1}$. At level k, each cluster contains 2^k points, or original site variables, and there are 2^{M-k} clusters, $k = 1, \ldots, M$.

We let S be the sum of all s_i, $i = 1, \ldots, N$, and denote the Gibbs distribution by $P_{N,f}(S)$. They show that by defining $t_j = (s_{2j-1}+s_{2j})\sqrt{c}/2$, $j = 1, \ldots, N$, the integral

$$\int ds_1 \cdots ds_{2N} F\left(\sum_{j=1}^{2N} s_j\right) \exp[-\beta H_{2N,f}(s_1, \ldots, s_{2N})]$$

---

[10] These variables correspond to the block-spin variables in the Ising model literature.

can be written as

$$\int dt_1 \cdots dt_N \, F\left(2c^{-(1/2)} \sum_{j=1}^{N} t_j\right) \exp[-\beta H_{N,g}(t_1, \ldots, t_N)],$$

where the function g is defined by

$$g(t) = -t^2/2 - \beta^{-1} \ln(2/\sqrt{c})$$
$$- \beta^{-1} \int du \, \exp[-\beta f(tc^{-0.5} + u) - \beta f(tc^{-0.5} - u)].$$

The above equation defines a transformation of f into g. The Gibbs distribution is transformed by

$$P_{2N,f}(S) = (c^{1/2}/2) P_{N,g}[(c^{1/2}/2)S].$$

They have shown that the probability distribution for a system with $2N$ agents can be made to correspond to that with N agents through a change of scale and a change of the Hamiltonians.

7.3.3   Idiart–Theumann model

Here, we explain the model of Idiart and Theumann (1990). Even though they proposed the model as a model of associative memory of neural networks, this model is sufficiently general to permit its reinterpretation as a model of economic agents (firms) that may be grouped into clusters according to similarities, technical or otherwise, and grouped into larger clusters as macroeconomic models. Their sites are to be interpreted as microeconomic agents.

There are a total of r levels of hierarchy in the model. At the bottom, or at the most disaggregated level, there are $N = N_1 2^{r-1}$ sites grouped into 2^{r-1} disjointed clusters, each consisting of N_1 sites.

For each cluster, we define a cluster variable (which is an intermediate macrovariable) by

$$S_{1,l_1}^{\mu} = \sum_{N_1(l_1-1)+1}^{N_1 l_1} w_i^{\mu} \sigma_i$$

where l_1 ranges from 1 to 2^{r-1}.

Here σ_i is the state variable of agent i. In the simplest case, the values are binary, 1 or -1. The weight w_i^{μ} depends on the parameter μ, which refers to the pattern in their model but can be reinterpreted as the label for local equilibria in economic context. Its value ranges from 1 to p.

The cluster variable thus defined corresponds to a block spin variable in Ellis (1985, p. 170). It is an intermediate variable of interest, and may be a sectorial average of some economic quantity, for example, when the hierarchy is built up by aggregating firms into sectors, and sectors into a countrywide macroeconomic model. Next, we posit an interaction potential, or some functions of the cluster variables to be minimized by configurations on level 1 as

$$H(1) = -(J/N)g^{r-1} \sum_{\mu=1}^{p} (S_{1,l_1}^{\mu})^2.$$

Here, g is an arbitrary coupling variable between levels.

On level 2, two neighboring clusters are joined to form a larger cluster consisting of $2N_1$ states. The kth-level cluster variables are defined analogously at level k by adding two neighboring cluster variables of level $k-1$:

$$S_{k,l_k}^{\mu} = S_{k,2l_k-1}^{\mu} + S_{k,2l_k}^{\mu}$$

for l_k ranging from 1 to 2^{r-k}.

The k-level interaction energy is taken to be

$$H(k) = -(J/N)g^{r-k} \sum_{l_k} \sum_{\mu} \left(S_{k,l_k}^{\mu}\right)^2.$$

The total interaction potential is the sum of the above from k of one to r.

This can be written as

$$H = \sum_{k} g^{r-k} \sum_{l_k} \sum_{i=j} J_{i,j}(l_k)\sigma_i\sigma_j,$$

where

$$J_{i,j}(l_k) = -(J/N) \sum_{\mu} w_i^{\mu} w_j^{\mu}.$$

A more convenient reformulation of the expression for the Hamiltonian is

$$H = -(J/N) \sum_{\mu} \sum_{l,n} a_{l,n}(r) S_l^{\mu} S_n^{\mu},$$

where we simply write S_l^{μ} for S_{1,l_1}^{μ} dropping the subscript 1 from l.

The matrix A with elements $a_{l,n}(r)$ has a special structure and we can calculate its eigenvalues and eigenvectors analytically. This matrix has a structure very similar to the matrix of transition probability rates that appears in Ogielski and Stein (1985) and in the Dyson (1969) model.

CHAPTER 8

Self-organizing and other critical phenomena in economic models

We sometimes observe major or drastic qualitative changes in the behavioral pattern or response of economic systems. Some of these changes are apparently triggered by minor changes in economic environments or policy parameters. For convenience, we call these responses "critical phenomena," which are economic phenomena that are overly sensitive to changes in environments or policies.

We mention two types of such phenomena. One type involves sudden changes in structure: An equilibrium may suddenly bifurcate when some model parameter crosses a critical value. Organized markets may suddenly emerge when none existed before, or may suddenly disappear. There are many examples of these types of critical phenomena.

The other type of events is also well known. We call it a piling-up phenomena. These events are often marked by crazes or fads: A significant fraction of agents suddenly have the same opinion or make a same choice, or otherwise occupy the same configuration or state, while they were more or less evenly distributed among several states in the absence of whatever triggered this sudden shift. (Recall that a state could refer to economic or expectational conditions or both.) For lack of a better term we call them piling-up of agents, or dense occupancy of a state by agents.[1]

8.1   Sudden structural changes

There are two senses in which sudden structural changes are relevant in economic modeling. One sense is familiar. Loosely put, discontinuous or major changes are produced in some properties or characteristics of systems or models as some parameter values are changed slightly near a so-called critical value. Examples are numerous both inside and outside economics. Outside of the field of economics, we observe water becoming vapor or ice at certain critical

---

[1] Events that we have in mind are similar to those called condensation phenomena in the physics literature.

temperatures, or sudden changes in electric conductivity or magnetic properties occurring in response to a slight change in temperature near critical temperatures, or an external magnetic field. Inside the realm of economics, phenomena of self-organization of agents are of this type. An example is Whittle's two-role model applied to farmers and traders. In his model, under certain technical condition a market may suddenly emerge where there were only itinerant traders (Whittle 1986, p. 381). Vriend (1994) has another example of this kind of self-organization. Hierarchically organized dynamic systems are another example of organizations in which we observe sudden structural changes. In the physics literature, it is known that critical points are associated with fixed points of renormalization group transformations in connection with certain coarse-graining, that is, aggregation of microunits. Dyson (1969) discussed a tree of Ising spins in this way, which was later taken up by the mathematicians Moore and Snell (1979) and, more recently, Bleher and Major (1987). In percolation models, critical points are associated with emergence of infinite aggregates. See Grimmett (1989, Sec. 1.4). Clearly, these are relevant to our discussion of hierarchical dynamics.

Another class of examples is that of optimization problems being solved by the simulated annealing method. This technique is introduced to avoid being stuck in local equilibria while searching for a global minimum of objective functions which have many local equilibria. With some positive probability controlled by a parameter β, simulated annealing algorithms explore neighboring solutions that are inferior to the ones already found in an effort to get out of neighborhoods of local equilibria that are not globally optimal.

At zero β, which corresponds to high temperature, there is only one solution. As β increases (as the temperature is reduced), there is a critical β value at which one equilibrium splits into two or more equilibria, or one cluster of states may split into several subclusters of states, and so forth. There may be a sequence of critical points and an associated sequence of clusters or equilibria. See Rose, Gurewitz, and Fox (1990) for an example. They discuss clustering of points in terms of such phase transitions that split the original data points belonging to one cluster into successive subclusters.

There is a second, perhaps less well known, sense in which these types of structural changes are relevant to economic modeling. It is based on the observation that chaotic behavior or systems are frequently found in natural organisms and are easily induced in man-made systems. Complex macroscopic systems in nature are found most frequently at the border of chaos and nonchaos, that is, at or near the region of the critical phenomena. These observations are available in the literature of geophysics and ecology, for example, and in the cellular automata literature such as Kauffman (1991, 1993).

We do not explore self-organizing phenomena since we will be led outside of what we have set out to cover.

8.2 Piling-up, or dense occupancy, of a common state

There are well-documented historical instances of speculative bubbles or some fads sweeping through regions or countries.[2] These events are marked by the fact that a large fraction of a population share the same beliefs, views, or expectations about something, or a large fraction of a group of people decide, choose, or act the same way. Put differently, a large percentage of population of agents occupy the same state, or dense occupancy of a state occurs. This phenomenon of gathering of agents in the same economic or expectational states also may be essential in understanding processes involved in deep recessions or in hyperinflation states, or economic circumstances that are marked by high degrees of uncertainty about economic prospects and large-scale disappearance of normal economic activities.

In Chapters 4 and 5 we discuss how to model some aspects of these phenomena, where group sentiments or pressures, also called bandwagon effects, are modeled as field effects which affect the transition rates of the jump Markov processes underlying them.

The degree of uncertainty beyond some threshold level seems essential to the occurrence of these phenomena. These economic phenomena would be loosely analogous to physical or chemical critical phenomena where phase transitions occur when temperatures, pressures, or some other key variables cross threshold values. We translate these phenomena into economic terms here.

In this section we focus on a special case in which particular economic or expectational states are occupied by a disproportionately large fraction of interacting agents.[3]

We let n_s be the number of agents in state s, where s is one of the states of the model. The number of states is, at most, denumerable. States could be economic, expectational, or a combination of both. The total number of agents is $N = \sum_l n_l$, where n_l can take on any nonnegative integer value.

Suppose that a macroeconomic variable, aggregate (deviational) output is available where $Y = \sum_l n_l y_l$, where we assume that each agent in state l has y_l. We let $Y_l = n_l y_l$.

We consider one state, s, in which there are n_s agents, each producing output y_s. The probability that this particular combination (n_s, y_s) is realized is proportional to the degree of multiplicity or degeneracy of the remainder of the system, denoted by $W(N - n_s, Y - Y_s)$, where $\ln[W(N, Y)]$ is proportional to the entropy of the system with N agents and with output Y,

---

[2] Montroll and Badger (1974) and Kindleberger (1989) give several accounts of these historical events.

[3] We pattern our analysis after Bose–Einstein condensation in physics. This is a phenomenon in which a large number of particles are found in a ground state below a critical temperature.

because each state is equiprobable by assumption, or rather by the definition of states.

We note that each (equilibrium) macrostate is equiprobable (by construction), and that the total system is composed of one subsystem in state (n_s, Y_s) and the rest of the system in state $(N - n_s, Y - Y_s)$. The probability $P(n_s, Y_s)$ of the subsystem in state (n_s, Y_s) is proportional to the partition number $W(N - n_s, Y - Y_s)$. Expanding this in a Taylor series, we obtain

$$\ln[W(N - n_s, Y - Y_s)] \approx \ln[W(N, Y)] + \beta\mu n_s - \beta Y_s,$$

where we introduce parameter β by

$$\beta = \partial \ln(W)/\partial Y,$$

which is positive because W increases with Y, and another parameter μ by

$$\partial \ln(W)/\partial N = -\beta\mu,$$

which is negative since W is increasing in N.

Hence, the probability is of the form

$$P(n_s, Y_s) \propto \exp[\beta(\mu n_s - Y_s)].$$

By normalizing this expression by the sum of the right-hand side[4] with respect to the state with n_s and Y_s, we obtain

$$P(n_s, Y_s) = \frac{1}{\Xi} \exp[\beta(\mu n_s - Y_s)].$$

Noting that the exponent can be written as $\beta \sum_l (n_l - y_l)$, we see that

$$\Xi = \prod_l \Xi_l,$$

---

[4] We can perform this summation in two steps. First, we keep n_s fixed, and sum over Y_s to define

$$Z(n_s) = \sum_s e^{-\beta Y_s}.$$

Recall our discussion of Laplace transforms in the example in Chapter 2. We proceed analogously in the general case. The partition function of the system composed of N agents is obtained by keeping the number N fixed to define

$$Z_N = \sum_{\sum n_s = N} \exp\left(-\beta \sum_s n_s y_s\right),$$

and then summing over N to define

$$\Xi = \sum_N e^{\beta\mu N} Z_N = \prod_s \sum_{n_s=0}^{\infty} \exp[\beta n_s(\mu - y_s)].$$

where[5]

$$\Xi_l = \sum_{n_l} e^{\beta n_l (\mu - y_l)} = \left[1 - e^{\beta(\mu - y_l)} \right]^{-1}.$$

For this to make sense, we require that $y_l \geq \mu$ for all l. This inequality is satisfied because μ is negative and y_l is nonnegative for all states. This expression can be interpreted as the probability-generating function of the Bose–Einstein statistics. See, for example, Whittle (1992, p. 112) for the expression of the probability-generating function.

The probability that n_l of the agents are in category l is given by

$$P(n_l) = e^{\beta \mu n_l} Z(n_l) / \Xi,$$

where $Z(n_l)$ is defined in footnote 8.4. The average number of agents in category l is given by

$$\langle n_l \rangle = \frac{1}{\beta} \frac{\partial}{\partial \mu} \ln \Xi_l = (e^{\alpha + \beta y_l} - 1)^{-1},$$

where we define $\alpha = -\beta \mu$, and its variance is given by

$$\text{var}(n_l) = \frac{1}{\beta^2} \frac{\partial^2}{\partial \mu^2} \ln \{\Xi\}_l = \langle n_l \rangle (1 + \langle n_l \rangle).$$

We note that the standard deviation (fluctuation) is of the same order as the mean in the case of the Bose–Einstein allocation scheme, since the average is greater than one.[6] Since the number of agents is nonnegative, we must have $\alpha \geq 0$. This condition is satisfied by our assumption on the signs of β and μ.

We separate the number of agents in the zero-output state from the positive-output states

$$N = \frac{1}{e^{\alpha} - 1} + \sum_{s=1}^{\infty} \frac{1}{e^{\alpha + \beta y_s} - 1}.$$

We denote the first term on the right by N_0, which is the number of firms that are not producing. We consider a situation in which α is close to zero. For convenience, we replace the sum with an integral. We define a density $d(\eta)$ to be that of the number of states with the output in the range $(y, y + dy)$. The total output is then given by

$$Y = \int_0^{\infty} \frac{\eta d(\eta)}{e^{\alpha + \beta \eta} - 1} d\eta,$$

---

[5] Here we assume $g_s = 1$ in the notation of the example in Chapter 2.

[6] In the Maxwell–Boltzmann allocation scheme, the average is less than one and the fluctuations are of the order of the square root of the mean.

and the number of agents is

$$N = \frac{1}{e^\alpha - 1} + \int_0^\infty \frac{d(\eta)}{e^{\alpha + \beta\eta} - 1} d\eta. \tag{8.1}$$

We assume that the density for η is of the form

$$d(\eta) = c\eta^s,$$

where c is a constant, and $s \geq 0$. It is important to realize that this integral for N undercounts the number of agents by the number of agents who are in zero-output state, since those in the zero-output state are not describable by a continuous density.

To carry out the integral, we use an Appell function, which is defined by

$$\phi(s, \xi) = \frac{1}{\Gamma(s)} \int_0^\infty \frac{x^{s-1}}{\xi^{-1}e^x - 1} dx,$$

where we let $\xi = e^{-\alpha} \leq 1$. By expanding the integrand in powers of ξ, we see that

$$\phi(s, \xi) = \sum_{k=1}^\infty \xi^k / k^s.$$

This function is monotone-increasing in ξ. We note that

$$\int_0^\infty \frac{\eta^s}{e^{\alpha + \beta\eta} - 1} d\eta = \phi(s + 1, \xi)\Gamma(s + 1)\beta^{-s-1}.$$

We define β_c, a critical value of β, by

$$N = \Gamma(s + 1)\phi(s + 1, \xi)\beta^{-s-1}.$$

Then, we can express Eq. (8.1) as

$$N = \xi/(\xi - 1) + N(\beta/\beta_c)^{-s-1}\phi(s + 1, \xi)/\phi(s + 1, \xi).$$

To see the dependence of ξ on β/β_c, it is convenient to rewrite the above as

$$\frac{\xi}{N(1 - \xi)} = 1 - \frac{\beta^{-s-1}}{\beta_c} \frac{\phi(s + 1, \xi)}{\phi(s + 1, 1)}.$$

When $\beta \leq \beta_c$, both sides intersect on the ξ axis, that is,

$$N_0/N = 0.$$

With $\beta \geq \beta_c$, both sides intersect at ξ close to 1. Approximately, we have

$$N_0/N = 1 - (\beta/\beta_c)^{-s-1},$$

which indicates that N_0 can be quite large when N is large.

We see that the behavior of the industry is quite different depending on whether β is above or below the critical value.

The two macrovariables determine two parameters α and β in the range $\beta \leq \beta_c$.

8.3   Phase transitions in the Ising tree model

Since we take trees as our basic structures of hierarchy, we summarize the known facts on the Ising tree models, drawing from the results of Spitzer (1975), Sawyer (1978), Moore and Snell (1979), and Kindermann and Snell (1980, Chap. V).[7] We discuss only binary trees in which every node including the root has two branches.

A state (configuration), ω, is an assignment of $+1$ or -1 (or more simply $+$ or $-$) to each node in the tree. The Hamiltonian is defined as in the usual Ising tree as:

$$H = \frac{J'}{2} \sum_{|i-j|=1} x_i x_j - h' \sum_j x_i,$$

where $J_{i,j} = J'$ if $|i - j| = 1$, and 0 otherwise. When no confusion is likely, we do not explicitly show dependence of H and x_i on ω.

The corresponding Gibbs distribution is

$$P(\omega) = e^{-\beta' H}/Z,$$

where the partition function is

$$Z = \sum_{\omega} H(\omega).$$

This probability distribution also can be written as

$$P(\omega) = e^{-\beta n_o(\omega) + h M(\omega)},$$

where $\beta = \beta' J'$, $h = \beta' h'$, $n_o(\omega)$ is the number of odd bonds in the configuration ω, and $M(\omega) = \sum_i x_i(\omega)$ is called magnetization.

---

[7] Kindermann and Snell (1980) remark that it is hard to derive some of the basic results for Ising models defined on sets of lattice points, but those defined on trees, that is, hierarchies, are easier to handle.

We let Z_n denote the partition function of an n-level tree, and write

$$Z_n = Z_n^+ + Z_n^-$$

where Z_n^+ is the sum over the states when the root node is in $+$ state, and Z_n^- is defined likewise when the root is in $-$ state. We define the ratio

$$U_n = Z_n^- / Z_n^+.$$

Given the state of the root node, there are exactly three distinguishable states at level 1, that is, the microstates of the two nodes at level 1 may be $(+, +)$, $(+, -)$, or $(-, -)$. The partial sum of the partition function is thus seen to be

$$Z_n^+ = e^{-2\beta + h} \left(Z_{n-1}^- \right)^2 + 2e^{-\beta + h} Z_{n-1}^+ Z_{n-1}^- + e^h \left(Z_{n-1}^+ \right)^2$$
$$= e^h \left(e^{-\beta} Z_{n-1}^- + Z_{n-1}^+ \right)^2,$$

and similarly

$$Z_n^- = e^{-h} \left(Z_{n-1}^- + e^{-h} Z_{n-1}^+ \right)^2.$$

The ratio U_n is governed by the recursion

$$U_n = f(U_{n-1}),$$

where

$$f(x) = \frac{(x + e^{-\beta})^2}{e^{2h}(e^{-\beta} x + 1)^2}.$$

By taking n to be one, we have $U_1 = e^{-2\beta - 2h}$, when all leaves are set to be $+$, since Z_1^+ represents the sum of a tree with all nodes being $+$, and Z_1^- is a tree with a negative root and two positive leaves. When leaves are all set to be $-$, $U_1 = e^{2\beta - 2h}$.

When the leaves are free to assume any state, then we consider a tree with only the root, that is, $n = 0$. Then, we have $U_0 = e^{-2h}$.

With a positive β, U_n has a limit U as n goes to infinity, and the limit satisfies

$$U = f(U).$$

By examining the shape of the map f, we note that there are, at most, three fixed points.

One of the advantages of using Ising tree models is that probabilities of all configurations can be evaluated by means of a transition matrix Q,

$$Q = \begin{pmatrix} s & 1 - s \\ 1 - t & t \end{pmatrix}$$

which we interpret to mean that a negative node produces another negative node with probability s, a positive node will produce a negative node with probability $1 - t$, and so on.

If we denote probability of a negative root by ω_-, then the probability of a two-level tree with two states on level 1 being $(+, -)$, and the four states on level 2 being $(+, +, -, +)$ is

$$\omega_-(1 - s)\, s\, t\, t\, s(1 - s) = \omega_-(1 - s)^2 s^2 t^2.$$

The resulting measure is a Markov random field, and the measure obtained on the finite-tree form can be applied to cylinder sets. We can check that the cylinder measure does not depend on the location of the starting point. This is a property analogous to the stationarity of the lattice model. In this tree model, there is no long-range order in the sense that $P(\omega_m \mid \omega_n = +)$; and $P(\omega_m \mid \omega_n = -)$ becomes the same as m goes to infinity for any finite n, because the measure is isomorphic to an ordinary two-state Markov chain with the transition matrix Q.

8.3.1 *Phase transitions in a random cost model*

Another example of economic phase transition can be constructed along the line of the random energy model discussed by Derrida (1981) by recasting the energy model into a random cost model that we introduce in Section 7.1.7.1. In short, there are N agents in a system, each of whom can be in one of two possible states.

Corresponding to 2^N configurations of the system, there are as many cost levels for the system. We assume that these costs (measured from some standard level as deviations) are normally distributed with mean zero and variance that is proportional to N. The random costs are generally correlated across agents. However, the assumption of independence lose no essential feature of this model. Therefore, we assume that the costs are independent across agents.

We define $n(c)dc$ as the number of configurations with costs in the range of $(c, c + dc)$. For technical reasons, we choose $dc = O(N^\alpha)$, where α is between 0 and 1.

The average number of configurations is

$$\langle n(c) \rangle = 2^N (\pi N J^2)^{-1/2} e^{-c^2/NJ^2}$$
$$= \exp\{N[\ln 2 - (c/NJ)^2] + O(\ln N/N)\},$$

from which we see that

$$c_0/N = J\sqrt{\ln 2},$$

defines a critical value, because above this value of $c\langle n(c) \rangle = o(1)$, and below this value there are many configurations, $\ln\langle n(c) \rangle = O(N)$.

Since the standard deviation of $n(c)$ is of $O[\langle n(c)\rangle^{1/2}]$, we have an approximate expression

$$n(c) \approx \langle n(c)\rangle,$$

for $c \leq c_0$.

When N approaches infinity, the (Boltzmann) entropy term approaches the limit

$$S(c)/N \sim \ln 2 - (c/NJ)^2.$$

We introduce a parameter β by the relation

$$\frac{dS(c)}{dc} = \beta,$$

which is analogous with the thermodynamics relation for the temperature, that is, we think of β as the inverse of something representing the level of economic activity. We obtain the relation

$$c/NJ = -\beta J/2,$$

or an alternative expression for the entropy term

$$S(c)/N \sim \ln 2 - (\beta J/2)^2,$$

if the right-hand-side expression is positive. The value of β,

$$\beta_c = 2(\ln 2)^{1/2}/J,$$

defines the critical value corresponding (loosely speaking) to the inverse of a critical temperature in physics or chemistry.

Free energy per agent is defined by

$$f(\beta) = -(1/\beta)S(c)/N = -(1/\beta)\ln 2 - \beta J^2/4,$$

for the values of β less than its critical value.

For a large value of β, the entropy term is negligible because $\langle n(c)\rangle$ is very small and we get

$$f(\beta) = -c_0/N = -J(\ln 2)^{1/2}.$$

8.4 Example of a two-level model

Suppose we have a two-level tree, and examine configurations of the system when the total cost is equal to C. We factor 2 as a product $2 = \alpha_1\alpha_2$. At level 2, the tree has α_1^N clusters. The cost of each cluster is randomly distributed with mean zero and variance $NJ^2a_1/2$. Then, within each cluster, the cost of each configuration is distributed normally according to

$$p(C, c) = (\pi NJ^2a_2)^{-1/2} \exp[-(C - c)^2/NJ^2a_2]$$

with the normalization condition $a_1 + a_2 = 1$.

Next, we estimate the number of clusters having the cost in the interval $(c, c + dc)$. We denote this by $N_1(c)dc$. Since there are α_1^N clusters, each with the normally distributed cost density, the average number is given by

$$N_1(c) \approx E[N_1(c)] \sim \exp\{N[\ln\alpha_1 - a_1^{-1}(c/NJ)^2]\},$$

if the exponent is positive, that is, if

$$|c|/NJ \le \sqrt{a_1\ln\alpha_1},$$

and if this condition is not met, then $N_1(c)$ is approximately zero.

We make a typical value of $N_1(c)$ equal to its expected value because the expected value is large (we deal with models with large N), and the fluctuation of $N_1(c)$ is of the order of the square root of the expected value. See Derrida (1981).

Knowing the density $N_1(c)$, we can calculate the density of the configurations having the cost C as follows:

$$q(C) \sim \int N_1(c)\exp\left\{N\left[\ln\alpha_2 - a_2^{-1}\left(\frac{C - c}{NJ}\right)^2\right]\right\}dc,$$

where the limits of the integration are $\pm NJ(a_1\ln\alpha_1)^{1/2}$.

A typical value of the density of $N_2(C)$ is proportional to $q(C)$, above, if the exponential part is positive, that is, if

$$\ln\alpha_1 + \ln\alpha_2 \ge a_1^{-1}(c/NJ)^2 + a_2^{-1}[(C - c)/NJ]^2,$$

and is nearly zero otherwise. For large N, this expression is approximately equal to the average partition function and, therefore, the expression

$$N^{-1}\ln N_2(C)$$

is approximately equal to the per-unit entropy, $S(C)/N$, where S denotes the entropy. As N goes to infinity, we can use the method of Laplace, or the large-deviation principle to see that the limit is given by

$$\sup\{\ln\alpha_1 + \ln\alpha_2 - a_1^{-1}(c/NJ)^2 - a_2^{-1}[(C - c)/NJ]^2\},$$

where the supremum with respect to c is in the ranges of $\pm NJ(a_1\ln\alpha_1)^{1/2}$. We denote this expression by $\psi(C)$. Otherwise, the limit is $-\infty$.

The expression inside the curly brackets is maximized by c, which is equal to a_1C, recalling that, by normalization, $a_1 + a_2 = 1$. When this value of c is substituted into the curly brackets, we see that one of the critical values of C is given when $\psi(C)$ vanishes. We denote this by C':

$$C' = NJ(\ln \alpha_1 + \ln \alpha_2)^{1/2}.$$

The other value of C is when c is such that the mean of $N_1(c)$ vanishes, that is,

$$c = a_1 C'' = NJ(a_1 \ln \alpha_1)^{1/2},$$

namely,

$$C'' = NJ(\ln \alpha_1/a_1)^{1/2}.$$

These are the two critical values of C. The model behaves differently when $C' \geq C''$ or $C' \leq C''$. This is exactly the same situation that we discuss in connection with partitioning of clusters and equilibria in the annealing. When we have

$$a_1/\ln \alpha_1 \geq a_2/\ln \alpha_2,$$

we have the former situation, and when the inequality is reversed, we have the latter situation.

When C' is not greater than C'', the model becomes degenerate and the two levels collapse to one level. The entropy (free energy) of the model is the same as that of the one-level model (called the random energy model by Derrida [1980]).

8.5   Random cost model

In the example in Section 7.1.7.1, the costs C_1 and C_2 share a common component ϕ, which explains a fraction v of the variances of the costs. In this section, we consider costs associated with 2^N configurations, using a simplifying assumption that the cost of each configuration is independent. In other words, we ignore correlations among costs associated with different configurations.

We define a random cost model as a system that has 2^N configurations and 2^N cost levels, and each deviational cost, c_i, is a Gaussian random variable with mean zero and variance proportional to N – say, $NJ^2/2$.

The configurations have a Gibbs distribution, and the partition function of a given sample of the 2^N costs is

$$Z(\{c_i\}) = \sum_{i=1}^{2^N} \exp(-\beta c_i),$$

and has the average free energy given by

$$F = -\beta^{-1}\langle \ln Z \rangle,$$

where, using $\langle \cdot \rangle$ to denote the expected value, the average is taken over energy values

$$\langle \ln Z \rangle = \int \prod_i p(c_i) \ln Z(\{c_i\}) dc_i.$$

We denote the number of cost levels between c and $c + dc$ by $n(c)\, dc$. Then, its average is given by,

$$\langle n(c) \rangle = \text{const } 2^N \exp(-c^2/NJ^2) = \text{const } \exp\{N[\ln 2 - (c/NJ)^2]\}.$$

This expression shows the existence of a critical cost level $c_0 = NJ(\ln 2)^{1/2}$, such that if c is above this critical value, then $\langle n(c) \rangle$ is very small, and it is much larger than 1 for $c < c_0$.

Because of the assumed independence, the fluctuations of $n(c)$ are of $O[\langle n(c) \rangle^{1/2}]$ for almost all samples, and hence we have

$$n(c) \sim \langle n(c) \rangle.$$

The entropy per configuration, then, is given by

$$S(c)/N \approx \ln\langle n(c) \rangle / N = \{\ln 2 - (c/NJ)^2\},$$

for $c \leq c_0$.

We introduce a parameter β to indicate degree of economic activities (analogous to the inverse of temperature in the thermodynamic relations) by the relation

$$\beta = \frac{dS(c)}{dc}.$$

We have

$$c/NJ = -\beta J/2,$$

or

$$S(c)/N \sim \ln 2 - (\beta J/2)^2,$$

if the right-hand-side expression is positive.

Therefore, the value

$$\beta_c = 2(\ln 2)^{1/2}/J.$$

For $\beta \geq \beta_c$, we have

$$f = F/N = -c_0/N = -J(\ln 2)^{1/2},$$

and for the values of $\beta < \beta_c$,

$$f = \beta^{-1}S(c)/N = \beta^{-1}\ln 2 - \beta J^2/4.$$

Elaborations and future directions of research

We collect here some items that are a further elaboration of topics discussed in the main body of this book, and to suggest potentially useful and important topics for the reader to develop further. We have consistently viewed dynamics as stochastic and we continue this view in this chapter as well.[1]

One of the major aims of this book is to examine consequences of changing patterns of agent interaction over time. We view these patterns as distributions of agents over possible types or categories over time, and we endevour to discover stable distributions of patterns of interactions among agents.

Equilibrium distributions of patterns of classification describe stable emergent properties of the model. Some simple and suggestive examples are discussed in Chapters 4 and 5.

In models with a small number of types, choices or classes, the methods developed in Chapter 5 are quite effective. When the number of classes becomes large, (numerical) solutions of the master equations may become cumbersome. An attractive alternative is to examine equilibrium distributions directly. We outline this method in Section E.2 by drawing on the literature of population genetics and statistics.

Interactions among several types of large numbers of agents may sometimes be modeled as Markov processes on exchangeable random partitions of a set of integers. Aldous (1985) mentions J. Pitman for the name, "Chinese restaurant process" which models how a restaurant with a large number of initially empty tables is sequentially filled up as customers arrive. By classifying customers by the tables they seat, there are a large number of agents of a large number

---

[1] One way to relate stochastic models to deterministic ones is to let the number of agents in the model increase, possibly without bound. We construct macroeconomic models this way in Chapter 5. As we have done in Chapter 4, models described by jump Markov processes may thus be related to ones described by deterministic ordinary differential equations, see Kurtz (1970). Stochastic models are sometimes easier to analyze than the corresponding deterministic models. See Kendall and Saunders (1983) for such an example.

of types. By interpreting tables as boxes and customers as indistinguishable balls a connection with the classical occupancy problem can be made, as well as with the problem of determining distributions of agents by types or classes. Aldous also describes random maps as examples of random partitions. This approach views patterns as partitions of a set of balls (agents) as in Kingman (1978b). The same kinds of random maps are also discussed by Derrida and Flyvbjerg (1987a, b) who apparently are not aware of the Aldous reference. We describe their analysis in Section E.4 and show that their problem and the Ewens distribution belong to the same class of distributions, that is, they have frequency spectrum functions, discussed in Section E.3, of the same class.

We have not discussed pure death processes as such. Pure death processes are important in stochastic processes introduced by Kingman (1982b) and called "coalescent"; they are Markov chains on hierarchy. In applications, pure death processes are useful in examining spread of defects such as bankruptcy in a network of financial institutions, for example. Linear stochastic models do not fully explain variability of observations in some fields, as noted by Ball and Donnelly (1987). They show that nonlinear models are better in explaining variability in pure death models, and also prove that if the sequence $\{\mu_k / k\}$ increases (decreases) with k, where μ_k is the transition rate from k agents to one fewer agent (death), then the states of the agents are negatively (positively) correlated.

We have not discussed simulation studies of collective dynamic behavior of a large number of agents. Simulation studies by a network of stochastic automata, such as Kauffman models, are definitely useful. In such models, state spaces contain many valleys, that is, many local equilibria. A statistical description of relative sizes of basins of attraction of stochastic dynamics is outlined in section at the end of this book. Sizes of basins of attraction are studied in the physics literature, which indicates that the multivalley structures of state spaces of random networks of automata share some common features with infinite-range spin glasses (Ising models with random interaction coefficients). Hierarchical dynamics, which we discuss in Chapter 7, also arise in discussing dynamics of random equivalence classes or random partitions. Coalescent processes are introduced by Kingman (1982b) to study these. Such statistical studies may be helpful in simulation studies of large stochastic dynamic systems. In studying statistical distributions of relative sizes of basins of attraction of random dynamics, the Poisson–Dirichlet processes of Kingman (1978a, 1982a) are useful. Some indication of this is found later in Section E.1.

E.1   Zipf's distribution in economic models

In the economic literature, a device is often employed to represent agents as points or subsets on the unit interval with a Lebesque measure, for example, agents are uniformly arranged on the unit interval. Is this scheme of introducing a distribution on the set of agents as inocuous as the economic profession seems to assume? Is there some interesting economic phenomenon we miss by assuming uniform distributions?[2]

This section considers distributions of agents by some attributes, or of some economic variables, following Hill (1970, 1974, 1982), Hill and Woodroofe (1975), and Chen (1980). We see that a variety of interesting distributions arise, in particular, Zipf's distribution.

In the simplest version, there are N agents (entities, units, or quanta) to be allocated among M non-empty classes or categories, which correspond to the urns in the well-known occupancy number problem discussed by Feller (1957, p. 39), for example, subject to the requirement that none of the categories is empty. We let $(L_1, L_2, \ldots, L_M)$ be a vector of occupancy numbers, and order them by the largest to the smallest. The distribution of the rth largest occupation number, $L^{(r)}$, against r is of interest. Another quantity of interest is the fraction $g(s)/M$, where $g(s)$ is the number of categories with exactly s agents.

By interpreting N and M appropriately, a number of interesting problems can be so represented. Besides the well-known examples of firm size distributions or income distributions by Simon and Bonini (1958), Ijiri and Simon (1964), Steindl (1965), Lucas (1978), and others in addition to the original work by Pareto, sizes of cities or word usage frequencies have been examined. Zipf (1949) also contains a large number of examples. Subject to verification of the key assumption used by Hill (1970), a number of other applications seem possible, and we indicate some below. We use the word "units" to cover various contexts in which the same procedure can be interpreted.

Three-level hierarchies arise by building on the two-level trees described previously. Hill (1974) mentions an example of K regions in each of which classifications proceed as in two-level trees. We have $\sum_i^K M_i = M$, and $\sum_i^K N_i = N$. Cities are classified by populations in each region, and regions are level 1 categories of a nation. There are K regions. In region i, there are M_i cities with total population N_i, $i = 1, \ldots, K$. Here is another possible example. By measuring outputs with a small enough basic unit (output quanta), output can be measured as a positive integer, which is allocated into K sectors. Output of sector i is contributed by M_i industries, each of which contains N_i numbers of firms. This is a three-level classification of firms' outputs.

As explained by Hill (1975), what is crucial is the assumption that the ratio $\theta_i = M_i/N_i$ can be regarded as asymptotically independent random variables and governed by the same distribution. Under this assumption, Hill deduces limiting distributions as N and M becomes large. What is novel is the fact that the number of categories is treated as random.

---

[2] See Hill (1968, 1970, 1975).

E.1.1 Bose–Einstein allocations

In modeling a set of allocations or assignments of agents or units, it is crucial to decide on the type of allocations that we regard to be equally probable. One possibility is to postulate that agents are indistinguishable in that permutation of their labels leaves situations invariant, for example, and governed by exchangeable processes. Then, the distributions of agents among categories or classes to form hierarchy are governed by the Bose–Einstein allocation.[3] If agents are assumed to be distinguishable, then we have the Maxwell–Boltzmann allocations or statistics.

If N agents are distributed into M categories or classes in such a way that none of the M classes is empty, then there are $_{N-1}C_{M-1}$ ways of distributing N indistinguishable or exchangeable agents into M categories or cells. This is so because when we want none of M cells empty, we first allocate M units to M cells. Then, there are this many ways of allocating the remaining ($N - M$) agents to M categories without any constraint, since $_{N-M+M-1}C_{N-M} = {}_{N-1}C_{N-M} = {}_{N-1}C_{M-1}$. In other words, this many configurations are possible, each of which defines a microstate of the model with N indistinguishable agents in M non-empty categories. When each of these microstates is regarded as equally probable, we have agents distributed according to the Bose–Einstein statistics or allocation. See Gnedenko (1962, p. 33), Feller (1957, p. 39).

A microstate of the model is the vector of occupancy numbers, $L = (L_1, L_2, \ldots, L_M)$. When these L_i are exchangeable, that is, any permutation of them has the same probability, we have

$$Pr(L \mid M, N) = {}_{N-1}C_{M-1}{}^{-1}.$$

By exchangeability, we see that

$$E(L_i \mid M, N) = M^{-1}E\left(\sum_i L_i \mid M, N\right) = N/M,$$

that is, the mean of L_i/N is $1/M$.

In the Maxwell–Boltzmann allocation, after M agents are allocated to ensure non-empty categories, the remaining $N - M$ agents are allocated to M categories as distinguishable agents. Then, the same microstate has the probability

$$Pr(L \mid M, N) = (N - M)!\left[\prod_{i=1}^{M}(L_i - 1)!\right]^{-1} M^{-(N-M)}.$$

---

[3] In the physics literature, it is called Bose–Einstein statistics. As remarked by Gnedenko (1962, p. 33) and others, the meaning of statistics here is peculiar to the literature of statistical mechanics. We use the word allocation instead.

Here, $L_i - 1$ units or agents have the binomial distribution based on $N - M$ trials with probability $1/M$ of success on a given trial. Hence the mean of L_i/N is the same $1/M$. However, the variances of these two distributions are different. The Maxwell–Boltzmann distribution represents sharper knowledge of L_i/N than the Bose–Einstein allocation.

From now on, we mainly discuss the Bose–Einstein allocation cases since they are the ones that correspond to the exchangeable agents, and point out occasionally the different implications of these two distributions.

E.1.1.1 Two-level hierarchy

To present a simpler case first, we discuss a two-level classification following Hill (1970). As before, we let L_i be the number of agents in category i, $L_i \geq 1$, $i = 1, \ldots M$. Naturally, $\sum_i L_i = N$. These L_i are exchangeable, that is, any permutation of them has the same probability.

The number of cells with exactly s agents, denoted by $g(s)$, is such that

$$Pr(G \mid M, N) = \frac{M!}{\prod_{s=1}^{\hat{s}} g(s)!} {}_{N-1}C_{M-1}{}^{-1},$$

where $\hat{s} = N - M + 1$, $G = [g(1), g(2), \ldots, g(\hat{s})]$, and we note that $\sum_s g(s) = M$, and $\sum_s s g(s) = N$, by definition.

Using the indicator functions $\chi_j(s)$ which are one if the classification cell j has exactly s agents in it, we express $g(s)$ as the sum $\sum_{j=1}^{M} \chi_j(s)$, and we have

$$M^{-1}E[g(s) \mid M, N] = {}_{N-s-1}C_{M-2}/{}_{N-1}C_{M-1},$$

and

$$E[g(s)g(t) \mid M, N] = M(M-1){}_{N-s-t-1}C_{M-3}/{}_{N-1}C_{M-1}$$
$$+ \delta_{s,t}E[g(s) \mid M, N].$$

If we let M and N go to infinity, keeping the ratio M/N at θ, then Hill (1970) shows that

$$g(s)/M \to \theta(1 - \theta)^{s-1},$$

in probability. With the Maxwell–Boltzmann distribution, the same ratio converges to

$$g(s)/M \to e^{-\lambda}\lambda^{s-1}/(s - 1)!,$$

where $\lambda = (1 - \theta)/\theta$.

Hill also establishes that if $F_N(x) = Pr(M/N \leq x \mid N)$ converges to a proper distribution function $F(x)$ with $F(0) = 0$, then $Pr[g(s)/M \leq x \mid N]$ converges to the distribution function $Pr[h_s(\theta) \le x]$, where θ is distributed according to F and

$$h_s(\theta) = \theta(1 - \theta)^{s-1}.$$

See our discussion on the Dirichlet–multinomial distribution in Section E.1.2 and at the end of Elaborations section for further detail. Hill (1974), shows that if M is random with $F_N(x) = Pr[M/N \le x \mid N]$ converging to an absolutely continuous distribution $F(x)$, then we have the limiting case:

$$Pr[L^{(r)}/\ln N \le a \mid N] \to Pr(\Theta \ge 1 - e^{-1/a}).$$

Here, Θ is a random variable having distribution F.

E.1.1.2 Three-level hierarchical classification
We can write the ratio of cells with s units as

$$g(s)/M = \left[\sum_{i=1}^{K} \frac{N_i}{N} \frac{M_i}{N_i} \frac{g_i(s)}{M_i}\right] \Big/ (M/N).$$

From our discussion of two-level trees, the right-hand side is approximately given by

$$\left[\sum_i \frac{N_i}{N} \theta_i^2 (1 - \theta_i)^{s-1}\right] \Big/ \sum_i \frac{N_i}{N} \theta_i.$$

Hill and Woodroofe (1975) show that if

$$\ln M_i = c + \delta \ln \theta_i + e_i,$$

for all i, where e_i are independent, then if $F_N(x)$ is asymptotically proportional to x^γ for $x \to 0$, and $G(s)/M$ is approximately proportional to $s^{-(1+\delta+\gamma)}$. This was generalized from a two-level classification to a three-level hierarchy in Hill and Woodroofe (1975). One of their interesting results is the following.

We let k be the number of the first-level classification, that is, the coarsest classification, which we call a category (e.g., a family in biological classification), and we let $N_i(k)$, $i = 1, \ldots, k$, be the number of agents in category i. We define $\beta_i(k) = N_i(k)/E(N_i(k))$, and

$$\theta_i(k) = M_i(k)/N_i(k),$$

where $M_i(k)$ corresponds to M_i of two-level hierarchy, which now carries an argument k since we are interested in letting k grow. Further, we define

$$g(s; k) = \sum_{i=1}^{k} g_i(s; k),$$

and let $M(k) = \sum_{i=1}^{k} M_i(k)$. Then, writing

$$g(s; k)/M(k) = \sum_i \beta_i(k)\theta_i(k)[g_i(s; k)/M_i(k)] \bigg/ \sum_i \beta_i(k)\theta_i(k),$$

we show that this converges in probability to

$$\int_0^1 t^2(1 - t)^{s-1}dH^*(t) \bigg/ \int_0^1 tdH^*(t),$$

where $H^*(t) = \lim_k E[\beta_1(k)I_k(t)]$, on the assumption that

$$[M_1(k), N_1(k)], \ldots [M_k(k), N_k(k)]$$

form a triangular array in which each row is an exchangeable process, and other technical conditions.

Alternatively, they show that if $M_i(k) = X_i(k)\theta_i(k)^{\gamma}$ and if $X_i(k)/E[X_i(k)]$ is asymptotically independent of $\theta_i(k)$ in the sense that the sequences are stochastically bounded as $k \to \infty$, and the covariances go to zero as well, then

$$E\{M_i(k)I_k(t)/E[M_i(k)]\} \approx \int_0^t y^{\gamma}dF(y) \bigg/ \int_0^1 y^{\gamma}dF(y),$$

if t is a continuity point of F, and $G(s; k)/M(k)$ converges in probability to

$$\int_0^1 t^{1+\gamma}(1 - t)^{s-1}dF(t) \bigg/ \int_0^1 t^{\gamma}dF(t).$$

We next derive some of the results mentioned above, following Chen (1980).

E.1.2 Dirichlet–multinomial model of Chen

Given $\mathbf{p}$, a vector of probabilities p_i that allocates a unit to category i, a multinomial distribution $MN(N, M; \mathbf{p})$ assigns probability

$$\frac{(N - M)!}{\prod_{i=1}^{M} \Gamma(L_i)} \prod_i p_i^{L_i-1}$$

to the allocation $(L_1, L_2, \ldots, L_M)$. This allocation ensures at least one unit in each of M categories or cells.

Next, we assume that the p_i have a symmetric Dirichlet distribution[4] on the $(M - 1)$-dimensional simplex with a single parameter β,

$$f(p_1, p_2, \ldots, p_M) = \frac{\Gamma(M\beta)}{\Gamma(\beta)^M} \prod_{i=1}^{M} p_i^{\beta-1},$$

where $p_i \geq 0$, $\sum_i p_i = 1$.

Chen (1978) defines a Dirichlet–multinomial distribution, $DM(N, M, \beta)$. It assigns to $L = (L_1, L_2, \ldots, L_M)$ the probability

$$Pr(L \mid N, M, \beta) = \int Pr(L \mid N, M, \beta, P) f(P) \, dp_1 \cdots dp_{M-1}, \quad (E.1)$$

where the integral is over the simplex. When the integration is carried out[5], we obtain

$$Pr(L \mid N, M, \beta) = \frac{(N - M)!\,\Gamma(M\beta)}{\Gamma(N - M + M\beta)\Gamma(\beta)^M} \frac{\prod_i \Gamma(L_i + \beta - 1)}{\prod_i \Gamma(L_i)}.$$

We note that this probability reduces to that of the Bose–Einstein allocation model when β is set to one, and to the Maxwell–Boltzman distribution when β goes to infinity.

There is an important relationship between this Dirichlet–multinomial model and the set of random variables with negative binomial distributions that is exploited by Chen. A nonnegative integer-valued random variable X has a negative binomial distribution, $NB(p, \beta)$, with parameter p and β, when

$$Pr(X = k) = {}_{k+\beta-1}C_k\, p^k (1 - p)^\beta, \quad k = 0, 1, \ldots, \; \beta \geq 0, \; 0 \leq p \leq 1,$$

where ${}_{k+\beta-1}C_k = \Gamma(k + \beta)/[\Gamma(k + 1)\Gamma(\beta)]$. If β is some positive integer, then we can interpret this probability as that of an event of successes and failures in which kth success occurs at exactly $k + \beta$ trials, that is, exactly β failures precede the kth success. See Feller (1957, p. 155), for example. In other words, when $Y_1, Y_2, \ldots, Y_M$ is a sequence of independent and identically distributed random variables following a geometric distribution with parameter p, the sum $\sum_i Y_i$ has the negative binomial distribution

$$Pr\left(\sum_i Y_i = S\right) = C_{S-1, r-1}\, p^r (1 - p)^{S-r}, \quad S = r, r + 1, \ldots,$$

[4] A Dirichlet distribution is given by $P(p_1, \ldots, p_M) = [\Gamma(\Sigma_j \alpha_j)/\Pi_\Gamma(\alpha_j)]\Pi_i p_i^{\alpha_i - 1}$. See Kingman (1975).

[5] See Copson (1955, p. 213) for a hint of changes of variables to carry out the integration. Alternatively, from the expression for the general Dirichlet distribution, we see that the product $\Pi_j p_j^{\beta-1}$ integrated over the $(M - 1)$-dimensional simplex is equal to $\Gamma(\beta)^M / \Gamma(M\beta)$.

which is seen to be NB(p, β), by setting $\beta = S - r$. Given X_i which is an independent and identically distributed NB(p, β) distribution, $\sum_{i=1}^{M} X_i$ has NB$(p, M\beta)$ distribution, as can be readily verified by calculating the moment-generating function or probability-generating function (Whittle 1992, p. 62).

We note that for X_i independent and identically distributed NB(p, β), their conditional probability, given that the sum, is independent of the value of the parameter p in the negative binomial distribution, and is equal to the distribution of L_i which can be verified easily by direct calculation:

$$Pr\left(X_i = a_i, \ i = 1, \ldots M \ \middle| \ \sum_{i=1}^{M} X_i = N - M \right)$$

$$= \frac{Pr(X_i = a_i, \ i = 1, \ldots M)}{Pr(\sum_{i=1}^{M} X_i = N - M)}$$

$$= Pr(L_i = a_i + 1, \ i = 1, \ldots, M \mid N, M, \beta).$$

To discuss distributions on two- and three-level trees of exchangeable units, we need the next fact: We let $X_i, i = 1, \ldots, M$ be a sequence of independent and identically distributed NB(p, β). We let N and M approach infinity in such a way that the ratio M/N converges to θ, where $\theta = (1 - p)/(1 - p + \beta p)$, or $p = (1 - \theta)/(1 - \theta + \theta\beta)$. We note that θ is between 0 and 1. Then, for any fixed K, $K \leq M$, and $a_i \geq 0, i = 1, \ldots, K$,

$$\lim_{N \to \infty} Pr\left(X_i = a_i, \ i = 1, \ldots, K \ \middle| \ \sum_{i=1}^{M} X_i = N - M \right) = \prod_{i=1}^{K} Pr(X_i = a_i),$$

where N and M go to infinity with a finite ratio θ. Namely, the X's are asymptotically independent (Chen 1980, Lemma 2).

This asymptotic independence is due to the result of the local-limit theorem of lattice distributions (see Gnedenko 1962, p. 295; Breiman 1968, Sec. 10.4; or Chung 1968, p. 161):

$$Pr\left(\sum_{i=1}^{M} X_i = N - M \right) = (2\pi M\sigma^2)^{-1/2}[1 + o(1)],$$

and

$$Pr\left(\sum_{i=K+1}^{M} X_i = N - M - \sum_{i=1}^{K} a_i \right) = [2\pi(M - K)\sigma^2]^{-1/2}[1 + o(1)],$$

where $\sigma = \text{var}(X_1)$.

From the local-limit theorem,

$$\lim_{N\to\infty, M\to\infty} \frac{N-M-a+(M-K)\beta C_{(M-K)\beta}}{N-M+M\beta C_{M\beta}} = p^a(1-p)^{K\beta},$$

where $a = \sum_{i=1}^{K} a_i$, and $p = (1-\theta)/(1-\theta+\theta\beta)$.

As before, $g(s)$ is the number of categories with exactly s units in them. Since there are M categories in a two-level hierarchy, $g(s)/M$ is the fraction of categories with exactly s units in them, and $G = [g(1), g(2), \ldots, g(\hat{s})]$, where $\hat{s} = N - M + 1$ is the maximum possible number of units in any category.

To obtain the distribution of the fraction $g(s)/M$, we define the indicator $\chi_j(s)$ as one when $L_j = s$, and zero otherwise. Then, by exchangeability we have

$$E[g(s)/M \mid N, M, \beta] = E\left[(1/M) \sum_{j=1}^{M} \chi_j(s) \mid N, M, \beta \right]$$

$$= E[\chi_1(s) \mid N, M, \beta] = Pr(L_1 = s \mid N, M, \beta)$$

$$= Pr\left(X_1 = s - 1 \mid \sum_i X_i = N - M \right),$$

where the last equality is by Chen (1980, Lemma 1). By Lemma 2 of Chen, this probability asymptotically approaches that of $Pr(X_1 = s - 1)$, when the ratio $M/N = \theta$ is held fixed in letting N and M go to infinity, that is,

$$E[g(s)/M \mid N, M, \beta] \to_{s+\beta-1,} C_{s-1} p^{s-1}(1-p)^\beta.$$

When β is equal to one, this expression reduces to $\theta(1-\theta)^{s-1}$, which is obtained by Hill (1970). This is the expected fraction under the exchangeability assumption of the units. If the units are distinguished, then we are using the Maxwell–Boltzmann distribution and the expected fraction is given by letting β go to infinity, which is $[1/\Gamma(s)]\lambda^{s-1}e^{-\lambda}$, with $\lambda = (1-\theta)/\theta$, which is entirely different from the Bose–Einstein allocation result.

Chen (1980) also calculates that the variance vanishes asymptotically,

$$\text{var}[g(s)/M \mid N, M, \beta] \to 0,$$

and hence $g(s)/M$ converges in probability to the mean shown above.

The joint distribution of G can be obtained by noting that there are $M!/\prod_s g(s)!$ allocations $L = (L_1, \ldots L_M)$ to realize a given G, where s ranges from 1 to $\hat{s} = N - M + 1$. Rewriting Eq. (E.1) in notation s as

$$Pr(L \mid N, M, \beta) = \frac{(N-M)!\Gamma(M\beta)}{\Gamma(N-M+M\beta)\Gamma(\beta)^M} \prod_{s=1}^{\hat{s}} \left[\frac{\Gamma(s+\beta-1)}{\Gamma(s)} \right]^{g(s)}, \quad \text{(E.2)}$$

we derive the distribution of G,

$$Pr[g(1), g(2), \ldots, g(\hat{s}) \mid N, M, \beta] = \frac{M!}{\prod_s g(s)!} \times \text{(E.2)},$$

if $\sum_{s=1}^{\hat{s}} sg(s) = N$, and zero otherwise.

For three-level hierarchies, by using triangular arrays of random variables, Chen shows that

$$\phi(s) \sim As^{-(1+\alpha)}, \ s \rightarrow \infty.$$

This is Zipf's weak law. The parameter α arises as follows. We let M be a random variable with distribution $F_N(x) = Pr(M/N \leq x \mid N, \beta)$ which is assumed to converge weakly to $F(x)$, with $F(0) = 0$, such that

$$F(x) \sim cx^{\alpha}$$

as x approaches zero.

E.1.3   Applications

All symmetric Dirichlet–multinomial models yield a Zipf's law (excluding only the Maxwell–Boltzmann distribution). This means that conclusions based on Bose–Einstein allocations or distributions are robust. As mentioned at the beginning of Section E.1.1, a number of applications of these results seem possible. M_i may be the number of firms in industry i, and N_i could be the workers in industry i. Then, $1/\theta_i$ is the average number of workers per firm. M_i could be output quanta of sector i, and N_i is the number of workers of sector i. Or, M_i could be wage rate quanta of sector i.

Similar interpretations seem possible in asset market modeling.

We offer some points that touch on econometric analysis of a large collection of agents of several types. In some applications, it may be important to treat the population and samples separately. For example, consider an economy with many agents who are of one of K types (choices). The relative frequencies of the types are $X_1, \ldots, X_K$, which are unknown. The number of agents also may be unknown except that it is large. Because the labeling is immaterial, these X_j are exchangeable random variables. Suppose we observe this economy by taking a sample of size n. In this sample, the composition of each type is known to be $n_i, i = 1, \ldots, K$, with $\sum_{i=1}^{K} n_i = n$.

Suppose that these n_i are distributed by a multinomial distribution

$$Pr(n_1, \ldots, n_K \mid X) = \frac{n!}{\prod_i n_i!} \prod_i X_i^{n_i}.$$

Next, we assume that X has a symmetric Dirichlet distribution

$$\phi(x_1, \ldots, x_K) = \frac{\Gamma(K\alpha)}{\Gamma(\alpha)^K}(x_1 \cdots x_K)^{\alpha-1}.$$

By averaging the first conditional distribution with this distribution, we obtain

$$Pr(n_1, \ldots, n_K) = \frac{n!}{\prod_i n_i!} \frac{\Gamma(K\alpha)\Gamma(\alpha+n_1)\cdots\Gamma(\alpha+n_K)}{\Gamma(\alpha)^K\Gamma(K\alpha+n)}.$$

Next, we suppose that only k of K types are present in this sample of size n. We arrange n_j in the descending-order statistics: $n_{(1)} \geq n_{(2)} \geq \cdots \geq n_{(k)}$. Their joint probability is given by

$$Pr[k; n_{(1)}, \ldots, n_{(k)}] = \frac{n!}{\prod n_{(i)}} \frac{\Gamma(K\alpha)\Gamma[\alpha+n_{(1)}]\cdots\Gamma[\alpha+n_{(k)}]}{\Gamma(\alpha)^k\Gamma(K\alpha+n)}M,$$

where M is the number of ways the order statistics $n_{(1)} \geq \cdots \geq n_{(k)} \geq 0, 0,$ $\ldots 0$ can be distributed among K types, that is,

$$M = \frac{K!}{(K-k)!} \frac{1}{a_1!a_2!\cdots a_n!},$$

where a_i is the number of n_j that are equal to j, that is, $\sum_{j=1}^{n} ja_j = n$, and $\sum_{i=1}^{n} a_i = k$.

If we let K go to infinity while keeping $K\alpha$ constant at θ, then

$$\frac{K!}{(K-k)!\Gamma(\alpha)^k} \to \theta^k,$$

and we obtain a limiting expression

$$Pr[k; n_{(1)}, \ldots, n_{(k)}] = \frac{\theta^k\Gamma(\theta)}{\Gamma(\theta+n)} \frac{n!}{\left\{\prod n_{(i)}\right\}a_1!a_2!\cdots a_n!}.$$

Alternatively, the expression

$$n_{(1)}n_{(2)}\cdots n_{(k)} = 1^{a_1}2^{a_2}\cdots n^{a_n}$$

may be used instead. See David and Barton (1962, p. 15) and Watterson (1974).

This alternative expression is a link to Kingman's notion of random partition. Any positive integer n can be partitioned several ways. For example, $5 = 4 + 1$ $= 3 + 2 = 3 + 1 + 1 = 2 + 1 + 1 + 1 = 1 + 1 + 1 + 1 + 1$. Kingman (1978b) introduces an equivalence class of the set $\{1, 2, \ldots, n\}$ and the induced partition of the integer n. See Ewens (1990) for an alternative expression for the sampling distribution, known by his name in the population genetics literature. This distribution has applications outside the original genetics literature as discussed in Aoki (1995c). Kingman (1982b) introduces the notion of n-coalescent as a discrete-state Markov process to describe hierarchical relations similar to the ones we use in this book. A node is partitioned further into nodes at a lower level of a tree counting from the root down. Hoppe (1986, 1987) presents related material as well.

Keener, Rothman, and Starr (1988) describe a family of two-parameters distributions that can encompass Maxwell – Boltzmann, Bose – Einstein and Dirichlet distributions depending on parameter values.

E.2   Residual Fraction Model

We follow Hoppe (1987) to model many finite populations of agents of different types whose sampling properties in the limit of large population size are described by the Ewens sampling formula (Kingman 1977).

Using independent and identically distributed random variables U with probability density $\theta(1 - u)^{\theta-1}$, $0 \le u \le 1$, we define random variables $Q_1 = U_1$, $Q_i = U_i \prod_{j=1}^{i-1}(1 - U_j)$, $i \ge 2$. These probabilities may be interpreted as those assigning agents to different types. When there are a finite number, K, of types, we impose $U_K = 1$.

We form the size-biased permutation of the sample by first selecting one agent at random from the population, and removing all V_1 agents of the same type from the population. Then, we select another agent at random from the remaining or residual $N - V_1$ agents, and remove all V_2 of agents of the same type. We continue in this manner until the entire population has been removed and allocated into K types. We have $V_1 + V_2 + \cdots + V_K = N$.

Hoppe (1987, Theorem 4) shows that

$$V_1 = 1 + \text{Bin}(N - 1, Z_1),$$

and

$$V_i = 1 + \text{Bin}(N - 1 - V_1 - \cdots - V_{i-1}, Z_i),$$

where Z_i are independent and identically distributed random variables with the same probability density function as the Us, and where $\text{Bin}(r, Z)$ denotes a binomial random variable on r trials with success probability Z. Both of r and Z may be random.

We allocate a finite N numbers of agents to K types by a randomized procedure which depends on the previous assignments only through their cumulative total. When types 1 through $i - 1$ have $n_1, n_2, \ldots n_{i-1}$ agents respectively, we assign

$$n_i = R_i \left(N - \sum_{j=1}^{i-1} n_j \right)$$

to type i, where $R_i(n)$ is a family of integer valued random variables between 0 and n. In the case of the Ewens distribution, we use

$$R_i(n) = 1 + \text{Bin}(n-1, Z_i).$$

As shown by Hoppe, this assignment has the probability

$$Pr[n_1 = x_1, \cdots n_K = x_K] = E\left[\binom{N}{\mathbf{x}} \prod_{i=1}^{K} Q_i^{x_i}\right],$$

where $\mathbf{x} = (x_1, \cdots x_K)$. Here the first notation on the right means the multinomial coefficient $N!/x_1! \cdots x_K!$.

By changing the variables to $y_0 = 0$, $y_i = x_1 + x_2 + \cdots + x_i$, we can rewrite the right-hand side as

$$E\left[\prod_{i=1}^{K} \binom{N - y_{i-1}}{x_i} U_i^{x_i} (1 - U_i)^{N-y_i}\right]$$

because the factor $1 - U_i$ appears in Q_j, $j \geq i+1$ with power $x_{i+1} + \cdots + x_K = N - x_1 - \cdots - x_i = N - y_i$.

By letting $S_i(N)$ denote the number of agents of type i in a sample of size N, we can calculate its probability as

$$Pr[S_1(N) = i] = \int_0^1 {}_{N-1}C_{i-1}x^{i-1}(1-x)^{N-i}\theta(1-x)^{\theta-1}dx.$$

Then the joint probability is given by

$$Pr[S_1(N) = x_1, \cdots S_K(N) = x_K]$$

$$= \prod_{i=1}^{K} {}_{N-1-y_{i-1}}C_{x_i-1} \int_0^1 u^{x_i-1}(1-u)^{N-y_{i-1}-x_i}\theta(1-u)^{\theta-1}du.$$

When the integration is carried out, the probability is given by

$$\frac{\theta^K N! \Gamma(\theta)}{\Gamma(N+\theta)} \prod_1^K \frac{1}{t_i},$$

with $t_i = N - y_{i-1} = x_i + x_{i+1} + \cdots + x_K$.

When we let N goes to infinity, the expression $(V_1/N, V_2/N, \cdots V_K/N)$ converges almost surely to $\{Z_1, Z_2(1 - Z_1), \ldots \prod_1^{K-1}(1 - Z_i)\}$ by the strong law of large numbers for binomial random variables.

E.3   Frequency Spectrum

We define the size-biased permutation of frequencies (fractions) $\{P_i\}$ by randomly selecting an agent from the population and denoting its frequency or fraction as P_1^s, and then removing all agents of the same type from the population and selecting another agent at random. The fraction of this second agent's type is denoted by P_2^s, and so on. For any positive integer i and distinct subscripts $\sigma(1), \sigma(2), \ldots \sigma(i)$, we have

$$Pr[P_j^s = P_{\sigma(j)}, j = 1, \ldots, i | \{P_k\}] = P_{\sigma(1)} \prod_{j=2}^{i} P_{\sigma(j)} \left(1 - \sum_{k=1}^{j-1} P_{\sigma(k)} \right)^{-1}.$$

Let $Q_1 = P_1^s$. Then for any bounded measurable function f on $[0, 1]$

$$\sum_i f(P_i) P_i = E[f(Q_1)|\{P_k\}] = \int_o^1 f(x)\theta(1 - x)^{\theta-1}dx.$$

By specializing the function f to be zero from 0 to t and equals $1/x$ for x larger than t, we obtain

$$E[\text{number of types whose fraction exceeds } t] = \int_t^1 \theta x^{-1}(1 - x)^{\theta-1}dx.$$

This relation shows that the integrand $\theta x^{-1}(1 - x)^{\theta-1}$ is the frequency spectrum. See Kingman (1980), Aldous (1985) or Hoppe (1987).

E.4   Statistical distribution of relative sizes of attractive basins

Some models exhibit many locally stable equilibria. Each locally stable equilibrium has a basin of attraction associated with it. In stochastic dynamics, a state in a basin of attraction does not necessarily remain in it, but may move to the basin of attraction of the locally stable equilibrium, overcoming the barrier separating the two basins. See Chapter 5 and van Kampen (1992, Chap. XIII).

Information on relative sizes of basins of attraction and their distributional properties, such as probabilities of two states falling in the same basin or two separate basins, are useful in analyzing behavior of dynamics with many local extrema. We briefly mention three approaches. One is the probability (called splitting probabilities by van Kampen [1992]). Given a set of locally stable equilibria, we calculate the probabilities that a state is captured in the domain of attractions of the respective equilibria. We use this approach in Chapter 5.

The second approach is to analyze random maps of a set of points that are assumed to be uniformly distributed in the state space, Ω, consisting of N points. We consider a function, called random mapping, of Ω into itself. See Katz (1955) and Harris (1960). This function is chosen randomly, but once chosen, it usually is kept fixed. These results are used by Derrida and Flyvbjerg (1987) to attach a weight $W_s = N_s/N$, where N_s is the number of points that fall in the basin. They derive the distribution of the average number of attractors with weights in the interval $(W, W + dW)$. Then they calculate the probability that a randomly chosen configuration belongs to a basin of attraction of weight W. They derive

$$f(w) = \frac{1}{2}w^{-1}(1 - w)^{-1/2},$$

and

$$g(w) = wf(w),$$

where $f(w)$ is the probability density of having the basin of attraction of relative size w, and $g(w)$ is the probability density of a randomly chosen state falling in this basin of attraction. The probability density of two states falling in the basins of relative size w_1 and w_2 is

$$g(w_1, w_2)dw_1dw_2 = g(w_1)w_1\delta(w_1 - w_2)dw_1dw_2$$
$$+ g(w_1)(1 - w_1)g\left(\frac{w_2}{1 - w_1}\right)dw_1d\left(\frac{w_2}{1 - w_1}\right),$$

where the first term is the probability that both states fall in the same basin of relative size, w_1. To interpret the second term, we note that when one state falls in the basin of relative size w_1, there are Nw_1 points of the state space Ω falling in this basin. We restrict the random map to the remaining $N(1 - w_1)$ points that are not in this basin. The probability of finding a basin of attraction of relative size w for this restricted map is again $f(w)$. The relative weight of the restricted map, w, is equal to the relative weight, for the unrestricted map, $(1 - w_1)w$. The idea is clearly the same as that of the residual allocation model in Section E.2.

In the Kauffman model that generalized this random map model, there are K inputs randomly chosen from N points for each point in the state space. A Boolean function is randomly chosen and is usually kept fixed.

The third approach is an explicitly statistical one using the Poisson–Dirichlet distribution introduced by Kingman (1975, 1977).

In simulation studies of large stochastic dynamics with many local extrema, it is important to statistically characterize distributions of sizes of basins of attraction. We outline an approach following Watterson and Guess (1977) and Kingman (1978b, 1980) who developed the tools in an entirely different – field – population biology. As we show, their tools are just the right ones in our investigation of models composed of microeconomic agents of several types or agents with a finite set of choices. The results of Derrida and Flyvbjerg (1987) can be thought of as special cases of the Watterson and Guess (1977) approach.

In our applications, a positive integer K is the number of basins of attraction. Parameter θ appears in the probability density function of a basic random variable to be described below, and can be interpreted as the parameter in the transition rates associated with random partitions or equivalence relations introduced by Kingman (1980, 1982a, b).

We start with a generalization of the Dirichlet distribution, called Poisson–Dirichlet distributions by Kingman. Kingman (1978b) mentions four ways that such a distribution arises. One of them, which he attributes to Patil and Taillie (1977), is the one that we sketch here. It is the random alms problem in which random portions of the initial unit amount of money are distributed to beggars as the owner of the money encounters them sequentially. We let V_i, $i = 1, 2, \ldots,$ be independent and identically distributed random variables with probability density

$$h(v) = \theta(1 - v)^{\theta-1},$$

for a positive θ with v between 0 and 1. We define

$$U_1 = V_1; \; U_2 = V_2(1 - V_1); \ldots, U_j = V_j \prod_{k=1}^{j-1}(1 - V_k), \ldots.$$

These U_j are the amount that each beggar gets in the alms problem.

Then, the descending-order statistics of the U_j have a joint Poisson–Dirichlet distribution. We now illustrate the derivation of the density for the order statistics, following the approach of Watterson and Guess (1977). We call the order statistics W_i, $W_1 \geq W_2 \geq \ldots$, which arrange U_j in the descending order. We think of these as relative sizes of basins of attractions normalized to sum to one. Watterson and Guess show that

$$f(w_1) = \theta w_1^{-1}(1 - w_1)^{\theta-1}$$

is the frequency spectrum of the relative size of the largest basin of attraction.[6] We can interpret the expression $wf(w)$ as the probability that a randomly chosen state of the dynamics belongs to a basin of the largest relative size w (see also Ewens 1990).

We let $w_1 \geq w_2 \geq \cdots \geq w_K$ with $\sum_{i=1}^{K} w_i = 1$ be distributed with density $\phi(w_1, \ldots, w_k)$, which is the Dirichlet distribution for the exchangeable random variables, since U_j are exchangeable:

$$\phi(w_1, w_2, \ldots, w_K) = \frac{\Gamma(K\alpha)}{\Gamma(\alpha)^K}(w_1 w_2 \cdots w_K)^{\alpha-1}.$$

[6] A frequency spectrum is a positive function defined on the unit interval with $\int_0^1 xf(x)dx = 1$ (see Kingman 1980, p. 32).

The density is therefore symmetric. The density $p(w)$ is the first descending-order statistic among the normalized sizes of basins of attraction, $W_1, \ldots, W_K$,

$$p(w_1) = \int \cdots \int \phi(w_1, w_2, \ldots w_K) dw_2 dw_3 \cdots dw_{K-1},$$

where the integration is over the simplex mentioned above, and w_K is substituted out by the condition that the w_j sum to one, that is, $w_K = 1 - w_1 - \cdots - w_{K-1}$. In particular, we note that $w_1 \geq w_K \geq 1 - w_1 \geq 0$, that is, $1 \geq w_1 \geq 1/2$.

We introduce new variables $y_j = w_j / w_1$, $j = 2, \ldots, K - 1$. In particular, $w_K = 1 - w_1 - w_1(y_2 + \cdots + y_{K-1})$. In these new variables, the density is given by

$$p(w_1) = \frac{K \Gamma(K\alpha)}{\Gamma(\alpha)^K} w_1^{(K-1)(\alpha-1)} I,$$

where the expression I is the integral

$$I = \int \cdots \int (y_2 \cdots y_{K-1})^{\alpha-1} (1 - w_1 - w_1 z)^{\alpha-1} dy_2 \cdots dy_{K-1},$$

where $z = y_2 + \cdots + y_{K-1}$, and the integration is taken over the region $A_1 - A_2$, where

$$A_1 = \left(0 \leq y_i \leq 1, \ i = 2, \ldots K - 1; 0 \leq z \leq \frac{1 - w_1}{w_1} \right),$$

and

$$A_2 = \left(0 \leq y_i \leq 1, \ i = 2, \ldots K - 1; z \leq \frac{1 - 2w_1}{w_1} \right).$$

We denote the integral over A_i as I_i, $i = 1, 2$ and note that $I = I_1 - I_2$.

To evaluate I_1, we introduce independent and identically distributed random variables $Y_2, \ldots, Y_{K-1}$ with density

$$q_1(y) = \alpha y^{\alpha-1},$$

over $[0, 1]$. Then, the expression $(y_2 \cdots y_{K-1})^{\alpha-1}$ in I is the product of the probability densities for these variables when multiplied by α^{K-1}. The random variable $Z = \sum_{i=2}^{K-1} Y_i$ has the density that is the $K - 2$ fold convolution of $q_1(\cdot)$ denoted by q_{K-2}. We express the integral $I = I_1 - I_2$ with

$$I_1 = \alpha^{-(K-2)} \int_0^{(1-w_1)/w_1} q_{k-2}(z)(1 - w_1 - w_1 z)^{\alpha-1} dz,$$

and

$$I_2 = \alpha^{-(K-2)} \int_0^{(1-2w_1)/w_1} q_{k-2}(z)(1 - w_1 - w_1 z)^{\alpha-1} dz.$$

In the Dirichlet distribution, we let the product

$$\theta = K\alpha$$

remain fixed in letting K become large. We may interpret θ as the transition rate of an underlying continuous-time Markov process. See Kingman (1980). Watterson and Guess (1977) show that q_K has a limiting density expression as K goes to infinity. We denote the limiting density by q. Since α is going to zero, the integrand has a pole at $z = (1 - w_1)/w_1$, which is the upper limit of integra of I_1, but I_2 is not affected by this pole. Thus, we have

$$I_1 \approx \alpha^{-(K-1)} w_1^{-1} q\left(\frac{1 - w_1}{w_1}\right),$$

and

$$I_2 \approx o\left[\alpha^{-(K-1)}\right].$$

The constants in the Dirichlet distribution become

$$\Gamma(K\alpha) \approx \Gamma(\theta),$$

and

$$\Gamma(\alpha)^K = \left[\frac{\Gamma(1 + \alpha)}{\alpha}\right]^K,$$

which, for large values of K, is approximately equal to

$$\frac{[\Gamma(1) + \alpha\Gamma'(1)]^K}{\alpha^K} = \left(\frac{1 - \gamma\alpha}{\alpha}\right)^K \approx e^{-\gamma\theta}\alpha^{-K},$$

where $\gamma = -\Gamma'(1)/\Gamma(1)$ is Euler's constant.

We next calculate the convolution of densities by the Laplace transform:

$$E(e^{-sZ_K}) = [E(e^{-sY_1})]^{(K-1)},$$

where $Z_K = Y_2 + \cdots Y_K$.

Noting that

$$\int_0^1 e^{-sy} \alpha y^{\alpha-1} dy = 1 + \alpha \int_0^1 (e^{-sy} - 1) y^{\alpha-1} dy,$$

and letting K go to infinity, we obtain

$$Ee^{-sZ} = \exp\left[\theta \int_0^1 (e^{-sy} - 1) y^{-1} dy\right]$$

as the Laplace transform of the limiting random variable Z of Z_K as K goes to infinity.

We can give an alternative expression using the exponential integral

$$E_1(s) = \int_s^\infty \frac{e^{-x}}{x} dx,$$

(see Abramovitz and Stegun 1968, Sec. 5.1.1), by noting that

$$\int_0^1 (e^{-sy} - 1) y^{-1} dy = \sum_{n=1}^\infty \frac{(-s)^n}{nn!} = -\gamma - \ln s - E_1(s).$$

By equating this to the known form

$$p(w_1) = \Gamma(1 + \theta) e^{\gamma\theta} q\left(\frac{1 - w_1}{w_1}\right) w_1^{\theta-1} = \theta w_1^{-1} (1 - w_1)^{\theta-1},$$

we identify the limiting density as

$$q(z) = \frac{z^{\theta-1}}{\Gamma(\theta) e^{\gamma\theta}}.$$

More generally, using this limiting density expression, the joint density of the normalized r largest basins of attractions is given by

$$p(w_1, w_2, \ldots, w_r) = \theta^r \left(\prod_{i=1}^{r-1} w_i^{-1}\right) (1 - w_1 - \cdots w_r)^{\theta-1},$$

over the region $w_1 + \cdots w_{r-1} + 2w_r \geq 1$.

See Aoki (1995c) for discussions of a connection between logarithmic series distributions and Dirichlet distributions.

E.5 Transient Distributions

When we allow the number of types to become unbounded, a diffusion process in the infinite-dimensional ordered simplex

$$\Delta_\infty = \left\{ \mathbf{x} = (x_1, x_2, \ldots) : x_1 \geq x_2 \geq \cdots \geq 0; \sum_{i=1}^\infty x_i = 1 \right\}$$

can be shown as the limit in distribution of several sequences of discrete stochastic models. See Griffiths (1979a, b) and Ethier and Kurtz (1986, Section 10.4).

Griffiths (1979b) also extends the Ewens distribution which is a stationary distribution to transient sampling distributions. One of his major conclusions is that the non-stationary expected number of types in a large sample at any time differs little from that in the stationary distribution when K goes to infinity and α in the Dirichlet distribution goes to zero in such a way that $K\alpha \to \theta$.

Appendix

A.1 The method of Laplace

We often need an asymptotic expression for an integral that depends on one or more parameters, that is, for large or small values of the parameter values. The method of Laplace is employed to derive such asymptotic expressions of integrals.

As an easy example, we consider an integral with a positive parameter v

$$w(v) = \int_\alpha^\beta g(x)e^{-vh(x)}dx$$

as the parameter v goes to infinity.

We let the minimum of $h(x)$ be attained at x^*. When it is at an interior point of the integration, $w(v)$ is straightforward to evaluate. We assume that $h''(x^*) \geq 0$, and change the variable of integration to $v = (x - x^*)\sqrt{vh''(x^*)}$. Then we have

$$w(v) = \frac{e^{-vh(x^*)}g(x^*)\sqrt{2\pi}}{\sqrt{vh''(x^*)}}[1 + O(v^{-1})].$$

When the minimum of h is attained at either limit of integration, and when h has continuous derivatives up to the second order in α and β, there is a simple way of evaluating the expression of Pólya and Szegö (1925, Vol. 1), quoted in Copson (1965, p. 36). Here, we give a heuristic argument from Copson by assuming without loss of generality that the minimum is attained at the lower limit of integration, α, that is,

$$h'(\alpha) = 0,$$

and

$$h''(\alpha) \geq 0.$$

246

Over a small interval $[\alpha, \alpha + \eta)$ of x, we introduce a new variable of integration t by

$$t^2 = -h(\alpha) + h(x) \geq 0,$$

over an interval $[0, \tau)$, for some positive τ since the right-hand side is nonnegative. Then, the integral can be rewritten as

$$\int_\alpha^{\alpha+\eta} g(x)e^{-vh(x)}dx = \int_0^\tau g(x)e^{-vh(\alpha)-vt^2}\frac{2t\,dt}{h'(x)}$$

where, for sufficiently small η, we have

$$\frac{2t}{h'(x)} = \frac{[2h''(\xi)]^{1/2}}{h''(\zeta)} \approx \frac{[2h''(\alpha)]^{1/2}}{h''(\alpha)},$$

since, by the mean-value theorem,

$$t^2 = -h(\alpha) + h(x) = (1/2)(x - \alpha)^2 h''(\xi)$$

for some ξ between α and $\alpha + \eta$, and similarly,

$$h'(x) = (x - \alpha)h''(\zeta)$$

for some ζ between α and $\alpha + \eta$. Carrying out the integration, we obtain an asymptotic expression

$$w(v) \approx g(\alpha)e^{-vh(\alpha)}\left[\frac{\pi}{2vh''(\alpha)}\right]^{1/2}.$$

See Copson (1965) for more precise bounds. Barndorff–Nielsen and Cox (1989, Sec. 3.3) also present several related techniques for asymptotic expansions of integrals with parameters. Several examples of the method are shown in the next subsections.

A.1.0.1 Example of error integral
A simple change of variable $y = z + x$ in

$$e(z) = \sqrt{2/\pi}\int_z^\infty e^{-y^2/2}dy = \sqrt{2/\pi}e^{-z^2/2}\int_0^\infty e^{-xz}e^{-x^2/2}dx$$

can give bounds on the error integral when we use the fact

$$w(z) = \int_0^\infty e^{-zx}g(x)dx = g(0)/z + g'(0)/z^2 + g''(0)/z^3 + \cdots,$$

which is obtained by repeated integrations by parts as $z \rightarrow \infty$.

A.1.0.2 Example of Stirling's formula

The integral representation of the gamma function, when evaluated by the method of Laplace, yields Stirling's formula. We start from the definition

$$\Gamma(\nu + 1) = \int_0^\infty x^\nu e^{-x} dx.$$

To put this integrand into a form to which the method of Laplace is applicable, we change the variable of integration to $\nu t = x$. Thus, the integral is

$$\Gamma(\nu + 1) = \nu^{\nu+1} \int_0^\infty e^{-\nu h(t)} dt$$

where $h(t) = -\ln t + t$, which has a unique maximum at $t = 1$. The Taylor series expansion at $t = 1$ can be used to obtain

$$\Gamma(\nu + 1) \approx (2\pi\nu)^{1/2} \nu^\nu e^{-\nu},$$

which is Stirling's formula.

We encounter more sophisticated applications of the method of Laplace, for example in Varadhan's version of the Laplacian asymptotic formula in evaluating the partition functions of some Gibbs distributions (see Deuschel and Strook 1989, p. 43, or Ellis 1985, p. 38).

A.1.0.3 Example of the partition-function evaluation

We let $X_i, i = 1, \ldots, n$ be independent binary-valued (1 and -1), identically distributed random variables. We denote its arithmetic average by

$$m_n = (1/n) \sum_1^n X_i$$

and let the potential (energy) of the configuration be given by

$$H_n(m_n) = -(n/2)m_n^2.$$

When k of the X_i take on the value 1, the average m_n is equal to $[k - (n-k)]/n$.

The partition function of the corresponding system is given by

$$Z = (1/2n) \sum_x e^{-\beta H_n(x)} = \int_{-\infty}^\infty q(x) \exp(\beta n x^2/2)\, dx$$

where $q(x)$ is the probability density function of m_n, which we derive next, and we note that $dx = 2/n$.[1]

---

[1] The limits of integration are actually from -1 to 1.

Assuming that the values of 1 and -1 are equally likely, we have

$$Z = \sum_{k=0}^{n} 2^{-n}\,{}_nC_k \exp\left(\beta n m_n^2/2\right)$$

where ${}_nC_k$ is a binomial coefficient. We express k in terms of $m_n = x$ as $n(1 + x)/2$, and use Stirling's formula as in Section 3.1 to approximate the probability density function of m_n by

$$q(x) \approx \exp[-nc^*(x)]$$

where

$$c^*(x) = (1/2)[(1 + x)\ln(1 + x) + (1 - x)\ln(1 - x)],$$

for $|x| < 1$. Finally, we have

$$Z \approx \int_{-\infty}^{\infty} \exp[n(\beta x^2/2 - c^*(x)]\,dx.$$

We apply the method of Laplace to see that as n goes to infinity,

$$\lim_{n}(1/n)\ln Z = \sup_{x}[\beta x^2/2 - c^*(x)].$$

This holds since the expression in the parenthese on the right-hand side has a continuous second-order derivative in $|x| < 1$.

Differentiating the expression in the parentheses, we obtain

$$\beta x = (1/2)\ln\frac{1 + x}{1 - x},$$

which can be alternatively put as

$$x = \tanh(\beta x),$$

which has two nonzero solutions in addition to the origin, if and only if β is greater than $1/2$. See Ellis (1985, p. 101) for drawings of this functional relation.

A.1.1 Rate functions

We encounter a more sophisticated statement of the method of Laplace, in, for example, Varadhan's version of the Laplacian asymptotic formula (see Deuschel and Stroock 1989, p. 43, or Ellis 1985, p. 51). Here, we give a version of Varadhan's integration formula (Varadhan 1984).

We let X be a complete separable metric space, and P_n be a sequence of probability measures on the Borel σ-fields of X. In our economic applications, X is often R^d, and P_n is distribution of a random vector z_n. A function $I(x)$ from X to reals is called a rate function if

(i) $I(x)$ is nonnegative,
(ii) $I(x)$ is lower semi-continuous, and is called a good rate function if in addition,
(iii) the level set $x : I(x) \leq c$ is a compact set in X for all c.

The sequence of probability measures is said to obey a principle of large deviations with rate function $I(\cdot)$ if

(i)   For every closed set F of X, as n goes to infinity

$$\limsup_n n^{-1} \ln P_n(F) \leq - \inf_{x \in F} I(x)$$

(ii) For every open set G of X, as n goes to infinity,

$$\liminf_n n^{-1} \ln P_n(G) \geq - \inf_{x \in G} I(x).$$

In particular, if a Borel set A is such that the infimum of the rate function over the interior of A and that over the closure of A are the same, then the limit exists and is equal to

$$\lim_n n^{-1} \ln P_n(A) = - \inf_x I(x).$$

When P_n satisfies a principle of large deviations, one of the results corresponding to the asymptotic evaluation of integrals by the method of Laplace is

$$\lim_{n \to \infty} n^{-1} \int \exp[ng(x)] \, dP_n(x) = \sup_x [g(x) - I(x)],$$

where g is a bounded continuous function on X. This relationship is known as Varadhan's integral lemma. See Varadhan (1984, Theorem 2.1).

When probability measure P_n on X satisfies the large-deviation principle with rate function $I(x)$, we let f be a map from X to another complete separable metric space Y, and we let $Q_n = P_n \cdot f^{-1}$ be the measure induced on Y. Then, Q_n satisfies the large-deviation principle with rate function $I'(\cdot)$ defined by

$$I'(y) = \inf_{x : f(x) = y} I(x),$$

and takes on the value $+\infty$, if no such x exists (see Varadhan 1984, Theorem 2.3).

A.1.1.1 *Example of partition function evaluation*
We approximate the average of the partition function,

$$\Xi_N = \sum_m e^{-\beta H_N(m)},$$

by an integral where m has a probability density function of the form

$$p(m) \approx e^{-Nc^*(m)},$$

and by Varadhan's integral lemma we can write

$$-\beta f(\beta) = \lim_{N \to \infty} \frac{1}{N} \ln \int N \exp[F(m) - c^*(m)] \, dm,$$

as

$$-\beta f(\beta) = \sup_m [F(m) - c^*(m)],$$

since the function $F(m)$ is bounded and continuous. In the above, we use the relation $-\beta H_N = NF(m)$ to define a function F.

A.2 First-passage times

This section collects some facts on first-passage times or times to absorption, which are used in Chapter 5.

A.2.1 Discrete-time Markov chains

We let X_n, $n = 0, 1, \ldots$, be a discrete-time Markov chain on a denumerable set of states that can be taken to be a set of positive integers. We call state i persistent or recurrent if the probability of eventual return to the initial state is one, that is,

$$Pr(X_n = i, \text{ for some } n \geq 1 \mid X_0 = i) = 1,$$

and we call state i transient if not persistent, that is, if the above probability is strictly less than one.

We can decompose the set of states into a transient set T and a persistent set, since the set of persistent states is closed, that is, once in the set, the transition probability to a state outside the set is zero.

We let $N_j(n)$ be the occupation time of state j in the first n transitions of the Markov chain, and let

$$N_j = \lim_{n \to \infty} N_j(n)$$

be the total occupation time of state j. We now call

$$N = 1 + \sum_{j \in T} N_j$$

the time to absorption from a transient state to the set of recurrent states.

We can calculate the expected time of absorption from a transient state by means of the conditional characteristic function

$$\phi_j(u) = E(e^{iuN} \mid X_0 = j),$$

which satisfies

$$\phi_j(u) = \sum_k p_{jk} E(e^{iuN} \mid X_1 = k)$$

$$= \sum_{k \in T^c} p_{jk} e^{iu} + \sum_{k \in T} p_{jk} [e^{iu} \phi_k(u)].$$

We denote the mean time to absorption from state j by

$$m_j = E(N \mid X_0 = j).$$

Then, differentiating the above with respect to u and setting u to zero, we obtain

$$m_j = 1 + \sum_{k \in T} p_{jk} m_k,$$

for all j in T. This is the set of equations to determine the mean first-passage time to the class of recurrent states. Collecting them into a column vector $\mathbf{m}$, we have

$$\mathbf{m} = \mathbf{1} + \mathbf{Q}\mathbf{m},$$

where $\mathbf{1}$ is a column vector of ones, and $\mathbf{Q}$ is the matrix made up of p_{jk} for $j, k \in T$. It can be solved for $\mathbf{m}$.

By differentiating the characteristic equation twice with respect to u and denoting $E(N^2 \mid X_0 = j)$ by $m_j^{(2)}$, we obtain

$$m_j^{(2)} = 2m_j - 1 + \sum_{k \in T} p_{jk} m_k^{(2)}.$$

A.2.2   *Example of a random-walk model*

We let the set of states be $\{1, 2, \ldots, K\}$ where K is the absorbing state and the rest of the states are transient. The equation for the mean first-passage times is

$$m_j = 1 + q_j m_{j-1} + r_j m_j + p_j m_{j+1},$$

where $p_j + r_j + q_j = 1$, for $j = 2, 3, \ldots K - 1$. At the states $j = 1$ and $j = K$, obvious modifications hold.

We next solve this set of equations. For example, we can let $d_j = m_j - m_{j-1}$, $j = 2, 3, \ldots, K - 1$. This satisfies the first-order difference equation

$$p_j d_{j+1} = q_j d_j - 1,$$

which has the solution

$$d_{j+1} = \frac{q_j q_{j-1} \cdots q_2}{p_j p_{j-1} \cdots p_2} d_2$$
$$- \frac{1}{p_j}\left(1 + \frac{q_j}{p_{j-1}} + \frac{q_j q_{j-1}}{p_{j-1} p_{j-2}} + \cdots + \frac{q_j \cdots q_3}{p_{j-1} \cdots p_2}\right),$$
$$j = 2, \ldots, K-1.$$

A.2.3 Continuous-time Markov chains

A.2.3.1 Simple random walks

We let $S_0 = 0$, and $S_n = \sum_1^n X_i$, where the X_i are independent and identically distributed and $X_1 = \pm 1$ with probability p and $q = 1 - p$, respectively. We let T be the first exit time from the interval $(-a, b)$, where a and b are both positive, that is, $T = \min\{n : S_n \leq -a, \text{ or } S_n \geq b\}$. We define $Y_0 = 0$, and for $n \geq 1$,

$$Y_n = e^{tS_n}/M(t)^n,$$

where $M(t) = E(e^{tX_1})$. This defines a martingale $\{Y_n, F_n\}$, where $F_n = \sigma(X_1, X_2, \ldots, X_n)$.

When T is a stopping time with finite mean such that $|S_n| \leq c$ for $n < T$, where c is a constant, then

$$E[e^{tS_n}/M(t)^n] = 1,$$

whenever $M(t) \geq 1$. See Wald's inequality in Grimmett and Stirzaker (1992, p. 467) or Whittle (1992, p. 256). For the simple random walk, the mean of T is shown to be finite. We apply this equality with $t = \theta$ where $M(\theta) = 1$. Then, $E(e^{\theta S_T}) = 1$, or

$$\eta_a P(S_T = -a) + \eta_b P(S_T = b) = 1,$$

where $\eta_a = E(e^{\theta S_T} \mid S_T = -a) = e^{-\theta a}$, and similarly $\eta_b = e^{\theta b}$. Since $P(S_T = -a) + P(S_T = b) = 1$, we have

$$P(S_T = -a) = \frac{e^{\theta b} - 1}{e^{\theta b} - e^{-\theta a}}.$$

The probability $f_b(n)$ that a random walk hits point b for the first time at the nth step, having started from 0, is given by

$$f_b(n) = \frac{|b|}{n} P(S_n = b),$$

for $n \geq 1$. For the simple random walk, we have $P(S_n = b) = C_{n,b} p^{(n+b)/2} q^{(n-b)/2}$.

A.2.4   *A standard Wiener process*

We let $W_t, t \geq 0$, be a standard Wiener process, that is, W_t is normally distributed with mean 0 and variance t.

We denote the first-passage time to the point x on the real axis by

$$T(x) = \inf\{t : W_t = x\}.$$

We let

$$M_t = \max\{W_s : 0 \leq s \leq t\}.$$

Suppose that x is positive. Then, $P[W_{T(x)} = x] = 1$ because the sample path of a Wiener process is continuous with probability one, and the event $T(x) \leq t$ occurs if and only if the event $M_t \geq x$ occurs. Then,

$$P(M_t \geq x) = P(M_t \geq x, W_t \geq x) + P(M_t \geq x, W_t \leq x, W_t \neq x)$$
$$= 2P(M_t \geq x, W_t \geq x) = 2P(W_t \geq x)$$

since, by definition, $W_t \leq M_t$. It follows that

$$P\{T(x) \leq t\} = P\{M_t \geq x\} = P\{|W_t| \geq x\}.$$

See Grimmett and Stirzaker (1992, p. 500).

By symmetry of W_t, this last probability can be evaluated as

$$P(|W_t| \geq x) = 2P(W_t \geq x) = \left(\frac{2}{\pi t}\right)^{1/2} \int_x^\infty e^{-u^2/2t} \, du,$$

which, on substituting $y = x^2 t / u^2$, becomes

$$P[T(x) \leq t] = \int_0^t \frac{|x|}{\sqrt{2\pi y^3}} e^{-x^2/2y} dy.$$

Thus, the probability density of the first-passage time to x is obtained by differentiating the above expression with respect to t as

$$f_{T(x)}(t) = \frac{|x|}{\sqrt{2\pi t^3}} e^{-x^2/2t},$$

for all $t \geq 0$.

A.2.5   *First-passage times to absorbing barrier*

Suppose that a Wiener process has a drift rate μ so that W_t is normally distributed with mean μt and variance t. Suppose that $W_0 = d$, where d is positive and there is a barrier at the origin in the sense that its density is zero at 0 for all $t \geq 0$, and initially it is at d.

Any Wiener process with the same drift rate μ and variance rate 1, starting from the initial position x has the density

$$g(y, t \mid x) = \frac{1}{\sqrt{2\pi t}} \exp[-(y - x - \mu t)^2/2t].$$

A linear combination of two such densities

$$f(y, t) = g(y, t \mid d) - e^{-2\mu d} g(y, t \mid -d)$$

satisfies the boundary condition imposed by the barrier,[2] and the initial condition.

The density function of the first-passage time to the barrier, T, can be obtained from the above. At time t, either the process has reached the boundary, or its position has the density function given by $f(y, t)$; hence,

$$P(T \leq t) = 1 - \int_0^\infty f(y, t)\, dy.$$

Taking the derivative of this with respect to t, we obtain the density function of the first passage to the barrier

$$f_T(t) = \frac{d}{\sqrt{2\pi t^3}} \exp[-(d + \mu t)^2/2t].$$

When the process starts at the origin, and the barrier is placed at some positive distance d, then the idea of superposition still works, and we have

$$f(y, t) = g(y, t \mid 0) - e^{2\mu d} g(y, t \mid 2d)$$

as the correct expression for the density.

A.3   Exchangeable processes

In economic modeling, as well as in many other modeling situations, members of a population, or members of some categories of the population may be indistinguishable. Rather than assuming them to be identical as in the framework of representative agents in economics, and rather than assuming their attributes to be independent and identically distributed random variables, it may be more appropriate to assume them to be exchangeable, as exposited by Galambos in Johnson and Kotz (1977, Sec. 2.9), in Kingman (1978a), or Diaconis and

---

[2] That $f(0, t) = 0$ is the correct boundary condition is easy to grasp intuitively. See Grimmett and Stirzaker (1992, p. 506), or Cox and Miller (1965, p. 220).

Freedman (1981). For a central-limit theorem for exchangeable random variables, see Chernoff and Teicher (1958), or Loève (1963, p. 365). See also Koch and Spizzichino (1982) for several applications.

Here we provide an introductory account following Galambos and Kingman. A finite or countably infinite sequence of events, $A_1, A_2, \ldots,$ is called exchangeable if, for any choice of n subscripts, $1 \leq j_1 \leq j_2 \leq \cdots \leq j_n$, the joint probability $Pr(A_{j_1} \cap A_{j_2} \cap \cdots \cap A_{j_n})$ depends only on n and not on the actual subscripts. In the case of a sequence of random variables $X_1, X_2, \ldots,$ they are called exchangeable if the events $\{X_1 \leq x_1\} \ldots$ are exchangeable, that is, a set of random variables $(X_1, X_2, \ldots, X_n)$ is said to be exchangeable, if the joint distribution of these random variables is the same as that of $(X_{\pi_1}, \ldots, X_{\pi_n})$ for all permutations π of $(1, 2, \ldots, n)$. Therefore, for any $Z = \phi(X_1, \ldots, X_n)$, such that $E(Z)$ exists, and $(X_1, \ldots, X_n)$ exchangeable, we have

$$E(Z) = \frac{1}{n!} \sum_{\pi} \phi(X_{\pi_1}, \ldots, X_{\pi_n}) = E[\psi(X_1, \ldots, X_n)],$$

where

$$\psi(x_1, \ldots, x_n) = \frac{1}{n!} \sum_{\pi} \phi(x_{\pi_1}, \ldots, x_{\pi_n}).$$

An infinite sequence of random variables, $(X_1, X_2, \ldots)$ is said to be exchangeable if the first n random variables are exchangeable for any $n \geq 2$.

A related notion is that of n-symmetry. A random variable is said to be n-symmetric if it is a function of a sequence of the X that is unchanged if the first n variables are permuted in any way. For example, $X_1 + X_2 + 5X_3$ is two-symmetric but is not three-symmetric.

We let F_n be the smallest σ-algebra with respect to which all the n-symmetric random variables are measurable. We note that the σ algebra is non-increasing with n, and the limit,

$$F_\infty = \bigcap_{n=1}^{\infty} F_n,$$

is well defined.

If f is a measurable function such that $|E[f(X_1)]|$ is finite, and if we let $Y = g(X)$ be a bounded n-symmetric random variable, then by the exchangeability of a sequence of X, we note that

$$E[f(X_j)g(\mathbf{X})] = E[f(X_1)g(\mathbf{X})],$$

because exchanging X_j with X_1 leaves g unchanged, and where $\mathbf{X}$ stands for the sequence of the X.

Then, letting Y stand for g, and summing the above with respect to j and dividing by n, we see that

$$E\left[(1/n)\sum_{j=1}^{n}f(X_j)Y\right] = E[f(X_1)Y].$$

Now let Y be the indicator function of any set A in F_n. Then, the above relation becomes

$$\int_A (1/n)\sum_{j=1}^{n}f(X_j)\,dP = \int_A f(X_1)\,dP, \forall A \in F_n.$$

Since the integrand on the left is n-symmetric, and hence F_n measurable, this is the same as

$$\frac{1}{n}\sum_j f(X_j) = E[f(X_1)\,|\,F_n].$$

By the Doob "Forward" Convergence theorem (Doob 1953, Theorem 4.3; Williams 1991, Sec. 11.5), we obtain the strong law of large numbers for an exchangeable sequence

$$\lim_{n\to\infty}(1/n)\sum_j f(X_j) = E[f(X_1)\,|\,F_\infty],$$

almost surely.

A special case is obtained by letting f be the indicator function of $(-\infty, x]$. Then, the above specializes to

$$\lim_{n\to\infty}\frac{1}{n}|(j \le n; X_j \le x)| = F(x),$$

where

$$F(x) = P(X_1 \le x\,|\,F_\infty),$$

is a random distribution function.

By the same reasoning, the above relation generalizes to a joint random distribution function of k random variables. First, we note that

$$\frac{1}{n(n-1)\cdots(n-k+1)}\sum f(X_{j_1},\ldots,X_{j_k})E[f(X_1,\ldots,X_k)\,|\,F_n],$$

and hence the strong law of large numbers takes the form

$$E[f(X_1,\ldots,X_k)|F_\infty]$$
$$= \lim_{n\to\infty}[n(n-1)\cdots(n-k+1)]^{-1}\sum f(X_{j_1},\ldots,X_{j_k}),$$

where the right-hand side can be replaced by taking the summation over 1 to n, independently for each index

$$\lim_{n} n^{-k} \sum_{j_1=1}^{n} \sum_{j_2=1}^{n} \cdots \sum_{j_k=1}^{n} f(X_{j_1}, \ldots X_{j_k}),$$

because the contributions of $O(n^{k-1})$ vanish in the limit.

By taking $f(x_1, x_2, \ldots, x_k) = \prod_{r=1}^{k} f_r(x_r)$, where $f_r(x_r)$ is the indicator function of $(-\infty, x_r]$, we have with probability 1,

$$P(X_1 \leq x_1, \ldots, X_k \leq x_k \mid F_\infty) = \prod_{r} F(x_r).$$

Kingman (1978a) shows that the above remains valid if it is replaced by

$$P(X_1 \leq x_1, \ldots, X_k \leq x_k \mid \zeta) = \prod_{r} F_\zeta(x_r),$$

where ζ is a single random variable and the distribution function now depends on it.

A.4   Low-frequency behavior

In the macroeconomic time series literature in the 1980s, low-frequency behavior of some macroeconomic variables is often said to have unit roots. The economic literature explains the presence of unit or near-unit roots with various devices, such as the exogenous technical progress factor in real business-cycle models, or fractional Brownian motion in time-series literature. Montroll and Shlesinger (1984) show how lognormal distributions may mimic $1/f$ noise over certain ranges of low frequencies.[3] Marinari et al. (1983) propose a model of $1/f$ noise based on a random walk in the presence of a potential function that has a certain scaling property for large deviations.

In macroeconomics, many variables are transformed into their logarithms and many are assumed either to be subject to Gaussian disturbances directly or are governed by some linear dynamics with Gaussian disturbances as forcing terms. Therefore, we feel that Montroll and Shlesinger's (1984) approach using lognormal distributions is natural, and we follow them first, and make a brief comment on Marinari et al. (1983) later.

Suppose that $\ln(x/\bar{x})$ is normally distributed with its density given by

$$F[\ln(x/\bar{x})] = (2\pi\sigma^2)^{-1/2} \exp\{-[\ln(x/\bar{x})]^2/2\sigma^2\} d[\ln(x/\bar{x})].$$

---

[3]   Many fluctuating natural phenomena have power spectra that behave like $1/f$ at low frequencies. Since the integral diverges, $1/f$ is not valid over the whole range of zero to infinity of frequencies.

We define the left-hand side above as $g(y)\,dy$, where $y = x/\bar{x}$, and introduce another random variable $z = \ln(y)$. Then, we take the logarithm:

$$\ln[g(y)] = -z - (1/2)(z/\sigma)^2 - (1/2)\ln(2\pi\sigma^2).$$

Therefore, if

$$(1/2)(z/\sigma)^2 \le \theta|z|,$$

then, except for the constant term, $\ln(y)$ is linear in z within a fraction θ. The larger the σ, the more orders of magnitude the approximation persists.

To see how the power spectra mimic $1/f$ noise, Montroll and Shlesinger use the device of superimposed autocorrelation functions with the time constant being lognormally distributed. We let a basic autocorrelation be given by

$$c(t, \tau) = e^{-t/\tau},$$

where τ is called the time constant or the relaxation time. After the elapse of time of about four time constants, the autocorrelation is nearly zero, since $e^{-4} = 0.0183$.

Its power spectrum is

$$S(f, \tau) = 4Re \int_0^\infty e^{-t/\tau} e^{2\pi i f t}\,dt = \frac{4\tau}{1 + (\omega\tau/\bar{\tau})^2},$$

where $\omega = 2\pi f \tau$.

Next, we assume that τ is distributed with density $\rho(\tau)$ and average $S(f, \tau)$ with respect to this density:

$$S(f) = \int_0^\infty S(f, \tau)\rho(\tau)\,d\tau.$$

We specialize the density to the lognormal one,

$$\rho(\tau/\bar{\tau}) = \frac{\exp\{-[\ln(\tau/\bar{\tau})]^2/2\sigma^2\}}{(2\pi\sigma^2)^{1/2}} d[\ln(\tau/\bar{\tau})].$$

We let $u = \ln(\tau/\bar{\tau})$. Then, renaming $S(f)$ as $S(\omega, \sigma)$, we have

$$S(\omega, \sigma)/4\bar{\tau} = \frac{1}{\omega(2\pi\sigma^2)^{1/2}} \int_{-\infty}^\infty \frac{e^{-u^2/2\sigma^2}}{\omega e^u + (\omega e^u)^{-1}}\,du.$$

At this stage, we already see that if σ is very large, then

$$S(\omega, \sigma) \sim (2\pi\sigma^2)^{-1/2} \int_0^\infty \frac{du}{1 + (\omega u)^2} = \frac{(\pi/2)^{1/2}}{2\omega\sigma}.$$

Montroll and Shlesinger expand the integral in the powers of $|\ln(\omega)/\sigma|$. If this is less than 2σ, then, carrying out the integration, they show that the spectrum indeed behaves like $1/\omega$.

Marinari and co-workers' arguments are more involved conceptually, because they use the scaling relation. Consider a system with a finite dimensional state vector that is changing as a diffusion process (a limiting case of a random walk on a lattice with the nearest-neighbor transitions proportional to the exponential function of the potential difference). In the equilibrium, the probability flux is proportional to $\exp[-\beta V(x)]$, where it is assumed that $V(x)$ scales, at least for large $|x|$ as $V(\lambda x) = \lambda^{\alpha}(x)$, for some α.

In the landscape created by this potential function, one expects that $x(t)$ will occasionally go through a "mountain" pass to go from one basin of attraction to a neighboring one. The probability flux through a mountain pass scales from $g(1)\exp[-\beta V(x)]$ to $g(\lambda)\exp[-\beta(\lambda^{\alpha}-1)V(x)]$, where $g(\lambda)$ is a polynomial in λ to account for volume normalization and change in the width of the pass.

Because the diffusion equation involves a single time derivative, time scale is correspondingly multiplied by the ratio

$$g(1)/g(\lambda) \times \exp[\beta(\lambda^{\alpha} - 1)V(x)].$$

Conversely, multiplication of the time by τ corresponds to scaling the distance by a factor $\lambda(\tau)$, which for large τ, after letting β be absorbed into $V(x)$, is given by

$$\lambda(\tau) = [V^{-1}\log\tau + 1 + O[\log\log(\tau)]^{1/\alpha},$$

which is approximately equal to $\log(\tau/\tau_0)$, for some constant τ_0.

The power spectral density of $x(t)$ is given by

$$S(f) = \lim_{T\to\infty}\left|\int_0^\infty e^{ift}x(t)\,dt\right|^2.$$

We note that the scaling property of the potential is converted into scaling of x, which produces

$$S(f/\tau) = \tau\lambda(\tau)^2 S(f).$$

In the above, we set f to 1, and τ to $1/f$. Then, for small values of f, we obtain

$$S(f) = S(1)\lambda(1/f)^2/f.$$

Thus, except for the numerator, the power spectral density is seen to be proportional to $1/f$. Their simulation seems to show that this nonconstant numerator does not contribute anything significant.

A.5   Lyapunov functions

In physical systems, (free) energy is usually the criterion to be minimized over possible configurations, that is, the system settles toward that configuration with the smallest (free) energy.

Lyapunov functions play a similar role in nonphysical deterministic systems. If a Lyapunov function can be constructed for a given dynamic, then we know that the system moves toward equilibria along a path on which the Lyapunov function is monotonically nonincreasing. Similar statements can be made about stochastic systems where expected values of Lyapunov functions conditional on the present state vectors of the systems decrease monotonically with time, as discussed by Aoki (1989, Sec. 2.6), for example. In this section, we establish that free energy is a Lyapunov function in the Curie–Weiss model, and then we establish the same for the Kullback–Leibler distance.

We assume that each state of microunit can independently assume the value 1 or −1 with the probability of individual microstate variable x_i being given by

$$P(x_i = 1) = \frac{1}{\sqrt{2\pi}\sigma} \int_{\theta_i}^{\infty} \exp[-(x - m_i)^2/2\sigma^2]\,dx$$
$$\approx \frac{1}{2}\left[1 + \mathrm{erf}\left(\frac{\bar{x}_i - \theta_i}{\sqrt{2}\sigma}\right)\right],$$

where erf is the error function introduced in Section 6.3. This probability can be approximated by

$$P(x_i) \approx \frac{e^{\beta h_i x_i}}{e^{\beta h_i} + e^{-\beta h_i}}$$

where $\beta^{-1} = 2\sqrt{2}\sigma$, and where

$$h_i = \sum_{j \neq i} J_{i,j} x_j,$$

with the assumption that $J_{i,j} = J_{j,i}$, and where the summation is over all configurations.

We denote by X the set of configurations (macrostate variable) in which x_i is fixed. We call the set of configurations Y in which x_i is changed into $-x_i$. By assumption, individual microstate variables are independent. Then,

$$w(Y \mid X)/w(X \mid Y) = Pr(-x_i)/Pr(x_i) = \exp(-2\beta h_i).$$

We associate the Hamiltonian to the macrovariable X by

$$H(X) = -(1/2) \sum_{j \neq i} J_{i,j} x_i x_j = -(1/2) \sum h_i x_i.$$

We do likewise for $H(Y)$.

Configurations X and Y differ only in the state variable at the ith component. We assume that the detailed balance condition holds, such that

$$W(Y \mid X)e^{-\beta H(X)} = W(X \mid Y)e^{-\beta H(Y)}.$$

The equilibrium distribution is then Gibbsian:

$$P_e(X) = \exp[-\beta H(X)]/Z,$$

where

$$Z = \sum_Y \exp[-\beta H(Y)].$$

We define potential (free energy) by

$$\beta F = \beta H - S,$$

where S is the Boltzmann entropy, that is, proportional to the logarithm of the number of configurations at a given H value. The average potential is defined by

$$\beta F(\{P\}) = \beta H(\{P\}) + \sum_X P_e(X) \ln P_e(X),$$

with

$$H(\{P\}) = \sum_X P_X H(X).$$

The master equation for the probability distribution (mass function) is given by

$$\frac{dP(X)}{dt} = \sum_{Y \neq X} [w(X \mid Y)P(Y) - w(Y \mid X)P(X)],$$

with a suitable choice of time unit.

Since the Hamiltonian of each configuration is fixed, the free-energy change with time is given by

$$\frac{dF}{dt} = \sum_X \frac{dP(X)}{dt} H(X) + (1/\beta) \sum_X \frac{dP(X)}{dt} [H(X) + \ln P(X)],$$

since $\sum_X dP(X)/dt = 0$.

Substituting the master equation into the above to rewrite the time derivative of the probabilities, we obtain

$$\beta \frac{dF}{dt} = (1/2) \sum_X \sum_Y w(Y \mid X)e^{-\beta H(X)} \left[e^{\beta H(Y)} P(Y) - e^{\beta H(X)} P(X) \right]$$
$$\times [\beta H(X) + \ln P(X) - \beta H(Y) - \ln P(Y)].$$

This expression is obtained by substituting the master equation for the time derivative of the probabilities, and averaging the two expressions that result by interchanges of two dummy variables X and Y on the right-hand side. We note that the last two expressions in brackets are of opposite signs. Hence, we conclude that the time derivative of free energy is nonpositive, that is, F monotonically decreases until the distribution reaches equilibria.

Next, we show that Kullback–Leibler information measures are nonincreasing with time and hence are Lyapunov functions. We let (X_t) be a Markov chain with discrete states, $j \in S$, and denote

$$u_j(t) = Pr(X_t = j),$$

for $j \in S$.

The master equation for the probabilities is

$$\frac{du_j(t)}{dt} = \sum_k [u_k(t)w_{kj} - u_j(t)w_{jk}],$$

where w_{ij} is the probability transition rate.

For any strictly concave function $h(\cdot)$, we define the negative of the Kullback–Leibler distance as

$$H = \sum_j \pi_j h[u_j(t)/\pi_j],$$

where the probability distribution π is defined by the equilibrium condition

$$\sum_k (\pi_k w_{kj} - \pi_j w_{jk}) = 0.$$

If we set $u_j(0) = \pi_j$, then

$$H(t) = H(0) = \sum_j \pi_j h(\pi_j/\pi_j) = \sum_j \pi_j h(1).$$

We let

$$p_{jk} = Pr(X_{t+\tau} = k \mid X_t = j),$$

for fixed $\tau \geq 0$.

Then,

$$u_k(t + \tau) = \sum_j u_j(t)p_{jk}.$$

We let

$$a_{kj} = \frac{\pi_j p_{jk}}{\pi_k},$$

where we note that it is positive and sums to one with respect to j.

We see that

$$\frac{u_k(t+\tau)}{\pi_k} = \sum_j \frac{u_j(t)p_{jk}}{\pi_k} = \sum_j a_{kj}\frac{u_j(t)}{\pi_j}.$$

By concavity,

$$h\left(\sum_j a_{kj}x_j\right) \geq \sum_j a_{kj}h(x_j),$$

unless x_j is a constant for all j.

Thus,

$$H(t+\tau) = \sum_k \pi_k h\left[\frac{u_k(t+\tau)}{\pi_k}\right] \geq \sum_j \sum_k \pi_k a_{kj} h\left[\frac{u_j(t)}{\pi_j}\right]$$

$$= \sum_j \sum_k \pi_j h\left[\frac{u_j(t)}{\pi_j}\right] = H(t).$$

For a special case, we take $h(\cdot)$ to be $-x \ln x$. Then,

$$H(t) = -\sum_j u_j(t) \ln\left[\frac{u_j(t)}{\pi_j}\right]$$

is the Kullback–Leibler distance between the two distributions, u and π.

A.6   Fokker–Planck equations and detailed balance

A.6.1   *Fokker–Planck equations and stochastic dynamics*

Fokker–Planck equations describe probability densities of state vectors of systems governed by stochastic differential equations of Ito or Stratonovich type. Here, we illustrate how a dynamic equation described by an Ito–stochastic differential equation,

$$dx_i(t) = K_i[x(t)]dt + \sum_j g_{i,j}[x(t)]dw_j(t),$$

for $i = 1, \ldots, n$, generates a Fokker–Planck equation.

We let $u(\cdot)$ be an arbitrary function of a macroeconomic state vector x. We write its differential retaining terms of $o_p(dt)$ as:

$$du = \sum_i (\partial u/\partial x_i)\,dx_i + (1/2)\sum_{i,j}(\partial^2 u/\partial x_i \partial x_j)\,dx_i dx_j,$$

by substituting the expression for dx's in the above.

Using the relation $\langle dw_j \rangle = 0$ and $\langle dw_i dw_j \rangle = \epsilon dt \delta_{i,j}$, where the terms in the angle brackets denote the average over x, we note that, given

$$\langle u(x) \rangle = \int u(x) p(x, t \mid x_0, t_0) \, dx,$$

its time derivative

$$\frac{d \langle u \rangle}{dt} = \int u(x) \partial p(x, t \mid x_0, t_0) / \partial t \, dt$$

is rewritten as

$$\frac{d \langle u(x) \rangle}{dt} = -\sum_i \int u(x) \frac{\partial}{\partial x_i} [K_i(x) p] \, dx$$

$$+ \epsilon / 2 \sum_{i,j} \int u(x) \frac{\partial^2}{\partial x_i \partial x_j} \left(\sum_m g_{i,m} g_{j,m} p \right) dx.$$

Since u is arbitrary, this relation yields the Fokker–Planck equation:

$$\frac{\partial p}{dt} = -\sum_i \frac{\partial}{\partial x_i} [K_i(x) p] + (\epsilon / 2) \sum \frac{\partial^2}{\partial x_i \partial x_j} (Q_{i,j} p),$$

where we define the matrix Q by

$$Q_{i,j} = \sum_m g_{i,m} g_{j,m}.$$

A.6.2 *Detailed balance and the Fokker–Planck equation*

We have shown elsewhere that Gibbs distributions arise as the stationary solutions of Fokker–Planck equations. Here, we give a little more background on the Gibbs distribution and show how potential functions are introduced.

We call a variable an even variable if its sign remains unchanged when the direction of time flow is reversed. An odd variable changes its sign when the flow of time is reversed. Economic variables in level form are even variables, and their rates of change are odd variables according to this definition. We introduce a matrix Θ by

$$\Theta = \text{diag}(\theta_1, \dots, \theta_n),$$

where θ_k is 1 or -1 according to the kth variable x_k is an even or odd variable.

Given two macroeconomic state vectors x^1 and x^2 of dimension n, the detailed balance conditions in dynamics are stated as

$$w(x^1, t \mid x^2, 0) p_e(x^2) = w(\Theta x^2, t \mid \Theta x^1, 0) p_e(x^1),$$

where p_e is a stationary solution of the Fokker–Planck equation, which we write as

$$\frac{\partial p}{\partial t} = -\sum_i \partial I_i / \partial x_i,$$

where

$$I_i = K_i(x)p - \frac{\epsilon}{2}\sum_j \frac{\partial}{\partial x_j}\{Q_{i,j}p\}.$$

Assuming a regularity condition that the probability density and its partial derivative with respect to components of the vector x both approach zero as $\|x\|$ goes to infinity, p_e is a stationary solution if and only if

$$\sum_i I_i = \sum_i K_i(x)p_e - \frac{\epsilon}{2}\sum_i\sum_j \frac{\partial}{\partial x_j}[Q_{i,j}(x)p_e(x)] = 0.$$

If $I_i = 0$ for all i, then the above reduces to

$$\frac{\epsilon}{2}\sum_j Q_{i,j}(x)\frac{\partial p_e(x)}{\partial x_j} = p_e(x)\left[K_i(x) - \frac{\epsilon}{2}\sum_j \frac{\partial Q_{i,j}}{\partial x_j}\right],$$

for all i.

Assuming the existence of the inverse of matrix $Q(x)$, we can solve the above as

$$\frac{\partial \ln p_e(x)}{\partial x_i} = (1/\epsilon)\sum_k\left[2K_k(x) - \epsilon\sum_j \frac{\partial Q_{k,j}}{\partial x_j}\right].$$

We define the right-hand expression in brackets as $Z_i(K, Q, x)$.

The left-hand side is a gradient vector, and so is the right-hand side if and only if

$$\frac{\partial Z_i}{\partial x_j} = \frac{\partial Z_i}{\partial x_i},$$

for all i, j pair.

Then,

$$p_e(x) = \exp[-\phi(x)/\epsilon]$$

where

$$\phi(x) = -\int^x Z(K, Q, x')\, dx'$$

is the potential function.

If the function $K_i(x)$, above, can be written as

$$K_i(x) = d_i(x) + r_i(x),$$

with the condition that

$$\sum_i \frac{\partial r_i(x)}{\partial x_i} = 0,$$

then Z_i simplifies to

$$Z_i^* = \sum_k Q_{i,k}^{-1}\left[2d_k(x) - \epsilon \sum_j \frac{\partial Q_{k,j}}{\partial x_j}\right],$$

and the condition for the existence of potential functions is restated in terms of Z^*'s rather than Z's. The stationary probability density function is then equal to

$$p_e(x) = \exp[-\phi^*(x)/\epsilon],$$

where

$$\phi^*(x) = -\int^x Z^*(K, Q, x')\, dx'.$$

References

Abramovitz, M., and I. A. Stegun (1968). *Handbook of Mathematical Functions* (Dover Publications, Inc., New York).

Agliardi, E. (1993). "Essays on the Dynamics of Allocation under Increasing Returns to Adoption and Path Dependence," Ph.D. dissertation, University of Cambridge, Cambridge, England.

Agliardi, E., and M. S. Bebbington (1994). "Self-Reinforcing Mechanisms and Interactive Behavior," Mimeograph, Department of Applied Economics, University of Cambridge, Cambridge, England.

Akerlof, G. A. (1980). A theory of social custom, of which unemployment may be one consequence, *Q. J. Econ.* **94**, 749–75.

Akerlof, G. A., and R. D. Milbourne (1980). The short run demand for money, *Econ. J.* **90**, 885–900.

Aldous, D. J. (1985). Exchangeability and related topics, in P. L. Hennequin ed., *Lecture Notes in Mathematics*, **1117** (Springer–Verlag, Berlin).

Aldous, D. J. and U. Vazirani (1993). "Introducing Interactions into Randomized Optimization Algorithms," Mimeograph, University of California, Berkeley.

Amemiya, T. (1985). *Advanced Econometrics* (Harvard University Press, Cambridge, MA).

Amit, D. (1989). *Modeling Brain Function* (Cambridge University Press, New York).

Anderson, S. P., A. de Palma, and J.-F. Thisse (1993). *Discrete Choice Theory of Product Differentiation* (MIT Press, Cambridge, MA).

Arnold, L. (1974). *Stochastic Differential Equation: Theory and Applications* (John Wiley and Sons, Inc., New York).

Aoki, M. (1975a). Control of linear discrete-time stochastic dynamic systems with multiplicative disturbances, *IEEE Trans. Autom. Control* **AC-20**, 388–92.

(1975b). Customer arrival rate as a signal to economic agents with imperfect information, Paper presented at the Third World Congress of the Econometric Society, Toronto, Ontario, Canada.

(1976). On fluctuations in microscopic states of a large system, in *Directions in Large-Scale Systems*, edited by Y. C. Ho and S. K. Mitter (Plenum Press, New York).

(1981). *Dynamic Analysis of Open Economies* (Academic Press, New York).

(1989a). *Optimization of Stochastic Systems: Topics in Discrete-Time Dynamics, 2nd Ed.* (Academic Press, New York).

(1989b). Short and longer-run dynamics of the real GNP and unemployment rate of the USA and West Germany, Paper presented at the Meeting of the Far Eastern Econometric Society, Kyoto, Japan.

(1994a). "New Macroeconomic Modeling Approaches: Hierarchical Dynamics and Mean Field Approximation," *J. Econ. Dynamics and Control* **18**, 865–77.

(1994b). "Group Dynamics When Agents Have a Finite Number of Alternatives: Dynamics of a Macrovariable with Mean Field Approximation," Discussion Paper No. 13, Center for Computable Economics, University of California, Los Angeles.

(1995a). Economic fluctuations with interactive agents: Dynamic and stochastic externalities, *Jpn. Econ. Rev.* **46**(2), 148–65.

(1995b). "Stochastic Interactive Dynamics: Effects of Multiplicity of Microeconomic States," Working Paper No. 20, University of California, Los Angeles, Center for Computable Economics, presented at the 1995 World Econometric Congress, Tokyo, Japan.

(1995c). "Statistical description of market shares in emergent markets," Working Paper No. 26, UCLA Center for Computable Economics, Nov.

(1996). "Shares in emergent markets: Dynamics of classification of agents in evolutionary model," in *Statistical Methods in Control and Signal Processes*, edited by T. Katayama and S. Sugimoto (Marcel Dekker, New York).

Aoki, M., and Y. Miyahara (1993). "Stochastic Aggregation and Dynamic Field Effects," Working Paper No. 3, University of California, Los Angeles.

Arthur, W. B. (1988). Self-reinforcing mechanisms in economics, in *Economy as an Evolving Complex System*, edited by P. W. Anderson, K. J. Arrow, and D. Pines (Addison–Wesley, Redwood City, CA).

(1989). Competing technologies, increasing returns, and lock-in by historical events, *Econ. J.* **99**, 116–31.

Bachas, C. P., and B. A. Huberman (1987). *Complexity and Ultradiffusion*, SLAC-PUB 4077 (Stanford University, Stanford, CA).

Baker, A. J., and R. J. Plymen (1992). *P–adic Methods and Their Applications*, (Clarendon Press, New York).

Baldwin, R., and P. Krugman (1989). Persistent trade effects of large exchange rate shocks, *Q. J. Econ.* **104**, 635–54.

Ball, F., and P. Donnelly (1987). Interparticle correlation in death processes with application to variability in compartmental models, *Adv. Appl. Probab.* **19**, 755–66.

Barndorff-Nielsen, O. E., and D. R. Cox (1989). *Asymptotic Techniques: For Its Use in Statistics* (Chapman and Hall, London).

Becker, G. S. (1974). A theory of social interactions, *J. Political Econ.* **82**, 1063–93.

(1990). A note on restaurant pricing and other examples of social influences on price, *J. Political Econ.* **99**, 1109–16.

Bellman, R. E. (1961). *Adaptive Control Processes: A Guided Tour* (Princeton University Press, Princeton, N. J.).

Berg, S. (1985). Paradox of voting under an urn model: The effect of homogeneity, *Public Choice* **47**, 377–87.

Bernasconi, J., and W. R. Schneider (1983). Diffusion on a one-dimensional lattice with random asymmetric transition rates, *J. Phys. A: Math. Gen.* **15**, L729–34.

Bertola G., and R. J. Caballero (1990). Kinked adjustment costs and aggregate dynamics, in *NBER Macroeconomics Annual 1990*, edited by O. J. Blanchard and S. Fischer (MIT Press, Cambridge, MA).

Besag, J. E. (1977). Statistical analysis of non-lattice data, *Statistician* **24**, 179–95.

Blanchard, O., and N. Kiyotaki (1986). Monopolistic competition and the effects of aggregate demand, *Am. Econ. Rev.* **77**, 647–66.

Bleher, P. M. (1982). Construction of non-Gaussian self-similar random fields with hierarchical structure, *Commun. Math. Phys.* **84**, 557–78.

Bleher, P. M., and P. Major (1987). Critical phenomena and universal expressions in statistical physics. On Dyson's hierarchical model, *Ann. Probab.* **15**, 431–77.

Blinder, A. S. (1981). Retail inventory behavior and business fluctuations, Brookings Papers on Economic Activity No. 2, pp. 443–505.

Blinder, A. S., and L. J. Maccini (1991). Taking stock: A critical assessment of recent research on inventories, *J. Econ. Perspect.* **5**, 73–96.

Blum, J., J. Chernoff, M. Rosenblatt, and H. Teicher (1958). Central limit theorem for interchangeable random variables, *Can. J. Math.* **10**, 222–9.

Bös, S., R. Künh, and J. L. van Hemmen (1988). Martingale approach to neural networks with hierarchically structured information, *Z. Phys. B Condensed Matter* **71**, 261–71.

Breiman, L. (1968). *Probability Theory* (Addison–Wesley, Reading, MA).

Brock, W. A. (1993). "Pathways to Randomness in the Economy: Emergent Nonlinearity and Chaos in Economics and Finance, Working Paper, Social Systems Research Institute, University of Wisconsin.

Brock, W. A., and S. N. Durlauf (1995). "Discrete Choice with Social Interactions I: Theory," Mimeograph, Social Systems Research Institute, University of Wisconsin, Madison.

Buchanan, J. M., and W. C. Stubblebine (1962). Externality, *Economica* **10**, 371–84.

Bucklew, J. A. (1990). *Large Deviation Techniques in Decision, Simulation, and Estimation* (John Wiley & Sons, New York).

Caballero, R. J. (1992). A fallacy of composition, *Am. Econ. Rev.* **82**, 1279–92.

Caballero, R. J., and E. M. R. A. Engel (1992). Beyond the partial-adjustment model, *Am. Econ. Rev., Papers Proc.* **80**, 360–4.

Caballero, R. J., and R. K. Lyons (1990). Internal versus external economies in European industry, *Eur. Econ. Rev.* **34**, 805–30.

(1992). External effects in U.S. procyclical productivity, *J. Monetary Econ.* **29**, 209–25.

Callen, E., and D. Shapero (1974). A theory of social imitation, *Phys. Today* July, 23–8.

Caplin, A. S., and D. Spulber (1987). Menu costs and the neutrality of money, *Q. J. Econ.* **102**, 703–26.

Caplin, A. S., and H. Nalebuff (1991). Aggregation and social choice: A mean voter theorem, *Econometrica* **59**, 1–23.

Caplin, A. S., and J. Leahy (1991). State-dependent pricing and the dynamics of money and output, *Q. J. Econ.* **106**, 683–708.

(1995). "Aggregation and Optimization with State-Dependent Pricing, Mimeograph, Department of Economics, Yale University, New Haven, CT.

Carroll, C. D. (1992). The buffer-stock thoery of saving: Some macroeconomic evidence, Brookings Papers on Economic Activity, No. 2, pp. 61–156.

(1994). Buffer stock saving and the life cycle/permanent income hypothesis, Paper presented at 1994 Annual Meeting of the Society for Economic Dynamics and Control, University of California, Los Angeles.

Ceccatto, H. A., and B. A. Huberman (1989). Persistence of nonoptimal strategies, *Proc. Nat. Acad. Sci. USA* **86**, 3443–6.

Champernowne, D. G (1953). A model of income distribution, *Econ. J.* **63**, 318–51.

Chen, W-C. (1978). "On Zipf's Law," Ph.D. dissertation, University of Michigan, Ann Arbor, MI.

(1980). On the weak form of Zipf's Law, *J. Appl. Probab.* **17**, 611–22.

Chernoff, H., and H. Teicher (1958). A central limit theorem for sums of interchangeable random variables, *Ann. Math. Stat.* **29**, 118–30.

Cho, J-O., and R. Rogerson (1987). Familty labor supply and aggregate fluctuations, *J. Monetary Econ.* **5**, 233–45.

Chow, Y., and H. Teicher (1978). *Probability Theory: Independence, Interchangeability, Martingale* (Springer, New York).

Chung, K. L. (1968). *A Course in Probability Theory* (Harcour, Brace & World, Inc., New York).

Clarke, F. (1992). The Gray code function, in *P-adic Methods and Their Applications*, edited by A. J. Baker and R. J. Plymen (Clarendon Press, New York).

Collet, P., and J-P. Eckmann (1978). *A Renormalization Group Analysis of the Hierarchical Model in Statistical Mechanics*, Lecture Notes in Physics, No. 74 (Springer, Heidelberg, Germany).

Conlisk, J. (1980). Costly optimizers versus cheap imitators, *J. Econ. Behav. Org.* **1**, 275–93.

Constantinides, G. M., and S. F. Richard (1978). Existence of optimal simple policies for discounted-cost inventory and cash management in continuous time, *Oper. Res.* **26**, 620–36.

Copson, E. T. (1955). *An Introduction to the Theory of Functions of a Complex Variable* (Clarendon Press, Oxford, England).

Copson, E. T. (1965). *Asymptotic Expansions* (Cambridge University Press, Cambridge, England).

Cornell, B., and R. Roll (1981). Strategies for pairwise competitions in markets and organizations, *Bell J. Econ.* **12**, 201–13.

Cover, T., and J. A. Thomas (1991). *Elements of Information Theory* (John Wiley & Sons, New York).

Cox, D. R., and H. D. Miller (1965). *The Theory of Stochastic Processes* (Methuen, London).

Csiszár, I. T. (1984). Sanov property, generalized I-projection and a conditional limit theorem, *Ann. Probab.* **12**, 768–93.

Csiszár, I. T., and J. Körner (1981). *Information Theory: Coding Theorems for Discrete Memoryless Systems* (Academic Press, New York).

Csiszár, I. T., M. Cover, and B.-S. Choi (1987). Conditional limit theorems under Markov conditioning, *IEEE Trans. Inf. Theory* **IT-33**, 788–801.

David, F. N., and D. B. Barton (1962). *Combinatorial Chance* (Hafner Publishing Co., New York).

Davis, M. H. A. (1993). *Markov Models and Optimization* (Chapman & Hall, London).

Davis, S. J., and J. Haltiwanger (1990). Gross job creation and destruction: Microeconomic evidence and macroeconomic implications, in *NBER Macroeconomic Annual 1990*, edited by O. J. Blanchard and S. Fisher (MIT Press, Cambridge, MA).

Dawson, D. A. (1983). Critical dynamics and fluctuations for a mean field model of cooperative behavior, *J. Stat. Phys.* **31**, 29–85.

Dawson, D.A., and J. Gartner (1989). *Large Deviations, Free Energy Functional and Quasi-Potential for a Mean Field Model of Interacting Diffusions* (American Mathematical Society, Providence, RI).

DeLong, J. B., and L. H. Summers (1986). Are business cycles symmetrical? in *The American Business Cycle*, edited by R. J. Gordon (University of Chicago Press, Chicago).

Dempster, A. P., N. M. Laird, and D. B. Rubin (1977). Maximum likelihood from incomplete data via the EM algorithm (with discussion), *J. Roy. Stat. Soc.* **B-39**, 1–38.

Dembo, A., and O. Zeitouni (1993). *Large Deviations; Techniques and Applications* (Jones and Bartlett Publishers, Boston).

Derrida, B. (1981). Random energy model, *Phys. Rev. B* **24**, 2613–26.

Derrida, B., and H. Flyvbjerg (1987a). The random map model: A disordered model with deterministic dynamics, *J. Physique* **48**, 971–8.

(1987b). Statistical properties of randomly broken objects and of multivalley structures in disordered systems, *J. Phys. A* **20**, 5273–99.

(1986). Multivalley structure in Kauffman's model: Analogy with spin glasses, *J. Phys. A: Math. Gen.* **19**, L1003–8.

Deuschel, J. D., and D. W. Stroock (1989). *Large Deviations* (Academic Press, Boston).

Diaconis, P., and D. Freedman (1981). Partial exchangeability and sufficiency, in *Proceedings of the Indian Statistical Institute Golden Jubilee International Conference on Statistics: Applications and New Directions*, Indian Statistical Institute, Calcutta, pp. 205–36.

Dixit, A. (1989a). Entry and exit decisions of firms under fluctuating real exchange rates, *J. Political Econ.* **97**, 620–37.

(1989b). Hysteresis, import penetration, and exchange rate pass-through, *Q. J. Econ.* **104**, 205–28.

Dixit, A., and J. Stiglitz (1977). Monopolistic competition and optimum product diversity, *Am. Econ. Rev.* **62**, 297–308.

Doob, J. L. (1953). *Stochastic Processes* (John Wiley & Sons, New York).

Doyle, P. G., and J. L. Snell (1984). *Random Walks and Electric Networks* (America Mathematical Association, Providence, RI).

Durlauf, S. N. (1991). Multiple equilibria and persistence in aggregate fluctuations, *Am. Econ. Rev.* **81**, 70–4.

Durrett, R. (1991). *Probability: Theory and Examples* (Wadsworth and Brooks/Cole Advanced Books and Software, Pacific Grove).

Dybvig, P. H., and C. S. Spatt (1983). Adoption externalities as public goods, *J. Public Econ.* **20**, 231–47.

Dyson, F. J. (1969). Existence of phase transition in a one-dimensional Ising ferromagnet, *Commun. Math. Phys.* **12**, 91–107.

Eckstein, Z., and K. I. Wolpin (1989). The specification and estimation of dynamic stochastic discrete choice models, *J. Human Resources* **24**, 562–98.

Ellis, R. S. (1985). *Entropy, Large Deviations, and Statistical Mechanics* (Springer, New York).

Ethier, S. N., and T. G. Kurtz (1986). *Markov Processes* (John Wiley & Sons, New York).

Evans, C. L. (1992). Productivity shocks and real business cycles, *J. Monetary Econ.* **29**, 191–208.

Ewens, W. J. (1990). Population genetics theory – The past and the future, in *Mathematical and Statistical Developments of Evolutionary Theory*, edited by S. Lessard (Kluwer Academic Publishers, London).

Feigelman, M. V., and L. B. Ioffe (1987). Hierarchical organization of memory, in *Models of Neural Network*, edited by E. Domany, J. L. van Hemmen, and K. Schulten (Springer–Verlag, Berlin).

(1991). Hierarchical organization of memory, in *Models of Neural Networks*, edited by E. Domany et al. (Springer–Verlag, Berlin).

Feller, W. (1957). *An Introduction to Probability Theory and Its Applications*, Vol. I, 2nd ed. (John Wiley & Sons, New York).

Fleming, W. H., and R. W. Rishel (1975). *Deterministic and Stochastic Optimum Control* (Springer–Verlag, New York).

Foley, D. (1994). A statistical equilibrium theory of markets, *J. Econ. Theory* **62**, 321–45.

Föllmer, H. (1973). On entropy and information gain in random fields, *Z. Wahrscheinlichkeitstheorie. verw. Geb.* **26**, 207–17.

(1974). Random economies with many interacting agents, *J. Math. Econ.* **1**, 51–62.

Föllmer, H., and S. Orey (1988) Large deviations for the empirical fields of a Gibbs measure, *Ann. of Probab.* **16**, 961–77.

Foster, D., and P. Young (1990). Stochastic evolutionary game dynamics, *Theor. Popul. Biol.* **38**, 219–32.

Freedman, D. (1971). *Brownian Motion and Diffusion* (Holden-Day, San Francisco).

Freidlin, M. I., and A. D. Wentzell (1984). *Raondom Perturbations of Dynamical Systems* (Springer, New York).

Frenkel, J. A., and B. Jovanovic (1980). On transactions and precautionary demands for money, *Q. J. Econ.* **95**, 25-43.

Friedman, D. (1991). Evolutionary games in economics, *Econometrica* **59**, 637–66.

(1993). "On Economic Applications of Evolutionary Games," Mimeograph, University of California, Santa Cruz.

Friedman, D., and K. C. Fung (1994). "International Trade and the Internal Organization of Firms: An Evolutionary Approach," Mimeograph, University of California, Santa Cruz.

Friedman, D., and M. Aoki (1992). Inefficient information aggregation as a source of asset price bubbles, *Bull. Econ. Res.* **4**, 251–79.

Fukao, K., and R. Benabou (1993). History versus expectations: A comment, *Q. J. Econ.* **108**, 535–42.

Fukao, T. (1987). *Theory of Distributed Systems* (in Japanese) (Sho Ko Do, Tokyo).

(1990). Stochastization of optimization problems and thermodynamics, *Soc. Inst. Autom. Contr.* **29**, 1077–83.

Galambos, J. (1987). *The Asymptotic Theory of Extreme Order Statistics* (Wiley, New York).

Geman, S., and D. Geman (1984). Stochastic relaxation, Gibbs distributions, and the Bayesian restoration of images, *IEEE Trans. Pattern Anal. Machine Intelligence* **PAMI-6**, 721–41.

Georgescu-Roegen, N. (1976). *Entropy Law and the Economic Processes* (Harvard University Press, Cambridge, MA).

Geweke, J. (1985). Macroeconometric modeling and the theory of the representative agents, *Am. Econ. Assoc. Papers Proc.* **75**, 206–10.

Glance, N. S., and B. A. Huberman (1993). The outbreak of cooperation, *J. Math. Sociol.* **17**, 281–02.

Glaeser, E. L., and D. C. Mare (1994). "Cities and Skills," NBER Working Paper No. 4728,

Gnedenko, B. V. (1962). *The Theory of Probability* (Chelsea Publishing Co., New York).

Griffiths, R. C. (1979a) A transition density expansion for a multi-allele diffusion model *Adv. Appl. Probab.* **11**, 310–25.

(1979b) Exact sampling distributions from the infinite neutral alleles models *Adv. Appl. Probab.* **11**, 326–54.

Grimmett, G. (1989). *Percolation* (Springer, London).

Grimmett, G. R., and D. R. Stirzaker (1992). *Probability and Random Processes* (Oxford University Press, Oxford, England).

Haken, H. (1977). *Synergetics: An Introduction* (Springer, New York).

Hajek, B. (1988). Cooling schedules for optimal annealing, *Math. Oper. Res.* **13**, 311–29.

Hamilton, J. D. (1989). A new approach to the economic analysis of nonstationary time series and business cycle, *Econometrica* **57**, 357–84.

Hammermesh, D. S. (1989). Labor Demand and the Structure of Adjustment Costs, *Am. Econ. Rev.* **79**, 674–89.

Hansen, L. P., and R. Jagannathan (1991). Implications of security market data for models of dynamic economies, *J. Political Econ.* **99**, 225–62.

Harris, B. (1960). Probability distributions related to random mappings, *Ann. Math. Stat.* **31**, 1045–62.

Haugen, R., E. Talmor, and W. Torous (1991). The effect of volatility changes on the level of stock prices and subsequent expected returns, *J. Finance* **46**, 985–1007.

Head, K., J. Ries, and D. Swenson (1994). "Agglomeration Benefits and Location Choice: Evidence from Japanese Manufacturing Investment in the United States," NBER Working Paper No. 4767,

Henderson, V. (1994). "Externalities and Industrial Development," NBER Working Paper No. 4730.

Hildendbrand, W. (1971). Random preferences and equilibrium analysis, *J. Econ. Theory* **3**, 414–29.

Hill, B. M. (1968). Posterior distribution of percentiles: Bayes' theorem for sampling from a population, *J. Am. Stat. Assoc.* **63**, 677–91.

(1970). Zipf's law and prior distributions for the composition of a population, *J. Am. Stat. Assoc.* **65**, 1220–32.

(1974). The rank-frequency form of Zipf's law, *J. Am. Stat. Assoc.* **69**, 1017–26.

(1975). A simple general approach to inference about the tail of a distribution, *Ann. Stat.* **3**, 1163–74.

(1982). A theoretical derivation of the Zipf (Pareto) law, in *Studies on Zipf's Law*, edited by H. Guiter and M. V. Arapov (Studienverlag Dr. N. Brockmeyer, Bochum, Germany).

Hill, B. M., and M. Woodroofe (1975). Stronger forms of Zipf's law, *J. Am. Stat. Assoc.* **70**, 212–19.

Hoel, P. G., S. Port, and C. Stone (1972). *Introduction to Stochastic Processes* (Houghton–Mifflin, Boston).

Hopfield, J. (1982). Neural networks and physical systems with emergent collective computational abilities, *Proc. Nat. Acad. Sci. USA* **79**, 2554–8.

Hoppe, F. M., (1984). Pólya-like urns and the Ewens' sampling formula, *J. Math. Biol.* **20**, 91–94.

(1986). Size-biased filtering of Poisson-Dirichlet samples with an application to partition structures in genetics, *J. Appl. Probab.* **23**, 1008–12.

(1987). The sampling theory of neutral alleles and an urn model in population genetics, *J. Math. Biol.* **25**, 123–59.

Huberman, B. A., and M. Kerszberg (1985). Ultradiffusion: The relaxation of hierarchical systems, *J. Phys. A: Math. Gen.* **18**, L331–6.

Huges, B. D., E. W. Montroll, and M. F. Shlesinger (1982). Fractal random walks, *J. Stat. Phys.* **28**, 111–26.

Idiart, M. A. P., and A. Theumann (1990). Hierarchical model of neural networks, in *Neural Networks and Spin Glasses*, edited by W. K. Theumann and R. Köberle (World Scientific, NJ), pp. 244–51.

Ijiri, Y., and H. Simon (1964). Business firm growth and size, *Am. Econ. Rev.* **54**, 77–89.

Ingber, L. (1982). Statistical mechanics of neocortical interactions, *Physica D* **5**, 83–107.

Iwai, K. (1981). *Disequilibrium Dynamics*, Monograph 27 (Cowles Foundation, Yale University, New Haven, CT).

Jardine, N., and R. Sibson (1971). *Mathematical Taxonomy* (John Wiley, London).

Jaynes, E. (1957). Information theory and statistical mechanics, *Phys. Rev.* **106**, 620–30.

(1979). Where do we stand on maximum entropy? in *The Maximum Entropy Formalism*, edited by R. D. Levine and M. Tribus (MIT Press, Cambridge, MA).

(1985). Macroscopic predictions in complex systems–operational approach, in *Complex Systems, Operational Approaches*, edited by H. Haken (Springer–Verlag, Berlin).

Jeong, U. (1993). "The Aggregate Behavior of a Large Number of Interacting Agents in Dynamic Stochastic Economies, Ph.D. thesis, University of California, Los Angeles.

Johnson, N., and S. Kotz (1977). *Urn Models and Their Application: An Approach to Modern Discrete Probability Theory* (John Wiley & Sons, New York).

Jona-Lasinio, G. (1975). The Renormalization Group: A Probabilistic View, *Nuovo Cimento* **26B**, 99–119.

Jones, L. K. (1989). Approximation-theoretic derivation of logarithmic entropy principles for inverse problems and unique extension of the maximum entropy method to incorporate prior knowledge, *SIAM J. Appl. Math.* **49**, 650–61.

Jovanovic, B. (1982). Selection and the evolution of industry, *Econometrica* **50**, 649–70.

Justesen, J., and T. Hohold (1984). Maxentropic Markov chains, *IEEE Trans. Inf. Theory* **IT-30**, 665–7.

Kabashima, Y., and S. Shinomoto (1991). Asymptotic dependence of the residual energy on annealing time, *J. Phys. Soc. Jpn.* **60**, 3993–6.

Kauffman, S. A. (1991). Antichaos and adaptation, *Sci. Am.* **65** (August) 78–84.

(1993). *The Origins of Order: Self-Organization and Selection in Evolution* (Oxford University Press, New York).

Karlin, S. (1966). *A First Course in Stochastic Processes* (Academic Press, New York).

Karlin, S., and H. Taylor (1981). *A Second Course in Stochastic Processes* (Academic Press, New York).

Kapur, N. N., C. R. Bector, and U. Kumar (1984). A generalization of the entropy model for brand purchase behavior, *Nav. Res. Logis. Q.* **31**, 183–98.

Katz, L. (1955). Probability of indecomposability of a random mapping function, *Ann. Math. Stat.* **20**, 512–17.

Kean, M. P., and K. I. Wolpin (1992). The solution and estimation of discrete choice dynamic programming models by simulation: Monte Carlo evidence, Mimeograph,

Keener, R., Rothman, E, and Starr, N. (1988). Distributions on partitions, *Ann. Statist.* **15**, 1466–81.

Kelly, F. P. (1979). *Reversibility and Stochastic Network* (Wiley, New York).

Kelly, F. P. (1976). On stochastic population models in genetics, *J. Appl. Prob.* **13**, 127–31.

Kelly, M. (1990) "Phase Transition in Dynamic Stochastic Economies with Many Interacting Agents," Ph.D. dissertation, Cornell University, Department of Economics, Ithaca, NY.

Kendall, W. S., and I. W. Saunders (1983). Epidemics in competition II: The general epidemic, *J. R. Stat. Soc. B.* **45**, 238–44.

Khinchin, A. I. (1949). *Mathematical Foundations of Statistical Mechanics* (Dover Publications, New York).

Kindleberger, C. (1989). *Manias, Panics, and Crashes: A History of Financial Crises* (Basic Books, New York).

Kindermann, R., and J. L. Snell (1980). *Markov Random Fields and Their Applications* (American Mathematical Society, Providence, RI).

Kingman, J. F. C. (1982a). On the genealogy of large populations, *J. Appl. Probab.* **19A**, 27–43.

——— (1982b). The coalescent, *Stochastic Processes* **13**, 235–48.

——— (1980). *Mathematics of Genetic Diversity* (Society for Industrial and Applied Mathematics, Philadelphia).

——— (1978a). Uses of exchangeability, *Ann. Probab.* **6**, 183–97.

——— (1978b). Random partitions in population genetics, *Proc. R. Soc. London Ser. A* **361**, 1–20.

——— (1977). The population structure associated with the Ewens sampling formula, *Theo. Popu. Bio.* **11**, 274–83.

——— (1975). Random discrete distributions, *J. R. Stat. Soc.* **B-37**, 1–22.

——— (1969). Markov population processes, *J. Appl. Prob.* **6**, 1–18.

Kirkpatrick, S., C. D. Gelatt, Jr., and M. P. Vecchi (1983). Optimization by simulated annealing, *Science* **220**, 671–80.

Kirman, A. (1992a). Variety: The coexistence of techniques, *Rev. Econ. Ind.* **59**, 62–74.

——— (1992b). Whom or what does the representative individual represent? *J. Econ. Perspect.* **6**, 117–36.

——— (1993). Ants, rationality and recruitment, *Q. J. Econ.* **108**, 137–56.

——— (1994). "Economies with Interacting Agents," Mimeograph, The European University Institute,

Klenow, P. J. (1992). "Multiple Steady States and Business Cycles," Mimeograph, University of Chicago.

Koch, O., and F. Spizzichino (Eds) (1982). *Exchangeability in Probability and Statistics* (North-Holland, Amsterdam).

Kokotovic, P. V., R. E. O'Malley, Jr., and P. Sannuti (1976). Singular perturbations and order reduction in control theory: An overview, *Automatica* **12**, 123–32.

Krugman, P. (1991). History versus expectations, *Q. J. Econ.* **106**, 651–67.

Kubo, R. (1975). Relaxation and Fluctuation of Macrovariables, in Lecture Notes in Physics No. 39, edited by H. Araki (Springer, Berlin).

Kubo, R., K. Matsuo, and K. Kitahara (1973). Fluctuation and relaxation of macrovariables, *J. Stat. Phys.* **9**, 51–96.

Kullback, S. (1959). *Information Theory and Statistics* (Wiley, New York).

Kullback, S., and R. A. Leibler (1951). On information and sufficiency, *Ann. Math. Stat.* **22**, 79–86.

Kurtz, T. G. (1970). Solutions of ordinary differential equations as limits of pure Markov processes, *J. Appl. Probab.*, **7**, 49–58.

——— (1971). Limit theorems for sequences of jump Markov processes appproximating ordinary differential processes, *J. Appl. Probab.*, **8**, 344–56.

——— (1978). Strong approximation theorems for density dependent Markov chains, *Stochastic Proc. Appl.*, **6**, 223–40.

Langton, C. G. (1991). "Computation at the Edge of Chaos: Transitions and Emergent Computation," Ph.D. dissertation, University of Michigan, Computer and Communication Sciences,

Leijonhufvud, A. (1993). Towards a not-too-rational macroeconomics, *South. Econ. J.* **60**, 1–30.

——— (1995). Adaptive behavior, market processes and the computable approach, Working Paper No.19, UCLA Center for Computable Economics.

Liebowitz, S. J., and S. E. Margolis (1994). Network externality: An uncommon tragedy, *J. Econ. Perspect.* **8**, 133–50.

Little, W. A. (1974). The existence of persistent states in the brain, *Math. Biosci.* **19**, 101–20.

Little, W. A., and G. L. Shaw (1978). Analytic study of the memory storage capacity of a neural network, *Math. Biosci.* **39**, 281–90.

Loève, M. (1963). *Probability Theory, 3rd ed.* (Van Nostrand Reinhold Co., New York).

Lucas, R. E., Jr. (1978). On the size distribution of business firms, *Bell J. Econ.* **9**, 508–23.

McCall, J. (1992). Exchangeability and the structure of the economy, in *Themes in Modern Macroeconomics*, edited by H. Brink (Macmillan Press, London).

Mahler K. (1973). *Introduction to p-adic Numbers and Their Functions* (Cambridge University Press, Cambridge, England).

Marinari, E., G. Parisi, D. Ruelle, and P. Windey (1983). On the interpretation of $1/f$ noise, *Commun. Math. Phys.* **89**, 1–12.

——— (1987). *Spin Glass Theory and Beyond* (World Scientific, NJ).

Merton, R. C. (1973). The theory of rational option pricing, *Bell J. Econ. Manage. Sci.* **4**, 141–83.

Mezard, M., and M. A. Virasoro (1985). The microstructure of ultrametricity, *J. Phys.* (Paris) **46**, 1293–1307.

Mezard, M., G. Parisi, and M. A. Virasoro (1986). SK Model: The replica solution without replicas, *Europhys. Lett.* **1**, 77–82.

Miyahara, Y. (1990). An essay on the models of disequilibrium dynamics: From micro-dynamics to macrodynamics (in Japanese), *Oikonomika* **27**, 115–23.

Montroll, E. W., and M. F. Shlesinger (1984). On the wonderful world of random walks, in *From Stochastics to Hydrodynamics*, edited by J. L. Lebowitz and E. W. Montroll (North-Holland Physics Publishing, Amsterdam).

Montroll, E. W., and W. W. Badger (1974). *Introduction to Quantitative Aspects of Social Phenomena* (Gordon and Breach Science Publishers, New York).

Montroll, E. W., and B. J. West (1987). On an enriched collection of stochastic processes, in *Fluctuation Phenomena*, edited by E. W. Montroll and J. L. Lebowitz (North-Holland, Amsterdam).

Montroll, E. W., and J. L. Lebowitz (Eds) (1987) *Fluctuation Phenomena*, edited by E. W. Montroll and J. L. Lebowitz (North-Holland, Amsterdam).

Moore, T., and J. L. Snell (1979). A Branching Process Showing a Phase Transition, *J. Appl. Probab.* **16**, 252–60.

Mortensen, D. T. (1994). The cyclical behavior of job and worker flows *J. Econ. Dyn. Cont.* **18**, 1121–42.

Mortensen, D. T., and C. A. Pissarides (1993). The cyclical behavior of job creation and job destruction, in *Labor Demand and Equilibrium Wage Formation*, edited by J. C. van Ours, G. A. Pfann, and G. Ridder (Elsevier Science Publishers, Amsterdam).

Murtagh, F. (1983). A survey of recent advances in hierarchical clustering algorithms, *Comput. J.* **26**, 354–9.

Neftci, S. N. (1984). Are economic time series asymmetric over the business cycle? *J. of Political Econ.* **92**, 307–28.

Øksendal, B. (1989). *Stochastic Differntial Equations: An Introduction with Applications, 2nd ed.* (Springer, Berlin).

Ogielski, A. T., and D. L. Stein (1985). Dynamics on ultrametric spaces, *Phys. Rev. Lett.* **55**, 1634–7.

Parga, N., and M. A. Virasoro (1986). The Ultrametric Organization of Memories in a Neural Network, *J. Phys.* Paris **47**, 1857–64.

Parisi, G. (1987). Spin glasses and optimization problems without replicas, in *Chance and Matter*, edited by J. Souletie, J. Vannimenus, and R. Stora (North–Holland, Amsterdam).

Parzen, E. (1962). *Stochastic Processes* (Holden-Day, San Francisco).

Patil, G. P., and C. Taillie (1977). Diversity as a concept and its implications for random communities, *Bull. Inst. International Stat.* **47**, 497–515.

Peck, S. C. (1974). Alternative investment models for firms in the electric utilities industry, *Bell J. Econ.* **5**, 420–458.

Peretto, P. (1984). Collective properties of neural networks: A statistical physics approach, *Biol. Cybernetics* **50**, 51–62.

Pollett, P. K. (1986). Connecting reversible Markov processes, *J. Appl. Probab.* **23**, 880–900.

Pólya, G. and G. Szegö (1925). *Aufgaben und Lehrsätzen aus den Analysis* (Springer, Berlin).

Rammal, R., and G. Toulouse (1986). Ultrametricity for physicists, *Rev. Mod. Phys.* **58**, 765–88.

Rohlfs, J. (1974). A theory of interdependent demand for a communications service, *Bell J. Econ.* **5**, 16–37.

Rényi, A. (1970). *Foundations of Probability* (Holden-Day, Inc. San Francisco).

Rose, K., E. Gurewitz, and G. C. Fox (1990). Statistical mechanics and phase transitions in clustering, *Phys. Rev. Lett.* **65**, 945–8.

Sanov, I. N. (1957). On the probability of large deviations of random variables, *Mat. Sb.* **42**, 11–44, (English translation, *Selected Translations in Mathematical Statistics and Probability* **1**, 213–44.)

Sawyer, S. (1978). Isotropic random walks in a tree, *Z. Wahr. und Verw. Gebiete* **42**, 279–92.

Scarf, H. (1960). The optimality of (S, s) policies in the dynamic inventory problem, in *Mathematical Methods in the Social Sciences*, edited by K. Arrow, S. Karlin, and P. Suppes (Stanford University Press, Standford).

Schelling, T. C. (1978). *Micromotives and Macrobehavior* (W. W. Norton & Co., New York).

Schikhof, W. H. (1984). *Ultrametric calculus: An Introduction to p-adic Analysis* (Cambridge University Press, London).

Schreckenberg, M. (1985). Long range diffusion in ultrametric spaces, *Z. Phys. B. Condensed Matter* **60**, 483–8.

Sheshinski, E., and Y. Weiss (1977). Inflation and costs of price adjustment, *Rev. Econ. Stud.* **44**, 287–303.

    (1983). Optimum pricing policy under stochastic inflation, *Rev. Econ. Stud.* **50**, 513–29.

Shwartz, A., and A. Weiss (1995). *Large Deviations for Performance Analysis* (Chapman & Hall, London).

Simon, H., and C. P. Bonini (1958). The size distribution of business firms, *Am. Econ. Rev.* **48**, 607–17.

Sinai, Ya. G. Self-similar probability distributions, *Theor. Probab. Appl.* **21**, 64–80.

Smith, G. W. (1989). Transactions demand for money with a stochastic, time-varying interest rate, *Rev. Econ. Stud.* **56**, 623–33.

Sokal, R. R., and P. H. A. Sneath (1963). *Principles of Numerical Taxonomy* (W. H. Freeman and Co., San Francisco).

Sommerfeld, A. (1949). *Partial Differential Equations in Physics* (Academic Press, New York).

Spitzer, F. (1972). A variational characterization of finite Markov chains, *Ann. Math. Stat.* **43**, 303–7.

—— (1975). Markov random fields on an infinite tree, *Ann. Probab.* **3**, 387–98.

Srinivasan, T. N. (1967). Geometric rate of growth of demand, in *Investments for Capacity Expansion*, edited by A. S. Manne, (MIT Press, Cambridge, MA).

Steindl, J. (1965). *Random Processes and the Growth of Firms: A Study of the Pareto Law* (Hafner Publishing Co., New York).

Stoker, T. M. (1993). Empirical approaches to the problem of aggregation over individual, *J. Econ. Literature* **31**, 1827–74.

Strauss, D. (1986). On a general class of models for interactions, *SIAM Rev.* **28**, 513–27.

—— (1993). The many faces of logistic regression, *Am. Stat.* **46**, 321–7.

Stutzer, M. (1994). "The statistical mechanics of asset prices," in *Differential Equations, Dynamical Systems, and Control Science*, edited by K. D. Elworthy, W. N. Everitt, and E. Bruce, *Lecture Notes in Pure and Applied Mathematics No. 152* Marcel Dekker.

—— (1995). A Bayesian approach to diagnosis of asset pricing models, *J. Econ.* **68**, 367–97.

Suzuki, M. (1978). Thermodynamic limit of non-equilibrium systems: Extensive property, fluctuation and nonlinear relaxation, in *Lecture Notes in Physics No. 38* (Springer, Berlin).

Tijms, H. C. (1994). *Stochastic Models: An Algorithmic Approach* (Wiley, Chichester, England).

Tikochinsky, N., N. Z. Tishby, and R. D. Levine (1984). Alternative approach to maximum-entropy inference, *Phy. Rev. A* **30**, 2638–44.

van Campenhout, J. M., and T. M. Cover (1981). Maximum entropy and conditional probability, *IEEE Trans. Inf. Theor.*, **IT-27**, 483–9.

van Hemmen, J. L., and R. Kühn (1991). Collective phenomena in neural networks, in *Models of Neural Networks*, edited by E. Domany, J. L. van Hemmen, and K. Schulten et al. (Springer, New York).

van Hemmen, J. L., A. C. D. van Enter, and J. Canisius (1983). On a classical spin glass model, *Z. Phys. B Condensed Matter* **50**, 311–36.

van Kampen, N. G. (1965). Fluctuations in Nonlinear Systems, in *Fluctuation Phenomena in Solids*, edited by R. G. Gurgess (Academic Press, New York), Chap. V.

van Kampen, N. G. (1992). *Stochastic Processes in Physics and Chemistry* (North Holland, Amsterdam, revised edition).

Vannimeus, X., and M. Mezard (1984). On the statisitcal mechanics of optimization problem of the traveling salesman type, *J. Phys.* **45**, L1145–53.

Varadhan, S. R. S. (1984). *Large Deviations and Applications* (Society for Industrial and Applied Mathematics, Philadelphia).

Vasicek, O. A. (1980). A conditional law of large numbers, *Ann. Probab.* **8**, 142–7.

Vriend, N. J. (1994). "Self-Organized Markets in a Decentralized Economy," Working Paper No. 94-03-013, Santa Fe Institute Economics Research Program, Santa Fe, NM.

Watterson, G. A. (1974). The sampling theory of selectively neutral alleles, *Adv. Appl. Probab.* **6**, 463–88.

Watterson, G. A., and H. A. Guess (1977). Is the most frequent allele the oldest? *Theor. Popul. Biol.* **11**, 141–60.

280   References

Weiss, A. (1986). A new technique for analyzing large traffic systems, *Adv. Appl. Probab.*
    18, 506–32.
Weidlich, W. (1974). Dynamics of interacting social groups, in *Synergetics –
    Cooperative Effects*, edited by H. Haken (North Holland, Amsterdam).
    (1994). Synergetic modelling concepts for sociodynamics with application to col-
    lective political opinion formation, *J. Math. Sociol.* **18**, 267–91.
Weidlich, W., and G. Haag (1983). *Concepts and Models of Quantitative Sociology: The
    Dynamics of Interacting Populations* (Springer, Berlin).
Weidlich, W., and M. Braun (1992). The master equation approach to nonlinear eco-
    nomics, *J. Evol. Econ.* **2**, 233–65.
Weiss, A. (1986). A new technique for analyzing large traffic systems, *Adv. Appl. Probab.*
    18, 506–32.
Whittle, P. (1985). Partial balance and insensitivity, *J. Appl. Probab.* **22**, 168–76.
    (1986). *Systems in Stochastic Equilibrium* (John Wiley & Sons, New York).
    (1992). *Probability via Expectation, 3rd ed.* (Springer, New York).
Wiener, N. (1948). *Cybernetics* (John Wiley & Sons, New York).
Williams, D. (1991). *Probability with Martingales* (Cambridge University Press, New
    York).
Woodroofe, M., and B. M. Hill (1975). On Zipf's law, *J. App. Probab.* **12**, 425–34.
Wright, R. (1995). Search, Evolution, and Money *J. Econ. Dyn. Contr.* **19**, 181–206.
Zipf, G. K. (1949). *Human Behavior and the Principle of Least Effort* (Addison–Wesley,
    New York).

Index

Printed in the United States
By Bookmasters